Leadership and Cooperation in Academia

Leadership and Cooperation in Academia

Reflecting on the Roles and Responsibilities of University Faculty and Management

Edited by

Roger Sugden

Faculty of Management, University of British Columbia, Okanagan Campus, Canada

Marcela Valania

Stirling Management School, University of Stirling, UK

James R. Wilson

Orkestra – Basque Institute of Competitiveness, Spain and Deusto Business School, Spain

Edward Elgar
Cheltenham, UK • Northampton, MA, USA

Published by
Edward Elgar Publishing Limited
The Lypiatts
15 Lansdown Road
Cheltenham
Glos GL50 2JA
UK

Edward Elgar Publishing, Inc.
William Pratt House
9 Dewey Court
Northampton
Massachusetts 01060
USA

A catalogue record for this book
is available from the British Library

Library of Congress Control Number: 2012948846

This book is available electronically in the ElgarOnline.com
Business Subject Collection, E-ISBN 978 1 78100 182 0

MIX
Paper from
responsible sources
FSC
www.fsc.org
FSC® C018575

ISBN 978 1 78100 181 3 (cased)

Typeset by Servis Filmsetting Ltd, Stockport, Cheshire
Printed by MPG PRINTGROUP, UK

Contents

Figures

Tables

Contributors

Mari Jose Aranguren
Orkestra – Basque Institute of Competitiveness, Spain and Deusto Business School, Spain

David Bell
Stirling Management School, University of Stirling, UK

Gert Biesta
Faculty of Language and Literature, Humanities, Arts and Education, University of Luxembourg, Luxembourg

David G. Blanchflower
Department of Economics, Dartmouth College, US; Stirling Management School, University of Stirling, UK; NBER, IZA and the Federal Reserve Bank of Boston

Philip Cooke
Centre for Advanced Studies, Cardiff University, UK

Thomas Docherty
Department of English and Comparative Literary Studies, University of Warwick, UK

Steve Fuller
Department of Sociology, University of Warwick, UK

Hans Chr Garmann Johnsen
University of Agder, Norway and Agderforskning, Norway

Gordon Graham
Princeton Theological Seminary, USA

Sonja Grönblom
Department of Economics, School of Business and Economics, Åbo Akademi University, Finland

Elspeth Jones
Emerita Professor of the Internationalisation of Higher Education, Leeds Metropolitan University, UK

James Karlsen
Agderforskning, Norway and Orkestra – Basque Institute of Competitiveness, Spain

Fumi Kitagawa
Manchester Business School, University of Manchester, UK

Miren Larrea
Orkestra – Basque Institute of Competitiveness, Spain and Deusto Business School, Spain

Roger Normann
University of Agder, Norway and Agderforskning, Norway

John Rogers
University of Stirling, UK

Silvia Sacchetti
Stirling Management School, University of Stirling, UK

Eileen Schofield
University of Stirling, UK

Roger Sugden
Faculty of Management, University of British Columbia, Okanagan Campus, Canada

Keith Tribe
Independent scholar, professional translator and rowing coach at King's School, Worcester, UK

Marcela Valania
Stirling Management School, University of Stirling, UK

Johan Willner
Department of Economics, School of Business and Economics, Åbo Akademi University, Finland

James R. Wilson
Orkestra – Basque Institute of Competitiveness, Spain and Deusto Business School, Spain

Introduction: origins, purpose and an overview

Roger Sugden, Marcela Valania and James R. Wilson[1]

> We didn't wait to look at one another. I took Irene's arm and forced her to run with me to the wrought-iron door, not wanting to look back . . . I still had my wrist watch on and saw that it was 11 p.m. I took Irene round the waist (I think she was crying) and that was how we went into the street. Before we left I felt terrible; I locked the front door up tight and tossed the key down the sewer. It wouldn't do to have some poor devil decide to go in and rob the house, at that hour and with the house taken over.
> Julio Cortázar, *House Taken Over* (1967, p. 16)

The origins of this volume lie in our belief that the university as an academic institution is an essential ingredient of vibrant societies, and in our fears over the appropriateness of the development paths that universities and university systems have been taking over recent years. Most especially, we are concerned that people working in universities have had disturbingly little space to think about and shape those paths, perhaps partly because they have not been given the space, partly because they have chosen – consciously or otherwise – not to take the space for themselves.

In his short story 'House Taken Over', Julio Cortázar tells of a man and his sister Irene living in a large family house that 'apart from its being old and spacious . . . kept the memories of great-grandparents, our paternal grandfather, our parents and the whole of childhood' (Cortázar, 1967: p. 10). They spent their time in a routine of house cleaning and idle pursuit, obtaining income from farms that others worked. One day they hear the noise of intruders in the back part of the house. They rush to bolt an oak door that shuts off that area, opting to live in the parts of the house that remained. 'The first few days [that followed] were painful, since we'd both left so many things in the part that had been taken over . . . But there were advantages too. The cleaning was so much simplified that, even when we got up late, nine thirty for instance, by eleven we were sitting around with our arms folded' (*ibid.*, p. 14). But then, 'except for the consequences' (*ibid.*, p. 16), the same thing happened again. This time the brother and sister heard noises in their area of the house, the front part, so they left altogether, locking the wrought iron front door to prevent intruders, even though the house was now taken over.

Some have interpreted the story as a comment on Peronism in Argentina, a possibility that Cortázar himself does not exclude.[2] Without wishing to push the analogy too far, we wonder if it has resonance in universities. Are we in academia tending to stand by whilst our houses are being taken over? This is a question of not only failing to reject unwanted intruders but also, for example, ignoring benefits from shared occupancy; or lacking the imagination to modify the architecture, so as to engage better with visitors.

We are at a point in history when, across the world, academic institutions are being questioned by their so-called stakeholders and pressured to change. We would assert that answering these questions and understanding these pressures require that everyone working in universities – including professional managers as well as academics – be in positions to think about their work, its value and organization. They need the space and stimulus to reflect on the responsibilities, roles and expectations that they identify for themselves, and that others place upon them. Then, they would not be bolting the doors and hiding away. They might be better able to understand and to act.

The purpose of this volume is to call for such space and provide stimulus for reflection.

The contributors are colleagues with whom we have shared thoughts on these issues over recent years. Some were participants in the Birmingham Workshops on Academic Freedom and Research/Learning Cultures, which we initiated in 2007 at the University of Birmingham (with Silvia Sacchetti, also a contributor to this volume). Those Workshops were conceived as a forum for rigorous analysis and thinking on academic cultures and environments. Some contributors joined in the 2009 EUNIP (European Network on Industrial Policy) Workshop hosted by Orkestra in San Sebastián; for us, this was an important point for debating aspects of university activity in relation to territory and policy stakeholders. Some were participants in the four-day programme on Cooperation and Leadership in Academia that we hosted in 2010 at the University of Stirling. This programme was designed explicitly with the prospect of the current volume firmly in mind. It was also intended to provide a space for those working in universities to reflect on their roles; on how those roles might be developed and on how they might be carried out more successfully.

In editing the volume we had no intention of requesting contributions that would be comprehensive on the key issues facing universities and those who work in them. Nor did we ask any contributors to be exhaustive in addressing any one issue. We simply intended to cover an interesting array of topics and urged authors to do so in any ways that they thought would be stimulating for readers. Our objective is to leave each contribution to be enjoyed on its own merits, to speak for itself in feeding reflection about the roles and responsibilities of university faculty and management.

Accordingly, by way of further introduction all that we now offer is the briefest of overviews as a flavour of the material that follows.

The volume begins with a set of contributions focusing on conceptions and types of university. Gordon Graham (Chapter 1) contends that:

> universities as we have come to know them do not have a single 'inner pulse'. Rather, there are at least three rationalized models of the university, all of which can be found to have played a significant part in the history of higher education. These are the university as college, as research center, and as polytechnic. (p. 3)

Exploring these three types, he contemplates tensions in choosing between and ordering 'research, teaching and practical relevance' (p. 8). Graham suggests that the main problem confronting academia 'is the difficulty of continuing to assert the university's valuable social role, while resisting two recurrent threats to its autonomy – "the state as social engineer" and "the student as customer"' (p. 15). He argues for a revitalized notion of the university as college.

University types, including university as college, are also addressed by Keith Tribe (Chapter 2). He studies the establishment of a set of new universities in 1960s Britain. Tribe suggests that, over time, those universities lost sight of their original purpose, which had been to be 'experimental, to provide scope for innovation in teaching and learning' (p. 17). Instead they converged on uniformity, 'increasingly' reshaping themselves according to 'what were conceived to be the values and imperatives of the private sector' (p. 23). Through this process there was an undermining of collegiality as a foundation for the governance of scholarship and teaching. Tribe's warning is that:

> [r]eforms to a [university] system in the absence of any substantial understanding of the evolution and present structure of that system hardly ever turn out in the way intended. The only sure thing is that reforms of that kind merely prepare the ground for future waves of reform. (p. 30)

In important respects Tribe is especially concerned with teaching, which can also be said for Gert Biesta (Chapter 3) in his consideration of balancing the core activities of universities. He questions 'what the university is *for*' (p. 32), looking at the rise of the so-called global university and considering the 'different ways in which the university has emerged in differing (national) contexts' (p. 33). He suggests 'that the global university is mainly adapting to private interests rather than supporting *public projects and the common good*' (p. 36). Distinguishing between three models – the economic, the professional and the democratic educational – he analyses 'the difference ... between a university that has a service-orientation towards private wants and a university that has a service-orientation towards the public good' (p. 38). This takes him to the significance of teaching. Biesta argues 'that if we want to conceive of the university as a public institution, that is as an institution with a public "task" and responsibility ... we need to conceive of its first priority as that of *teaching*' (p. 39).

A concern with public good is also central to the argument offered by Roger Sugden (Chapter 4). Having explored current reality, he challenges societies to evolve a new model of socio-economic development, one that would better accommodate the interests of publics. Consequently he suggests 'that a task facing universities is to provide people with the creative space to meet that challenge' (p. 43). He cautions universities against choosing business models that use large, transnational corporations as role models: 'a university adopting such corporate logic would be unlikely to have as one of its broad objectives the serving of publics' (p. 50). Rather, Sugden advocates 'the possibility that a university might choose to adopt *public interests logic*; it might organize itself so as to enable people to think about, analyse and understand ways in which the interests of publics might be better satisfied' (p. 51). That takes him to comments on values, academic freedom and creativity, thus to asides on Docherty's (2008) analysis of sense and sensibility.

Thomas Docherty takes his earlier analysis of sense and sensibility further in this volume (Chapter 5), and in doing so considers the relevance of the economic model, notably its stress on achieving efficiencies in ways that, for him, actually result in *inefficiencies*. The reason for that outcome is the failure 'to address the question of the regulation of sense and sensibility', in particular 'to recognize the value of sensibility, a sensibility that requires play, which "wastes time"' (p. 58). He criticizes the 'contemporary utilitarian and instrumentalist ideology of education' (p. 64), and the free-market conservative thinking that rewards productivity and disallows play. For Docherty, play is:

> a kind of radical release of the very energies that are required for committed learning and teaching in the first place. It is in play that we see the play of sensibility and that we therefore engage the body with the mind in embodied learning or sense-making. Without play, there can be no experience. (p. 65)

Moving to Chapter 6, Philip Cooke and Fumi Kitagawa maintain the concern with conceptions and types of university. In the context of UK experience, they describe and discuss three related agendas: 'massification, marketization and privatization' (p. 70); corporatization, based upon new public management; and 'the questionable ethics associated with the global procurement of students and research income' (p. 70). They argue that in now privatized universities 'academic expenditure has risen at a far slower and lesser pace than administrative and largely administratively related expenditure' (p. 85). These newly employed administrative staff are said to be 'engaged in recruiting overseas, especially Asian students, managing financial flows, managing assessment procedures and auditing financial flows' (p. 85). Most damningly, Cooke and Kitagawa conclude that:

> universities over-rode basic ethical requirements in a democracy of denying support to non-democratic and repressive regimes by accepting major financial transfers from regimes that in some cases were, in 2011, to be seen to turn guns upon their own protesting citizens. (p. 86)

Marketization and new public management also concern Sonja Grönblom and Johan Willner (Chapter 7). They offer an appreciation of the historical development of universities and then explore impacts on work motivation, employment and performance. For them, 'marketization has usually been advocated through economic arguments related to cost efficiency. In particular, the new public management is based on theories where employees are seen as driven only by a desire to earn money and avoid effort' (p. 101). In contrast, they see it as realistic that people may have other motivations. Grönblom and Willner therefore use a formal economic model including intrinsic motivation to analyse universities with and without marketization, and thereby challenge recent developments. They conclude that their 'formal analysis suggests that sticks and carrots can make sense only when the intrinsic motivation is weak, but in other cases they tend to reduce the work effort' (p. 101). Grönblom and Willner also show circumstances in which, for example, a Vice Chancellor may gain from a weakening of employees' intrinsic motivation.

The focus on motivation is maintained in the contribution by Silvia Sacchetti (Chapter 8). She also explores motivation in the context of current changes in academia, which she sees as including a mimicking of business and the prioritization 'at a growing rate across national systems of' an incentive system that serves the aim of revenue increase (p. 122). In particular, Sacchetti aims at 'providing a way of understanding whether enquiry-led academics are an endangered species and how motivations can be kept alive (p. 122). To analyse motivation she draws an analogy from physics, exploring the idea of thermodynamics. Sacchetti calls for peer support in academia, rather than peer evaluation, as a way to 'respect-fully encourage enquiry and the development of new ideas. In this way, researchers can renew their intrinsic motivations and, as a consequence, their commitment to academic enquiry' (p. 114). She suggests that the role of senior staff and leaders be that of giving support and of upholding the support network among peers.

A particular aspect of peer relationships is addressed by Steve Fuller (Chapter 9). He argues that in the context of 'calls for academic inquiry to be more "open sourced" and "publicly oriented", it has been common for academics who either uphold or oppose the neo-liberal mode of knowl-edge production to agree on the inviolability of "peer review" as a core academic value' (p. 128). However, for Fuller 'the value of peer review in the larger political economy of knowledge production is rather circum-scribed and typically conservative in effect' (p. 128). He is quite damning of its use, and thus calls for change. For example, he writes of an 'authori-tarian appeal to peer review, so alien to the early modern science societies, that needs to be ended, and preferably replaced' (p. 143). Fuller's analysis leads him to wonder about playing 'the natural openness of entrepre-neurial publishers against the natural public-mindedness of Humboldtian scholar–teachers' (p. 145). He even contemplates 'bringing publishers into the governing structure and staffing of the university' (p. 145).

In Chapter 10, John Rogers and Eileen Schofield shift our attention to the role of non-academic staff, and to their relationships with academics. They point to a 'deep and unhelpful divisiveness within university com-munities' (p. 147) that has tended to be emphasized and perpetuated by the literature. They argue that the functions and activities of non-academic staff 'are not generally discussed in terms of their nature, merits or contri-bution. Rather, they tend to be portrayed as an impediment to the pursuit of scholarship' (p. 147). Looking to present a more balanced view, Rogers and Schofield consider the rise of managerialism, the professionalization of university administration and the criticisms that have been levelled at non-academic staff. They endorse the prospects for working in the so-called 'third space' – i.e. 'between academic and professional domains, across and outwith boundaries and hierarchies' (p. 156). They identify the role of the leader as that of 'ensuring that all of the talents available within a university are engaged effectively in pursuit of shared goals' (p. 159).

Whilst maintaining an explicit concern with the contributions of all talents, Elspeth Jones (Chapter 11) moves our attention to what has com-monly become, albeit in often limited respects, one of the more pressing issues for universities over recent years: internationalization. She advocates an integrated approach, suggesting that internationalization can facilitate 'an inclusive, intercultural dimension to the teaching, research, service, and the commercial and entrepreneurial pursuits of a contemporary university' (p. 162). She argues that this approach implies that a university's '"global reach" involves not only international undertakings but also local, regional, national and, crucially, internal systems, processes and organizational culture' (p. 162). Jones sees a consequent need to engage all university staff in the internationalization agenda, and her view is that 'an internationalization strategy that does not give sufficient attention to the leadership and development of staff is unlikely to achieve its aims' (p. 165). She suggests how to evaluate progress in achieving such integrated internationalization, and offers possible indicators of success.

Another pressing concern for universities over recent years has been the funding of higher education. That is the subject of David Bell's contribution (Chapter 12). Concentrating on the 'almost unprecedented fiscal austerity' (p. 184) following the 2007 financial crisis, he presents a somewhat bleak yet varied picture of the realities in the US and Europe. For example, in 2009/10 alone, the state's contribution to the University of California's budget fell by $813 million and approximately 1900 employees were laid off. Bell observes that, 'as it should be within a democratic state' (p. 184), government/higher education relationships have tended to be uneasy. However he also perceives that 'the new financial pressures are leading to realignments of these relationships and a consequent redistribution of power that will affect both higher education itself and, through it, society in general' (p. 184). Which is not to imply a necessarily negative outcome: 'in some sense, these changes provide an opportunity for those who can use a time of significant change to effect improvements in the system' (p. 196).

Aspects of the relationships between universities and societies are taken up by Roger Normann and Hans Chr Garmann Johnsen (Chapter 13). They argue that understanding what happens when university and society meet is underdeveloped, because 'this meeting is not of one type only, but rather represents a plurality of interaction forms' (p. 197). For them, such meetings are 'very context-specific' and 'can put many different role dimensions into play, such as institutional, communicative, power, identity and culture, as well as more formal and structural elements' (p. 197). They denote this plurality the 'third place'. Their concern is to improve understanding of the third place, what happens there in terms of knowledge development and learning, and how it is organized and managed. Normann and Johnsen explore these issues from the perspectives of, on the one hand, universities and, on the other hand, business communities and regions. They do so by drawing on data from a particular region in Norway, namely Agder.

Mari Jose Aranguren, James Karlsen, Miren Larrea and James Wilson (Chapter 14) also contribute to the debate about university–society relations, especially regarding territorial socio-economic development. Addressing their concern that 'there is little written around the practical aspects of achieving more "relevant" research that is at the same time independent and academically rigorous' (p. 216), they analyse three long-running cases of 'action research' involving researchers and regional development agents in the Basque Country. Their contention 'is that action research can contribute to opening up the black box of interactive learning processes between academic research and regional actors' (p. 217). Reflecting on the cases, Aranguren et al. stress that '[k]nowledge co-generation is a social and an emotional process' p. 229 that demands change: from practitioners, who need to get away from wanting 'to get knowledge from the researchers in a linear way as a recipe of what to do' (p. 230); from researchers, who need to appreciate that their theoretical knowledge is 'not enough to have real-world impacts' (p. 230). Aranguren et al. emphasize that such change necessitates time, among other things.

David Blanchflower (Chapter 15) takes up the issue of relevance, depicting the absence of academics in periods of social need. Reflecting on recent macro-economic crises and the 'need for engagement and involvement of the economics profession in the problems of our day' (p. 237), he asks academics: where were you? Blanchflower observes, for example, that for him 'sitting at the Bank of England as a member of the Monetary Policy Committee (MPC) from 2006 to 2009, trying to make interest rate decisions every month, was a lonely task; there was little or nothing academic economists had to contribute' (p. 235). The consequence of their absence is said to be 'some of the worst economic policy errors in a generation' (p. 265). He wonders if 'the great fear' is due to lack of self-confidence, or possibly worry 'that they will be forced to move outside their comfort zone and be asked questions about something else' (p. 237). In certain respects his chapter is a call to arms, his aim being 'to discuss the policy mistakes' and, most importantly, 'look for help' (p. 238).

To conclude the volume we move away from the particular illustrations provided by economics and economists to a more general issue that is a recurring theme across the chapters: leadership in universities. We finish with a contribution on this topic because of the especial importance that we believe it has not only in explaining the successes, failures and development paths that universities have experienced, but also in determining their future.

Thomas Docherty (Chapter 16) begins with a discussion of the meaning of education, drawing examples from the literary work of Muriel Spark and Seamus Heaney to suggest 'that leadership and followership are charged with meanings well beyond the simple idea of being at the head or tail of a race, or of an army, or of a group or institutional body' (p. 271). He explores these meanings, thus issues of responsibility, answerability and experience. For him, '[p]erhaps above all, to lead means to assert a particular kind of break; and, in this, it is clear that the leader, insofar as she or he leads, cannot be simply the agent of another, more powerful force' (p. 271). He sees 'a crisis of leadership' in higher education, 'provoked' by a managerialism implying 'that instead of leaders, we have managers; instead of followers, we have resources' (p. 277). For Docherty, 'leadership is leadership if and only if it enhances freedom and extends it. It is not enough simply to protect existing freedom; the point of leading is to offer freedom more widely' (p. 281). Asking what that might mean in a university, he points to the necessity of 'encouraging dissent rather than conformity' and of 'challenging authorities, especially those that are illegitimate' (p. 281).

We urge that you, reader, use not only Docherty's contribution on leadership but also each of the following chapters as a stimulus to your thinking about the work, value and organization of universities. On such foundations we hope that there might be a bright future for our houses.

NOTES

1. Thanks to Mari Jose Aranguren for comments on an earlier draft of this introduction.
2. Interview of Julio Cortázar in 'A fondo', 20 March 1977, accessed on 16 April 2012 from *Escritores en el archivo de RTVE* (*Writers in RTVE Archive*) at www.rtve.es/alacarta/videos/escritores-en-el-archivo-de-rtve/entrevista-julio-cortazar-programa-fondo/1051583/. In the interview Cortázar also says that he dreamt the story – it was the result of a nightmare.

REFERENCES

Cortázar, Julio (1967), 'House Taken Over', in: Julio Cortázar, *Blow-Up and Other Stories*, New York: Pantheon Books.
Docherty, T. (2008), *The English Question or Academic Freedoms*, Brighton: Sussex Academic Press.

1. The university: a critical comparison of three ideal types

Gordon Graham

What is a university? More contentiously, what is a *real* university? It is reasonable to regard these questions as either rhetorical or empty. Even a brief glance at institutions of higher education in the modern world will show them to be astonishingly varied in size, history and function. For example, the Indira Ghandi Open University has approximately 3 million students; the University Center in Svalbard, the world's most northerly university, has about 300. Harvard, established in the seventeenth century, is universally acknowledged as an international leader in the advancement of the arts and sciences; the much larger Technical University of Uttar Pradesh, established in Lucknow at the start of the twenty-first century, serves largely local educational needs and does not figure at all in international research tables. Ave Maria University in Florida (founded 2003) is one of America's newest universities and its sole PhD programme is in Theology; Princeton (founded 1726) is one of America's oldest universities and theology is not studied there at all. All these institutions, despite the radical differences between them, have been accorded the title 'university' and are recognized as such. Who then is to say which of them is a 'real' university? Besides, what is the point of such a question? What's in a name, after all?

1 THE ACTUAL AND THE IDEAL

Liberal nominalism of this kind often has something to commend it. Yet it cannot be the whole story in this context. The title 'university' does not merely classify; it accords a special status, and this means we can always ask if the status is warranted. This is shown by the fact that in a few instances, the title 'university' is at best parasitic. Consider the case of Hamburger University in Oak Brook, Illinois, a suburb of Chicago. This training facility of McDonald's Corporation has 30 resident professors, classes in 28 different languages, and over 80000 graduates. Although its purpose is undoubtedly an educational one – to instruct personnel employed by McDonald's in various aspects of the business – its use of the title 'university' is in some way whimsical. There is no serious intention here to enter the lists with Harvard, Cambridge, Tokyo or ANU.

These great four universities, of course, are special by any standard. They appear in the top 25 of the 2010 *Times* and QS World University rankings of the world's universities. It is not this fact that marks the crucial difference with Hamburger University, however. The *Times* list runs to 400, and the QS list to 1248, and in both lists a very large number of universities fall far short of Harvard and Cambridge in terms of reputation and attainment. Yet even those that come in at the bottom differ importantly from McDonald's Hamburger University. Even universities that get no higher than six hundredth share something important with Harvard. In contrast to even the very best educational institutions at primary and secondary level, they aim to be the *sort* of thing that Harvard is. That is to say, despite radical differences in their self-understanding and aspiration, they see themselves, not merely as part of a 'higher' or tertiary level of education, but as academic institutions that have ultimate responsibility for determining their own academic goals and standards. This is commonly realized in a commitment to free inquiry, and an authority to confer degrees. These familiar facts show that the title 'university', properly accorded, bestows a certain status, because it invokes an educational ideal and not just a sociological classi-fication. Consequently, understanding what a university is, is not simply a matter of empirical investigation; it requires an exploration of educa-tional norms.

To ask what the ideal of a university is, is at the same time to ask what it ought to be. Yet framing a conception of that ideal cannot be undertaken in abstraction from empirical facts and historical realities. If we are to avoid the danger of utopianism – i.e. inventing a concept that has never existed and precisely for that reason never will – we must somehow abstract critically from the past to the present and to the future. Philosophically speaking, what is required is neither the idealistic rationalism of Plato, nor the empiricism of Locke and Hume, but the philosophical historicism of Hegel. As I understand it, Hegelianism seeks to determine the essential nature of things with the benefit of hindsight. Famously, the owl of Minerva takes its flight at dusk, which is to say that philosophical understanding consists in a conceptual reconstruction of entities in their historical maturity. Applied to the idea of a university, this means we need to abstract from *extraneous* detail while according full weight to the character of the university as it has developed historically. In Hegel's own terms, we must avoid any inquiry in which 'the *Idea* is seen as "only an idea", a representation in the realm of opinion'. The formulation of a mere 'idea' in this sense is fruitless because 'what matters is to recognize in the semblance of the temporal and transient the substance which is immanent and the eternal which is present' (Hegel, 1991: 20). This recognition requires us to give due weight to empirical facts about actual universities, while at the same time according them a greater degree of coherence than they have ever actually possessed in any specific historical realization.

Hegel is well aware that conceptual ideals so construed emerge 'in an infinite wealth of forms, appearances, and shapes'. What we are in search of is a 'core' concept that will enable us to 'find the inner pulse' of the reality we want to idealize. Now it is arguable, it seems to me, that universities as we have come to know them do not have a single 'inner pulse'. Rather, there are at least three rationalized models of the university, all of which can be found to have played a significant part in the history of higher education. These are the university as college, as research centre, and as polytechnic. Although none of them has ever been fully realized (and is unlikely ever to be so), setting them out as contrasting models can nonetheless be illuminating. It provides a conceptual orientation to the many problems that commonly confront contemporary universities, and it helps to clarify the potential choices that those with responsibility for the future of the university must make. The core differences between them have proved to have important social and economic ramifications, and these have occasioned further differences in administrative style, social role and financial structure that are often taken to be characteristic. But for present purposes, I shall leave these aside and focus exclusively on more strictly educational and intellectual differences.

2 THE UNIVERSITY COLLEGE

The university as college is the oldest conception of the university. Its roots are Christian, and the pursuit of the ideal that underlies it shaped the universities of Europe for 600 years or more. Education as the pursuit of learning lay at its heart. This is reflected in the fact that the distinctions between bachelor, master and doctor did not separate members of the university in the way the class of 'student' is separated from the profession of 'teacher'. Bachelors, masters and doctors were in the original sense *colleagues*, members of a single body and related in an ascending order of educational accomplishment in which, nevertheless, those at the highest level were just as much engaged in learning as those at the lowest.

The purpose of this learning was not simply knowledge for its own sake.

Given the college's Christian origins, this could hardly be the case. What drives us to seek knowledge of God is not intellectual curiosity as such, but the hope of salvation. Accordingly, a division between useful knowledge and theoretical inquiry, often taken for granted today, is deeply alien to the college ideal, and as a matter of fact, from earliest time, the universities of Europe were as much professional schools for priests and lawyers (and later for physicians), as they were centres of biblical and theological scholarship. Even the arcana of logic, at which the Scholastics excelled, served a practical purpose, since the value of logic ultimately lay in its power to assist theology in avoiding heretical errors.

Although the model of the university as college has medieval origins, its realization cannot be confined to the pre-modern period. The universities of the eighteenth-century Scottish enlightenment – all of them colloquially referred to as 'Colleges' – while undergoing radical curricular and institutional change that left scholasticism behind, nevertheless preserved certain key elements, notably the integration of teaching and learning and the combination of the academic with the practical. It was people educated in these Scottish colleges who established fledgling institutions of higher education in the American colonies. They thus laid the foundations of several important universities in post-colonial America, all of which took the college model as their template. Among the most famous are Princeton University in New Jersey, Columbia University in New York, 'U. Penn' (the University of Pennsylvania) in Philadelphia, and the College of William & Mary in Virginia.

What subsequently became known as the 'American College Ideal' departed from the medieval conception insofar as it separated liberal from professional education. This came to be provided for in separate law schools, medical schools and seminaries. Nevertheless, an education in the liberal arts was regarded as a necessary preliminary to professional training. Furthermore, liberal education retained an importantly practical orientation. A curriculum based upon mathematics, the classical languages and philosophy, and informed by religion, concluded in the final year with lectures on Ethics and Politics. Usually taught by the President of the College, the purpose of this course was to ensure that students emerged from their education well versed in their civic and social responsibilities.

The College ideal struggled to survive in the second half of the nineteenth century. Across Europe, the connections between Church and University were seriously weakened, but the main pressure came from two disparate sources – an alternative conception of the university as research institution, and an increasing demand for more severely practical and technical education.

3   THE RESEARCH UNIVERSITY

An early manifestation of the modern 'research' university can be found in the establishment of the Lucasian Professorship of Mathematics at Cambridge in 1664. Henry Lucas, the founder, had made it a condition of his gift that the holder should not be active in the Church, and Isaac Newton, as its potential occupant, although himself a Christian, persuaded King Charles II that this provision should enable him (and his successors) to hold the Chair without submitting to the hitherto uniform requirement that Cambridge professors be ordained to the priesthood. Subsequently, thanks in no small part to Newton's own occupancy, The Lucasian became one of the most prestigious scientific chairs in the world, whose holders were (like Stephen Hawking) exceptionally gifted individuals engaged in scientific inquiry.

The most famous, and perhaps founding instance, of an entire institution intended exclusively for such individuals was the University of Berlin. Created in 1810 by William von Humboldt, this was, by intention, primarily a community of scholars and scientists devoted to intellectual inquiry for its own sake, and without any special emphasis on educational value or wider social function. Since lectures were given and students enrolled at Humboldt's university, the 'German' model may have found its purest example 60 years later in the United States. The establishment of the Johns Hopkins University in 1876 was accompanied by a statement of purpose in which its Board deliberately rejected the traditional American college model in favour of what it understood to be the 'German' research university. In language characteristic of the time, its first President – Daniel Coit Gilman – expressly drew a distinction between the old-style 'college' and the ambition to be a 'university'. The aims of a university, he declared, were 'the encouragement of research . . . and the advancement of individual scholars, who by their excellence will advance the sciences they pursue'. Despite appearances, this declaration was not in fact made in complete indifference to social and educational role. Rather, it rested upon the conviction that the best way to fulfil both these functions was to create an institution that would be wholly devoted to intellectual research by gifted individuals. Universities were for the production and transmission of knowledge, and they served society best by sticking to this role.

Elements of the German or Humboldtian model have gained great prominence – one might say dominance – in the world of modern universities. Evidence of this lies in the emphasis that is given to research activity and reputation in the construction of comparative league tables such as the *Times* and QS rankings cited earlier. This emphasis both reflects, and in turn strengthens, a policy within institutions of hiring leading scholars and researchers first and foremost, and only determining their contribution to the undergraduate curriculum thereafter. In effect, this makes additional measures of excellence – in student teaching, knowledge transfer, or impact within the wider community for example – secondary, despite the lip service that is often paid to them.

Generally speaking, then, in current thinking 'first-class university' means first-class research institution. The model has never been without its critics, however. To begin with, it rather too easily fits the negative image of the 'ivory tower', a place for the pursuit of arcane interests that have no connection with or value for the business of ordinary life. The pejorative description, 'ivory tower', is especially damaging to universities dependent upon the public purse. Why should taxpayers be expected to pay the occupants of ivory towers? Johns Hopkins, of course, was founded on a private donation – worth the equivalent of several trillion dollars today (on some measures). Donations on this scale are exceptional, and almost all universities that aspire to something like the Johns Hopkins model rely to some degree upon state finance, either directly or indirectly. This makes them susceptible to other demands than that of pure inquiry. But even where there is no call upon the public purse, the perception that universities are ivory towers is sufficient to incline more practically minded people to seek both knowledge and education elsewhere.

4   THE TECHNICAL UNIVERSITY

In 1796, John Anderson, a professor at the University of Glasgow, left a substantial sum of money for the establishment of an alternative 'university' that, freed from the Scottish liberal arts curriculum, could devote itself to 'useful' knowledge and thus serve the needs of tradesmen and industrial workers. Initially known as 'Anderson's University', the name had to be changed in acknowledgement that the institution actually lacked the legal status of a university (and did not gain that status until 1964, when it became the University of Strathclyde). 'The Andersonian' was the first of a large number of 'mechanics institutes' that came into existence in the course of the nineteenth century, not just in the United Kingdom, but also in Australia, Canada and other parts of the British Empire. Though many amounted to little more than reading rooms, some of them were subsequently incorporated into universities, or, like the Andersonian itself, became fully-fledged universities in their own right.

The counterparts to the mechanics institutes in the United States were a deliberate creation of an Act of Congress, signed into law on 2 July, 1862. What came to be known as the Morrill Act gave grants of land to individual states to use as a means of financing new institutions of higher education. The aim of these 'Land Grant' universities was 'to teach such branches of learning as are related to agriculture and mechanical arts . . . in order to promote the liberal and practical education of the industrial classes in the several pursuits and professions in life'. Although this severely utilitarian conception of a university was tempered somewhat by the provision that agricultural and mechanical studies should be promoted 'without excluding other scientific and classical studies', the spirit of the Morrill Act was to ensure that public resources devoted to universities would be used in a way that generated public benefit. One of the earliest universities founded under this initiative was Texas A&M, which was established, as it happens, in the very same year as Johns Hopkins – 1876. For the first decades of its existence, Texas A&M combined practical education with military training, so that the State of Texas could be adequately provided with soldiers as well as farmers and mechanics.

The Morrill Act was passed during the American Civil War, and post-war reconstruction prompted important debates between competing conceptions of the university. In California the liberal arts College of California somewhat reluctantly agreed to merge with a new 'Land Grant' state university, on the understanding that the resultant University of California would be more than simply a school of agriculture, mining and mechanics. Perhaps it is a measure of the difficulty this amalgamation presented, that Daniel Coit Gilman, the UC's second President, served less than ten years before moving to the East Coast as the founding President of the new 'research only' Johns Hopkins.

In Princeton, Harvard and Yale the old colleges acknowledged the need for change, but differed about what form it would take. James McCosh, President of the College of New Jersey, strove to transform it into Princeton University with a new emphasis on research and postgraduate education, while at the same time remaining faithful to the College ideal that he had inherited from his predecessors. In a series of public debates, he crossed swords with Charles Eliot, his counterpart at Harvard, who believed that a more radical break with the past (and with religion) was required.

The end result, almost inevitably, was an official subscription to all three models. Today, in addition to educating 39 000 students, Texas A&M describes itself as a 'research-intensive flagship university', thereby revealing the extent to which the Johns Hopkins model has been influential. Johns Hopkins, on the other hand, although starting out with an exclusive focus on graduate education, soon went the way of 'useful education' by establishing America's first university-based School of Nursing in 1889. A short time after, the venerable College of New Jersey celebrated its one hundred and fiftieth anniversary by becoming Princeton University, and to this day describes itself as a 'world-renowned research university' with a 'distinctive commitment to undergraduate teaching'.

5   COMPARING THE MODELS

This express commitment to elements drawn from the three models I have described is consonant with the methodological principles deployed by both QS and *Times* in their compilation of world rankings. Universities, it seems, must aspire to combining intellectual research for its own sake, supplying and transferring useful knowledge for the benefit of society as whole, and providing an undergraduate education that will enrich the lives of the individuals who undergo it. But while this is a multiple imperative by which academic managers universally feel driven, a question arises about the extent to which it is truly realizable. Those who work within universities are well aware that aspirations to excellence in intellectual research, student education and practical relevance generate competing demands on time and resources. The tension lies deeper than this, however. Often the competition for resources between these various purposes brings to the fore deep differences in the values that underlie them.

Open debate about these competing values is not easily conducted. The ever-present internal demands for academic significance and student satisfaction, alongside the external pressures brought to bear by official accreditors, financial auditors and public relations departments, give university leaders powerful reason to gloss over them. It is more politic, for the most part, to give general acknowledgement to academic research, student education and social relevance, than to confront the difficult decisions generated by any serious attempt to order them. Yet in view of the debates and disagreements that were of such concern to their counterparts in times past, it is not implausible to think that in reality modern universities embody unresolved allegiances to incompatible models.

The now dominant ideal of a research-intensive university is in large part sustained by a belief that there is an essential connection between free inquiry and the growth of human knowledge and understanding. This belief explains the supposition of the founders of Johns Hopkins that untrammelled inquiry by gifted individuals is the best way to maximize a university's contribution to human well-being. The contention draws much of its plausibility from a common perception that academic freedom of this kind has underlain the exceptional advances made by the natural sciences in the nineteenth and twentieth centuries. The same ideas underlie contemporary defences of 'blue skies' scientific research supported by the public purse: scientific discoveries are necessarily unpredictable; accordingly, research has to be entrusted to a gifted few if society is to reap the benefits that new knowledge brings.

Widespread as this way of thinking is, as an account of the 'inner pulse' of a university, it is highly problematic. To begin with, although the general picture fits the sciences since the Enlightenment rather well, it fits the traditional liberal arts over the same period only by stretching and straining the concepts of research and knowledge. Adam Smith, Immanuel Kant, Max Weber, Margaret Mead and Suzanne Langer, for instance, who all worked at some point in universities, must number among the most gifted minds of their generations. Yet it is highly implausible to regard their studies in philosophy, history, literature and social inquiry as 'research' that resulted in a body of 'knowledge' comparable to established results in physics, geology or biology.

Some simple facts underscore the truth of this. Aristotle's physics is now of interest only to historians of science, but his philosophical endeavours continue to provide material for contemporary philosophical education and reflection. Historical and archeological investigation has certainly substantially increased our knowledge of the past, but historians invariably insist on the necessity of new 'perspectives' for the interpretation of this knowledge. In the most 'scientific' of social studies – econometrics – sophisticated theoretical developments are evident, certainly, but those who favour 'political economy' will deny that these developments are in any sense advances. While there is no turning the clock back when it comes to the theory of evolution, say, many students of literature have gladly abandoned 'literary theory' and returned to the kind of textual criticism that preceded it. And so on.

Still less can we say that in general work in the humanities (or even social sciences) produces 'useful' knowledge in any straightforward sense. Indeed, this cannot plausibly be said about science in general either. From time to time Nobel prizes in the natural sciences are awarded to highly innovative work that has huge technological potential. But the major advances made in cosmology, evolutionary biology, and plate tectonics have no evident practical application. It might be, of course, that implications with practical consequences emerge. Such a possibility cannot be ruled out. It took almost a century for James Clerk Maxwell's innovative work in electro-magnetism to gain practical value. It remains true, nonetheless, that the intellectual value of Einstein's theory of relativity, or Darwin's theory of evolution, remains intact, whether or not they ever prove to have practically valuable consequences. Conversely, immensely important, even world-changing technologies, can owe little to scientific research – the telephone, motorcar and airplane being especially striking examples. Third, it is not true that 'pure' research, even in expensive cutting-edge science, must take place within the institution of the university. Many pharmaceutical laboratories, defence contractors, art museums and charitable foundations undertake fundamental research in biochemistry, engineering, history, archeology and the social sciences. There is no reason to think, in other words, that significant or successful research has any necessary connection with educational function. It may in general be true that commercial laboratories rely on university-educated people, but some of the most innovative work in computer technology shows that this need not be the case.

6   RESEARCH AND EDUCATION

It is with regard to the connection between research and education that the deepest problem lies. McCosh and others were especially anxious that a strong emphasis on the university as primarily a place of research would introduce a radical division between researchers and teachers. This division, of course, found institutional expression in Johns Hopkins, where initially there was no provision for undergraduate education at all. The educationalists' worry was that with the elevation of the research university the institution of the liberal arts college would come to be regarded as second class precisely because of its commitment to undergraduate education. The possibility remains a common source of concern in many quarters today, and it is not difficult to find evidence that the adage 'Those who can, do, and those who can't (or can't yet), teach' has made an appearance in universities. The result is that research has come to overshadow education in determining the academic status of both institutions and individuals.

One strategy for offsetting this distortion might be thought to lie in making it a requirement that even the most active university researchers continue to teach students at all levels. But this does not really touch the source of the difficulty. What is to determine the content of the curriculum that is taught? Once again, the issue can be seen to surface with particular clarity in late nineteenth-century debates in the United States. A key element in Charles Eliot's modernization at Harvard was the introduction of electives in place of the core curriculum, which had hitherto been characteristic of the American college, and a direct result of the Scottish model that it copied. McCosh's objection to electives was twofold. First, electives presuppose that students know what is worth studying in advance of studying it. Second, electives leave faculty free to offer courses based on research interests rather than the educational needs of the student.

It is the second possibility that is most significant in the present context. An important step in the move from liberal arts college to research university was the introduction of postgraduate courses, whose purpose was to provide higher level study and instruction for new generations of scholars and scientists. McCosh oversaw the introduction of such courses at Princeton, but the danger he saw with electives was that they would transform undergraduate courses into preparation for postgraduate study. This is of course what has happened quite widely within universities. The curriculum in most subjects is structured so as to enable students to move up through the subject from introductory to advanced levels. The natural trajectory of such a structure leads to graduate work and eventually to original research. The absurdity of this as a *general* curricular structure, and what puts it at odds with the college ideal, is the fact that only a tiny proportion of students will ever enter the ranks of professional scientists and scholars. It is not so much that one size is being made to fit all, but that a size *already known* to fit only a minority is allowed to determine the general provision for all.

In such circumstances, the values that underlie a liberal education have been effectively abandoned, and no amount of emphasis on pedagogical skill will counter this. The issue is not about excellence in teaching, but the value and relevance of what is taught. However brilliant the instruction, basic biochemistry cannot be of much value to those who never become biochemists, and a grounding in the techniques of formal logic is of equally limited value to those who will never become logicians.

7   RESEARCH AND PRACTICALITY

At this point in the argument appeal is likely to be made to the doctrine of transferable skills, which alleges that an education in biochemistry or logic can generate intellectual skills that will prove serviceable in a wide range of other contexts. This is very dubious claim, in my view, but even if we accept it, there is still the unanswerable objection that John Henry Newman brings in his lectures on *The Idea of a University* (Newman, 1852/1982). If there are these transferable skills, why not teach them through the medium of knowledge that is also useful in itself? Let us suppose it is true that a biochemistry course teaches such things as analytical clarity, conceptual imagination, cogency and rigour of thought, even to those who never go on to work as biochemists. Newman's point is that these skills can also be taught in what he (unhappily perhaps) calls 'servile' subjects like mechanical engineering, accountancy, architecture and pharmacy, where what is learned will be directly useful in the occupations at which these subjects are directed.

This observation turns attention to the third model – the technical university – a place where practically useful knowledge is taught at an advanced level and in such a way that it inculcates the virtues of clarity, cogency and so on. This model need not be exclusive. The protagonist of the technical university can allow that there is a place for 'pure' research in institutions that do not aim to generate practical benefit to either individual careers or society at large. Yet if the alternative separation between instruction and inquiry is to be avoided, the protagonist of the technical university must find a place for research there too. This is relatively easy to do, in a general way. The difficulty lies in finding a place for research of a certain kind – commonly referred to as 'pure' research – and for wholly free inquiry. The two concepts are related, of course, since one condition of an inquiry being free is that it is not restricted by considerations of practical relevance.

Now it seems evident that much scholarly activity that is traditionally believed to be the proper province of universities is without immediate practical worth. This is especially true of research in the arts, humanities and social sciences. Even where economic connections with, for instance, tourism, publishing, historic conservation, or the 'leisure industry' can plausibly be anticipated, it seems perverse to claim that this is where the chief value of the research lies. The slogan 'knowledge for its own sake' is not as easily endorsed as is often supposed, since it is easy to find examples of real, but trivial knowledge. Yet it does gesture in a plausible direction. There is a clear difference between the pursuit of knowledge for the purposes of deepening our understanding, and its pursuit for advancing our practical projects. The clearest illustration comes from the study of history. The past is unalterable and thus beyond our practical reach. Nevertheless, historical inquiry can enhance and enrich our understanding of times and cultures of which we cannot be a part.

The general point does not apply to the arts and 'soft' sciences only. The same may be said of physics, chemistry and biology, where many of the most striking advances have had no practical relevance. Of course, in this context the 'blue skies' concept is often invoked to remind us that the practical value of scientific research cannot be known in advance, and that some of the most arcane inquiries have proved of immense practical value in the end. But this appeal does not really help. If what matters is a value that may or may not be realized, this requires us to suspend judgement on whether even the most innovative scientific discoveries are of any value.

In short, the rationalizing appeal to 'practical knowledge' renders even the greatest scientists and scholars mere 'underlabourers' (to use John Locke's term) in the service of others. Thus, life of the mind and the calling of the intellectual have no value in their own right. This I take to be a *reductio ad absurdum* of the conception of university as exclusively a technical institution.

Taken in combination, these reflections suggest that two of the idealizations of the university that I have been exploring are internally defective. The research university can find a place for undergraduate education, but only insofar as it constitutes the first stages of an intellectual trajectory that only a tiny minority of students will ever follow. By contrast, the technical university can provide educational courses across a very wide range, but the intellectual investigations of its faculty can be legitimated only insofar as they serve external purposes.

8 REVITALIZING THE UNIVERSITY COLLEGE

Can the third model of university as college do any better? On the face of it, the answer would appear to be 'no'. The history of higher education in Europe and North America is one in which the traditional college has gradually been sidelined, the result in part of the generalist nature of a liberal arts education that does not easily lend itself to research specialization it seems, and especially the sort of advanced scientific inquiry that is highly esteemed. In addition, at least as traditionally conceived, education of this sort seems possible only for a minority. It is thus readily perceived as 'elitist' in the negative sense of that word, because suited to levels of participation that have become politically and socially unacceptable. Taken together, modern university 'systems' have seen increasing emphasis on highly specialized research and a major expansion in state provision for higher education. These create a context in which the college model seems ever more antiquated – for the most part, the vestige of a by-gone era. Liberal arts colleges survive, of course, and they remain highly valued, especially in the United States, but even there they now constitute a very small proportion of the higher education system as a whole.

However, sometimes things that appear headed for the dustbin of history may have properties of particular value to the culture that is sending them there. There is an element in the college model that potentially offers a solution to the current problem of integrating the competing demands of research, teaching and practical relevance. This element is *professional* education, something that potentially combines all three. The medieval university aimed to offer professional education from the first, though the profession in view was primarily that of priest – now of marginal interest to the world of universities – although as noted earlier, the education of lawyers and 'mediciners' (physicians) also made an early appearance. There is no return to such a world, yet the *general* concept of professional education, as the college model understood it, may still be able to provide valuable pointers.

Professional education is practical, but it is not technical. We can best bring out the point at issue by exploring the contrast between a trade and a profession. The distinction is an interesting one, and repays sustained reflection. In this context, however, and for reasons of space, I shall simply have to assert that the core of the difference lies in this. It is enough for a trade to aim at technical excellence. By contrast a profession must have intrinsic values that go beyond technical excellence. Consider two examples. The pursuit of excellence in information technology requires education to a very high level in computer science. In itself, though, such excellence is indifferent to the purposes to which it is applied. We can assume that computer IT specialists should keep within the law like everyone else, but there is no conceptual barrier to their skills reaching the highest levels of excellence in service to criminals as much as to the police. And we do find, as a matter of fact, that equally astonishing levels of technical achievement underlie the most trivial computer games as much as the most intellectually significant scientific experiments. The pursuit of excellence in medicine, by contrast, cannot be indifferent to purpose in this way. Central to it is the promotion of a non-technical value – health. That is why health professionals cannot countenance the use of medical skill to other ends – judicial amputations, for example – and why there is always some pressure on cosmetic surgeons to connect their work with psychological or emotional 'health'.

In a similar fashion, 'bent' lawyers can be exceptionally skilled in law. The administration of justice is not just one among a number of ends that lawyers may have. It is intrinsic to the profession. The defect in rogue lawyers is not their incompetence, but their willingness to use their knowledge and skill to unjust ends. The same point applies, if anything even more forcibly to the profession of priest. This is revealed in the intriguing fact that a properly ordained priest fully conversant with the theology and liturgical practices of the Church was required for the celebration of the 'black' mass. The liturgical acts had to be faultless to be effective; their corruption lay in their being directed to the worship of Satan.

What all this shows is that professional education requires what the modern world calls 'values education'. This is not significantly different from an education in the liberal arts. To serve justice we have to know what it is. This is not empirical knowledge in any straightforward sense. It requires the sort of philosophical reflection and historical understanding characteristic of jurisprudence, alongside the study of criminology, broadly construed. So too with medicine. Contemporary curricular reform in medical schools has given new emphasis to 'medical humanities' in the education of physicians.

These examples serve to reveal a connection between a liberal and a practical education. This is a salutary counter to some of the divisions with which we are currently familiar. Nevertheless, it goes a very small way towards addressing the further matters of research excellence and large-scale tertiary education. Unfortunately, these further connections can only be hinted at here. It will have to suffice to note that the ideal of the college, as exemplified in eighteenth-century Scotland and post-colonial America, understood education for citizenship and civil leadership as a key part of its role. The expression 'political education' can have unwelcome connotations, but in *this* sense it has just the same sort of structure as professional education – special competence informed by philosophical, historical and sociological reflection on ethics, politics and the arts, as well as a sufficient knowledge of, for instance, mathematics, the sciences, economics, and technology. The purpose of such an education is to form an intelligently responsible citizenry across all classes and groups, one that will be able to resist both tyranny and the sort of populism that can corrupt democracies. The role of free inquiry central to the idea of a university is to ensure that intelligent citizenship never degenerates into received opinion or ossified dogma.

This is a very brief sketch, but I think it is possible to elaborate this revitalized version of the university as college in a way that throws new and more profitable light on many of the problems that currently confront the academy. Chief among these, in my estimation, is the difficulty of continuing to assert the university's valuable social role, while resisting two recurrent threats to its autonomy – 'the state as social engineer' and 'the student as customer'.

BIBLIOGRAPHY

Burgh, H., A. Fazackerly and J. Black (eds) (2007), *Can the Prizes Still Glitter?* Buckingham: University of Buckingham Press.

Carter, J. and D. Witherington (1992), *Scottish Universities: Distinctiveness and Diversity*, Edinburgh: John Donald.

Graham, Gordon (2008), *Universities: the Recovery of an Idea* (second edition), Exeter: Imprint Academic.

Hofstadter, R. and W. Smith (eds) (1961), *American Higher Education: a documentary history*, in two volumes, Chicago: Chicago University Press.

Newman, John Henry (1852/1982), *The Idea of a University*, Martin Svaglic (ed.), Indiana: Notre Dame University Press.

Sloan, Douglas (1971), *The Scottish Enlightenment and the American College Ideal*, New York: Teachers College Press.

Hegel, G. W. F. (1991), *Elements of the Philosophy of Right*, Wood, Allen W. (ed.), translated by H. B. Nisbet, Cambridge: Cambridge University Press (originally published 1821).

2. The 'form' of 'reform'. The postwar university in Britain, 1945–1992

Keith Tribe

The nature and purpose of university education in Britain is much misunderstood. The current prevailing evaluation of universities as machines for the production of human capital is a relatively new one, inapplicable to the quite recent past, as the recent writings of Stefan Collini have sought to emphasize.[1] But given the rapidity of changes to British higher education since the later 1980s, not all directly related to the 1992 Act, it is very difficult to form a clear picture of the development of the British university system during the second half of the twentieth century, especially since there has always been so little informed discussion. In addition, while it might be assumed that well-found reform must necessarily be based upon a sound understanding of the object of reform – the historical reasons for the existence of the object in a particular given form – in the sphere of British higher education this amounts to a quite novel and radical idea.

This chapter seeks to address the problem in a limited and particular way: by considering the history of the post-war New Universities, the green-field campus universities mostly associated with the 1960s, but initiated in 1950 with the opening of Keele University. The primary purpose of these new foundations was not to provide capacity for an overstretched system; their purpose was experimental, to provide scope for innovation in teaching and learning. By considering some of these initiatives we can perhaps broaden our understanding of the possibilities of university education, what it might offer to students, and also importantly, the scope it offers to teachers for innovation. As it happens, none of these early experiments have lasted: patterns of teaching and learning in all of the New Universities are now similar to anywhere else. And so the trajectory that these institutions have followed is also instructive of the fate of reform. I present here some case studies in the economy of reform,[2] so that we might better understand why it is that the aspirations attached to university institutions find fulfilment in the management rhetoric of 'academic excellence' instead of the real experience of students.

I will begin with some general remarks on education and educational achievement in post-war Britain, followed by some more specific comments on the evolution of the university as an institution. My discussion of the New University foundations will be related to those institutions in which I have spent most of my academic career: Essex, Keele and Sussex. This somewhat personal view is moderated by my extensive research on the development of the modern research university since the later nineteenth century, in particular, the formation and development of the economics discipline, which is itself a creature of the twentieth-century university.

SCHOOLING AND THE MODERN UNIVERSITY

In the later 1940s there were broadly four routes to a university degree: by attending an institution that awarded its own degrees, not necessarily on a full-time basis (Oxford or Cambridge, London, Glasgow, Birmingham, Queen's Belfast for example); by attending a university institution through which one might study for a London external degree (a university college such as Leicester or Reading); by attending a local authority Technical College and studying for an external London degree (typically a BSc, but not necessarily so); or indeed by not attending any institution at all and taking a London external degree by private study, whether living in Britain, or in Accra or Montréal.

Summarized in this way it already becomes apparent that access to the university system was not then as socially elitist as is often assumed. While it was true that only a small proportion of young people either studied for, or achieved, a university degree, this was not so much for lack of access to higher education on the part of those who might benefit from it, but for the more prosaic reason that most professional and administrative employers placed no great value on a university education, preferring instead their own professional training and qualifications (banking, accountancy, the law, teaching, local administration).[3] Such employers recruited school-leavers aged 14–17[4] and gave them appropriate training; someone in their early twenties with a university degree simply did not fit into such a path from schooling to employment, being too old and overqualified. This was rather different in Scotland, whose ancient universities were more akin to the Continental European model, providing the medical and legal education that in England was the province of teaching hospitals and the Colleges of Law.

Links between the English universities and the professions were indirect; William Ashley's purpose in founding the Birmingham Faculty of Commerce in 1902 was to provide a training for managers and administrators, but this foundered on the general lack of interest on the part of employers for university-level recruits to industry. This if nothing else highlights the way in which a university education was not then conceived as necessarily linked to employment in industry, commerce and public administration. In any case, as late as 1961–2, 73 per cent of pupils in England and Wales left school without having sat for any public examination;[5] while moderated by the fact that most universities had their own matriculation procedures and did not rely for selection on national qualifications alone, the fact that the vast majority of school leavers lacked any such qualification suggests that any direct linkage between formal education at any level and the labour market was of marginal significance. It does however go some way to explain why such a small proportion of the population attended university. Although it was true that in 1959 less than 4 per cent of the 18-year-old cohort attended university,[6] the same source records that in 1956 only 10.5 per cent of the cohort attended school to the age of 17 in any case (Murray, 1959: 393).

It is also generally supposed that the socio-political experience of the Second World War initiated a wide-ranging modernization of Britain, the creation of a welfare state being associated with greater social mobility and the establishment of a universal right to education and healthcare. As far as the development of British universities is concerned, this is also somewhat misleading, since reforms to training and the creation of new institutions mooted in the 1930s were delayed until after the war. Moreover, there was at this time little impetus for expansion since it was widely supposed that the population was declining,[7] there being therefore little incentive to extend university provision in anticipation of a growth in numbers of young people.[8] Finally, the baby-boom of the immediate post-war years is only the second of three such booms in the twentieth century: apart from a short sharp boom following the First World War peaking in 1920, the post-war boom peaking in 1947 is eclipsed numerically by a subsequent boom that peaked only in 1964.[9]

This is not to deny that the social changes of the 1940s and 1950s were driven by the cultural legacy of the war, an increasing and hence younger population, and a bipartisan political emphasis on equality of access to welfare, housing, health and education. But the planning and foundation of new modern campus universities during this period, beginning with the inauguration of the University College of North Staffordshire in 1950, was not a response to a perceived lack of capacity in the existing higher education system, but to enable experimentation with new ideas for the structure and purpose of a university. The established stock of university-level institutions was thought to be quite capable of absorbing any rise in demand for student places. It should also be emphasized that the endorsement of the extension of the university system given by the Robbins Report

(Committee on Higher Education, 1963) appeared well after all the New Universities in England – Keele, Sussex, York, Lancaster, East Anglia, Kent, Essex, Warwick – were established, if not actually opened.

The chief impact of the Robbins Report was on what became the polytechnic sector, associated also with the formation of the Council for National Academic Awards in 1965 to provide degree-level qualifications for these upgraded institutions. While the university sector did expand considerably during the later 1960s, the principal source of expansion in British higher education at this time was access to local authority institutions, which generally demanded two, rather than three, 'A' levels as a condition of entry. Alongside these institutions most schoolteachers were trained in Teacher Training Colleges, which subsequently became transformed into Colleges of Higher Education, and then, after 1992, universities. Nursing training was not rolled into this system until 2000. One little-noted impact of this process of consolidation imposed upon what had been a diverse system, both in terms of academic level and of funding, has been the extension of direct central government control to include all post-school education.

These developments from the 1960s until the 1990s are significant, but neglected. However, the new polytechnic institutions were not conceived as sources of new models for higher education; this was the task of the new university foundations. Since this chapter seeks primarily to identify what was 'new' about the New Universities, and suggest why they followed a common path to uniformity, my focus is necessarily limited to these new foundations, and specifically to Essex, Keele and Sussex. My discussion here centres on Keele; this is because it was the first of the new universities and there is clarity about the intentions (or indeed lack of them) that initially shaped it, while its longer history permits a clearer perspective on the subsequent unravelling of the original goals. And to understand what was 'new' about these foundations we first need to form an idea of the nature of the system into which they were inserted.

THE EVOLUTION OF THE BRITISH UNIVERSITY – A BRIEF HISTORY

Another prevailing and widespread misconception regarding the development of the British university system is that far into the twentieth century Oxford and Cambridge dominated, both numerically and culturally. This not only neglects the role of the four ancient Scottish universities, it also underestimates both the role of the University of London from the mid-nineteenth century and that of the new civic universities of the later nineteenth century. The University of London as founded in 1826 was both secular and open to both men and women; Oxbridge took the rest of the century to catch up. The original University of London (what is now known as University College, London) also taught 'modern' subjects, unlike Oxford and Cambridge ('Oxbridge'), which until mid-century confined themselves to the teaching of classics and mathematics; it introduced written examinations in place of the oral Oxbridge examination;[10] and, when the University of London became an examining institution with provincial centres in the mid-nineteenth century it gave the modern British university a curricular and institutional structure that persisted throughout the twentieth century. Oxford and Cambridge maintained their leading position by successfully adapting to all of these changes, none of which they initiated; once so adapted Oxbridge became at best *primus inter pares*, and in particular areas of study and research no longer the leading institutions.

The model from which the universities of Oxford and Cambridge adapted was one whose chief role was producing clerics and teachers – hence the religious tests applied to candidates (in Oxford) and graduates (in Cambridge), and the exclusion of women. The gradual addition of the natural sciences and engineering to the range of subjects taught naturally involved changes to the organization of teaching and learning, but very significantly the British university system as a whole remained almost exclusively wedded to undergraduate rather than graduate study well into the later twentieth century. It was not until the later 1960s that a postgraduate qualification generally became a requirement for junior staff, and it was somewhat later that a doctorate became the standard qualification for recruitment into university academic employment. Nonetheless, university staff were contractually obliged to pursue independent research, and so to this extent the conditions established in the new American research university of the later nineteenth century were met: that university teachers were scholars engaged in their own research, their teaching thus reflecting this engagement. As an institution of teaching and learning, this principle was well established by mid-century: that a university student pursued a course of study the greater part of which was conducted independently, guided by lectures, classes and supervisions but not dependent on them in the manner of a school pupil. Organized in department and faculty, a 'professor' was usually a departmental head and so responsible for the teaching of a particular subject within the university as conducted by the senior and junior members of a given department. Described in this way it is easier to conceive the internal power structure of a mid-century university: as a series of fiefdoms in which the professoriate headed their subject areas and collectively as the Senate directed the course of university development.

In Britain a university is an independent institution enjoying the legal status of a perpetual trust dedicated to teaching and scholarship and licensed to grant its own degrees. While the Scottish universities enjoyed central government funding as part of the Union Settlement, London and the new civics – Owens/Victoria/Manchester, Liverpool, Birmingham, Sheffield, Leeds – were privately endowed and also supported by fees and local administration funding. A small amount of central government funding was introduced at the very end of the nineteenth century, and by the 1920s London took the lion's share of this. Private funding continued to be important in the interwar years: virtually all of the London School of Economics' interwar building programme was funded by the Rockefeller Foundation, which also made a major contribution to the New Bodleian Library extension in Oxford and the new University Library in Cambridge. However, in 1919 the Cabinet had explicitly rejected a proposal to make domestic charitable giving to universities tax-deductible, on the grounds that any resulting funds in fact belonged to the government and so was not at the disposal of individual taxpayers. Instead, the University Grants Commission was established to disburse funds and to assess standards of teaching and research, removing the management of government funding from direct political control. With the postwar growth of universities the role of government funding increased, and the role of the UGC extended, until in 1989 it was abolished and replaced, initially by the Universities Funding Council, and then by an ever-proliferating number of short-lived quangos known chiefly by their acronyms.[11] The new regulatory framework created and regularly rebuilt since 1992 has principally had the effect of re-establishing direct government control of universities, exerted through the new university managerial structures that were first developed in the later 1980s.

For by the time that the 1992 Act converted various institutions of higher education into universities the established universities had already begun the process of managerial restructuring. During the preceding 100 years the executive head of a university was the Vice-Chancellor who chaired a Senate, the principal decision-making body composed of the university's professors. All significant decisions regarding finance and university development were here made collectively.[12] The Vice-Chancellor had of course substantial powers to direct the development of the institution, but had no more than a small staff with which to do this, and was furthermore answerable to a University Council and University Court composed of local worthies, business representatives and local government officials. During the later 1980s, and mostly anticipating the fact that the government would eventually get around to reorganizing higher education in much the same *dirigiste* fashion inflicted upon schooling and vocational training, university administrations increasingly began to reshape themselves according to the values and imperatives of the private sector – or more precisely, what were conceived to be the values and imperatives of the private sector, as few university administrators had any direct business experience. University Vice-Chancellors now began to see themselves as the chief executives of their institutions, managing the business of the Senate more directly, and developing a central office for this purpose. However, the introduction of a private-sector ethos, which was eventually to undermine the prevailing collegiate principles governing scholarship and teaching, was not linked to the development of established structures of governance. Professorial positions were created as a means of developing new areas of expertise, so that departments were no longer led by a single professor, but rather by a Head of Department appointed from among the senior staff. The role of the professoriate in directing university policy was thereby diminished, since they were now simply better-paid versions of university lecturers;[13] Senate was increasingly sidelined by the office of the Vice-Chancellor, the academic staff treated simply as a workforce and the professoriate transformed into line managers. There was a universal failure to develop an executive board capable of checking the centralization of executive power in the office of the Vice-Chancellor, as existed for example by the later 1990s in the NHS for all Trusts. Theoretically of course the Vice-Chancellor remained answerable to Court and Council, but these bodies were too large, diffuse and disengaged to either assess independently or act in concert against executive decision-making. These developments combined to create a serious problem of governance in the higher reaches of British universities that emerged independently of the post-1992 reorganization of higher education, but which that reorganization has greatly amplified. There is today no greater a supply of competent, let alone charismatic, university Vice Chancellors than there was 20 years ago, but they are spread over a far greater number of institutions; and unlike any NHS Chief Executive, there are few real checks on their power, and little prospect that they could be summarily dismissed for abusing this power.

This story can be elaborated in detail across an academic landscape differentiated by subject areas, institutions, and student intakes; but the rapidity of the changes undergone in British higher education since the early 1990s, not all related directly to the 1992 Act itself, has all but obliterated a clear view of what went before. I will now turn to sketch in some of the bright futures envisaged for universities and university education in the 1950s and 1960s, in the ruins of which we now live.

THE NEW UNIVERSITIES OF POSTWAR BRITAIN

During the 1930s discussion of the future of universities laid emphasis upon the need to resist specialization in undergraduate training and promote breadth, Adolf Löwe's influential *Universities in Transformation* (Löwe, 1940) arguing for instance that students should spend two out four years on a broadly-based introductory course, rather on the model of the present-day American liberal arts college. Interest was also expressed in expanding student numbers – in the immediate postwar years the Barlow Report (Committee on Scientific Manpower, 1946) recommended that the existing output of graduates in science and technology be doubled, and that there be significant increases in the number of students studying in the humanities. The Committee also proposed the early foundation of at least one new university, a proposal that was opposed by existing universities, arguing that available resources would better used on existing institutions. The UGC accepted that resources were constrained, but determined that an exception be made in the case of what later became Keele University. This decision clearly illustrates the way that this initiative was unrelated to considerations of capacity; and it was not until the 1970s that real concern was expressed about the relatively small size of all the new foundations.

As elsewhere in the country there were in the Potteries local proposals to found a new university, together with newly vacated wartime sites thought suitable for this purpose.[14] The Potteries had a long history of adult education initiated by R. H. Tawney in 1908, and this educational tradition plus the fact that Tawney was a member of the UGC from 1943 to 1948 lent this particular project traction. A. D. Lindsay, the eventual founding Principal of the University College of North Staffordshire, was not directly involved in the initial planning, but his educational background in Glasgow and Oxford had led him to favour a broad, modern curriculum over increasing specialization. As Vice-Chancellor of Oxford from 1935 he had also persuaded Lord Nuffield that his endowment to the university should be used to found a new college devoted to the social sciences, and not for the natural sciences. His longstanding interest in extending the range of subjects studied at university level was reflected in his participation in the University Committee established by the British Military Government in Germany, which in 1949 published reform proposals including the establishment of a new *Studium Generale* course in the German university. In May 1947 he had opened a House of Lords debate on education, arguing that the number of students in England and Wales would have to double to reach the proportion of young people studying in Scottish universities, suggesting that the expansion of the university system was the natural corollary of the 1944 Education Act.[15] On a number of levels Lindsay's ideas regarding universities and learning were formally realized in the structure of Keele University, but in fact he had little to do with the actual shaping of the curriculum.

Those in the Potteries who supported the idea of founding a new university based upon modern principles of learning and teaching succeeded in gaining support from the universities of Oxford, Manchester and Birmingham, and it was in joint meetings with representatives of these universities that the actual structure was devised: a four-year degree course based on Joint Honours, with a common Foundation Year reviewing the history of Western Civilization, and three subsidiary subjects of study to run alongside the subjects studied for joint honours. The composition of subjects studied was to be constrained only by the timetable; students themselves would select the combinations which could cross the division of the arts from the natural and the social sciences, but were to be constrained by, for example, a student studying for an arts-based degree having to take a subsidiary course in a natural or life science. Quite how this would be realized was in fact never worked out until the students arrived and were inducted into the Foundation Year in the autumn of 1950. Nor did Lindsay himself play a major role in the detailed design of the teaching programme: much of that work was done by Roy Pascal, Professor of German at the University of Birmingham, who outlined a workable teaching model in a memorandum of 17 February 1949. Indeed, teaching plans were still vague when the advertisement for the first 12 professors was published in December 1949. It later became plain that the Joint Honours system, with students themselves selecting the combinations to be studied, required clear departmental direction so that teaching might convey to students the core of any particular subject. But since this did not become obvious until well into the second year of the University's existence[16] the founding professors stumbled into this particular problem unawares.

Despite many years of discussion, there was a clear lack of forethought regarding the resources that this curricular structure required. From the very first the Foundation Year and Joint Honours programme called for the immediate appointment of staff across a wide range of subjects. A gross imbalance between staff and students emerged: planned for an annual intake of 150 students (thus a total student body of 600), by 1952–3 there were already 44 fulltime staff and 415 students, by 1955 (the year following the first full cycle) 564 students and 80 fulltime staff. Keele had not many more students than the average contemporary secondary school had pupils, and sited on what remains the largest campus in Britain had a student/staff ratio of 7:1.[17] Since however the Foundation Year and honours courses were lecture-based, and students allocated themselves randomly across subjects, this did not permit a more tutorial-based system to emerge. Indeed, for the first 30 years the Foundation Year was run rather like a resident distance-learning course, students posting their essays to tutors who marked and returned them in like manner. Furthermore, despite the university having been sited west of the Potteries on account of the local tradition of adult education, local student recruitment was quickly eclipsed: only 62 of 153 students admitted in 1951 came from the West Midlands, and of these only 23 from the Potteries. The following year only 41 of 140 students admitted originated in the West Midlands. Within a few years of its founding the local character of the institution had all but disappeared.

By the later 1970s it was plain that a compulsory Foundation Year was financially unsustainable, and so it became an optional access course followed by a conventional three-year joint honours degree. The possibility of eccentric combinations of subjects – Russian and Electronics, or Economics and Music – was eroded simply through student choice. Increasingly students opted for closely related subjects, such as Economics and Management Science, and eschewed experimentation. Student choice put an end to the diversity of studies envisaged by the founders. The lack of effective cross-departmental links inherent in the original model prevented the teaching staff from adapting to such changes. The centralization of student recruitment left the departments without any real control over the students recruited to their subject. These and other factors combined to undermine the original vision of its founders; through the 1990s, Keele University became distinguished from other institutions merely by the fact that it was small, campus-based and retained a joint honours programme. Indeed, the underlying imperative that departments teach to the core of their subject area while leaving individual students to do the connecting hampered departmental specialization and inter-departmental collaboration. A broad division into three faculties had originally existed merely to determine the menu of subjects a student could choose; any possibility that a more substantial faculty structure might develop was undermined by the managerial revolution of the 1990s, since decision-making moved away from academic staff to university administrators.

The trajectory followed by Keele University in its first 40 years – from a tiny university with an unusually broad curricular spectrum to a small university offering much the same kind of range of studies as many other British institutions – is instructive, for this movement to the mean had many sources, most of which were strenuously but vainly resisted by teachers and administrators. The next new university founded in Britain, the University of Sussex, has followed much the same path, but for quite different reasons: the destruction of its founding principles was imposed upon it by university management in the early twenty-first century, with the connivance of some parts of its teaching staff who failed to appreciate properly what they were to lose until it was too late. In this case the university management argued that Sussex's profile as an educational establishment was too different from the norm to remain attractive to potential students, presenting the somewhat bizarre idea that in order to be competitive one institution has to look much the same as all the rest.[18]

The committee charged with planning the University of Sussex was formed in 1958, a Vice-Chancellor was selected in 1959, professors were appointed and then the first intake of 50 students arrived in October 1961.[19] In many respects the problems identified in Keele's development were avoided both in the planning and development of Sussex, although the actual lack of departments created different problems of their own. While assuming the viability of a very generous student–staff ratio of eight to one, at a time that the UGC was pressing Keele to expand to 1200 students in total,[20] it was originally envisaged that Sussex would quickly expand to 3000 students. The university was structured according to distinct 'civilizations', schools of study to which individual members of staff were appointed and in which students studied: European Studies, English and American Studies, Social Studies, African and Asian Studies, Educational Studies, Physical Science, Biological Science, Applied Science and Engineering Science. By throwing academics together in this way the problem identified at Keele – that academics were constrained to teach and work to a core of their subject and lacked inter-departmental structures – was overcome, but eventually as the university grew this created an opposite problem: that especially in the arts and social sciences, subject specialists in each school found it difficult to pool their resources and so develop their disciplines both inside and outside the university.

Whereas the central form of teaching at Keele was the lecture, at Sussex this was eschewed in favour of tutorials, seeking to reinforce a teacher–pupil relationship. In part this reflected the influence of Oxford on the new foundation, but in opting for a tutorial-based system Sussex was also reflecting contemporary thinking on learning and development, moving away from a strict pedagogy to a child/student-centred model. There was indeed a definite advantage in this model in that it relaxed the constraints of an orthodox teaching programme, giving a greater degree of flexibility to both teacher and student. Quite apart from this it was thought that a student programme organized in this way would counter persistently high wastage rates in British universities; running at some 14 per cent in England excluding Oxbridge, this in fact ranged between institutions and subjects from 3 per cent to 30 per cent (Corbett, 1964: 30) On the other hand, staff eventually rediscovered the merits of a lecture-based model for themselves: that it forces teachers to organize their thoughts, keep up with recent work, and reflect on the sequence in which students should be introduced to a subject. A mix of lectures and tutorials developed through the 1970s and 1980s.

The university retained its school structure, moderated by the introduction of a parallel major path, into the later 1990s. Internal pressure built up for a switch towards an emphasis on core principal subjects, reflecting the longstanding frustrations of disciplinary segmentation brought about by the school structure, but neglecting to consider the impact that such a shift would have on the profile of Sussex in the post-1992 landscape. Within a few years the university administration entirely remodelled the teaching structure of the university along faculty-departmental lines, presenting to the potential student a teaching programme that looked much the same as that offered in any other university: lecture-based with a few classes, and organized around one principal degree. This new structure lasted less than three years before it again required remodelling, creating new layers of managerial posts to carry out work that, in the older university, had merely been one part of a senior academic's duties. Sussex has therefore followed a similar path to that of Keele over 40 years, from an educational innovator to a degree factory,[21] with the difference that in Sussex the major changes have been imposed by the university administration, rather than emerging out of a number of cross-cutting trends.

Turning briefly to Essex, a similar arc can be detected, although its arrival at an institution very similar to Sussex and Keele so far as its teaching programme goes has involved less structural change. While the planning process for Sussex was far more focused and coherent than it had been at Keele, Essex advanced on both of these. The Academic Planning Board was established in October 1960 but it was not until June 1962 that Albert Sloman was appointed Vice Chancellor.[22] A professor of Spanish from the University of Liverpool, he was given carte blanche to give shape to the new foundation, and among his early decisions was to limit the university initially to eight departments or centres, each with its own professor to head it. These heads were in turn given a free hand to devise teaching as they thought appropriate, within a standard model of lecture and class. The first professors took up their appointments in 1963, and the first student intake was 1964. The teaching was school-based – so for example, one could study politics in the School of Social Studies or the School of Comparative Studies, the distinction being that in the former it would be linked with sociology and economics, in the latter with languages and literature. Serving this model were departments of the standard kind, overcoming the tensions between the constraints of student and staff that proved so damaging in Keele and Sussex. Entering the university four years after it had opened, I spent my first year in a common School of Social Studies course organized around a core programme of economics, sociology and government. In my first year, besides these subjects, I took two hours of mathematics and two hours of computer programming a week throughout the year. Other students in my first year took courses in French or Portuguese. Following on from this students specialized for two years in one of the three core subjects.

That has now all gone. A strictly departmental structure has reasserted itself, student learning being more or less entirely aligned with one department, so that a degree in economics, for example, now looks very much like one from any other university. As we have seen with Keele and Sussex, this is not for want of experimentation with interdisciplinary structures, rather from an inability to sustain an idiosyncratic pedagogic structure in the longer term. While there is no one source for this inability, the outcome is a university landscape of a remarkably uniform appearance. Every summer the announcement of 'A' level results is accompanied by a variety of guides for prospective students. None of these pays any attention to the individual merit of teaching and scholarship in any given university or department.

CONCLUSION

In June 2011 the opening in London of a New College of the Humanities was announced. Anthony Grayling, its prospective Master, demonstrated in his comments on his own time at Sussex and Oxford that he was as confused as anyone else about the purpose of the university education he had himself received. He commented that he had found his training at Sussex insufficiently specialized, and was of the view that the education he received at Oxford was more suited to a career as a scholar. Both are serious misapprehensions. Comparisons with major American liberal arts colleges made at the time likewise missed the point that the faculty of such institutions are expected to carry the core teaching functions with minimal assistance. The 'star academics' whose names were associated with the launch of the New College are the last people one could look to for the performance of such core functions. The real value of the education to be found in the American liberal arts colleges cannot be denied; the prospectus of the New College is a parody of that value.

But as this chapter has argued, perhaps that does not matter in any case. If the New College survives more than five or ten years it will eventually offer teaching largely indistinguishable from that available elsewhere, possibly more expensive, but also possibly not. Reforms to a system in the absence of any substantial understanding of the evolution and present structure of that system hardly ever turn out in the way intended. The only sure thing is that reforms of that kind merely prepare the ground for future waves of reform.

NOTES

1. See his 'From Robbins to McKinsey' (Collini, 2011).
2. 'Economy' not in the modern sense of 'efficiency', but of internal organization.
3. For some sense of clerical and administrative employment and the nature of qualifications in the 1920s and 1930s see Savage (1993), pp. 196–216.
4. While in England and Wales university entry has typically been at the age of 18 since the later nineteenth century, compulsory schooling ceased at 14 until the autumn of 1947 and at 15 until the autumn of 1972.
5. See Aldcroft (1992), p. 36. It should be noted that there was then an extensive network of voluntary part-time post-school education available, while a proportion of unqualified school-leavers would receive workplace training and qualification.
6. But as implied in the opening paragraph, this proportion is significantly smaller than those actually studying for university degrees; in comparisons of pre- and post-1992 participation rates this qualification is very often neglected, so that full-time students at university pre-1992 are compared with all students studying in higher education post-1992. Even in the 1950s these were two very distinct numbers, and by the 1980s such a comparison deflates the pre-1992 participation rate in higher education by up to 50 per cent.
7. Live births per 1000 of the total population were above 16 in the later 1920s, falling to 15 and then stabilizing around 14 during the 1930s.
8. See Reddaway (1939).
9. See Mitchell, (1988), Table 10, pp. 42–4.
10. Whence in Cambridge the term 'Tripos' for an honours degree, related to the custom of having the examinee sit on a three-legged stool.
11. Some of these are listed in Stevens (2004), p. xviii.
12. The Oxford Congregation and Cambridge Senate remain important bodies, the former being explicitly referred to as the University's sovereign body.
13. It might also be noted that when senior polytechnic teachers were 'promoted' after 1992 to the title of Professor they generally received little or no increase in pay, which by that time had become the only positive point of being a university professor. Professorial pay has usually been a matter of direct negotiation with the University, and not part of an established pay scale; in the case of polytechnics, this confidentiality served to conceal not their greater remuneration, but the fact that it remained the same.
14. Most of the new proposals were initiated and led at County level, each with a number of possible sites. Lancaster University, for instance, nearly ended up at Blackpool.
15. *Manchester Guardian* 15 May 1947, p. 6.
16. Keele was called a University College until the 1960s, due to its connection with Oxford, Manchester and Birmingham; but unlike other university colleges it was chartered from the beginning to award its own degrees, and therefore to devise its courses as it saw fit.
17. *Prospectus* 1952–3, pp. 9–10; *Annual Report* 1955, pp. 4–5. The compulsory common Foundation Year placed a definite constraint on expansion, since first-year numbers could not increase beyond the capacity of the largest lecture theatre.
18. While the source for such a belief most likely comes from a garbled understanding of perfect competition and its analytical purpose, some intellectual support for a related idea – that the competitive process itself diminishes differentiation among goods

and services supplied – can be found in the work of Harold Hotelling (for example, Hotelling, 1929).

19. See account of founding Vice-Chancellor Sir John Fulton (Fulton, 1964), pp. 9–10.
20. That is, 300 students in each year, a practical ceiling given the size of the largest lecture theatre available into which the first year could all fit to hear the Foundation Year lectures; duplication of the lecture course does not appear to have ever been seriously contemplated.
21. A 'degree factory' can be provisionally defined as an institution with: (1) instrumental and task-oriented students; (2) limited personal contact between teachers and students; (3) primarily lecture-based teaching; (4) limited control of what is taught by lecturers because of the dominance of textbooks and disciplinary models; both teaching and research controlled by a separate management hierarchy.
22. Sloman gives his own account of the establishment of Essex University in an interview printed in Tribe (1997), pp. 223–37.

REFERENCES

Aldcroft, D. H. (1992), *Education, Training and Performance 1944 to 1990*, Manchester: Manchester University Press.

Collini, S. (2011), 'From Robbins to McKinsey', *London Review of Books* **33** (16), 25 August, pp. 9–14.

Committee on Higher Education (1963), *Higher Education. Report of the Committee appointed by the Prime Minister under the Chairmanship of Lord Robbins 1961–63*, Cmnd. 2154, London: Her Majesty's Stationery Office.

Committee on Scientific Manpower (1946), *Scientific Manpower*, Cmd. 6824, London: Her Majesty's Stationery Office.

Corbett, J. P. (1964), 'Opening the mind', in D. Daiches (ed.) *The Idea of a New University. An Experiment in Sussex*, London: André Deutsch.

Fulton, John (1964), 'New universities in perspective', in D. Daiches (ed.) *The Idea of a New University. An Experiment in Sussex*, London: André Deutsch.

Harold, Hotelling (1929), 'Stability in competition', *Economic Journal,* **39**, pp. 41–57.

Löwe, Alfred (1940), *Universities in Transformation,* London: Sheldon Press.

Mitchell, B. R. (1988), *British Historical Statistics*, Cambridge: Cambridge University Press.

Murray, K. (1959), 'The development of the universities in Great Britain', *Journal of the Royal Statistical Society* Series A (General), **121**, p. 393.

Reddaway, Brian (1939), *The Economics of a Declining Population*, London: Allen & Unwin.

Savage, M. (1993), 'Career mobility and class formation: British Banking workers and the lower middle classes', in A. Miles and D. Vincent (eds), *Building European Society. Occupational Change and Social Mobility in Europe, 1840–1940*, Manchester: Manchester University Press.

Tribe, K. (ed.) (1997), *Economic Careers. Economics and Economists in Britain 1930–1970*, London: Routledge.

Stevens, Robert (2004), *From University to Uni. The Politics of Higher Education in England since 1944*, London: Politico's.

3. Balancing the core activities of universities: for a university that teaches

Gert Biesta

INTRODUCTION

The question as to how to balance the core activities of the university can be taken as a simple technical question. In that case – and on the assumption that there are three core activities: teaching, research and service – balancing would mean something like doing one-third of each. One may perhaps wish to argue that everything a modern university does should be research-led, research-based or research-driven, in which case the balancing would be a matter of putting research first and making sure that the other activities follow proportionally. Or one might want to make the case that the university should first and foremost provide service – service to the community, service to society, or service to the economy, for example – in which case considerations of service should drive teaching and research. Yet this already shows that the question of balancing is actually never simply an arithmetical issue but leads us straight to the question of what the university is *for*. This is the question I will pursue in this chapter in order to develop a line of thinking that may help in engaging with the question of balancing in a more imaginative way.

THE RISE OF THE 'GLOBAL UNIVERSITY'

To find out what the university is for, we might begin by looking at what it is that contemporary universities are actually aiming to achieve. When we look at a global scale, we can see that more and more universities in more and more countries are actually trying to achieve the *same* thing. They all want to become 'excellent' and 'world class'; they all want to be research-led; they all want to get to the top of the league table; they all are chasing publication in a small number of journals included in a small number of global citation indexes (and in some cases publication in such journals has even become mandatory for academics); they are all competing for the same financial resources; they are all competing for the same students; and – perhaps summing it all up – they are all competing for the same prestige.

Elsewhere (Biesta 2011) I have referred to this phenomenon as the rise of the 'global university'. The global university is not meant to refer to a particular kind of university but instead highlights a particular *modus operandi* of universities and the main characteristic of this *modus operandi* is that it is entirely self-referential. That is to say: the conception of a good university that underlies the global university is not based on a substantive set of values and principles but is articulated in terms of how one institution is positioned *in relation to* other institutions (on this phenomenon see also Simons and Masschelein 2009). The pseudo-substantive notion of 'quality' is often mobilized in this context, for example when the global university is saying that it strives for 'the highest quality in research and teaching'. But 'quality' is a problematic concept because it does not really mean anything until one begins to specify its qualities, so to speak, that is, until one begins to specify what kind of quality one is after. With respect to the notion of 'quality' there is also the problem that much of what the global university aims for in terms of quality is actually defined in terms of *indicators* of quality rather than quality itself, so that it is not uncommon to find the global university identifying its main strategic aim in terms of the league table position it seeks to achieve – often without being able to articulate what it will do once it has achieved that position, other than going ever more upwards and onwards.

While it seems to be perfectly clear, therefore, where the global university is going, it could be argued that *at the very same time* the global university lacks any sense of direction. The global university is, after all, only going where everyone else is going. It is a *responsive*, or perhaps even more a *reactive* and *adaptive* institution. And since everyone is reacting to everyone else, the system as a whole is slowly going nowhere – that is, it is drifting rather than that it has a sense of direction. It would be easy to conclude that the global university is therefore a perversion of the very idea of the university. But the difficulty with taking that angle is not only that the university is a historical construction and not a natural phenomenon – so that it is difficult to claim some kind of 'essence' of the university that can then become perverted – but also that the university has been constructed and is being constructed in a number of different ways. There is not *one* idea of a university, but there are several. In order to put the question of what the university is *for* in perspective, it is therefore useful to look briefly at some of the different ways in which the university has emerged in differing (national) contexts.

IDEAS OF THE UNIVERSITY

In a recent paper Zgaga (2009) makes a useful contribution to this task through a brief discussion of the history of the modern university in terms of four 'archetypes' to which he refers as the *Napoleonic*, the *Humboldtian*, the *Newmanian* and the *Deweyan* model respectively. Zgaga emphasizes that these models 'should not be taken as fixed and isolated patterns' (ibid.: 180) – in fact '(n)one of them can be associated with a single period of time, national context or distinguished scholar' (ibid.: 177) – but as analytical tools that can help to understand differences between universities and university systems and the differing conceptions of what a university is for that underlie these differences.

The Napoleonic model, which emerged in the wake of the French Revolution, conceives of the university as an institution *of* the state and *for* the state. In the words of Rüegg (2004: 45, quoted in Zgaga 2009: 178) it was:

> a corporation controlled by the state and incorporated into the hierarchy of the civil service [aiming at] three primary goals: first, to secure for the post-revolutionary state and its society the officials necessary for political and social stabilization; second, to make sure, that their education was carried out in harmony with the new social order and to prevent the emergence of new professional classes; and third, to impose limits on freedom of the intellect if it seemed likely to prove dangerous to the state.

The Napoleonic university is therefore very much a university focused on teaching rather than research, with its main aim to educate the 'leaders in industry, commerce, finance, expanding state bureaucracies, and the growing professions, including many kinds of engineering, accountancy, social administration, and education itself' (Perkin 2006: 175, quoted in Zgaga 2009: 178).

If the Napoleonic model gives us an idea of the university of a state institution focused on teaching and the education of state professionals, the Humboldtian model, connected to the opening of the University of Berlin in 1810, gives us a conception of the university that is different on precisely these two aspects. Here the idea of the university as an institution for 'the teaching of existing knowledge and the passing on of directly usable knowledge' (Zgaga 2009: 178) is replaced by an orientation towards the discovery of new knowledge, both as the purpose of the university and as its pedagogy – something expressed in the Humboldtian idea of *Bildung durch Wissenschaft*. 'Higher institutions of learning,' as von Humboldt wrote, 'treat all knowledge as a not yet wholly solved problem ... in contrast to the schools, which take as their subject only the completed and agreed upon results of knowledge', so that in the university 'the teacher no longer exists for the sake of the student; both exist for the sake of learning' (Von Humboldt 1963: 250–51, quoted in Zgaga 2009: 178). This mission of the university requires freedom of teaching and learning, which means that while the Humboldtian university is *of* the state in that the state both needs to secure its material conditions and its independence, it is not an institution *for* the state. The Humboldtian archetype needs, in other words, a conception of academic freedom.

But the training of professionals to protect and develop the nation state, and the conduct of research for its own sake in autonomous institutions were, as Zgaga's analysis makes clear, not the only answers to the challenges of the industrial age. The Newmanian archetype responds to a conception of the university that is too narrow, too specialist and too utilitarian by making a case for a university focused on the formation of the person and the cultivation of the intellect. John Henry Newman argued for a focus on liberal education by which 'the intellect, instead of being formed or sacrificed to some particular or accidental purpose, some specific trade or profession, or study or science, is disciplined for its own sake, for the perception of its own proper objects, and for its own highest culture' (Newman 1996: 109, quoted in Zgaga 2009: 179). While the Newmanian archetype entails an argument 'against Professional or Scientific knowledge as the sufficient end of University Education' (Newman 1996: 118, quoted in Zgaga 2009: 179), it is based on the idea that the cultivation of the intellect 'because it is a good in itself, brings with it a power and a grace to every work and occupation which it undertakes and [thus] enables us to be more useful' (ibid.). The Newmanian university is therefore neither a university of the state nor a university for the state but first and foremost a university for the person and the citizen, albeit on the belief that the cultivation of the person will, in the longer run, also benefit society.

Zgaga adds a fourth archetype to his overview to which he refers as the Deweyan model. This is a conception of the university that emphasizes the role of university education in the formation of citizens and the promotion of democracy, both at the level of society as a whole and in relation to the communities surrounding the university. Zgaga locates the roots of this conception in the North American context where, as he argues, 'higher education has never been understood as a predominantly "state affair"' (ibid.: 179). Whether the Deweyan model can be seen as distinctively different from the other models or whether it is a version of the Newmanian emphasis on liberal education infused with a more explicit focus on citizenship and democracy, is an issue for further discussion. Zgaga's point, however, is not to identify and characterize existing university systems but to distinguish between different conceptions of and rationales for the university. In actuality different universities, university systems and conceptions of the university will always combine aspects from the different models (see Zgaga 2009: 180).

PUBLIC GOOD OR PRIVATE BENEFIT?

As soon as we see that there is not one idea of the university but that there are many, it becomes difficult to argue that the global university is a perversion of the very idea of the university, because this idea only exists in *plurality*. While we might want to say that the global university is a perversion of a particular conception of the university, and while the foregoing could also help us to identify with much more precision which elements and aspects of the modern university are being eroded or undermined by the rise of the global university as the *modus operandi* of contemporary universities, I wish to highlight a more fundamental difference between the differing conceptions of the (modern) university on the one hand and the global university on the other. This difference has to do with the fact that the conceptions of the modern university outlined above all have an orientation towards the *public good*. All models see higher education first and foremost as a public good rather than as a provision entirely orientated towards individuals and their individual needs and benefits. Even the most utilitarian of the four archetypes, the Napoleonic university, is informed by a rationale in which the education of 'leaders' – and 'leaders' are explicitly different from 'elites' – is meant to support the public interest (or, to be more precise, the interest of particular publics).

One thing that is different about the current conditions under which universities operate in many countries, is the rise of the neo-liberal belief in the capacity of markets to produce beneficial outcomes for individuals in a range of non-economic domains. These developments help to explain the rise of the global university as an *adaptive* university, that is, a university trying to adapt to the 'demands' of, for example, global capitalism, economic 'realities', the 'needs' of students, and even the very 'logic' of the market itself. While one could see this as a way in which the global university is trying to be useful just as the models of the university presented above all try to be of use, what is different is that the global university is mainly adapting to private interests rather than supporting *public projects* and *the common good*.

FROM A UNIVERSITY THAT ADAPTS TO A UNIVERSITY THAT TEACHES

One could argue that a university that aims to be responsive and adaptive is a university that tries to take its service task seriously. After all, in being adaptive, the global university appears to service the needs of a wide range of different 'stakeholders' – both 'concrete' stakeholders such as students, companies or government agencies, and more 'abstract' stakeholders such as the knowledge economy, global capitalism or society at large. But the critical issue is *how* the university relates to its 'stakeholders' – and I put 'stakeholders' in quotation marks in order to indicate that the idea of 'stakeholders' is already part of the very logic I aim to question here. I wish to suggest that there are in principle three different ways in which an organization – or for that matter an individual – can engage with its 'stakeholders'. The first – and this is the model we can find in the global university as an adaptive university – follows the logic of an economic transaction. In an economic transaction there are two parties, customers and providers, and the transaction is based on the assumption that customers know what they want and that providers service these demands and compete in terms of price and quality. This is indeed what we can see the global university doing. It tries to service the needs of a wide range of stakeholders and clients – and does often refer to them as 'customers' – and, where possible, competes on price, but definitely competes in terms of quality, hence the strong emphasis on reputation and relative positioning in league tables.

Yet the economic model is not the only way in which organizations and individuals can engage with their 'stakeholders'. A second way of engagement is the one we can find in professional transactions. The main difference between economic and professional transactions is that in the latter it is the professional who defines what the client needs and it is the professional who subsequently also services this need. In most cases the servicing of these needs occurs without competition between professionals but on the basis of self-regulation of professional standards and financial compensation. If in the economic model the wants of the 'stakeholders' are simply accepted as their needs, and if in the professional model needs are defined by the professionals who service the need, the third model is the model where parties engage in a process of *collective* needs definition based on recognition of differential expertise. This is a process in which wants are *transformed* into needs rather than that wants are simply taken as needs or needs are defined by those who service the needs. There are two possible names for this third model. We can either call it a *democratic* model, on the assumption that democracy is not simply a question of the counting of preferences but rather of the transformation of individual preferences into collectively supported and supportable needs – and this is necessarily a public process that not so much takes place in the public sphere as that it actually constitutes the public sphere (see Marquand 2004). But we can also call it an *educational* model on the assumption that one of the key educational transformations is that of what is actually desired into what can be seen as legitimately desirable (see Biesta 2010).

By distinguishing between the economic, the professional and the democratic-educational model it becomes possible to see that the way in which the global university provides service to its 'stakeholders' is not the only way in which the university can engage with its service task. More importantly, the distinction between the three models makes visible what the difference is between a university that has a service-orientation towards private wants and a university that has a service-orientation towards the public good. The key distinction here is between an orientation that simply accepts – and thus adapts to – the ways in which customers define their wants and an orientation where the legitimacy of the wants is itself subject to educational and democratic transformation. While in the first mode the university gives to its stakeholders what they already know they want, the second mode operates on the assumption that there is a difference between wants and needs, between what is desired and what is desirable, so that the university does not simply give to its stakeholders what they already know they want, but gives something that, at the start, they do not know they want. Whereas in the first mode the university brings nothing new to the table, in the second mode it does. How might we call this latter relationship? I suggest that we call this *teaching.* Teaching, after all – if it is not just the facilitation of learning – is precisely the 'gesture' in which something *new* is brought to a situation. Teaching, to put it differently, is precisely the 'gesture' that *transcends* what is already there (see Biesta 2011). After all, when I teach you – and when you identify my activities as teaching – I do not tell you what you already know or give you what you already have; for my activity to count as teaching, I need to tell you something that you did not already know or bring you something that you did not already possess. Teaching, to put it differently, is *additive not adaptive*.

It is true that the democratic-educational mode is not the only way in which the university can teach. While the economic mode is one that makes teaching *im*possible (see also Biesta 2004), the professional mode is also one in which something new is brought to the table. In this respect the professional mode and the democratic-educational mode are both modes in which teaching is possible. The difference between the two is that the professional mode relies on the authority of the professional – and in this regard is based on an unequal power relationship between professionals and their clients – whereas the democratic-educational mode is after the constitution of what we might call an authority that authorizes (see Meirieu 2007). This is not a form of authority that takes its power from a source outside of the process – be it expertise, be it knowledge, be it social position – but rather sees the process of the transformation of wants into needs, and of what is desired into what is desirable, as a process in which all those involved eventually lend authority to the outcome of the process.

ARGUMENT FOR A UNIVERSITY THAT TEACHES

Against the trend of thinking of the university first and foremost as a research institution – something we can see very prominently in the ways in which the global university aims to position itself in relation to other universities and tries to gain prestige – but also against the trend of thinking of the university first and foremost as an institution that should be useful and functional for society, I wish to argue that if we want to conceive of the university as a public institution, that is, as an institution with a public 'task' and responsibility (see also Biesta et al. 2009), we need to conceive of its first priority as that of *teaching*. The 'if' is important here, as the global university seems to have given up on the need for the university to be a public institution. One can partly take this 'if' as an expression of commitment – in which case my argument for a university that teaches is mainly an argument for those who wish to understand the implications of one's commitment to the university as a public institution. But one can also ask what it would mean if we no longer thought of the university as a public institution – and here perhaps we might ask whether, if the university is just to be seen as a set of private functions, there would still be a reason to call this set of private functions 'a university' or whether it would not be more convenient and less expensive if the different functions of the university became independent of each other – in which case the whole question of the balancing of the core activities of the university would have disappeared.

To think of the first priority of the university as that of teaching means a number of things. It first of all means that the university needs to think of itself as an institution that has something new to offer to those it is in communication with. To see its first priority as that of teaching means, in other words, that it should establish teaching relationships with those it is in communication with, and that it should take a 'teacherly' attitude in those relationships. To take a teacherly attitude, that is, to operate on the assumption that one has something to say and to bring, means that those that the university is in communication with can no longer be understood as stakeholders and definitely not as consumers – which also means that the whole language of 'delivery' is probably not one that is appropriate for articulating what the university is after and about. Perhaps, following Dewey (1954), we should refer to those that the university is in communication with as 'publics' – also in order to highlight that what is at stake in the university that conceives of itself first and foremost as an institution that teaches is its public orientation, that is, its orientation towards the public good (see also Sugden, Chapter 4 in this volume).

To think of the first priority of the university as teaching does not simply mean that in terms of priority teaching should come first and research and service should follow. To think of the first priority of the university as that of teaching means to *rethink* the very nature of university research and university service. With regard to research the challenge is perhaps best expressed in Lawrence Stenhouse's definition of research as 'systematic enquiry made public' (Stenhouse 1983: 185). The point here is that research is not simply a form of systematic inquiry that meets all the methodical and methodological standards. Research – unlike systematic enquiry – always comes with the requirement to make one's systematic enquiries public. To make one's enquiries public is not a question of publishing one's findings but of making the whole research endeavour available for public scrutiny, that is, to see research in all its phases and aspects always as a public act with a public responsibility. With respect to service the challenge is not to approach the question of service in a servile manner, that is, entirely subordinated to the wishes and demands of others, but to see service in a teacherly way, that is, as a process in which one has something to offer and something to say, a process where one engages in (educational) needs definition and (democratic) needs transformation.

Some might say that this runs the risk of leading to a situation where the university becomes unaccountable. While the upshot of the idea that the first priority of the university is that of teaching is that the university becomes a critical rather than a docile institution, this doesn't mean that the university transforms itself into an ivory tower. The critical difference here is between democratic forms of accountability that carry a shared responsibility towards the common good, and technical–managerial forms of accountability that lack such an orientation (see Charlton 1999). While the university may well wish to become unaccountable in the technical–managerial sense – an accountability that is not orientated towards the public but towards quality controllers and inspectors – its orientation towards the public good requires that it not simply professes from a position of authority, but engages in the accountable establishment of authority that authorizes, which can only be an ongoing task and challenge.

Finally: should the taxpayer pay for such a university, that is, for a university that resists simply delivering what its 'stakeholders' demand? Putting the question in this way – and it is important to note that the question is very often put in this way – suggests that the relationship between citizens and the state can be expressed in economic terms, that is, as one where taxpayers pay in order to get individual benefits in return. But the relationship between citizens and the state is precisely not an economic relationship but should be conceived as a political relationship where what is at stake is the ongoing definition of public needs and of the common good. The question, therefore, is not whether taxpayers should be paying for a university that takes teaching as its first priority. The question rather is whether society would benefit from the presence of an institution that does not simply give society what it already knows that it wants and does not simply say what society already knows or already knows that it wants to hear. This, as I have suggested in this chapter, is the question of teaching and the teacher, which means that with regard to the university the critical question in the face of the rise of the global university is whether contemporary society wants to be open to the possibility of being taught, or whether it prefers to stay where it is, without challenge or interruption.

REFERENCES

Biesta, G.J.J. (2004), Against learning. Reclaiming a language for education in an age of learning. *Nordisk Pedagogik* **23**, 70–82.

Biesta, G.J.J. (2010), *Good Education in an Age of Measurement: Ethics, Politics, Democracy.* Boulder, CO: Paradigm.

Biesta, G.J.J. (2011), How useful should the university be? On the rise of the global university and the crisis in higher education. *Qui Parle: Critical Humanities and Social Sciences* **20** (1), 35–47.

Biesta, G.J.J., N. Kwiek, G. Locke, H. Martins, J. Masschelein, M. Simons and P. Zgaga, (2009), What is the public role of the university? A proposal for a public research agenda. *European Educational Research Journal* **8** (2), 250–55.

Charlton, B.G. (1999), The ideology of accountability. *Journal of the Royal College of Physicians of London* **33**, 33–35.

Dewey, J. (1954), *The Public and its Problems.* Chicago: Swallow Press.

Marquand, D. (2004), *The Decline of the Public.* Cambridge: Policy Press.

Meirieu, P. (2007), *Pédagogie: Le devoir de résister.* Issy-les-Moulineaux: ESF.

Newman, J.H. (1996), *The Idea of a University.* New Haven: Yale University Press.

Perkin, H. (2006), History of universities. In J.F. Forest and P.G. Altbach (eds), *International Handbook of Higher Education, Part 2.* Dordrecht: Springer.

Rüegg, W. (ed.) (2004), *A History of the University in Europe. Volume III. Universities in the Nineteenth and Early Twentieth Century (1800–1945).* Cambridge: Cambridge University Press.

Simons, M. and Masschelein, J. (2009), The public and its university. *European Educational Research Journal* **8** (2), 204–17.

Stenhouse, L. (1983), *Authority, Education and Emancipation.* London: Heinemann.

Von Humboldt, W. (1963), On the relative merits of higher institutions of learning. In *Collected Works*, vol. 10, trans M. Cowan, 250–60. Detroit: Wayne State University Press.

Zgaga, P. (2009), Higher education and citizenship: 'The full range of purposes'. *European Educational Research Journal* **8** (2), 175–88.

4. Space in an inferno? The organization of modern universities and the role of academics

Roger Sugden[1]

1 INTRODUCTION

We begin with a perhaps bleak view of people and of the sort of societies and economies that we, as people, have created, but also with rays of hope and thus questions for those of us with an interest in the organization of universities and the role of academics. For Italo Calvino, in the concluding paragraph of *Invisible Cities* (1972: 165):

> The inferno of the living is not something that will be; if there is one, it is what is already here, the inferno where we live every day, that we form by being together. There are two ways to escape suffering it. The first is easy for many: accept the inferno and become such a part of it that you can no longer see it. The second is risky and demands constant vigilance and apprehension: seek and learn to recognize who and what, in the midst of the inferno, are not inferno, then make them endure, give them space.

Could a university provide such space? Could it enable people to think about and understand who and what are not inferno? If so, what would that require for the organization of the university, and for the role of academics?

Using an analysis of socio-economic realities and potential, this chapter reflects on issues raised by these questions. In so doing it identifies a critical challenge that is currently facing societies, communities and territories: to evolve a model of socio-economic development that serves the interests of publics. We suggest that a task facing universities is to provide people with the creative space to meet that challenge, and we consider what more precisely this might involve.

2   SOCIO-ECONOMIC REALITY AND POTENTIAL

Section 2 of the chapter considers socio-economic realities and potential, focusing first on the governance of socio-economic activity, illustrating our arguments using Hymer's (1972) analysis of US transnational corporations and uneven development across the world. We then explore Dewey's (1927) appreciation of the public interest and, drawing arguments together, provide a characterization of current socio-economic development processes, i.e. of the inferno referred to by Calvino. We also consider the potential for a form that might better satisfy the interests of publics. We thereby provide a context to contemplate, in section 3 of the chapter, the organization of modern universities and the role of academics – the possibility of a space in the inferno.

Governance

Inspiration for our perspective on current realities comes in the first instance from Coase (1937), a contribution at the base of every rigorous consideration of the economic theory of the firm. His concern is the coordination of production activity, and his paper is typically presented as a classic, highlighting the significance of market versus non-market mechanisms for coordinating production. However, a different reading of Coase suggests that his analysis is essentially about planning (Cowling and Sugden, 1998a): Coase recognizes that coordination by the price mechanism entails 'planning by individuals' who 'exercise foresight and choose between alternatives' (387), but he is especially interested in the 'planning within our economic system which is quite different from . . . individual planning . . . and is akin to what is normally called economic planning' (388). For Coase (1937), power relations are at the heart of economic planning, and the problem of economic planning is the essence of the problem of organizing production.

   The language in which firm's planning has been considered over more recent years is one of 'strategy' (Zeitlin, 1974), and that is the concept which informs our distinguishing of different realities. Specifically, our perspective is provided by a focus on the governance of socio-economic processes and systems, and the actors therein, in the sense of analysing which people make strategic decisions, on what basis and to what effect. The contention is that the critical (but not exclusive) determinant of what does or might occur in production activity is its governance. Each and every type of socio-economic process, system and organization is argued to be characterized by a particular type of governance, and different types of governance are associated with different efficiency and distribution effects (Cowling and Sugden (1998a; 1998b); see also Sugden and Wilson (2002) on the aims of economic development). This analysis is applicable to varied types of firms, universities, hospitals, international organizations, industrial sectors, education systems, health systems, networks, local economies, national economies and so on. It asserts the importance of economic power, rejects determinism, embraces voluntarism (Bailey et al., 2006), and emphasizes people's positive freedom to act (Cowling and Sugden, 1998b).

In particular, we concentrate on two opposing types of governance, one hierarchical and one non-hierarchical (as identified by Sacchetti and Sugden (2003) for the case of networks):

Direction: a hierarchical system to plan activities according to the exclusive aims of a core, with or without the agreement of others; strategy making is dominated by the core, which directs resources.
Mutual dependence: an ideal type that is characterized by the absence of hierarchy and of a strategic decision-making core; strategies are determined through a process of diffused coordination amongst partners, each of which is allowed and encouraged to contribute to strategic choice through communication and deliberation.

To illustrate, consider Hymer's (1972) analysis of uneven development. His concern is a stylized version of the US economy, and in particular its evolution from a system in which small firms are especially influential into one in which certain forms of large corporation 'penetrate almost every nook and cranny' (ibid.: 48). The analysis focuses on a hypothetical situation: what the world economy would look like, if it were to be dominated by a 'regime' (ibid.: 38) of such corporations. Hymer argues that the governance by direction in the corporations would be reflected in governance by direction of the world economy.

His analysis focuses on layered decision-making in transnational corporations, most interestingly on two extremes: (1) the lowest levels of management, responsible for the coordination of day-to-day activities; (2) the most senior levels of management, concerned with goal determination and planning, i.e. strategy. He argues that whilst the lowest level would be spread throughout the world 'according to the pull of manpower, markets and raw materials' (ibid.: 50), the strategic planning activities would be concentrated in a handful of major cities, like London, New York and Tokyo:

> One would expect to find the highest offices of the [transnational] corporations concentrated in the world's major cities . . . These . . . will be . . . major centres

of high-level strategic planning. Lesser cities throughout the world will deal with the day-to-day operations of specific local problems. These in turn will be arranged in a hierarchical fashion: the larger and more important ones will contain regional corporate headquarters, while the smaller ones will be confined to lower level activities. (ibid.: 50)

What Hymer also argues is that an extreme system of governance by direction would have significant welfare consequences: 'income, status, authority and consumption patterns would radiate out from [the major] centres along a declining curve' (ibid.: 38), and 'the "best" and most highly paid administrators, doctors, lawyers, scientists, educators, government officials, actors, servants and hairdressers' (ibid.: 50) would agglomerate around those centres. His ultimate conclusion is that such governance has a systemic tendency to produce poverty as well as wealth, underdevelopment as well as development.

The interests of publics
To explore in more depth the 'winners' and 'losers' in different governance processes, consider Dewey's (1927) seminal analysis, in particular the idea of a public interests criterion for assessing socio-economic relations, behaviours and activities (Sacchetti and Sugden, 2009).[2]

For Dewey (1927), an act might have significant consequences both for those directly engaged in it, and for others. The direct participants are said to have private interests in the act, whereas the others have public interests. Dewey (1927) is also clear in acknowledging that an act might bring into existence more than one public, each of which, according to Long (1990: 171), has 'a shared concern with consequences' of the act. Referring to this literature – and recognizing that the making of a strategic choice is an act – Branston et al. (2006a: 195) identify 'the public interest in a corporation's activities in general and in its strategies in particular as the agreed upon, evolving concerns amongst all of those indirectly and significantly affected by those activities and strategies (wherever they live, whatever their nationality)'. For example, the consumers purchasing a corporation's outputs would form a public, as would (at least the mass of) the corporation's employees (i.e. all of those not actually making its strategic decisions).

To illustrate more specifically, consider the economic crisis that broke in 2008. Strategic choices in the banking and finance sector in London, New York and other leading centres impacted on interested parties in all sectors and in all corners of the world. Stiglitz (2008) refers to a global crisis and to 'families whose life dreams are destroyed as they lose their homes, their jobs, and their life savings'. Very few of the people losing their employment had a direct input to the strategic choices being made, but each clearly had an interest. When Bell and Blanchflower (2009) refer to the crisis impacting on youth unemployment and warn of the 'permanent scars' (ibid.: 26), they are identifying young people as an interested public.

By way of further illustration and explanation, Figure 4.1 positions reality under (the current form of) socio-economic development, and is in line with the depiction of Hymer (1972). It focuses on the parallel spectra of interests and governance possibilities that we have been discussing. On the left hand side of the figure we map governance, ranging from direction to mutual dependence. Parallel to this, on the right hand side we map the accommodation of interests.

The idea underlying the parallel spectra is as follows:

- One extreme is governance by direction, associated with the pursuit of specific private interests and the exclusion of publics.

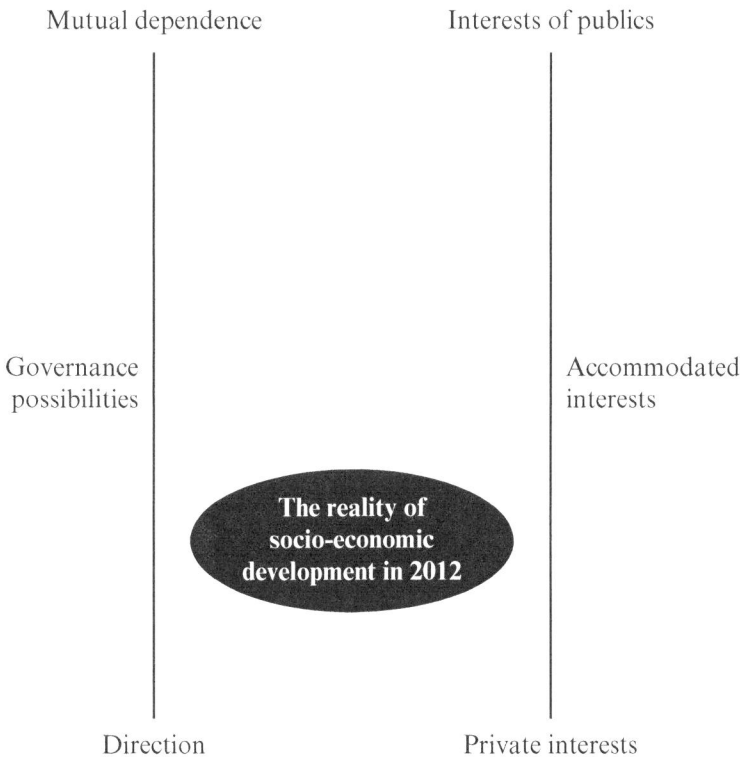

Mutual dependence   Interests of publics

Governance possibilities   Accommodated interests

The reality of socio-economic development in 2012

Direction   Private interests

Figure 4.1   Governance of, and interests in, socio-economic development

- The other extreme is governance by mutual dependence, associated with an awareness and accommodation of the interests of publics.

Between these two extremes are degrees of direction, corresponding with degrees to which specific private interests override the interests of publics (or, viewed from the opposite end of the spectrum, corresponding with degrees to which there is an awareness and accommodation of the interests of publics).

As for the current reality of socio-economic development, the sort of concentration of power and unevenness envisaged by Hymer (1972) is in many respects well recognized in the literature (Dicken, 1992; Cowling and Sugden, 1994). For example, Henderson et al. (2001) review analysis of uneven development across and within countries. For them, 'the most striking fact about the economic geography of the world is the uneven distribution of activity' (ibid.: 81), reflected in 54 per cent of world GDP being produced by countries occupying 10 per cent of the landmass. Similarly Coe and Yeung (2001), asserting that uneven development is 'the single most visible structural outcome of globalization processes' (ibid.: 370). Moreover, they relate development variations across territories to the 'uneven power relations underlying most global production chains such that some segments of these chains have disproportionately greater power and control over other segments' (ibid.: 371). This recognition of concentrated power applies not only to the power associated with particular regions, but also to that of particular firms. Consider for example Fold (2001), highlighting the impacts of large producers in the chocolate industry in Europe on cocoa production in West Africa, and linking those with the influences of the structural adjustment programmes stimulated by the World Bank and International Monetary Fund (IMF). More generally, Rothschild (2005: 445) views the large transnational corporations as having 'become – nationally and internationally – an especially powerful interest group'.

In short, on the basis of the theoretical and empirical evidence, we would argue that the world's economies have been driven by large and powerful firms that essentially follow their own private interests, with less regard for the publics upon which they impact. Hence we show reality in the late twentieth and early twenty-first centuries, in the space towards the extreme lower ends of the governance and interests spectra in Figure 4.1.[3]

Viewed from another perspective, we have identified a critical challenge for societies, communities and territories: the possibility of evolving a model of socio-economic development that better serves the interests of publics. Quite how this might be achieved, if in fact it could be achieved, would require further analysis and considerable thought. For example, we would need to explore precisely what is meant by 'public' (and, in doing so, distance it from the notion of 'public' meaning 'government'). We would need to understand how publics might identify both themselves and their interests; analysing what acting in public interests entails, Dewey (1927: 327) reasons that 'the prime difficulty' is discovery of 'the means by which a scattered, mobile and manifold public may so recognize itself as to define and express its interests'. Especially important, we would need to think about the importance of values in socio-economic activity (on which see Sacchetti and Sugden, 2009). Do people look to impose one on another? Do they focus on personal consumption for personal gratification? Do they value mutual respect, sharing, critical awareness and some notion of socio-economic democracy?

Another concern would be to consider varied types of enterprise, and indeed socio-economic systems comprising different mixes of enterprise types. Using Hymer's analysis, the chapter has offered criticism of a stylized form of large corporation, but that is not to argue that large corporations or large firms more generally do not have a place in a socio-economic system aiming to satisfy the interests of publics. It might be that we need to consider systems in which there are both large and small firms, as well as firms that seek profit and those that are non-profit. Perhaps we need to give particularly close thought to the role of so-called social enterprises and the third sector.

Moreover, if people are to rise to the challenge of evolving a socio-economic system that better serves the interests of publics, we might argue that the education system needs to be given considerable thought. It is with that in mind that we now turn to Section 3 of this chapter.

3 THE ORGANIZATION OF MODERN UNIVERSITIES AND THE ROLE OF ACADEMICS

Universities are not immune to impact from the socio-economic contexts within which they sit, and in fact have been strongly influenced by the emergence of a comparatively dominant set of market-based economic models throughout large parts of the world in the 1980s and 1990s. The end of the Cold War and transition in the old Soviet bloc marked the advent of hegemony for free market capitalism, for what Stiglitz (2002: 221) calls 'market fundamentalism', and this included the upholding of large, transnational corporations – the entities that both drove and epitomized free market economies – as role models for all organizations. The influence of that market logic has been felt in the education sector. For example, de Boer (1999: 132) argues that some people 'advocate business models of management' for universities, seeking to 'transform' them 'into organizations similar to ordinary commercial firms so that they can be assessed and managed in roughly similar ways'.

We urge caution with such an approach, most especially the necessity for discrimination in the choice of business model (Sugden (2004); see also Grönblom and Willner (2009), who question managerialism and performance management; and Wilson (2009), concerned with marketization, corporatization and globalization in the university sector. If a transnational corporation is governed by direction in the style depicted by Hymer (1972), it is designed to pursue private rather than public interests, with a structure, organization and management to suit. As Zeitlin (1974) observed, to govern in such a way is to have the power to determine broad corporate objectives despite the resistance of others, within and without the corporation. Power to determine the strategic direction of activity is concentrated in a core group pursuing aims and objectives that not only do not meet those of interested publics, but that do not even recognize the existence of those publics. An implication of the theoretical and empirical arguments underlying Section 2 of this chapter is that a university adopting such corporate logic would be unlikely to have as one of its broad objectives the serving of publics.

On a related theme, we would also urge caution in following the basis for management education in the US. Although Khurana (2007) sees market logic as especially influential towards the end of the last century, he identifies professionalization logic as a principal concern in earlier years. However, in doing so he argues:

> The goal of the professionalization project in American management, carried out by the university-based business school, was to achieve control in a specific area – the large, publicly traded corporation – and protect that control from competing groups, namely, shareholders, labour and the state. (ibid., 10)

The idea was to create institutions to maintain an appropriate social order, one based upon exclusion. Again, a university adopting that model would be unlikely to have as one of its broad objectives the serving of publics in a way that might shift reality up the spectrum depicted in Figure 4.1. Indeed, as with the corporate logic corresponding to Hymer's (1972) characterization, a university following that professionalization logic would be positioning itself towards the lower end of the governance/interests spectrum, as in Figure 4.2.

To reason against market/corporate logic of the 1980s/1990s is not to suggest that a university can draw no lessons from the experiences of corporations. Similarly, to argue against US professionalization logic is

Mutual dependence   Interest of publics

Governance   Accommodated
possibilities   ?   interests

UNIVERSITIES
market/corporate
logic of 1980s/1990s;
professionalization
logic re US
management

Direction   Private interests

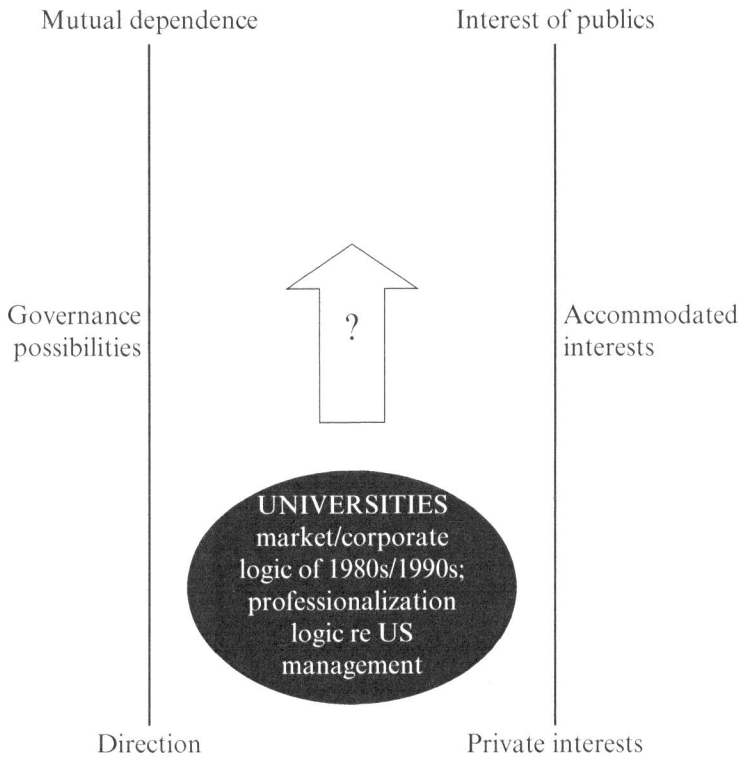

Figure 4.2   Public interests logic in the organization of universities

not to suggest that a university need be unconcerned with a professional approach to management. In each case, however, it is to say that public interests would not be served by following such logic.

In contrast, we consider the possibility that a university might choose to adopt *public interests logic*; it might organize itself so as to enable people to think about, analyse and understand ways in which the interests of publics might be better satisfied. We recognize that this would not be easily met, in part because it is currently unclear precisely what that would entail. It would surely depend upon the context, the particular mix of disciplines or subject areas under consideration, and the extant or potential university under review; requirements and outcomes would be determined by specific histories, relationships, cultural settings and socio-economic environments. However, there are some elements that can be identified as generally relevant, including the values that would have to underpin the organization of activities and the stress on creativity that would be required.

Values

Focusing especially on the state and political democracy, Dewey (1927) analyses what it would mean to satisfy public interests. Identifying '*the* problem of the public' as 'the essential need' for 'the improvement of the methods and conditions of debate, discussion and persuasion' (ibid.: 365), he views deliberation as particularly significant. Explicitly drawing on this analysis in considering the organization of production, Sacchetti and Sugden (2009) argue that effective Deweyan deliberation needs to be founded on particular values, notably: positive freedom; the rejection of controlling influences; inclusion on equal terms; informed participation; the desire to reach a consensus; sympathy; mutual respect; reciprocity; continuous learning.

We suggest that a university choosing to adopt public interests logic would need to organize and conduct itself according to the logic of such values. That would essentially necessitate a certain form of collegiality, a concept long associated with academic activity and one that is often used with positive connotations in today's debates, but one that is typically employed as rhetoric and without clear understanding of content and implications. Our suggestion is that collegiality should encompass a university's academic and support staff, its students and the publics with interests in its activities; and that this would necessitate an acceptance and embracing by all parties of positive freedom and of the other values of Deweyan deliberation.[4]

Consideration of these values takes us to an issue long debated in and around universities, that of 'academic freedom'. For Einstein (quoted in Child, 2007: 3), academic freedom is 'the right to search for the truth and to publish and teach what one holds to be true. This right also implies a duty; one must not conceal any part of what one has recognized to be true'. Such freedom has a clear negative dimension – a freedom from constraint – but it is essentially positive, in line with the values of Deweyan deliberation. There is a right to act, the capability 'to be somebody, not nobody; a doer deciding, not being decided for, self-directed . . . conceiving goals and policies on [one's] own and realising them'; and the capability 'to be conceiving of [oneself] as a thinking, willing active being, bearing responsibility for [one's] choices and able to explain them by reference to [one's] own ideas and purposes' (Berlin, 1969: 131).

Such academic freedom is not an open licence to undertake whatever activities an academic might wish. Rather, it carries explicit responsibilities. Rooted in his or her own ideas and aims, the academic must follow suitable methods and methodologies to search for and disseminate the 'truth'.[5] For a university intended to serve the interests of publics, and taking the academic body as a whole, that truth must not be confined to an understanding and pursuit of merely private interests. There would be a necessity to take full account of all publics, existing and potential, today and in the future, and indeed in the past. Viewed from this perspective, academics accepting a university organization according to the corporate logic of the 1980s and 1990s would be failing in their responsibilities. Likewise, there would be failure amongst academics embracing the sort of professionalization logic seen at the birth of US management schools.[6]

Creativity

In the context of organizing production in general, rather than universities in particular, deliberation and satisfying the interests of publics have been argued to relate to people's creativity (Sacchetti and Sugden, 2010). For Dewey (1927: 327), 'the prime difficulty' is for a public to recognize both itself and its interests (Dewey, 1927: 327). The problem is that people would be typically unaware that they have common – i.e. public – interests in a particular activity if they were unable to use their creativity in thinking about and assessing that activity. Moreover, even if a public had some sense of its own existence, its interests would be hidden if its members could not be creative in contemplating their concerns. In short, if the people in a particular society, community or territory sought to evolve a model of socio-economic development that better serves the interests of publics – if they wished to move in an upward trajectory in Figure 4.1 – then there would be a necessity to ensure that all of those people are enabled to be creative.

That conclusion has clear consequences for a university choosing to adopt public interests logic, namely: it would need to place the nurturing and stimulation of people's creativity at its heart.

Chomsky (1975: 164) is insightful in this respect. He suggests that each person has a creative impulse, the aim of education being 'to provide the soil and the freedom required for the growth of this creative impulse, to provide, in other words, a complex and challenging environment' that the person 'can imaginatively explore'. Moreover, he argues that the purpose of education is not 'to control' a person's 'growth to a specific, predetermined end, because any such end must be established by arbitrary authoritarian means; rather, the purpose of education must be to permit the growing principle of life to take its own individual course, and to facilitate this process by sympathy, encouragement, and challenge, and by developing a rich and differentiated context and environment' (ibid.: 164).[7] This reference to 'authoritarian means' is effectively a critique of systems designed to serve private (in this situation, authoritarian) interests, and he is explicit in his rejection of controlling interests, one of the values that we suggest for collegiality.[8]

4 CONCLUSION

This chapter has argued that there has been a failure over recent years to satisfy public interests in socio-economic development; that is a characteristic of the 'inferno' built by people. The origins of the failure are the governance processes characterizing socio-economic activity, in particular the ways in which choices have been made to determine the strategic direction of production. It has been suggested that a university needs to be careful not to copy failed models of governance, and that a university might organize itself so as to enable people to think about, analyse and understand ways in which the interests of publics might be better satisfied.

In more detail, we advocate a notion of the university as a collegial space to nurture the intrinsic, unique creativity of faculty, support staff, students and interested publics, so that each person is enabled to think critically, to analyse, to appreciate and to understand the ways in which the interests of publics might be better satisfied. Our analysis points to collegiality being founded on a rejection by all parties of controlling influences, alongside an embracing of positive freedom, inclusion on equal terms, informed participation, the desire to reach a consensus, sympathy, mutual respect, reciprocity and continuous learning. In such a university, outcomes would not be constrained to specific, predetermined ends.

NOTES

1. This chapter was first written as background to the author's University of Stirling Professorial Inaugural Lecture, 20 May 2009.
2. Policy-makers are sometimes heard to profess a concern with public interests as an assessment criterion, without necessarily being at all clear what such interests entail. By drawing on Dewey, we offer that clarification.
3. It might be argued that public interests are served in situations where all economic actors narrowly pursue their own private interests. For example, some might contend that public interests are reducible to Pareto optimality, and that the likes of Debreu (1959) and Arrow and Hahn (1971) show that an economy can be in Pareto optimality when actors pursue their narrow self-interests under conditions of perfect competition. However, the strategic choice approach is based upon the empirical validity of a reality characterized by power and imperfect competition. Even in such cases it might still be argued that public interests are served, for example through policies that seek to correct market failures, but the difficulty with that argument would be its presumption that policy makers know the interests of publics despite, according to Dewey (1927), those

publics often being themselves unaware of their own existence (Branston et al., 2006a; 2006b).

4. One implication is that, for a university adopting public interests logic, such values would underpin and define the style of leading and managing.

5. In arguing this we would also stress the significance of contesting the meaning of truth and the suitability of particular methods and methodologies.

6. Consider also the comments by Ajit Singh in a discussion of academic freedom and the study of economics at the EUNIP International Conference, San Sebastián, Spain (September 2008). He argued that academic advancement tends to come to those who promote and follow the dominant economic ideologies, and that those ideologies tend to be pursued in order to serve the ideologies rather than the interests of publics. According to the reasoning in this chapter, such an approach would amount to academic economists failing in their responsibilities.

7. Such arguments suggest the importance, for a university following public interests logic, both of what Veblen (1918: 20) terms 'idle curiosity' and of what Docherty (2008) refers to as sense and sensibility (see also Chapter 5 by Docherty, this volume). Referring to the study of English, more widely to 'the proper place . . . of literature . . . within a society', Docherty considers the deficiencies of having 'a form of knowledge that was not "lived", not actually "felt" at the inner level of sensibility' (2008: 4). The result of such a form might be seen as 'a triumph of the industrialisation of the human spirit', a failure to balance appropriately 'sense or reason and sensibility or feeling' (ibid., 4–5). The idea is that the study of literature might demand a balance, but we would argue that the same could be said for the study of other subjects, for example economics. One hypothesis is that an understanding of a poem, painting, machine, economy . . . that is not felt might be in some sense lacking. For example, an engineer or economist might first feel what is failing in a particular machine or economy and then make that feeling tangible, expressing it through reasoned argument and correcting the failure; but such reasoning and correction might not occur without the feeling, other than by chance. Another hypothesis is that sensibility is a determinant of people's capacity to be imaginative; that understanding of economies requires imagination; therefore that an academic studying an economy needs sensibility for the subject in order to unleash his or her full creative potential in exploring what is and might be happening in the economy. Without sensibility imagination is constrained and understanding limited.

8. Chomsky forsakes the certainty of predetermined outcomes, and Docherty (2008: 20) does something similar, rejecting the certainty associated with universities that hide behind paper trails and that therefore fail to pursue truth. He comments upon a reality in which

> [t]he teaching that is done in a particular institution might be in fact and in the experience of all concerned mediocre, but the audit-trail paperwork shows the steady and rhythmic pulse of 'excellence' in all things. In [this] and similar examples, we can say that it is 'administered form' that gives certainty and legitimacy. In our time we have learned to call this 'transparency', which we too often mistake for 'truth' or for 'justice'.

REFERENCES

Arrow, K. and F. Hahn, (1971) *General Competitive Analysis*, San Francisco: Holden-Day.

Bailey, D., L. De Propris, R. Sugden and J. R. Wilson (2006) Public policy for economic competitiveness: an analytical framework and a research agenda, *International Review of Applied Economics*, **20**(5): 555–72.

Berlin, I. (1969) *Four Essays on Liberty*, Oxford: Oxford University Press.

Bell, D. N. F. and D. G. Blanchflower (2009) What should be done about rising unemployment in the UK?, mimeo, University of Stirling.

Branston, J. R., K. Cowling and R. Sugden (2006a) Corporate governance and the public interest, *International Review of Applied Economics*, **20**(2): 189–212.

Branston, J. R., L. Rubini, R. Sugden and J. R. Wilson (2006b) The healthy development of economies: a strategic framework for competitiveness in the health industry, *Review of Social Economy*, **LXIV**(3): 301–29.

Calvino, I. (1997) *Invisible Cities*. London: Vintage (original editition 1972).

Child, J. (2007) Academic freedom – the threat from managerialism, paper presented at the Birmingham Workshops on Academic Freedom and Research/Learning Cultures, University of Birmingham, October.

Chomsky, N. (1975) Toward a humanistic conception of education, in: W. Feinberg and H. Rosemont (eds), *Work, Technology and Education: Dissenting Essays in the Intellectual Foundations of American Education*, Urbana: University of Illinois Press.

Coase, R. H. (1937) The nature of the firm, *Economica*, **IV**: 386–405.

Coe, N. M. and H. W. Yeung (2001) Geographical perspectives on mapping globalisation, *Journal of Economic Geography*, **1**: 367–80.

Cowling, K. and R. Sugden (1994) *Beyond Capitalism: Towards a New World Economic Order*, London: Pinter.

Cowling, K. and R. Sugden (1998a) The essence of the modern corporation: markets, strategic decision-making and the theory of the firm, *The Manchester School*, **66**(1): 59–86.

Cowling, K. and R. Sugden (1998b) Strategic trade policy reconsidered: national rivalry vs. free trade vs. international cooperation, *Kyklos*, **51**(3): 339–58.

de Boer, H. F. (1999) Changes in institutional governance structures: the Dutch case, in: J. Brennan, J. Fedrowitz, M. Huber and T. Shah (eds) *What Kind of University? International Perspectives on Knowledge, Participation and Governance*, Buckingham: SRHE and Open University Press.

Debreu, G. (1959) *Theory of Value*, New York: John Wiley & Sons.

Dewey, J. (1927) The public and its problems, in: J. A. Boydston (1988) *John Dewey. The Later Works, Volume 2: 1925–1927*, Carbondale and Edwardsville: Southern Illinois University Press. Page numbers refer to the reproduction.

Dicken, P. (1992) *Global Shift: The Internationalization of Economic Activity*, London: Paul Chapman.

Docherty, T. (2008) *The English Question or Academic Freedoms*, Brighton: Sussex Academic Press.

Fold, N. (2001) Restructuring of the European chocolate industry and its impact on cocoa production in West Africa, *Journal of Economic Geography*, **1**: 405–20.

Grönblom, S. and J. Willner (2009) Destroying creativity? Universities and the new public management, in: S. Sacchetti and R. Sugden (eds), *Knowledge in the Development of Economies: Institutional Choices under Globalisation*, Cheltenham: Edward Elgar.

Henderson, J. V., Z. Shalizi and A. J. Venables (2001) Geography and development, *Journal of Economic Geography*, **1**: 81–105.

Hymer, S. H. (1972) The multinational corporation and the law of uneven development, in: J. N. Bhagwati (ed.) *Economics and World Order: From the 1970s to the 1990s*, London: Macmillan. Page numbers refer to the reproduction in

H. Radice (ed.) (1975) *International Firms and Modern Imperialism*, London: Penguin.

Khurana, R. (2007) *From Higher Aims to Hired Hands. The Social Transformation of American Business Schools and the Unfilled Promise of Management as a Profession*, Princeton: Princeton University Press.

Long, N. E. (1990) Conceptual notes on the public interest for public administration and policy analysts, *Administration and Society*, **22**: 170–81.

Rothschild, K. W. (2005) New worlds – new approaches. A note on future research strategies, *Kyklos*, **58**(3): 439–47.

Sacchetti, S. and R. Sugden (2003) The governance of networks and economic power: the nature and impact of subcontracting relationships, *Journal of Economic Surveys*, **17**: 669–91.

Sacchetti, S. and R. Sugden (2009) The organization of production and its publics: mental proximity, markets and hierarchies, *Review of Social Economy*, **LXVII** (3): 289–311.

Sacchetti, S. and R. Sugden (2010) Creativity and the public interest in economic development: a knowledge governance perspective, *Ekonomiaz*, **74**: 36–49.

Stiglitz, J. E. (2002) *Globalization and its Discontents*, New York: Norton.

Stiglitz J. E. (2008) Global crisis – made in America, *Spiegel Online International*, http://www.spiegel.de/international/business/0,1518,590028,00.html, accessed on 14 December 2008.

Sugden, R. (2004) A small firm approach to the internationalisation of universities: a multinational perspective, *Higher Education Quarterly*, **58**(2/3): 114–35.

Sugden, R. and J. R. Wilson (2002) Economic development in the shadow of the consensus: a strategic decision-making approach, *Contributions to Political Economy*, 21: 111–34.

Veblen, T. (1918) *The Higher Learning in America*. Page numbers refer to the 2005 publication, New York: Cosimo.

Wilson, J. R. (2009) Higher education and economic development: do we face an inter-temporal trade-off?, in: S. Sacchetti and R. Sugden (eds), *Knowledge in the Development of Economies: Institutional Choices under Globalisation*, Cheltenham: Edward Elgar.

Zeitlin, M. (1974) Corporate ownership and control: the large corporation and the capitalist class, *American Journal of Sociology*, **79**(5): 1073–119.

5. Sense and sensibility in academia

Thomas Docherty

The governance of the modern University or Academy is, to some extent, haunted by an issue whose roots lie in the Enlightenment, where philosophers struggled to regulate the competing claims of sense (the operations of reason and intellect) and those of sensibility (the physical sensations of life as it is lived). One social model proposes the University as the site of Reason, of intellectual work untrammelled by the distractions of material accident; at the same time, the contemporary economic model sees the University as necessarily fully embroiled in the realm of 'life-as-it-is-lived', the life of productivity and of material wealth-production.

One contemporary answer to the problem of how we 'regulate' the claims of sense and sensibility is to find a new vocabulary: we no longer explore these issues, but rather we 'manage' them. Within this construction of management, we thus find 'reasonable' modes of behaviour that nonetheless address the question of economy; and the result of this is the so-called 'Value-for-Money' agenda. VfM operates, in standard form, by a concentration on 'the three Es': we begin by making Economies (i.e. we cut funding); we then address Efficiency (i.e. we maximize output while minimizing input); and, miraculously, we thereby improve Effectiveness (i.e. we achieve more despite the funding cut). Central to this is the idea of endlessly improving efficiency.

In what follows here, I want to address the two questions implicit in this depiction of our contemporary milieu: the regulation of sense and sensibility, and the implicit value of efficiency driving as a normative value. I will argue that the drive for efficiency is inefficient, and that it is so because it fails to address the question of the regulation of sense and sensibility: in short, I will show that it is inefficient because it fails to recognize the value of sensibility, a sensibility that requires play, which 'wastes time'. We might call this argument 'in praise of the coffee-bar'.

At one level, the question is extremely basic. Consider the excitement of research or of teaching. Which scientist would not feel a frisson – in the body – as they discover something previously undreamt of in our philosophies? Which critic is not moved – physically moved – to laughter, tears, and myriad physical responses in between, when they watch a performance of *King Lear* or listen to Bach's *Cello Suite no. 1 in G* or look at Picasso's *Guernica* (for random examples)? In these, there are visceral responses, felt sensitively on the pulse. Such responses appear just as surely in relation to the teaching and learning situation as well: who is not physically elated by the seminar in which genuine thinking has taken place?

The extreme rationalist will reply that these physical responses may be important; but, nonetheless, they are but 'accidentals', and are not a 'necessary' part of our work; and the University manager will say that they are interesting, but will ask how we can manage them (and measure them). I want to argue that, far from being contingent, such sensibilities are in fact integral to a University education or experience and that, properly understood, they are strictly unmanageable. In these days, when questions of a so-called 'student experience' have become of central importance, we should look closely at the nature of experience itself in the framework of learning and teaching. As we do so, we will open up the second issue, that of the relation between a contemporary political drive for 'efficiency' and what I will provocatively call 'wasteful play'; and in this, we will see that the prioritization of efficiency is, paradoxically, the least efficient mode of learning that we have.

1 EXPERIENCE

In 1916, just as America was about to enter the First World War, John Dewey published *Democracy and Education*. There, he pointed out that two meanings of 'experience' – an active sense and a passive sense – get mixed together in the word. Experience means trying something, as in an experiment whose outcome we cannot predict; but it also means undergoing something, and thus opening ourselves to the possibility of being transformed. As Dewey put it:

> When we experience something we act upon it, we do something with it; then we suffer or undergo the consequences. We do something to the thing and then it does something to us in return . . . The connection of these two phases of experience measures the fruitfulness or value of the experience . . . *We learn something*. (italics mine)

Learning, in this account, is precisely the negotiation of an experiment: teacher and student may have an idea of what we would like to achieve, but we cannot guarantee the outcome; and we will also potentially be surprised and even changed as we both work our way through the experimental process. In this, Dewey is starting to outline a pragmatic view of education: an education that is formed in and through activity and practice, material historical thinking. He establishes that there is an intrinsic link between learning and experience, arguing that 'to "learn from experience" is to make a backward and forward connection between what we do to things and what we enjoy or suffer from things in consequence'.

This is important in that it puts learning (the work of sense) into a historical situation (the realm of sensibility); and it places the subject who learns – the student (and the teacher is also a student here) – right at the centre of an experience. In this, the student finds that she or he has to negotiate material realities, and that she or he has to realize that there can be material consequences of thinking in certain ways. Dewey notes that 'under such conditions, doing becomes a trying: an experiment with the world to find out what it is like; the undergoing becomes instruction – discovery of the connection of things'. In short, there are material consequences to the ostensibly purely intellectual activities going on in education. There is a materiality to learning and teaching: they literally *matter*. 'Intelligence' is a material entity. It has a historical substance in and of itself. It is not a preparation for action, but is rather itself already constitutive of action. It does things, and changes not only minds but also other things as well.[1]

In all of this, Dewey counters that state of affairs in which a pupil was regarded simply as a passive recipient of knowledge (a knowledge supposedly 'transmitted' or transferred spiritually, as it were). He replaces that moribund and non-organic model of learning, in which knowledge is commodified into modularized and consumable items, with a radically healthier view of both pupil and teacher as active, physically and bodily present in the activity of learning and teaching. The account of learning that he rejects is one based upon a profound philosophical dualism, in which mind and body, sense and sensibility, are radically discrete. For Dewey, that was no mere or bland philosophical position: it had a profoundly ethical counterpart, for he saw the dualism of mind and body in these matters as incipiently evil, in fact.

The reasoning is clear: the acceptance of such a dualism led straight to a situation where the body (and with it the entire realm of an exterior or public sphere) is regarded as 'mere' physicality, and meaning (and with it the very identity of the Academy) becomes instead the province of a realm of spirit divorced from material and historical realities. In this condition, 'bodily activity becomes an intruder . . . it becomes a distraction, an evil to be contended with'. For those who subscribe to the evils of dualism, a major problem lies in the fact that students (and even teachers) have bodies. Their bodies are, self-evidently for Dewey, 'wellsprings of energy' and, as such a coiled or potential energy, the body is prone to do things, to act. It is now therefore regarded as the source of a certain potential indiscipline, a threat to the control of the teacher in the classroom; and teaching, in this situation, becomes – in some cases primarily – a policing of the body's physicality.[2]

In some ways, the dualism critiqued by Dewey lies at the root of the medieval academy, governed centrally by a religious impulse that is suspicious of the corporeality of experience, preferring to construe reality as that which is to be found in the realm of Ideas, of a mind divorced from history, a mind that has become equated with transcendent spirit. The religious aspect of this is that it prioritizes spirit with the extreme consequence of the total eradication of the bodily or historically material world. Such an attitude is also at the root of education conceived fundamentally in theological terms as a necessary policing of the bodily activity and energy that constitutes sensibility and even history itself. In this the 'good' pupil is 'educated not into responsibility for the significant and graceful use of bodily powers, but into an enforced duty not to give them free play'.[3] In many of the advanced societies, the governing myth here is to be found in the fundamentalist reading of the Adam and Eve myth, where a profound awareness of the body and a shame regarding it is the consequence of eating of the fruits of knowledge.

And yet, the body is at the foundation of all empirical perception, as of all aesthetics: it is through the body that we perceive the world in terms of our material engagements with it, in terms of our experiencing of it. If education, learning and teaching are to be experiences with a real and substantive historical material reality, then the body itself must be engaged. Imagine, for a simple example, the case of a musical education. Music usually involves notation on the page; but the real point of music is the experiencing and the sensation of physical vibration. We hear music thanks to the manipulation of air, the transmission of vibrations that are felt not just within the ear but also deep within the body itself. The response can be various: we dance, we sing, we clap hands, we weep; but all these are material and physical – aesthetically visceral– sensations or experiences.

If we isolate the mind from such bodily experience, Dewey argued, then it follows that we start to prioritize the objects of perception as things also in isolation: we see things, and we do not experience the world as constituted by the relations between things. If we cannot allow for a learning that depends upon the essential relation of our body with material activity, then we cannot hope to see the relations between things in the world. We become removed from the sphere of the social and of community; and the social becomes rapidly atomized. We end up lacking the possibility of sympathy, for we are reduced to living in the mental space of a now vacuous 'I', an 'I' crying out to be filled. Worse, we are an 'I' crying out to be intellectually manipulated into conformity with what already exists. 'Do I dare disturb the universe?' asked J. Alfred Prufrock in Eliot's poem.[4] In these cases, the answer is clearly negative. But real learning is indeed a shaking of the universe, a disturbing of the ground beneath the feet of *both* the learner and the teacher: it is a communal experience, and an experience of community. We usually simply call that something like 'communication'; and communication is central to education.

There is a difference, then, between what we can call the mechanized *management* of experience, which is achieved by the reduction of relations to discrete and atomized things; and, on the other hand, experience as learning, which is much less predictable and which involves the body in sensation. Within 'the student experience' it is the former that becomes the quarry, for it is the former that can be ostensibly 'measured' and quantified. It would be like trying to learn how to play the piano simply by reading musical notation, and without ever going through the physical changes required in feeling how to strike the keys, heavily or lightly (*forte* or *piano*); or how to stretch and coordinate the fingers; or how to sit or stand. What of those whose bodily sensations are limited or disturbed by some quality or other? What of Beethoven, say? The great percussionist, Evelyn Glennie, who is deaf, can feel and sense her music through the vibrations of the instruments around her: music is experienced neither just as notation nor as a discrete activity of the ear, but is instead an entire physical experience. That experience is itself at the root of Beethoven's own 'imagining' of his own music: the emancipation of the imagination itself has a profound and fundamental relation to experience. And if it is thus for a composer or performer as she or he learns the music that they will 'teach' us, then it is equally thus for the audience or the learner.

Any craftsperson knows this. Richard Sennett has recently written about the importance of understanding the hand itself in relation to learning. He, too, gives an example from music. As a cellist, he indicates that one learns to play the cello not by an abstract transferring of notation to sound, but actually through feeling how the hand itself makes the notes. Practice is just the name we give to that state of affairs in which our body starts to work as if intuitively in relation to the materiality of the objects (in this case, cello, bow) that it manipulates: the body learns to act in concert with something exterior to it, to make the third thing that we call 'music'. These musical examples are paradigmatic of all learning: ignore the role of the body, and both learning and teaching are radically limited and circumscribed.

Dewey relates his own idea of what constitutes thinking here explicitly to what is going on in the war. As he is writing *Democracy and Education*, 'the world is filled with the clang of contending armies', he says. In our response to this dread and factual state of affairs, it is not enough to register individual items (to take an atomized view), nor is it enough to ignore them (or to argue that this has no effect on our other activities, especially those that involve thinking and learning). He writes that, 'To fill our heads, like a scrapbook, with this and that item as a finished and done-for thing, is not to think. It is to turn ourselves into a piece of registering apparatus'. Doing that, of course, would allow us to consider knowledge as the purchasing of separate and atomized commodities that we register as we pay for them, and whose value we measure against our wallets; but this has nothing whatsoever to do with the transformative processes that we call learning or teaching. In short, the registering and 'managing' of experience is anathema to the university's primary purposes and identity.

Thinking is related not simply to registering what happens, or to registering the 'input' as it were; but it actually also implies the imagining of what might be the case, that is, to imagination as such (engaging output and input together). However, this is not some dreamy-eyed imagining, done in the seductive charm and cool of one's room late at night; rather, it is imagination as action, imagination in the midst of battle, as Dewey was writing in the midst of war. Edward Said always took the view that critical thinking – the only serious kind of thinking that there is – is tied up with the demand for liberation. As he put it, describing his own preferred modes of literary criticism, 'criticism must think of itself as life-enhancing and constitutively opposed to every form of tyranny, domination, and abuse; its social goals are noncoercive knowledge produced in the interests of human freedom'. This, together with his political writings, give a real substance to his view that 'even in the very midst of a battle in which one is unmistakably on one side against another, there should be criticism, because there must be critical consciousness if there are to be issues, values, *even lives* to be fought for'.[5]

The question of learning and teaching is really a matter of a battle, even a physical battle, a battle for the future control of our own bodies and thereby for the future ways in which we will occupy and relate to each other and to our environment or ecology. The University is thus primarily a site for experience, but experience construed now as an ongoing struggle between the rival demands of sense and sensibility, a struggle in which both sense and sensibility should be given full rein; and it is this that we call experience itself.

2   PLAY; OR, WASTING TIME PRODUCTIVELY

Our politicians tell us, now as so often, that we live in hard times; and in such times, the forces of conservatism always turn their attention to play. Especially in difficult financial times, play is regarded as suspect, frivolous. Governments, like latter-day Malvolios, regard playfulness with suspicion, righteously denying cakes and ale to a struggling population. Like the ghosts of Thomas Gradgrind in Dickens' *Hard Times* (Dickens, 1854) they leave no room for anything that can be regarded as excess. Gradgrind, remember, is:

> a man of realities. A man of fact and calculations. A man who proceeds upon the principle that two and two are four, and nothing over, and who is not to be talked into allowing for anything over . . . With a rule and a pair of scales, and the multiplication table always in his pocket, sir, ready to weigh and measure any parcel of human nature, and tell you exactly what it comes to.[6]

That is Dickens in 1854; but it could equally well be a contemporary utilitarian and instrumentalist ideology of education. While extolling the supposed virtues of modernization, we have caught up, in our official thinking about learning and teaching, with 1854.

This is the conservative view, and it has triumphed not just through conservative political administrations. In all cases, what it says is that there is no time for play. Children, students, teachers: there will be no easing up on productivity. The free-market conservative think-tank, the Centre for Policy Studies, was founded in 1974; and, under its aegis, Alfred Sherman posed a number of provocative questions. Among these was the question of when it is that we can say that workers are actually 'at work', for, allegedly, they cannot be said to be 'at work' when they are in the canteen or coffee-bar, say. It is this kind of thinking that starts to shape the 'Value-for-Money' agenda, the phrase itself being a Thatcherite mantra designed to justify the holding down of wages while simultaneously demanding higher output.

The more recent manifestation of this is the TRAC accountability system[7] through which academics must account for every hour of their work, and so-called Full Economic Costing of funded research activities. Behind both of these, and governing the entire mentality that gave them to us, is the Sherman question that would compartmentalize 'work' into atomized, and thus quantifiable units. Once such quantification is in place, a purely economistic model of University experience can be established. In this, play would be that which happens elsewhere, and would be seen as irrelevant to the operations of sense that are seen to be the intrinsic identity of the University. In this way, further, sensibility is either eliminated fully from the University or, if it is allowed continued existence, it is so only on condition that it is economically managed and controlled.

For a philosopher such as Schiller, play – *Spielen* – is central to education; for a psychologist such as Vygotsky, play is central to human development; for a historian such as Huizinga, *homo ludens* is a powerful agent of imagination in the rituals that determine the possibility of our living together in any social or public realm. In all of these, however, play is always threatening to escape our control: that is what makes it play in the first place. In Shakespeare's *Hamlet*, we find that 'the play's the thing'. When Hamlet says this, he is hoping that theatre will 'catch the conscience of the king' and reveal an underhand and occluded story of murder; but, more generally, what I argue here is that play is indeed the thing whereby we catch not just the conscience of kings and authorities, but also whereby we catch the very *consciousness* of participants in the University's activities.

Play, in short, is a kind of radical release of the very energies that are required for committed learning and teaching in the first place. It is in play that we see the play of sensibility and that we therefore engage the body with the mind in embodied learning or sense-making. Without play, there can be no experience.

And what now of our much-vaunted and debated 'student experience' crowed over by University marketing managers, surveyed endlessly by student associations whose surveys – perhaps ominously, and presumably not entirely disinterestedly – are sometimes financed by banks? Has it anything whatsoever to do with this? If it has not, then it is missing the point. And, of course, in the hands of those who describe and manipulate 'the student experience', it really does have nothing whatsoever to do with this. 'The student experience' is there, we might say, in order to ensure that our students *do not have any experience*. 'The student experience' is a myth designed to preclude the experiences of learning and teaching. Teaching and learning take place, certainly; but they do so *despite* the demands and norms of 'the student experience'; for it is really but an exercise in consumerist branding. As such, it is a sinister threat to the fundamental point and function of the University.

Real and genuine experience, we might say by contrast, is precisely contentiousness, the kinds of battle for and with the imagination – and for the possibilities of freedom in actual lives and futures – described by Dewey and Said; but it is a physical battle every bit as much as a mental or spiritual one. Dewey thought of it as an engaged thinking. He pointed out that, in a situation such as war, whether we are directly involved or not, we take sides, at least 'emotionally and imaginatively', for 'We desire this or that outcome'; and if we do not have such desires, then we are not thinking: 'One wholly indifferent to the outcome does not follow or think about what is happening at all'.

Importantly, this shows the consequentiality of thought, because in this state of affairs we share in the consequences of the action, of the experience. It follows from these observations that thinking, thus, happens always in a state of doubt, of uncertainty as to outcomes: 'all thinking is research, and all research is native, original, with him who carries it on, even if everybody else in the world is sure of what he is still looking for'. It thus follows that 'all thinking involves a risk' (Dewey, 1985: 154–5).

It is well known, at least since the time of Aristotle watching children learn by mimicry, that young children learn a great deal through play. It is perhaps not so often accepted that things are no different at any later stage in life. Play is central to learning and to teaching; for, in play, we exercise imagination and we explore possibility; we take the 'what is' and ask 'what if' instead. Play allows us not only to imagine the world and ourselves as other than we are, but actually to become other than we are. That, of course, is why it can be subversive; and that is why governments and administrations are suspicious of it. In its threat to control and regulation, it must be downgraded: it becomes 'frivolous' or 'unproductive' or 'a waste of time'. In hard times (and times are always Dickensian-hard, of course, when a powerful class wants to restrain possibilities that others might become free), play becomes construed and mediated as a threat to efficiency.

Yet, as even the mythmakers of 'the student experience' know, play is serious business. The 'student experience' is thus characterized not just in terms of teaching and learning; rather, it reaches out to embrace all that a student might want to engage with, including facilities of all sorts. Many of these facilities are what we might call 'hard-core': they include accommodation (for both living and teaching), libraries, refectories, shops on or near campus, and so on. There are also other facilities, including entertainment venues, as given by the Union and by all kinds of society; and, in these latter areas, we find 'the student experience' at play. The point, however, is that this is also 'contained' play: it, too, is regulated in ways that are designed to eliminate risk.

We can return to our quadruped graminivorous creature here. When Lev Vygotsky considered the development of the child, he looked at a young boy who was playing with a stick. The stick, in the hands of this boy, rapidly became something other than it was; and the young boy started to 'ride' it as if it were a horse. As a horse, the stick is now in a different physical relation to the body of the boy; and, through it, he can imagine his environment as other than it is. He can become a horse-rider, even though there is no horse there; but he is showing that he has the potential to do something new, and to transform his body and his world thereby. The stick is what Vygotsky calls a 'pivot'; and, around such a pivot, the boy not only learns, but also develops. This is what we might call *Bildung* or *formation*. It involves a transformation of boy and world; but a transformation that is effected through unregulated play.

By extension here, we might think of the café, or the photocopier or water-cooler where ostensibly inconsequential chat happens, as just such a pivot. In playful conversation, collegiality can be established – but equally, of course, it may not be. The point is the establishment of imaginative possibility. *Something* happens – even if we cannot know what it is – when bodies collide in the café; and that something, however evanescent, is of the very essence of the University.

Schiller, in his *Letters on Aesthetic Education* (Schiller, 1793), was also extremely aware of the power of play, or of *Spielen*. In Schiller, the play in question was both the childhood activity that would be later described by Vygotsky; but it was also theatre, play-acting. *Spielen* brings body and mind together in the form of action once more. Theatre, Schiller argues, is a prime location for the activity of learning and teaching as I have been describing it in these pages. The theatre in question might just be the café where our bodies enter into collegial relation with each other. The important thing about this kind of play, however, is that, by trying out a role, one can achieve not only knowledge but also *authority*.

Authority is the other side of experience. In saying this, I do not mean to suggest that we unquestionably grant authority to those more experienced than ourselves. In fact, in our time, this is extremely unlikely to happen: experience counts for little, if anything, in the question of authority. In our time, rather than listen to the voice of experience whose loss Benjamin lamented in his 1933 essay on 'Experience and Poverty', we are encouraged and enjoined to prefer the mathematical voice of abstract facts and computation. We do not listen to the voice of experience; rather, we manage and control it – and this means that we refuse to give it free rein, free play. In the consequent stifling or at least degradation of imagination, we also circumscribe possibility. Above all, we circumscribe the possibility that things tomorrow might be different from how they stand today; and this means that we refuse to grant authority and autonomy to the next generation of learners: our students.

Play, therefore – unregulated play, or, better, play that makes its own rules autonomously as it goes along – should be at the centre of a University. By this, I do not mean to suggest that the University is a site for frivolity, obviously: I have already rejected the description of play as frivolity as a conservative ploy that is designed to hamstring people and to force them into specific forms of 'efficient productivity', where everyone's productivity is policed more or less brutally. Play as *Spielen* however is axiomatic to learning and teaching; and this is especially so if we consider the importance of experiment to teaching and to learning. Not only Schiller and Vygotsky, but also Johan Huizinga would back this up, for the social is shaped to a large extent by the rituals that surround the modes of living produced by what he described as *homo ludens*. Play is that which disrupts the routines of mindless production, the mechanization of life, in order to produce *time*; and that time is where thinking – and thus also learning – can take place, as our bodies try out new roles, new languages, new stances or positions, new arguments, new battles, new loves.

Playful waste, as I am calling it, is that kind of activity that produces *time*, produces time even in the form of a 'waste of time', an expanse of time; but, for experience to happen at all, it is precisely time that we need. Time allows for the possibility of historical change. A University programme should be concerned with the production of time itself, and not with an alleged 'efficiency' model that says more must be crammed into less by eliminating the time required for play, or indeed for thinking. Voltaire once suggested, close to despair at the banalities of philosophical Optimism, that we might abandon the grand scheme of things and 'cultivate our own garden'.[8] The analogy here, for my own purposes, might very productively be made with gardening: playful waste is like compost: it needs time to settle in order to generate fresh life and growth. One word for such living growth is *Bildung*; and, without play, we will find no such edification in our academy at all.

Sense making depends first of all upon an acknowledgement of the realities of sensibility; and it is a negative move to corral such reality through a gesture of efficiency. It is time to allow for time itself, time in which play can allow the entire social sphere and public realm to benefit from the imaginative possibilities that edify our human being.

NOTES

1. See John Dewey, *Democracy and Education* (Dewey, 1985), 146–7.
2. Ibid., 147–8. For a prime literary example of this, see Charles Dickens, *Hard Times*, Chapter 2, 'Murdering the Innocents', where Gradgrind resents the fidgeting of his pupils, especially Sissy Jupe (1854, reprinted in Penguin, 1969).
3. Ibid., 148. It is this theology that shapes the barbarism that refuses an education to girls, as with the Taliban; but it is also an attitude that finds more subtle articulation in things such as single-sex schooling, or in male-only literary canons, or in glass-ceilings and employment legislation.
4. T. S. Eliot, 'The Love Song of J. Alfred Prufrock', originally published 1915.
5. Said, (1984), 28–9, italics added.
6. *Hard Times*, 1969 edition, p.48.
7. The acronym 'TRAC' stands for 'Transparent Approach to Costing'. It is a system of accounting used in the sector, and it claims to provide accurate actual costs of teaching and research. There are many controversies around its use.
8. In *Candide*, edited by J. H. Brumfitt, Oxford: Oxford University Press, 1968: 150 (originally published 1759).

REFERENCES

Benjamin, Walter (1999), 'Experience and Poverty', in Michael W. Jennings, Howard Eiland, Gary Smith (eds) *Walter Benjamin: Selected Writings, Volume 2: 1927–1934*, Cambridge, MA: Harvard University Press, 731–6.

Dewey, John (1985), *Democracy and Education*; Carbondale and Edwardsville: Southern Illinois University Press (originally published 1916).

Said, Edward (1984), *The World, The Text, The Critic*, London: Faber & Faber.

Schiller, Friedrich (1982), *On the Aesthetic Education of Man*, edited by Elizabeth M. Wilkinson and L. A. Willoughby. Oxford: Clarendon Press (originally published 1793).

6. From state to market via corruption: universities in an era of privatization

Philip Cooke and Fumi Kitagawa

INTRODUCTION

In this chapter, we will write about three sets of key agendas that have evolved in British academia in the past generation. These are: (1) its massification, marketization and privatization, (2) its 'corporatization' according to the 'administrative creep' determinants of 'new public management', and (3) the questionable ethics associated with the global procurement of students and research income. The chapter is written from the multiple perspectives of two authors – a UK academic who has worked in British academia for 40 years, beginning as a lecturer and ending as a research institute director; and a Japanese lecturer, who was once an international doctoral student studying changes in the UK academic system, and later recruited as 'international staff' to teach in the UK system. It may be worth noting that the recent transformation of the UK system contrasts with the Japanese system, which was changing rapidly by emulating the earlier UK reforms following 'New Public Management' (Ferlie et al., 1996), but has evolved relatively modestly in more recent years.

The chapter is constructed as follows. First, following this Introduction, we begin by setting out the broad landscape of 'marketization' of higher education in different parts of the world. The attention is drawn to the continued 'massification' of higher education in the UK combined with various forms of administrative and structural reforms of the sector. The detailed account of the evolving 'marketization' and 'privatization' of the UK system follows, especially the English higher education sector, which culminated in the White Paper, *Students at the Heart of the System* published in June 2011 (DBIS, 2011).

In the second main section, attention is drawn to the transformation and the changing roles of higher education in society as presented in broader institutional resource and management issues for UK universities in the recent past. The absolute rise in student numbers over the last 50 years has been accompanied by their requirements for special needs associated with quality assurance in teaching and learning. Through the massification process, there has been a constant cry from academic staff especially that university and government policies require them to teach hugely increased student numbers while retaining hitherto prevailing teaching quality standards.

In the third section, we highlight changes concerning human resource management including the increase in the number of both academic and administrative staff and their salaries over the last decade. Among the factors that seem to be responsible is the rise of the 'audit society' (Power, 1997), which affects particularly the vastly expanded quantity and volume of research and teaching contracts through the evolution of 'New Public Management' over the decades. While it was Philip Selznick (1949) who first recognized 'administrative creep' in his famed study of bureaucracy in the Tennessee Valley Authority, which he termed 'goal displacement', it is a modern irony that it has come full circle to arrive in academia, where it might have been thought enlightened study and informed opinion would have provided some protection from its worst effects. It also reflects the displacement effect of having increased quantities of public and private financial resources flowing through university coffers. Legal incrimination is the threat hanging over inadequately robust systems of financial management, not to mention the increased responsibilities academic functionaries, teaching and research staff face in terms of fortified health and safety legislation, from the administration of animal houses to the care of students in the field. At practically each step, administrative undergirding is in demand in ways that could hardly have been imagined a generation ago. The final section attends to the desirability or otherwise of the 'globalization' of universities, particularly involving the aforementioned pursuit of academic research largesse from political regimes with questionable records on human rights and returns to the theme of the quality of teaching experience 'bought' by large numbers of foreign students recruited to UK shores by the burgeoning international administrator cadre already mentioned.

THE TRANSFORMATION OF THE UK HIGHER EDUCATION – MASSIFICATION AND MARKETIZATION

In many countries across the world, there has been a common trend over the last three decades – governments are introducing more market-oriented national higher education systems. Marketization of the higher education sector is based on the belief that *demand* – whether 'of students for qualifications', 'of employers for skills', or 'of the economy for innovation' – can produce 'a coherent shape for such complex institutions as universities' (Anderson, 2010). It should be noted that there is not a single higher education market, but rather a multitude of markets: differentiated markets for students at different levels of programmes including undergraduates, graduates, a market for company training; a market for research staff, a market for lecturers and professors; a market for research grants and scholarships; a market for donations, and so on (Jongbloed, 2003).

The structure of the UK higher education system, the activities of UK academics and the nature of their work and profession have substantially changed over the past three decades. The higher education sector in the UK has been transformed into a 'diversified and increasingly stratified sector' (Brennan et al., 2007: 175). One of the main factors influencing this change is a transformation from an 'elite' to 'mass' system of higher education (see McNay, 2006; Scott, 2010). The age participation ratio has risen from 4 to over 40 per cent over the past 50 years. In parallel, the sector has been facing increasing competition and continuous 'marketization'. Through the process of marketization, there has been a race to attract and recruit foreign students, who have paid the full economic cost of their education since the 1980s. In recent years, UK universities have recruited large numbers of Asian, especially Chinese, students notably to graduate school courses. Consequently, there are concerns about students' limited competence in English, academic skills and issues related to teacher–student relationships for students coming from different cultural and educational backgrounds (Edwards and Ran, 2006). Further, the Research Assessment Exercise (RAE), first introduced in 1986, and to be replaced by the Research Excellence Framework (REF) in 2014, has placed institutions in competition with each other for 'research active' academics.

This transformation is testified to in the contrasting principles of the Robbins report into the expansion of UK higher education in 1963 and Dearing's more utilitarian and 'productivist' theses of 1997, reflecting the political view that in an age of globalized competition in the 'knowledge economy', the most important task of a higher education system is to contribute to the practical applications of knowledge, its service to national competitiveness and to society (see Lee and Miozzo, 2009). In 1963, the report of the Robbins committee on higher education presented the 'Robbins principle', that university places should be available to all who were qualified for them by ability and attainment (Anderson, 2010). In the

1963 Robbins Report the objectives of higher education were defined as follows:

- 'instruction in skills',
- 'to promote the power of mind',
- 'the search for truth', and
- 'the transmission of common culture and common standards of citizenship' (Robbins, 1963: 6–7) (cited in National Committee of Inquiry into Higher Education (aka the Dearing report), 1997: 71).

UK higher education went through a series of severe funding cuts during the 1980s combined with the 'massification' of the sector after the Robbins report. The amount universities had to spend on teaching had been halved and funding for infrastructure and research had been substantially reduced. Dearing's report was the first national comprehensive study on higher education commissioned by the government since Robbins. During an interview on the tenth anniversary of his report, Dearing (quoted in Crace and Shepherd, 2007) said:

> The crisis in 1996 was the result of a period of very fast growth in student numbers, financed in very substantial part by severe reductions in the unit of resource [the amount a university spends on each student] for teaching, and massive decay in research infrastructure.

In the 1997 Dearing Report, *Higher Education in a Learning Society*, the government perspectives had become:

- 'to enable individuals to develop their capabilities';
- 'to increase knowledge and understanding both for their own sake and for their practical applications';
- 'to serve the needs of a knowledge-based economy'; and
- 'to play a major role in shaping a democratic, civilised and inclusive society' (National Committee of Inquiry into Higher Education, 1997: 72).

The Dearing report emphasized eight key themes in its recommendations (Crace and Shepherd, 2007):

- all full-time undergraduates should contribute £1000 per year of study after graduation on an income-contingent basis;
- there should be a return to the expansion of student numbers;
- the world-class reputation of UK degrees must be protected;

- higher education should make greater use of technology;
- the government should increase funding for research;
- there should be more professionalism in university teaching;
- there should be a stronger regional and community role for universities; and
- there should be a review of pay and working practices of all staff.

Together with the aspiration that academic research could contribute to regional and national innovation processes and competitiveness in the UK as it had at some elite or technical universities in the US, the call for universities and academic research to be accountable, to be efficient, to consider user needs, to secure income from other sources and to collaborate with industry to foster knowledge transfer became institutionalized through government funding. The concept of a 'third mission' was initially about individual universities' revenue generation in the 1980s. Under the 1997 Labour government, the third mission was largely about generating 'public benefit' through subsidizing private profit by entrepreneurial exploitation of intellectual property. This was to be done by licensing, trade sale of licence value or creation of spin-off businesses supported by the state through public funding such as the Higher Education Innovation Fund (HEIF) in England, and various 'third mission' funding schemes in Northern Ireland, Scotland and Wales.

The institutional dimensions of devolution processes conditioned by different forms of 'economic governance' (Cooke and Clifton, 2005) and knowledge transfer and exchange between different actors constituting innovation systems warrants further investigation and analysis (Huggins and Kitagawa, 2012). Knowledge transfer refers to 'processes for capturing, collecting and sharing explicit and tacit knowledge' (European Commission, 2007) between higher education institutions (HEIs) and third parties, including industry and civil society organizations. The effects of devolution on higher education, research funding and the management of knowledge transfer are a growing area of policy concern (Universities UK, 2008). The economic and social contributions of universities were seen to be public goods, supported by a number of regional bodies in England (like the now defunct Regional Development Agencies and Regional Government Offices) and more centralized institutional mechanisms like the English, Northern Irish, Scottish and Welsh higher education funding councils (Lawton Smith, 2007). During the 2000s, a number of regional frameworks were built where different types of universities – with different strengths and weaknesses – supposedly worked together and helped economic growth and well being through knowledge exchange and outreach activities. A critical issue seldom addressed was how to connect such a third stream mission to the core activities of universities, namely, teaching and research. There was a new mantra for universities to create new institutional entrepreneurial architectures to define and achieve their new goals. This was: to exploit the gold in academic researchers' heads.

'PRIVATIZATION' OF UK UNIVERSITIES: WHO PAYS, WHO BENEFITS?

Administrative and structural reforms in the higher education sector over the decades have resulted in the general need for diversification of funding income in universities and encouragement towards sourcing of external funding through various market mechanisms. This began under the 1997–2010 Labour government, which accepted the findings of the Dearing Report (NCIHE, 1997) that first recommended charging fees for university education in the UK. In 1998, the Labour government introduced the student fees set at £1000, a figure that now seems ludicrously inadequate to the prevailing ambitions of the sector. In 2004, the government increased the level of tuition fees that universities were allowed to charge, up to £3000 a year. Following the 2007–10 recession, the new political economy surrounding UK universities will drastically transform the nature of the university again, and also the nature of their 'publicness'. The apotheosis of this escalating educational cost hyperinflation is the announcement in early 2011 that most English universities will charge up to £9000 (some US $15000) in annual fees per student from the start of the academic year in autumn 2012, raising the cap from the prevailing level of £3290. Following the report commissioned by the government (the Browne Report, 2010), in early 2011 universities in England announced in large numbers that they would be accepting the coalition government's proposal that they could triple annual fee charges to undergraduate students, up to £9000 per year. This supersedes the government's estimate of how many universities would charge the full amount by about 50 per cent, creating a requirement of a further £1 billion public support of the student loans scheme (Shepherd, 2011).

The government White Paper published in June 2011 sets out the new vision for higher education in England in the following way:

> We are reducing the block grant money that universities and colleges will get from the Higher Education Funding Council for England (HEFCE) and increasing to a maximum of £9,000 the tuition loans that students can borrow from Government. The precise amount they borrow will depend on how much their university or college decides to charge in graduate contribution; any waivers or discounts it offers; and the decisions of students themselves on how much they want to borrow. (DBIS, 2011, p. 15)

Table 6.1   Income and expenditure of UK HEIs, 2005/06–2009/10

Academic year	Total income (£000s)	Expenditure (£000s)
2009/10	26 798 894	25 845 920
2008/09	25 371 918	24 939 307
2007/08	23 428 930	22 877 440
2006/07	21 255 048	21 016 635
2005/06	19 528 413	19 352 832

Source: HESA (2011a).

This is based on the view that the public money should come predominantly in the form of 'loans to first-time undergraduate students', to take to the institution of their choice, rather than as grants distributed by a central funding council, as the White Paper *Students at the Heart of the System* sets out. It is also widely mooted that higher fees may reduce the supply of students, that this problem will fall mainly on the less privileged universities, notably the former polytechnics that gained university status in 1992 at the behest largely of the non-university trained Prime Minister of the day, the Conservative John Major, and that some of this group may go bankrupt and fail accordingly.

Ironically, this newly realized potential government funding crisis slightly delays the onset of the effective 'privatization' of the English universities, where 13 of the 20 self-defined research intensive institutions known as the 'Russell Group' announced, by March 2011, that they would charge the full amount, with the rest expected to follow. Naively, the coalition government of Conservatives and Liberal Democrats had assumed an average fee increase involving only a doubling of the hitherto prevailing £3000 per year. This will influence significantly the funding and institutional landscapes of higher education in the UK, especially in the English part of the realm. In addition to the changing regime of publicly funded institutions, new private providers of higher education are emerging. For example, in July 2010, BPP University College of Professional Studies was granted university college status, being the first private provider to gain university status in 30 years, and they will compete with the existing higher education sector.

If we look at the situation in the UK, we see the following overall picture (Table 6.1). First, in an era of relatively low inflation, there was a substantial budgetary rise, taking total income up by over a third (37.4 per cent) to £26.8 million in five years. Second, this period comes after 2004 and the previous tripling of university fees from the original 1998 Dearing level of £1000 to the 2010 rate of £3290. Accordingly, third, other factors

Table 6.2   Specimen Russell Group University income (£ million) from student fees, 2001–10

Student origin	2001	2003	2009	2010
UK	16.0	17.0	44.5	47.5 (53%)
EU	1.6	1.8	2.5	2.8
Non-EU	12.7	15.9	29.0	33.5 (37%)
Part-time	1.6	1.4	6.0	6.2
Total	31.9	36.1	82.9	90.0

Source: Calculated by the authors based on the university's own data.

Table 6.3   UK HEI income by source, 2009/10

Source	Income (£000s)	Percentage of total
Funding body grants	9 043 115	33.7
Tuition fees and education contracts	8 272 137	30.9
Research grants and contracts	4 345 421	16.2
Other income	4 915 913	18.3
Endowment and investment income	219 201	0.8

Source: HESA (2011a).

have contributed to the substitution effect of private money replacing at least part of the state's previous contribution.

Second, deducible from the out-turns evident in Table 6.2 are increasing UK full-time and, to a lesser extent, part-time student numbers, on the one hand, and, on the other increasing income from larger numbers and increasing fees for non-EU students. The data represent a specimen Russell Group student profile. Clearly, the undeflated student income rates for the two years at the beginning and at the end of the 2000s show significantly increased magnitudes of university income in these categories. Importantly, they show a near trebling of income from fees paid by non-EU students. Finally, again it should be noted on non-inflation adjusted figures, that the overall income of the specimen Russell Group University nearly trebled in the ten years from 2001 to 2010.

By 2009/10 the share of overall university income arising from the direct transfer of public funds by the UK government was only marginally the largest as Table 6.3 shows. This amounted to just over £9 billion (33.7 per cent) compared to £8.3 billion (30.9 per cent) from the market in privately funded fee income from students. With the trebling of a significant part of fee income, which Table 6.2 suggests could be at least some 53 per cent of fee income, a sum of roughly £45 million translates into one of £135 million for the average Russell Group University, less some quantity of transfer payments in the form of social inclusion bursaries and whatever arrangements prevail in the non-English nations of the UK. For instance, Higher Education Statistics Agency (HESA) data show that in Wales, for example, its university funding body took a cut of £65 million (8.5 per cent) for academic year 2011/12.

The HESA data for total English university income for 2009/10 were £22.2 billion from a UK total of £26.7 billion. Keep in mind that English universities have taken cuts of £2.34 billion in 2010–11, so let us say that reduces their overall future budgets to £20 billion (cuts elsewhere should also be included, although harder to identify). Tripling domestic fee income shifts the current share of public fee and other income down from 2009/10's £9 billion to £7 billion in the following year, while domestic fee income can be estimated to rise from £8.3 billion (some 37 per cent of which is non-EU in origin). Using the specimen Russell Group breakdown as a guide, the non-EU element is thus close to £3 billion (37 per cent of £8.3 billion), leaving the remainder as a conservative £5 billion of pre-Browne fee income.

This will now rise much closer to £15 billion, minus the aforementioned public funding cut, which has to be factored in with the other sources of income in Table 6.3 to give a guide to the new private/public income balance. Importantly, the other main private income source, which is non-EU fee income, can also be adjusted upwards. Of course, under UK coalition government plans, much direct state funding for degree courses is being scrapped. As Table 6.4 shows, the 2010 government spending review cuts the higher education budget from £7.1 billion to £4.2 billion by 2014.

However, if only the 'funding body grants' (down to £7 billion, then to £4 billion in 2014) and the domestic fee element of 'tuition fees and edu-

Table 6.4   Estimated UK university income shares, 2012/2013

Source	Income (£)	Estimated percentage of total as of 2014
Funding body grants	7 billion (to be reduced to 4 billion by 2014)	20.3 (12.7)
Tuition fees	18 billion	52.1 (57.1)
Research and endowments	4.5 billion	13.4
Other income	5 billion	14.2

Source: Calculated by the authors.

cation contracts' (up to £15 billion plus £3 billion non-EU) in Table 6.3 are adjusted, this gives a conservatively calculated private/public fees balance for the UK (some public fee transfer arrangements prevailing in the UK nations outside England) of 52.1 per cent private to 20.3 per cent public (57.1:12.7 per cent by 2014); and the privatization of the UK, especially English, university system becomes starkly apparent (Table 6.4). Moreover, in practice, much research, endowment (a tiny figure; Table 6.3) and 'other' income is private, so there needs to be an overall adjustment to the private/public income ratio closer to 70:30 (or with the 'funding body cuts' 80:20) to get a sense of how far market relations have penetrated the UK university system by 2012/13. A final point is that taking the Browne report limit to the full, £9000 represents a massive one-off windfall for the UK's universities. From 2012 to 2014 there is clearly a short-term windfall for universities until cuts are fully in place. The key question is, how many of the 166 currently independent recipients of university funding body income in the UK will charge Browne fees, how many can resist a share of the short-term privatization bonanza, and how many will survive if they do not?

THE EVOLUTION OF 'ADMINISTRATIVE CREEP' IN THE UK UNIVERSITY

Hence, the UK, especially English, university system seems to have been now 'privatized'. However, this is a process that has been evolving since at least 1998 and in relation to the demise of student grants which began much earlier, somewhat longer compared to the postwar days when only some 5 per cent of student-age cohorts actually sought a university education. Recall, in any case, the trebling of income for the specimen Russell Group University during the 2000s. During that period, as noted, there have been regular complaints from teaching staff that their numbers were not increasing at a pace concomitant with the rapid rise in the number of students they were expected to teach. Furthermore, improving the quality of the total had become the key mantra for higher education.

Adding to the newly wrought role of enhancing student experiences, those of the academics and their burgeoning managerial strata were also changing. That there have been solid grounds for the suspicion of 'administrative creep' in UK universities was testified to in HESA data (quoted in Tahir, 2010), that showed that there were 10740 managers in the UK higher education sector in 2003/04, while in 2008/09 this segment alone had grown to 14250, an increase of 33 per cent. During the same period the number of academics increased by 10 per cent from 106900 to 116495

Table 6.5   Comparative average incomes by staff type in UK HEIs

Academic year	Academic	Managers	Non-academic professionals
2009/10	£46 998	£48 575	£38 772
2008/09	£46 607	£48 088	£38 530
2007/08	£43 486	£44 667	£35 861
2006/07	£41 128	£42 724	£34 405
2005/06	£38 933	£40 981	£33 087

Source: Collated by the authors based on HESA (2011b).

while the total number of students rose by 9 per cent from 2 200 180 to 2 396 055. The HESA definition of manager is the new public management type of non-academic professional involved in finance, auditing, marketing, widening participation, human resources, student services, quality assurance and various other professional and academic evaluations. Table 6.5 shows that 'managers' maintained a salary advantage over academics and non-academic professionals between 2005/06 and 2009/10.

Were this to be exceptional compared to other administrative occupational change magnitudes, official statistics might be expected to reveal this. Predictably though, the indicators are rendered opaque by various classification anomalies. For example, one of these is the absence of a 'pure academic' indicator, obfuscated by 'academic-related' or 'clinical-related' sub-categories. Excluding 'clinical' is possible and gives a core academic UK staff of 110 535 in 2000/01. This compares with 117 930 full-time academic professional staff in 2009/10. However a significant category of 63 665 part-time academic staff now also exists. Meanwhile total non-academic staff amounted to 205 835 and a further 185 155 non-academic 'atypical staff' (mostly short-term contract) in 2009/10 compared to 120 625 (full-time) and 67 250 (part-time) in 2003/04 (HESA 2011b).

Accordingly, although precise comparison of categories over time is difficult, it can be at least suggested that full-time non-academic staff in UK universities grew from 120 625 to 205 835, a difference of 85 210. Between 2003/04 and 2009/10, the number of 'non-academic professionals' stayed almost the same (27 170 and 27 615 respectively) while core full-time academic staff grew by 7395 in the lengthier period 2000/01 to 2009/10.

This 33 per cent to 10 per cent growth asymmetry between academics and managers, with higher incomes for the latter, is instructive even though the relative numbers in the two categories massively favour the academics (in 2009/10, 14 290 managers, 117 930 academic professionals; HESA 2011b). Nevertheless, overall, academic professionals, at 117 930

Table 6.6   Expenditure by UK HEIs by activity, 2009/10

Category	Expenditure (£000s)	% of total
Staff costs – academic	8 139 223	31.5
Staff costs – other	6 503 678	25.2
Other operating expenses	9 363 684	36.2
Depreciation	1 396 584	5.4
Interest and other finance costs	453 204	1.8

Source: HESA (2011c).

in 2009/10 were outweighed by non-academic occupational categories of 205 835. Of course, the majority of the latter, as non-professional non-academics (some 168 475) were lower paid, sufficient to depress average non-academic incomes overall to £29 609 in 2009/10 (based on HESA 2011b). Hence, these data give an indication where a good portion of the UK university income increase has gone. Moreover, the significant 'other operating expenses' entry in Table 6.6 includes costs in respect of payments to non-contracted staff or individuals, all other non-staff costs incurred, maintenance contracts and infrastructure costs (e.g. communications), many of which contribute to administrative rather than strictly academic practice.

WHITHER 'PRIVATIZED' UNIVERSITIES?

Inside Job is a 2010 documentary film about the global financial crisis in 2007–10. Along with criticizing the financial and derivatives markets, the state regulations and incentive mechanisms that induced the crisis, the film highlights the role of academia in the recent financial meltdown. The director of the film, Charles Ferguson highlighted economist Martin Feldstein, Professor of Economics at Harvard University, and a former head of Ronald Reagan's Council of Economic Advisors. He was a director of mega-bankrupt derivatives insurer AIG, bailed out in 2008 at $49 billion by the US Treasury, and former board member of the financially healthier investment bank, responsible for inventing the very derivatives that brought the global financial system down, J. P. Morgan & Co. (G. Tett, 2009). Ferguson demonstrated that many leading professors and faculty in economics departments and business schools derived large proportions of their incomes from being engaged as consultants or conducting 'speaking engagements'. Thus, then Dean of Columbia Business School, Glenn Hubbard, is a paradigm case of engaging in these practices while also reaping emoluments from affiliations with private equity firm Kohlberg Kravis Roberts (KKR) and hedge fund BlackRock Financial. Hubbard and others, notably Harvard Business School's John Y. Campbell, denies a conflict of interest between academia and the banking sector.

On the other side of the Atlantic, in early March 2011, the director of the London School of Economics (LSE) resigned over donations made to the School by a charity associated with a son of the Libyan dictator Colonel Muammar Gaddafi. Former banker Sir Howard Davies recognized that his position *did* represent a conflict of interest among academic, political and business principles when he said the decision to approve acceptance of £300 000 in research funding from a foundation run by Gaddafi's son, Saif, had 'backfired', that the university's reputation had 'suffered' accordingly and that he had no option but to resign. The doctoral student had been feted when opening LSE's Centre for Global Governance headed by sociologist Professor David Held. It transpired that LSE had benefited to the tune of £3.7 million from its Libyan connection. Shortly after this event, at which Saif Gaddafi spoke of the importance of democracy for Libya's future, he was to be seen on TV News brandishing a machine gun and threatening 'to destroy' opponents of his father's regime. Dr David Starkey, a former LSE colleague, said on the BBC television programme, *Question Time* that the LSE 'sold degrees', invented useless degrees which they could sell to overseas students, to which he added the charge of 'intellectual corruption'. Starkey said: 'Because universities are starved of funds, they go out of their way to attract foreign students and they invent non-degrees, Masters' degrees that have got almost no meaning, so they get very large fees from it. So there was systemic corruption.'[1]

Now, like most privatized institutions that become 'market-facing' firms, universities must seek private or, indeed, public finance from elsewhere. This is also the case in regard to the part of perceived university under-funding that concerns the infrastructural support system for conducting research. Despite funding constraints in the UK, research has also become a success story there as well as for more affluent leading universities elsewhere in the advanced economies. This is for three reasons: first, universities recruited and retained top research talent from the 1970s onwards but especially from the 1990s when some (notably US) public and private research budgets for healthcare, energy and environment burgeoned with the end of the Cold War. Second, during that same period public research laboratories declined in influence because they were uneconomic and frequently locked into long term projects and lifetime employment. Private laboratories became perceived as equally expensive as non-university public ones and unproductive compared to university research, which benefited accordingly. Finally, the reason university research triumphed was because it was flexible, swift and cheap, something the emerging 'research market' was quick to recognize. Research thus became a major institutional quality driver even though teaching accounted economically for the main income of universities. High aspiration universities thus had to have a strong research base, for example, acquiring medical schools (not always wisely as they were expensive and shared many of the 'lock-in' characteristics of public and private laboratories), or at least portfolios of research institutes in leading edge research fields.

One source of funding for prestigious research institutes has always been the endowment market, particularly pronounced in north America and Israel more than, for example, the UK. However, ambitious UK universities found another lucrative source of targeted research and teaching funding in, amongst others, the repressive Arab regimes of north Africa and the Middle East. This came to light over the notorious case of the foundation of Colonel Gaddafi's son Saif al Islam, the Gaddafi International Charity and Development Foundation (GICDF), which funded teaching courses and the Centre for Global Governance research institute at the London School of Economics. Not only did the son of the Libyan dictator fund the research institute to the tune of £300 000, he was awarded the PhD in 2008 prior to making the donation. Although no proof has yet been forthcoming, anonymous LSE sources at 'pro-director' level, one rung below LSE Director Sir Howard Davies, openly joked that a solicitation for funding would follow the granting of the PhD. It was made to the tune of £1.5 million and granted accordingly the following year. This followed a £2.2 million LSE contract with Libya to train its civil servants. The head of the Global Governance centre Professor David Held subsequently became a trustee of GICDF in June 2009 but resigned following a conflict of interest decision made by the council of the LSE. A colleague and supervisor of the dictator's son's PhD reported to Owen (2011) 'I can hardly be confident that nobody else helped him since there's evidence that he lifted bits'. As noted earlier in this chapter, this incident was the proximate cause of Sir Howard's resignation and the setting up of an inquiry into the university's links with Libya, chaired by the former Lord Chief Justice, Lord Woolf.

Rapidly following on top of this scandal, other parts of the UK university system were found to have accepted comparable funding from other non-democratic regimes in the Arab world. In March 2011 Cambridge University was the target of attack over ethical funding of universities after accepting a new donation from the Oman government to promote religious understanding. The finance, from Sultan Qaboos was to establish a chair of the Abrahamic Faiths and Shared Values in the university's faculty of divinity. The donation was the second substantial one the university had received from the Sultanate – bringing his total funding to the university to well over £4 million. It followed the donation of £2.8 million for a chair in modern Arabic and a further £300 000 to support a fellowship in oriental studies at the university's Pembroke College. The university had also received £8 million from the House of Saud to set up a new centre for Islamic studies. The issue in these and other cases was picked up by Owen (2011) from a report by the conservative London Centre for Social Cohesion as follows: 'the UK's finest universities are taking money from some of the world's worst dictatorships. Iran, Saudi Arabia and China, all with appalling human rights records, are significant contributors to venerable UK institutions' (Garner, 2011a). Durham University was next to be identified as having taken £700 000 from Middle East sources, including £11 000 from the Iranian government. Moreover, Oxford University's Centre for Islamic Studies received £75 million from several Muslim countries. Even Liverpool John Moores University, recipient of £1.2 million for training, was implicated in links with the Libyan regime (Garner, 2011b). It subsequently emerged that Oxford University had accepted a doctoral proposal from the son of former Iranian president Akbar Rafsanjani under a pseudonym and with doubts about the provenance of its authorship (Syal, 2011).

CONCLUSIONS

In 2004, Derek Bok, the former President of Harvard University argued in his book, *Universities in the Marketplace: The Commercialization of Higher Education* (Bok, 2004) that universities have 'lost sight of any clear mission beyond a vague commitment to "excellence"' in their eagerness to make money by agreeing to more and more compromises with basic academic values. Calhoun (2006) in his paper 'Is the university in crisis?' noted that social scientists, who spend much of their lives in universities and who should know better, are often surprisingly oblivious to transformations of higher education.

We have shown two clear and key things about the evolution of the UK university system in the past decade or so. The first important thing we have demonstrated quite convincingly is that the UK system, especially its English part (which is easily the majority) will have been effectively privatized by 2012/13 with a further boost to privatization until 2014 according to announced government plans. The second thing we have shown is that university income will have risen even more quickly for the brief hiatus period from 2012–14 because public cuts will not yet have been implemented in full force and it is hard to see, under the circumstances how very many institutions will eschew charging the full £9000 annual undergraduate fee now allowed from 2012. This accelerates an already rising income trend based on (undeflated) HESA income statistics over the decade of the 2000s. The question we raised is 'where did that money go?' In large measure, our answer points to it going to fund the major 'administrative creep' that has befallen UK universities as they have grown and become marketized. Relatively speaking, academic expenditure has risen at a far slower and lesser pace than administrative and largely administratively related expenditure. Without arguing that the university has become a version of Weber's bureaucratic 'iron cage', everyday life in academia for those who have experienced it for the past 40 years can nevertheless feel closer to that condition now than at the outset of that period (Weber, 1994).

The UK higher education system has gone through constant 'marketization', combined with a series of 'reforms' since the 1980s and the relationship between the state and the higher education sector has been substantially transformed. These changes can be stated briefly, and address three key points about the evolution of the UK university system from an overwhelmingly state-funded to a privatized regime of management.

The first key point is that it is unquestionable that the UK system, especially in England, is well on the way to privatizing the hitherto publicly funded national higher education system. This has been managed through a triple process of 'system shock' dating from the 1980s, first, when the system was allowed to grow its finances mainly by means of the admission of non-EU graduates to undertake full fee expensive postgraduate education, followed by the gradual introduction of fees to home students. Second, along with the continuing 'massification' of higher education, particularly since the late 1990s, the sector was confronted with the governmental requirement to admit up to half the university-age cohort for university degree level instruction. However, adding this to the rise in domestic student numbers without substantially more sufficient resources to teach them adequately made the growth aspiration unviable. What in fact happened to much of the new resource was that instead of adequately supplementing teaching or research budgets it was allocated in large measure to the employment of new administrative strata engaged in recruiting overseas, especially Asian students, managing financial flows, managing assessment procedures and auditing financial flows. Expensive management tiers were added to 'manage the managers' according to the theory of 'administrative creep'. Finally, in their thirst for resources to replenish these demanding recipients of corporate resources, universities over-rode basic ethical requirements in a democracy of denying support to non-democratic and repressive regimes by accepting major financial transfers from regimes that in some cases were, in 2011, to be seen to turn guns upon their own protesting citizens. Concerned observers might agree that the time for 'educating the educators and their academic administrators' is long overdue.

NOTE

1.   http://www.mentorn.tv/news.aspx, accessed 30 March 2011.

REFERENCES

Anderson, R (2010), The 'idea of a university' today. Online at http://www.history andpolicy.org/papers/policy-paper-98.html, accessed 1 July 2011.
Bok, D. (2004), *Universities in the Marketplace: The Commercialization of Higher Education*, Princeton, NJ: Princeton University Press.
Brennan, J., W. Locke, and R. Naidoo (2007), 'United Kingdom: an increasingly stratified profession' in W. Locke and U. Teichler (eds) *The Changing Conditions for Academic Work and Careers in Select Countries*, Kassel, Germany: International Centre for Higher Education Research, pp. 163–76.
Browne, J. (2010), *Securing a Sustainable Future for Higher Education*, (Browne Report). Online at http://webarchive.nationalarchives.gov.uk/+/hereview.inde-pendent.gov.uk/hereview//report/ accessed 11 October 2012.
Calhoun, C. (2006), Is the university in crisis? *Society*, May/June 2006.
Cooke P. and N. Clifton (2005), Visionary, precautionary and constrained 'varieties of devolution' in the economic governance of the devolved UK territories, *Regional Studies* **39**, 437–51.
Crace, J. and J. Shepherd, (2007), Ten Years after the Dearing Report, *Guardian*, Tuesday 24 July. Online at http://www.guardian.co.uk/education/2007/jul/24/highereducation.tuitionfees, accessed 1 July 2011.
DBIS (2011), *Students at the Heart of the System*. Online at http://www.bis.gov.uk/news/topstories/2011/Jun/he-white-paper-students-at-the-heart-of-the-system, accessed 1 July 2011.
Edwards, C. and A. Ran (2006), Meeting the needs of Chinese students in British Higher Education. Online at http://www.ncll.org.uk/10_about/50_research/10_research_projects/MeetingTheNeeds.pdf, accessed 1 July 2011.
European Commission (2007), *Improving knowledge transfer between research institutions and industry across Europe: embracing open innovation.* Online at http://ec.europa.eu/invest-in-research/pdf/download_en/knowledge_transfe_07.pdf, accessed 10 July 2010.
Ferlie, E. L. Ashburner, L. Fitzgerald and A. M. Pettigrew (1996), *The New Public Management in Action*. Oxford, Oxford University Press.
Garner, R. (2011a), Fury at Omani sultan's cash for Cambridge, *The Independent*, 9 March, 6.
Garner, R. (2011b), Durham University accepted £11,000 donation from Iran, *The Independent*, 18 March, 19.

HESA (2011a), *HE Finance Plus 2009/10*. Online at http://www.hesa.ac.uk/
index.php?option=com_content&task=view&id=1985&Itemid=161, accessed
7 October 2012.

HESA (2011b), *Staff in Higher Education Institutions 2009/10*, Cheltenham,
Higher Education Statistical Agency.

HESA (2011c), *Finances of Higher Education Institutions 2009/10*, Cheltenham:
Higher Education Statistical Agency.

Huggins, R. and F. Kitagawa (2012), Regional policy and university knowledge
transfer: perspectives from devolved regions in the UK, *Regional Studies*, **46** (6),
817–32.

Jongbloed, B. (2003), Marketisation in higher education, Clark's triangle and the
essential ingredients of markets. *Higher Education Quarterly*, **57** (2), 110–35.

Lawton Smith, H. (2007), Universities, innovation and territorial development: a
review of the evidence. *Environment and Planning C: Government and Policy* **25**:
98–114.

Lee, H. and M. Miozzo (2009), The impact of university–industry collaboration on
academic research training and careers of PhDs in science and engineering: The
case of the UK. DRUID Summer conference paper.

McNay, I. (2006), Delivering mass higher education: the reality of policy in practice, in Ian McNay (ed.) *Beyond Mass Higher Education: Building on Experience*
SRHE/Open University.

National Committee of Inquiry into Higher Education (NCIHE) (1997), *The
Dearing Report: Higher Education in the Learning Society*, London: HMSO.

Owen, J. (2011), LSE insider claims Gaddafi donation was 'openly joked about',
Independent on Sunday, 13 March, 35.

Power, M. (1997), *The Audit Society*, Oxford, Oxford University Press.

Scott, P. (2010), Structural Changes in Higher Education: The Case of the
United Kingdom, in D. Palfreyman and T. Tapper (eds.) *Structuring Mass
Higher Education: The Role of Elite Institutions*, New York: Routledge.

Selznick, P. (1949), *TVA and the Grass Roots*, New York: Harper & Row.

Shepherd, J. (2011), Rush to charge £9,000 fees opens up £1bn gap in university
funding, *The Guardian*, 28 March, 10.

Syal, R. (2011), Oxford investigates Rafsanjani's son over PhD application, *The
Guardian*, 28 March, 8.

Tahir, T. (2010), The irresistible rise of academic bureaucracy, *The Guardian*, 30
March.

Tett, G, (2009), JP Morgan and the new masters of the universe, *Financial Times*,
29 September.

Universities UK (2008), *Devolution and Higher Education: Impact and Future
Trends*, London: Universities UK, London.

Weber, M. (1994), *Political Writings*, Cambridge: Cambridge University Press.

7. Marketization and alienation in academic activity

Sonja Grönblom and Johan Willner

1 INTRODUCTION

This chapter analyses the consequences for work motivation, employment and performance when a university is reorganized by the principles of the market, i.e. by *marketization*. In the context of public sector and non-profit organizations, marketization means attempts to improve economic performance through the alleged superiority of private sector practices (Lynch, 2006). Marketization is for example believed to strengthen customer orientation and cost awareness (Jongbloed, 2003). Few organizations offer a more striking contrast between old and new principles than the university.

There is a rich descriptive literature on university reforms, but few studies have seriously questioned their advantages by applying microeconomics. Our purpose is therefore to analyse how such dimensions of marketization as economic rewards and punishments, more powerful managers and eroded employment protection might affect the performance of a university in its core tasks, the work efforts of its employees and the size of its staff. In contrast to traditional agency theory, we emphasize potential intrinsic motivation. We ask whether marketization can be associated with alienation (i.e. estrangement from work, tasks or duties), not least because of the possibility that economic sticks and carrots crowd out the intrinsic motivation, as suggested by the literature on motivation in other organizations.

Our chapter is organized as follows. Sections 2 and 3 describe universities before and after marketization. Section 4 introduces intrinsic motivation, in order to amend the agency models that are applied in Sections 5 and 6 on different types of governance. Section 7 compares performance, while Section 8 provides a (non-technical) summary and discussion.

2   THE TRADITIONAL UNIVERSITY

The word university means a community of teachers and scholars, *universitas magistrorum et scholarium*. By a *traditional university* we mean an expert organization that conforms to this description, and is characterized by a combination of research and higher education, by *autonomy*, collegiality and *academic freedom*. Its working conditions include tenure and a fixed rather than performance-related wage.

Universities as degree-granting institutions can be dated back at least to the tenth century, when they were also given guaranteed legal status. The idea of academic freedom dates back to the twelfth century onwards. *Constitutio Habita*, which was issued by Frederic I Barbarossa, granted independence from church and state for the University of Bologna in 1158 (Hermans and Nelissen, 2005, pp. 26–30). In the middle ages, the universities provided mainly professional education, not least for the Church (see also Anderson, 2009). The combination of research and teaching became predominant during a long process that includes the Enlightenment and the French Revolution (and the subsequent reaction). This development has been described as essential for Europe's 'passage out of the Dark Ages' (Côté and Allahar, 2011, p. 9). Modern research suggests that the universities played a prominent part in the scientific revolution in the seventeenth and eighteenth centuries, in contrast to earlier views that emphasized the scientific research outside universities (Gascoigne, 1990).

Wilhelm von Humboldt's university reforms in Prussia, and in particular in the University of Berlin in the early nineteenth century, gave a more precize meaning to the concept of academic freedom. Humboldt's *idea of the university* included *Lehrfreiheit*, i.e. the freedom to teach, and *Lernfreiheit*, i.e. the freedom to learn.[1] *Lehrfreiheit* requires employment protection in the form of tenure, and hence freedom to express controversial views.[2] The idea of the university also includes collegiality (*Kollegialität*), i.e. academic self-governance and collective decision-making. This ensures that the university can be characterized as an expert organization, and gives the chairholders veto power through implicit non-aggression pacts (Schimank, 2005).[3] The traditional university can in fact be compared to a non-profit labour cooperative (James and Neuberger, 1981). This does not rule out hierarchies, but it is difficult for the deans or vice-chancellors of a traditional university to overrule a faculty majority, and the students can be described as partners in truth-seeking (Anderson, 2009).

The idea of a university soon gave Germany a leading position that was maintained until the Nazi regime, and set an example for the higher education system in Europe (Anderson, 2009), and later in the US (although mainly for the elite universities). During the nineteenth century, the powerful university presidents in the US usually decided in favour of interventionist donors and founders, and they saw the students as customers to be served, but the Johns Hopkins University was established in the 1870s as an early exception to the focus on teaching (see also Graham, Chapter 1 in this volume).

Three factors explain why a group of US universities – the Ivy League – gradually became world leaders during the twentieth century. First, private and non-profit universities became able to afford a stronger position for the academic staff, including more research time, because of endowments that had increased in value. A similar development occurred in the state universities because of more generous subsidies. This affluence made them resemble non-profit labour cooperatives (Glaeser, 2002). Second, deans and presidents began to use their power in favour of self-governance and academic freedom (Anderson, 2009). Tenure was implemented through an agreement in 1940 (Glaeser, 2002). Third, there was an inflow into the US of top scientists (which may have been influenced by the ideals of a traditional university) during the Nazi era.

The combination of collegiality, autonomy, academic freedom and research-led teaching is sometimes dismissed as an expensive way to teach those who are already privileged (see Lynch, 2006; Anderson, 2009). But the traditional university does not have to be socially exclusive. An expanding university sector in the presence of redistribution might explain the high intergenerational social mobility in the Nordic countries, in striking contrast to less egalitarian countries such as the UK and the US (Bratsberg et al., 2007). Because of their ability to develop sciences and humanities, and because of their potential contribution to social mobility, the traditional university does not have to be just an old-fashioned and inefficient luxury.

3   FROM UNIVERSITAS TO MARKETIZATION

Humboldt's idea of a university is now often perceived as outdated, and its professors are sometimes dismissively compared to colluding businessmen who cannot go bankrupt (Schimank, 2005). In most countries since the early 1990s, universities have therefore been restructured in a neoliberal spirit so as to resemble a firm subject to market pressures.[4] This process is alternatively described as marketization (Jongbloed, 2003; Lynch, 2006), the New Public Management (Evans et al., 2005, Newberry and Pallot, 2004; Hood, 1995; Schimank, 2005), or (in particular in the US) as corporatization (Scheuerman and Kriger, 2004).

While there are now some profit maximizing institutions such as Phoenix University in the US, with non-tenured staff and no research (Lynch, 2006), the sector is still dominated by non-profits. Universities have usually not been privatized (and many prominent US universities have been private from the beginning), but marketization has in most cases included several of the following features:

- Budget cuts and austerity (Rhoades and Slaughter, 2004).
- Managerialism instead of collegiality (Rhoades and Slaughter, 2004; Schimank, 2005; Bonewits and Soley, 2004), not least because of a desire to react flexibly to market pressures (Shattock, 1989).
- Erosion of tenure and an increased proportion of adjunct staff on short-term contracts (Lee and Clery, 2004; Scheuerman and Kriger, 2004).
- Restrictions on dissemination and in some cases ideological bias because of increased dependence on external funding (Shattock, 1989; Bonewits and Soley, 2004; Alternet/Ayn Rand Indoctrination, 2011).
- Output funding (for example in proportion to exams), performance-related pay and competition in order to create high-powered incentives for institutions, departments and individuals (Gruening, 2001; Hood, 1995; Schimank, 2005).
- A shift towards subjects and topics that are favoured by the business community, at the expense of other research and teaching (Bonewits and Soley, 2004).
- Vocationalism or pseudo-vocationalism rather than an emphasis on the *Bildungsuniversität* (Côté and Allahar, 2011)
- Consumer orientation, vouchers and/or tuition fees (Wright, 2000; Jongbloed, 2003; Lynch, 2006), and a business-oriented identity (Fairclough, 1993).

However, such a break with the idea of the university as implied by marketization can hardly be enforced without top-down micromanagement, not least in the form of red tape rather than freedom for the institutions and their employees.[5] Cases in point include restrictions on the maximum time allowed for research, and time-consuming forms and bureaucratic procedures associated with time management, quality assessments and performance-related wages. Rewards and punishments according to plans for the number of degrees likewise suggest associations to Soviet planning rather than free enterprise.

Inefficiency is the most important official reason that the traditional university is perceived as outdated. The new public management was meant to address inefficiency and was a reaction against *progressive public administration*, i.e. micromanagement of inputs rather than payment by results (Hood, 1995). Economic rewards and punishments, together with austerity, managerialism, centralization and reduced job security are all believed to promote efficiency. Such changes were first imposed under Margaret Thatcher in the UK and subsequently by governments in New Zealand and Australia, and now also for example in the Netherlands, Germany and the Nordic countries (Gruening, 2001; Huisman et al., 2006; Schimank, 2005).

But there has also been a mistrust focused directly on academic freedom, at least when there is a clash between the views inside academia and the dominant political ideology. An essential part of the New Right is an attempt to mould universities in the 'image of the establishment' (Alternet/Ayn Rand Indoctrination, 2011; Bonewits and Soley, 2004). The first signs of austerity in the US emerged as a reaction against student protests, for example against the war in Vietnam in the 1960s and 1970s, when the universities were accused of being populated by tenured radicals (Dawson, 2007). In the UK, austerity and top-down governance seem to be explained by Thatcher's ideological mistrust of the universities, which she believed were alien to the enterprise culture (Shattock, 1989).[6]

While Finland's legislation from 2010 will hardly set trends in the same way as reforms in the US or the UK, the country deserves attention because of its reputation until now for excellent education and an innovative ICT-sector. As in the other Nordic countries, tuition is still free (for EU residents), probably because fees might mean political suicide. But the universities' financial and administrative autonomy has increased through a reform in 2010. The state provides core funding according to performance, but universities are encouraged to apply for donations, mainly from the business community. Such reforms are believed to ensure more flexible reactions to changes, more international funding, and a more prominent role in the innovation system.

Finland's universities have therefore become independent legal entities, without proper privatization. However, the promised autonomy refers mainly to fund management. The vice-chancellors have become less dependent on faculty opinion, and the senate is reduced and consists of 40 per cent external representatives. Despite the rhetoric of autonomy, academics therefore now have less influence within their institutions than before. Furthermore, each working hour has to be reported (although there is passive resistance), and a highly bureaucratic wage-setting system (with no essential changes in the wage structure) was introduced prior to the reform. There are rules that restrict the lecturers' research time, and the true meaning of reacting flexibly to changes seems to be eroded tenure.

4 THE ROLE OF INTRINSIC MOTIVATION

Marketization and the new public management are partly inspired by mainstream principal–agent theory and partly by Public Choice and Chicago thinking (Hood, 1995; Gruening, 2001). These traditions have in common the assumption that civil servants and academics behave as the economic man (*homo economicus*) inside their organizations just as they do as actors in the market. The public sector would be inefficient under such conditions, at least if it did not introduce high-powered incentives (see Dixit, 1997). However, such simplified thinking on the relationship between sticks, carrots and work efforts is now also challenged within mainstream theory (see Frey, 1997; Bitzer et al., 2007; Murdock, 2002; Bénabou and Tirole, 2002, 2003).

Reforms aimed at bribing greedy and lazy agents to work harder, then, not only miss the point, but may also be counterproductive, by crowding out intrinsic motivation. In Bénabou and Tirole (2002, 2003), the principal knows more about the work assignments than the agents. To rely on intrinsic motivation signals that the task is associated with importance and responsibility, whereas economic rewards and punishments may cause *motivation crowding out* (MCO). Alternatively, utility functions may be additive, with one component reflecting intrinsic motivation, so that sticks and carrots mean that employees can increase overall utility by becoming less dedicated (James, 2005).

Many earlier contributions focus on commercial firms and are therefore not directly applicable to universities, where the academic staff have more knowledge than any principal about their work assignments. We therefore choose a different point of departure and assume specific overall utility function in effort and income. It works as the Nash-product of the utility of work efforts and a traditional expected utility that increases in income and decreases in efforts. This approach can also be interpreted as dealing with a personality with two sides (see, for example Elster, 1986a). One side is dedicated to the core activities of the organization, whereas the other side is like *homo economicus*. The decision is then reached through an internal game, as first analysed by Schelling (1978) in the case of a weakness of will.[7]

In Willner and Grönblom (2009) we use a similar framework but with a fixed number of employees. Any impact of budget cuts and incentive wages on staff size is therefore ignored, like the possibility that the employer might be able to influence the strength of the intrinsic motivation. A fixed wage and a reliance on intrinsic motivation can then under certain conditions yield higher efforts. Moreover, budget cuts can reduce efficiency, and there is MCO if the participation constraint is binding or if the employee's utility is for other reasons kept at a level that only just prevents quitting.

The present analysis focuses on the broader concept of marketization and not just budget cuts and extrinsic rewards and punishments. We also include managerialism (in the form of a performance-based salary and objectives that are not necessarily aligned with faculty) and eroded tenure (in the sense that redundancies are now not ruled out). We ask how such changes will affect effort and, because the staff size is no longer given, employment. We also ask whether the new type of managerial vice-chancellor would prefer stronger or weaker intrinsic motivation among the employees if motivation can be affected through changed working conditions. The key findings are summarized in a non-formal way in the concluding section.

5   AN ORGANIZATION WITH INTRINSIC MOTIVATION PRIOR TO MARKETIZATION

Given the economic arguments behind marketization, it makes sense to analyse how university reform works in a principal–agent setting, which is amended so as to include staff with intrinsic motivation. This section describes an organization that corresponds to a traditional university, as a contrast to the analysis of marketization in next section.

We model an organization that produces a single composite output x, thus ignoring the potential tension between different tasks such as teaching and research. Each employee i exerts an effort e_i, which yields either an output x_i or zero with probabilities q and $1-q$. Output in the good state (x_i) is proportional to effort and normalized so as to equal e_i. The organization maximizes expected output qx_i. There are l identical employees, so they will all choose the same effort e. The expected aggregate output is $Ex = qle$, because ql employees are successful. The employees are tenured, which means that the given budget B does not require anybody to be fired. The wage y does not depend on success or failure. There is asymmetric information, which means that the employer can observe output but not effort.

The employee maximizes a Nash product N, where one factor is increasing in effort (or expected output) and the other represents the traditional opportunistic notion of utility that is decreasing in effort and increasing in wage. In other words, N is a product of the satisfaction from work and the conventional payoff. This lends itself to an interpretation in terms of intra-personal bargaining. Let $\beta > 0$ denote the strength of the intrinsic motivation,[8] so that e^{β} represents potential intrinsic motivation, and let the traditional, opportunistic notion of utility be represented by the quasilinear function $v = y - ke^2/2$, where $k/2 > 1/2$ expresses the strength of the disutility of effort. The outside option utility is denoted by v_0. N then becomes:

$$N = e^\beta(v - v_0) = e^\beta\left(y - \frac{k}{2}e^2 - v_0\right) \tag{7.1}$$

The organization then maximizes its expected output subject to a number of constraints. The *incentive compatibility constraint* (ICC) implies that the employer must accept that the employee maximizes (7.1) with respect to e, which yields:

$$y - \frac{2 + \beta}{2\beta}ke^2 - v_0 = 0 \tag{7.2}$$

Use the abbreviation $(2 + \beta)k/\beta = \theta$ and rearrange:

$$y = \frac{\theta}{2}e^2 + v_0 \tag{7.3}$$

As for the *participation constraint* (PC), the inequality:

$$y - \frac{k}{2}e^2 \geq v_0 \tag{7.4}$$

must hold true, because the Nash-product is not otherwise defined. Note that it stands for the participation constraint that would apply if there were no intrinsic motivation ($\beta = 0$), and it can be given the same interpretation in this context as well. Note however that it follows from the ICC that the PC is always satisfied if the wage is fixed.

There is also a *budget constraint* (BC) that requires $B = ly$. This constraint is binding for obvious reasons. Many countries have in addition legislation or collective agreements that restrict the organization's wage setting. We therefore assume a *minimum-wage constraint* (MWC) that requires the wage to be at least y_0. However, there is no meaningful post-marketization solution unless $v_0 > y_0$. This implies that y is always strictly greater than y_0 according to (7.3), so the MWC is not binding in this context.

There is no managing director (MD) in this kind of university. One employee has the additional assignment of being the vice-chancellor for a limited period, with a salary increase that is negligible in this context.

Omitting those Lagrange multipliers that must be zero, the maximizing of expected output given the constraints BC and ICC yields the following Lagrange function, where λ_1 and λ_2 stand for the non-zero multipliers:

$$\Omega = qle + \lambda_1[B - ly] + \lambda_2\left[y - \frac{\theta}{2}e^2 - v_0\right] + \lambda_3 y_0 \qquad (7.5)$$

The optimal solution is then:

$$e^T = \sqrt{\frac{2v_0}{\theta}} = \sqrt{\frac{2\beta v_0}{(2 + \beta)k}} \qquad (7.6)$$

$$l^T = \frac{B}{2v_0} \qquad (7.7)$$

Thus, efforts depend on the size of the outside-option utility and the parameters that represent the strength of the intrinsic motivation and the disutility of effort. The employment level depends only on the budget and on the outside-option utility. We may think of tenure as a commitment from the decision-makers that B is sufficient for a given level l_0 of employees; no similar assumption is made in the next section. Note that the equilibrium wage is $y = 2v_0$, and hence independent of both β and k.

6   MANAGERIALISM, PERFORMANCE-RELATED PAY AND EROSION OF TENURE

Suppose now that the organization is affected by marketization, which here means performance-related wages, managerialism and lost tenure. Performance-related pay means that the wage depends on observed output, not effort. In other words, the employee gets a wage supplement with the probability q. Let w_0 stand for an intercept and b for a coefficient that expresses the impact of the expected output. The expected wage then becomes:

$$Ey = w_0 + qbe + (1 - q)0 = w_0 + qbe \qquad (7.8)$$

The president/rector or vice-chancellor has become managing director, MD. We assume that the MD gets an incentive salary that partly depends on output, but partly also on an ability to cut costs. Let Y_0 be an exogenous intercept reflecting the impact of the exogenous salaries in the business community, and let α express the impact on the MD's salary of a weighted sum of output and cost-savings, here the surplus after the wages are paid. Its weight is ρ. Higher values of α and ρ mean a more significant break with the traditional university. The expected managerial salary is then:

$$EY = Y_0 + \alpha[qle + \rho(B - lw_0 - lqbe)] \qquad (7.9)$$

so it follows from (7.9) that EY is decreasing in w_0, which is also the wage in the bad state of nature. The MWC is therefore always binding, so we replace w_0 by y_0. The Nash product that the employee maximizes then becomes:

$$N = e^\beta \left[y_0 + qbe - \frac{k}{2}e^2 - v_0 \right] \qquad (7.10)$$

which implies the following ICC and PC:

$$y_0 + qbe\frac{\beta + 1}{\beta} - \frac{\theta}{2}e^2 - v_0 = 0 \qquad (7.11)$$

$$y_0 + qbe - \frac{k}{2}e^2 - v_0 \geq 0 \qquad (7.12)$$

It follows from (7.11) and (7.12) that the ICC implies that the PC is also satisfied if and only if $e \geq qb/k$. Suppose first that this is the case. The effort level is then:

$$e^M = \frac{q(1 + \beta)}{\rho(2 + \beta)k} \qquad (7.13)$$

To get the number of employees, insert y_0 and the solution (7.13) into (7.9) to get the MD's expected salary, and solve the expression $B = lEy + EY$ for l:

$$l^M = \frac{(1 - \alpha\rho)B - Y_0}{(1 - \alpha\rho)\dfrac{y_0 + \beta v_0}{\beta + 1} + (1 + \alpha\rho)\dfrac{q^2(1 + \beta)}{2\rho^2 k(2 + \beta)}} \qquad (7.14)$$

It follows from (7.11) and (7.13) that the condition $e \geq qb/k$ means:

$$\frac{q^2(1 + \beta)^2}{\rho^2(2 + \beta)^2 k} > 2(v_0 - y_0) \qquad (7.15)$$

as when y_0 is close to v_0, or when the intrinsic motivation is strong.

In the opposite case, the PC is binding, which means that $e = qb/k$, and hence the following solutions:

$$e^{M^{PC}} = \sqrt{\frac{2(v_0 - y_0)}{k}} \qquad (7.16)$$

$$l^{M^{PC}} = \frac{B(1 - \alpha\rho) - Y_0}{(1 - \alpha\rho)(2v_0 - y_0) + \alpha q\sqrt{2(v_0 - y_0)/k}} \qquad (7.17)$$

Lost tenure means that staff reductions can cause redundancies and not only unfilled vacancies. For example, we might think of l_0 as $l^T = B/2v_0$, suggesting that there is no built-in guarantee that (7.14 and 7.17) are not lower than $l^T = B/2v_0$.

7   A COMPARISON

In this section we therefore analyse the impact of marketization (in the form described in Section 6) on effort levels, employment, and the nature of work motivation. Suppose first that the PC is not binding after marketization. To compare the intensity of work then means comparing (7.6) and (7.13). It follows that effort is actually higher before marketization if:

$$\frac{q^2}{\rho^2 k v_0} > \frac{2}{1 + [\beta(2 + \beta)]^{-1}} \qquad (7.18)$$

This holds true under reasonable conditions, i.e. if β is large and/or if k is low, as might be expected in a university.

If the PC is binding after marketization we compare (7.6) and (7.16), which yields the following condition for effort to be higher before marketization:

$$\beta > -2 + 2\frac{v_0}{y_0} \qquad (7.19)$$

Again, the condition is satisfied if β is large.

As for employment, marketization leads to redundancies if the optimal employment is below $B/2v_0$. Consider first the case where the PC is not binding. As follows from (7.14), the difference may go both ways. However, a high β and a low k would increase the denominator and hence lead to lower employment. This may also happen for low values of B, even if $B/2v_0$ meant full employment before marketization, and for high values of Y_0. No similar negative effects of higher intrinsic motivation and a lower disutility of effort on employment are present under the traditional organizational form.

If the PC is binding, it follows from (7.17) that the size of β plays no part. However, a lower disutility of effort would reduce employment and increase the likelihood of redundancies. As follows from (7.17), redundancies become more likely for low values of B and high values of Y_0 and ρ. The impact of α is ambiguous for some parameter values.

So far we have assumed that β and k are given. However, the employer may in practice be able to affect both work motivation and disutility of effort by changing working conditions and task assignments, for example through the amount of bureaucracy. Would a manager with a wage schedule such as (7.9) like the employees to be highly motivated and to have a low disutility of effort?

To answer this question, note that the variable part of the manager's salary is:

$$V = qle + \rho(B - lw_0 - lqbe) \tag{7.20}$$

Suppose first that the PC is not binding. Insert the solutions for l and e as expressed by (7.13) and (7.14), rearrange, and introduce the following abbreviation:

$$\psi(\beta) = \frac{(1 + \beta)^2}{(y_0 + \beta v_0)(2 + \beta)} \tag{7.21}$$

We get:

$$V = \rho B - \frac{\rho}{(1 - \rho\alpha) + \dfrac{q^2(1 + \rho\alpha)}{2\rho^2 k}\psi(\beta)} \tag{7.22}$$

It is obvious that V is decreasing in k, so the manager has no incentive to increase the disutility of effort. However, the impact of β is more complex. V is increasing in β if ψ is also increasing. Differentiating (7.21) shows that this is the case if:

$$\beta > -3 + 2\frac{v_0}{y_0} \tag{7.23}$$

The highest salary would be reached where $\beta = -3 + 2v_0/y_0$. It is unlikely that the MD would be able to affect employee motivation so

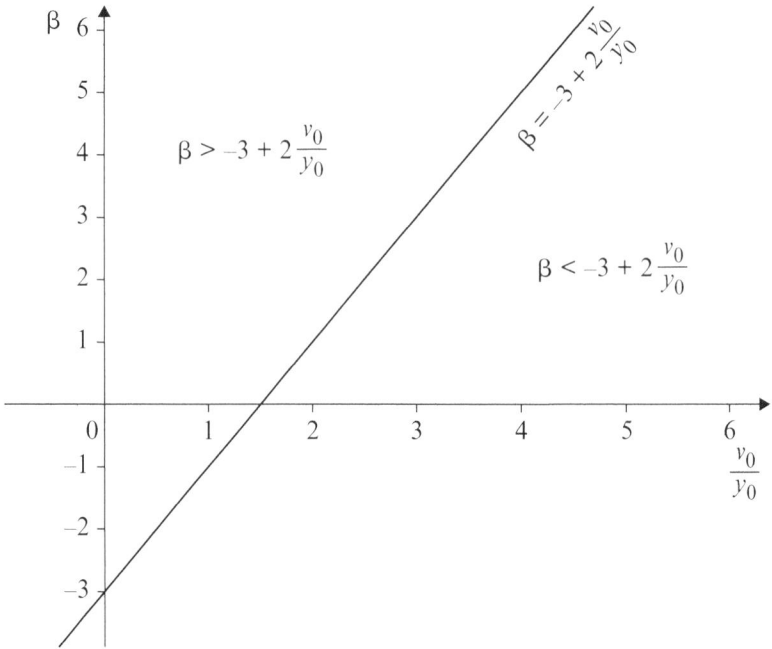

Figure 7.1   The incentive to change intrinsic motivation

as to get precisely the optimal value. However, suppose that the MD has some power to increase or reduce β. If v_0/y_0 is relatively low (i.e. if $1.5 > v_0/y_0 > 1$), (7.23) is satisfied for all values of β, in which case the MD would benefit from an increase in β.[9] However, in the case of large values of v_0/y_0 (i.e. if $v_0/y_0 > 1.5$) and if β is also large, the MD might gain by a reduction. This applies for example when $v_0/y_0 = 2.5$ and $\beta = 2$. Figure 7.1 illustrates the partition of the parameter space implied by (7.23).

Such an incentive among leaders to demotivate the organization's staff is explained by the fact that the employees' wages are increasing in β when the PC is not binding. To see that this holds true, note that the wage schedule implies that $qbe = y - y_0$ and use (7.13) and (7.11).

No such effect is present if the PC is binding, as follows from (7.12) and (7.16), and as above, the MD would not benefit from an increase in k. However, the case when the PC is binding is associated with alienation in another sense, because the effort level as expressed by (7.16) is the same as if there were no intrinsic motivation, i.e. as if $\beta = 0$.[10]

8   DISCUSSION AND CONCLUDING REMARKS

Marketization has usually been advocated through economic arguments related to cost efficiency. In particular, the new public management is based on theories where employees are seen as driven only by a desire to earn money and avoid effort. We have therefore attempted to perform an economic analysis using otherwise traditional methods, but amended with the more realistic assumption that employees have potential intrinsic motivation. While marketization has changed the university in several respects, we have focused on performance, work efforts, employment and the role of the manager (MD) in an organization that becomes subject to performance-related pay, managerialism and reduced tenure.

The formal analysis suggests that sticks and carrots can make sense only when the intrinsic motivation is weak, but in other cases they tend to reduce the work effort. This can be described as motivation crowding out, but there is motivation crowding out in another sense as well. If the participation constraint is binding, employees work as if there were no intrinsic motivation. This happens because any additional utility derived from higher efforts on the job leads to a wage reduction that keeps utility constant at a level where the employee only just refrains from quitting.

Managerialism in the model means a shift of emphasis from output – research and teaching – towards cost-cutting. It also means that the manager's salary is adjusted (through an intercept) to correspond to similar positions in the business community. The administration then becomes more expensive. But it also turns out that the leader – managing director or vice-chancellor – would under some circumstances benefit (through rewards for cost-cutting) by the employee's intrinsic motivation becoming weaker. For example, it is in the power of university leaders to increase the proportion of those assignments for which the intrinsic motivation is weak, such as bureaucracy, or to make other changes in the work environment. The intuition is based on the fact that the employees' wages are increasing on the strength of intrinsic motivation if the participation constraint is not binding.

As for reduced tenure, it is possible but not necessary that marketization leads to redundancies. There is a direct but small effect, because a high MD salary reduces the number of employees that the organization can afford. More importantly, under some circumstances marketization can cause the manager to hire fewer employees if their intrinsic motivation is high or if their disutility of effort is low. There are no such adverse employment effects of high intrinsic motivation without marketization. Another mechanism that can cause redundancies is a high reward for cost-cutting.

Real-world university reforms differ in many details. In Finland, budget cuts and a promise of no wage reductions limit the scope for individual wage setting.[11] In contrast to the still limited scope for individual wage setting in practice, sticks and carrots have a strong impact on departments, faculties and universities, in the sense that their funding depends on the number of degrees awarded (this applies to 80 per cent of funding in our university, for example). Finland conforms more closely to the formal model when it comes to the erosion of the tenure system, and also in the sense that the vice-chancellors have become like managing directors. Their remuneration is not transparent, but press reports suggest that the reform has led to a significantly higher wage; for example the vice-chancellor of the University of Helsinki had a wage increase of 61 per cent (*Ylioppilaslehti*, 2011).

As for empirical evaluations, a survey commissioned jointly by the unions representing professors and research staff one year after the far-reaching reform in Finland (*Professorit ja Tieteentekijät. Yliopistouudistusta koskeva kysely, 2010*) can be summarized as follows. One in ten who responded found the reform successful, and as many as 55 per cent thought that it was unsuccessful. Academic freedom was perceived by 59 per cent as reduced, and a majority experienced at least as much bureaucracy as before (89 per cent). A significant majority (79 per cent) responded that there was no increase in the number of employees. Fewer than 25 per cent were in favour of external representation in the senate. The reform was officially described as reducing the proportion of short-term contracts, but a majority did not experience any such effects, or any improvement in working atmosphere, transparency, leadership or job satisfaction. The highest response rates and the most critical opinions were found in education and the humanities. Another survey, commissioned by the lecturers' union, suggest that more than 60 per cent are dissatisfied both when it comes to research, teaching and working conditions (see *Akatiimi*, 2011). Both studies should however be interpreted carefully because of low response rates, but at least they do not contradict our formal analysis.

These studies also highlight some omitted topics. For example, what is the impact of more short-term contracts? Moreover, bureaucracy and other unproductive tasks seem (somewhat paradoxically) to be an integral part of marketization. We have included such issues in an article with a focus on budget cuts (see Willner and Grönblom, 2009), but not on why leaders may change the work assignments deliberately. Finally, given that efficiency is sometimes defined as student turnover, as in Finland, rather than in research output, it would also be important to analyse marketization when there is more than just one type of output, as in the present analysis.

ACKNOWLEDGEMENTS

We thank Niklas Grönblom for valuable research assistance. This research is part of the Academy of Finland project *Reforming Markets and Organisations* (REMO, 115003) funded 2007–2011. Work during Johan Willner's sabbatical 2009–2010, which was partly spent at the University of Warwick and funded through the Academy of Finland project *Motivation and the Organisation of Economic Activity* (MOE, 130986), has also contributed to the analysis. Financial support for Sonja Grönblom from Otto A. Malm's donation fund and the Waldemar von Frenckell foundation is gratefully acknowledged.

NOTES

1. Britannica Online Encyclopaedia/Academic freedom, online at http://www.britannica.com/EBchecked/topic/2591/academic-freedom, accessed 23 May 2011.
2. Without safe employment there would in addition be no incentive for an incumbent to choose the best candidates for junior positions (Carmichael, 1988).
3. For example, all-important decisions were traditionally made collectively by a Senate or Congregation consisting of the professors in the UK universities (see also Tribe, Chapter 2, this volume). However, junior staff and even students have been included in the decision-making committees in some countries, such as in Finland.
4. The ideology behind the US university reforms since the early 1990s represents 'a kind of accidental neoliberalism produced by the wildly inaccurate application to higher education working conditions of dimly remembered chestnuts from Econ 101' (Bousquet, 2008, p. 19).
5. Evans *et al.* (2005) describe the impact of neoliberalism on the non-profit sector as centralized decentralization.
6. Mrs Thatcher said in an interview: 'Some academics and intellectuals do not understand and are putting out what I call poison. Some young people who were thrilled to bits to get to university had every decent value pounded out of them. . . . Had we had another 10 years of that, it would have gone beyond repair.' (As quoted by Shattock, 1989, p. 35.)
7. This idea is related to *hyperbolic discounting* in Gintis (2006, p. 245).
8. The function e^β does not have to be concave. Suppose for example that there are exponents α and $1 - \alpha$ in the Nash product and that some other exponent $\gamma < 1$ stands for the strength of the intrinsic motivation. This would make the maximization of the Nash product formally equivalent to maximizing (1), with the interpretation that $\beta = \alpha\gamma/(1 - \alpha)$ can be greater than unity.
9. Note that (7.13) and (7.14) are based on the assumption $v_0/y_0 > 1$.
10. This can be seen as follows. Set $\beta = 0$, maximize (7.10) with respect to e and use the binding participation constraint (7.12) to eliminate b. This yields (7.16).
11. Combining a rhetoric of performance-based pay and limiting the scope for wage increases may also reduce motivation in a different way: the explanation for low wages appears to be low performance.

REFERENCES

Akatiimi (2011), 'YLL:n jäsenkysely osoitti: Palkkaus ja työmäärä ovat epätasa-painossa', **5**, 20, also via http://www.acatiimi.fi/5_2011/05_11_08.php, accessed 30 September 2012.

Alternet (Ayn Rand Indoctrination at American universities, sponsored by the right wing), http://www.alternet.org/teaparty/151066/ayn_rand_indoctrination_at_american_universities,_sponsored_by_the_right_wing/, accessed 29 May 2011.

Anderson, Robert (2009), 'The "idea of a university" today', in Withers, Kay (ed.), *First Class? Challenges and Opportunities for the UK's University Sector*, London: Institute for Public Policy Research.

Bénabou, Roland and Jean Tirole (2002), 'Self-confidence and personal motivation', *Quarterly Journal of Economics*, **CXVII** (3), 871–915.

Bénabou, Roland and Jean Tirole (2003), 'Intrinsic and extrinsic motivation', *Review of Economic Studies*, **70** (3), no. 244, 489–520.

Bitzer, Jürgen, Wolfram Schrettl and Philipp Schröder (2007), 'Intrinsic motivation in open source software development', *Journal of Comparative Economics*, **35** (1), 160–69.

Bonewits, Sarah and Lawrence Soley (2004), 'Research and the bottom line in today's university', *American Academic*, **1** (1), 81–92.

Bousquet, Marc (2008), *How the University Works. Higher Education and the Low-wage Nation*, New York: New York University Press.

Bratsberg, Bernt, Knut Roed, Oddbjorn Raaum, Robin Naylor, Markus Jäntti, Tor Eriksson and Eva Österbacka (2007), 'Nonlinearities in intergenerational earnings mobility: consequences for cross-country comparisons', *Economic Journal*, **117** (519), C72–C92.

Carmichael, H. Lorne (1988), 'Incentives in academics: why is there tenure?', *Journal of Political Economy*, **96** (3), 453–72.

Côté, James and L. Allahar Anton (2011), *Lowering Higher Education: The Rise of the Corporate University and the Fall of Liberal Education,* Toronto: University of Toronto Press.

Dawson, Ashley (2007), 'Another university is possible: academic labor, the ideology of scarcity and the fight for workplace democracy', *Workplace*, **14**, May, 91–105.

Dixit, Avinash (1997), 'Power of incentives in private versus public organizations', *American Economic Review*, **87** (2), 378–82.

Elster, Jon (ed.) (1986a), *The Multiple Self*, Cambridge: Cambridge University Press and Norwegian University Press.

Evans, Bryan, Ted Richmond and John Shields (2005), 'Structuring neoliberal governance: the nonprofit sector, emerging new modes of control and the marketisation of service delivery', *Policy and Society*, **24** (1), 73–97.

Fairclough, Norman (1993), 'Critical discourse analysis and the marketization of public discourse: the universities', *Discourse & Society*, **4** (2), 133–68.

Frey, Bruno S. (1997), 'On the relationship between intrinsic and extrinsic work motivation', *International Journal of Industrial Organization*, **15** (4), 427–40.

Gascoigne, John (1990), 'A reappraisal of the role of the universities in the scientific revolution', pp. 210–29 in Lindberg, David C. and Robert S. Westman (eds),

Reappraisals of the Scientific Revolution, Cambridge: Cambridge University Press.

Gintis, Herbert (2006), *Game Theory Evolving. A Problem-Centered Introduction to Modeling Strategic Interaction*, Princeton, NJ: Princeton University Press.

Glaeser, Edward L. (2002), 'The governance of not-for-profit firms', National Bureau of Economic Research, working paper 8921.

Gruening, Gernod (2001), 'Origin and theoretical basis of the new public management', *International Public Management Journal*, **4**, 1–25.

Hermans, Jos M. M. and Marc Nelissen (eds) (2005), *Charters of Foundation and Early Documents of the Universities in the Coimbra Group*, Leuven: University of Leuven Press.

Hood, Christopher (1995), 'The "new public management" in the 1980s: variations of a theme', *Accounting, Organizations and Society*, **20** (2/3), 93–109.

Huisman, Jeroen, Harry de Boer and Leo Goedgebuure (2006), 'The perception of participation in executive governance in Dutch universities', *Tertiary Education Management*, **12**, 227–39.

Innolink (2010), *Professorit ja Tieteentekijät. Yliopistouudistusta koskeva kysely 2010*, Helsinki: Innolink.

James, Estelle and Egon Neuberger (1981), 'The university department as a non-profit labor cooperative', *Public Choice* **36**, 585–612.

James, Harvey S. (2005), 'Why did you do that? An economic examination of the effect of extrinsic compensation on intrinsic motivation and performance', *Journal of Economic Psychology*, **26**, 549–66.

Jongbloed, Ben (2003), 'Marketisation in higher education, Clark's Triangle and the essential ingredients of markets', *Higher Education Quarterly*, **57** (2), 110–35.

Lee, John and Sue Clery (2004), 'Key trends in higher education', *American Academic*, **1** (1), 21–36.

Lynch, Kathleen (2006), 'Neo-liberalism and marketisation: the implications for higher education', *European Educational Research Journal*, **5** (1), 1–17.

Murdock, Kevin (2002), 'Intrinsic motivation and optimal incentive contracts', *Rand Journal of Economics* **33** (4), 650–71.

Newberry, Susan and June Pallot (2004), 'Freedom or coercion? NPM incentives in New Zealand Central Government Departments', *Management Accounting Research*, **15**, 247–66.

Rhoades, Gary and Sheila Slaughter (2004), 'Academic Capitalism in the New Economy: Challenges and Choices', *American Academic*, **1** (1), 37–59.

Schelling, Thomas C. (1978), 'Egonomics, or the art of self-management', *American Economic Review*, **69** (2), *Papers and Proceedings*, 290–94.

Scheuerman, William and Thomas Kriger (2004), 'Introduction – the concept of corporatization: a useful tool or a feel-good slogan?' *American Academic*, **1** (1), 7–19.

Schimank, Uwe (2005), '"New public management" and the academic profession: reflections on the German situation', *Minerva*, **43**, 361–76.

Shattock, Michael (1989), 'Thatcherism and British higher education. universities and the enterprise culture', *Change: The Magazine of Higher Learning*, **21** (5), 31–9.

Willner, Johan and Sonja Grönblom (2009), 'The impact of budget cuts and incentive wages on academic work', *International Review of Applied Economics*, **23** (6), 673–89.

Wright, Robert E. (2000), 'Student evaluations and consumer orientation at universities', *Journal of Nonprofit & Public Sector Marketing*, **8** (1), 33–40.
Ylioppilaslehti (2011), 'Yliopiston johdon palkkapussit lihoivat', **98** (6), 20–21, also via http://ylioppilaslehti.fi/2011/04/yliopiston-johdon-palkkapussit-lihoivat/, accessed 30 September 2012.

8. Motivational resilience in the university system

Silvia Sacchetti

A disposition to find your colleagues' work 'interesting' is about the most
important single attribute you can cultivate if you yourself want to be
a good colleague.
(Brennan, 2004: 89)

1 INTRODUCTION

Academia has been going through a process of change, which some
authors say is increasingly mimicking the aims, modalities and values
of traditional business (Sugden, 2004; Wedlin, 2008; Grönblom and
Willner, 2009; Wilson, 2009; Parker, 2011). In particular, the competition for funding has endorsed the use of specific incentive systems that
are aimed at influencing the motivations of academics and the capacity
of departments to obtain research funds. For the purpose of this work we
shall think of academics as individuals who can contribute to the creation
of novel explanations by means of enquiry, and comment on the possible implications that current incentive systems may have on academics'
endurance to problematize situations, raise questions and look for possible answers. Specifically, we explore the elements of the domains that
surround academics and how these interact with their motivations.

Across a number of disciplines, including management, psychology,
sociology and economics, there is an overarching agreement on the fact
that human motivations importantly shape the nature of social and economic action, determining the effectiveness of organizations and their
activities. Approaches however differ, not least in their basic assumptions. Whilst in economics it has been conventionally assumed that individuals are motivated by wealth maximization (Brennan, 2004), theories
of social psychology and organizational behaviour have addressed the
relationship between individuals and context, emphasizing the role of
non-economic motivational drivers (such as achievement, recognition,

professional growth, interest in the task performed) for the fulfilment of basic needs, such as competence (the mastering of abilities such as learning and creativity), autonomy (the feeling that an act is connected to the individual's will and critical judgement) and relatedness (the feeling to belong or being connected to a group) (Deci and Ryan, 2000). These constructs help to understand some of the considerations presented in the chapter. Deci and Ryan (1985; 2000) identified a major critical issue in the evolution of motivations. In contrast with external drivers, such as pay increase, intrinsic motivations have been argued to reflect the innate attitudes of the individual when performing an activity:

> Perhaps no single phenomenon reflects the positive potential of human nature as much as intrinsic motivation, the inherent tendency to seek out novelty and challenges, to extend and exercise one's capacities, to explore, and to learn. . . . The construct of intrinsic motivation describes this natural inclination toward assimilation, mastery, spontaneous interest, and exploration that is so essential to cognitive and social development and that represents a principal source of enjoyment and vitality throughout life. (Deci and Ryan, 2000: 70)

In line with social psychology approaches, in this work we recognize that explanations of the dynamics of motivations, including those of academics, require an understanding of the way in which individual motivations (exemplified as the intrinsic interest towards activities or by the pull of external drivers) evolve out of social and economic processes of interaction (exemplified by relationships with colleagues and paradigms within the discipline; or with the university organization and its incentive strategies).

The working hypothesis of this chapter is that individuals engage in a constant process of definition, achievement and critical assessment of their own aims. In doing so they interact with contextual conditions (Dewey, 1934). Motivations are the immaterial energy that is used for the pursuit and critical appraisal of valued objectives at each specific point in time. Motivations, therefore, can be considered as a specific type or resource in human action. We see them as inputs into processes as well as outputs, the idea being that motivations are not static but constantly evolving as individuals engage with the environment. Through action and interaction with the environment motivational energy, taken at any point in time, is subject to change, including dissipation and renewal. In particular, we build an analogy between motivations and energy-matter in thermodynamics, which serves the purpose of positioning the issue of motivational dissipation and renewal in academia. Given the nature of academia and its concern for scientific advancements, we assume that academic work is inherently aimed towards enquiry. We suggest that crucial in the renewal of motivational energy is access to an open environment where the critical appraisal of aims and values is supported by encouraging enquiry, imagination and creativity. In particular, based on experience and self-reflection, we argue that for the enquiry-led academic discovery is supported when, along the process, researchers can work in a space that welcomes the emergence of novel and critical approaches to academic activities (reflecting autonomy, relatedness and competence).[1]

At the same time, rather than looking at motivation renewal within a monolithic organizational context, we take a complex view of academia. Complexity requires decomposition. We therefore suggest a possible way to identify, within the university organization, specific subsystems and the interactions between pairs of subsystems. The utility of this approach, which is grounded on Simon's classic complex system theory, is that of identifying the flows of motivational energy from and to different subsystems and whether, within the same organization, subsystems differ in the way they contribute to motivational dissipation or renewal (Simon, 1973).

2 SOME CONTEXTUAL CONDITIONS: PEER EVALUATION, PEER SUPPORT AND MULTIPLE APPROACHES

As a way of introducing our analysis of motivational resilience within a complex system, we first look at some specific conditions in academia that can help to make sense of some of the circumstances that currently interact with academics and their motivations. In particular, in what follows we distinguish between peer evaluation and peer support as two academic institutions which influence academic activity and specifically research.

2.1. Peer Evaluation

Peer evaluation has a long history in academia. It determines access to faculty and legitimizes scientific work. If on the one hand peer judgement supports coherence of enquiry in those who have access to academia, yet on the other it also moulds the aspirations and choices of academics.

At an increasing rate across countries, higher education policy has embedded peer evaluation within the incentive system that guides the allocation of public resources. The system of institutional incentives works by allocating public funding to departments according to past outcomes and peer review, which mainly relies on publications.[2] This process is not without contradictions. In a special issue of the *American Journal of Economics and Sociology*, the editors offer a critical perspective on the impacts of the use of citation indexes, bringing together a number of bibliometric and network studies that emphasize how heterodox economists are in fact disadvantaged with respect to mainstream economists (Elsner and Lee, 2010). Strong criticisms have emerged that are sufficient to raise, not least, a number of question marks on the validity of the measures applied to the ex-post evaluation of academic work:

> [T]he International Mathematical Union, the International Council of Industrial and Applied Mathematics, and the Institute of Mathematical Statistics have argued in a joint report released in June 2008 that the belief that citation statistics are accurate measures of scholarly performance is unfounded. The use of such statistics is often highly subjective, the validity of these statistics is neither well understood nor well studied, and the sole reliance on citation data provides at best an incomplete and often shallow understanding of research (Adler, Ewing, and Taylor 2008: 2). In the same light, Bruno Frey and Katja Rost (2008: 1) found that publication and citation rankings do not effectively measure research quality and that career decisions based on rankings are dominated by chance. (Elsner and Lee, 2010: 1334)

Despite the doubts, the assessment system is at the moment based primarily on peer review and citations, with no hints towards a change in direction. On the contrary, an increasing number of countries are adopting similar criteria to support resource allocation in higher education. Post-performance evaluation of faculty have had a long-standing application in North America and the UK, and inspired policies have more recently in Australia, Belgium, Denmark, Italy, New Zealand and Norway.[3] Universities have adopted different strategies in response to such policies. In the UK, for example, universities tend to submit for evaluation only a selection of work, and then allocate research funds to the same researchers whose work has been submitted for assessment. One implication is that the others, the excluded, as Meyer (2012) notices, are bounded to enter a spiral of lack of funding, thus jeopardizing future research, their own career or even their tenure (ibid.).[4] Intrinsic motivation and research aspirations across the excluded can then be expected to decrease. More generally, when associated with access to the discipline or with particular benefits, peer review may favour extrinsic motivational drivers, particularly in younger academics.[5] With reference to the UK performance evaluation system, for example, Larkin (1999) observes how young talents feel under pressure to choose research topics that are consistent with the interests of evaluation panels. Untenured scholars may opt for lines of enquiry that are more likely to be acknowledged within established approaches or funding bodies, with the aim of demonstrating their suitability for academic organizations.

As it is, we can expect the pursuit of novelty to be channelled by extrinsic drivers and eventually slowed down. In a piece with clear Schumpeterian flavour, McKenzie and Galar (2004) addressed the question of paradigm shifts, and argued that should novelty emerge, it would do so from the work of those who deviate from known methods. They argue that the extent to which academia leaves space for unknown paths to be undertaken and radical innovations to develop and thrive, determines the survival of deviants and the introduction of novel ideas. Like past performance evaluation based on publications, peer assessment of research projects may reflect a preference of research bodies for projects that minimize risk by using a good fit with prevailing disciplinary paradigms. Since novelty introduces issues and methodologies that may have not been tried before, funding bodies tend to privilege established research areas and methodologies. The risk aversion of funding bodies is also reflected in the allocation of research funds to established academics who can offer a track record of past performance in the discipline. Further challenges would come also from the role that policy makers play in identifying elements of research programmes and, therefore, of research priorities promoted to government funding bodies, as research programmes that appeal to policy makers constitute a way of attracting research grants, access career advancements or maintain tenure (Smith, 2012).[6]

2.2. Multiplicity within Disciplines and Publics

In fact, from a substantive point of view, the use of peer assessment for ex-post evaluation and project funding implies more than a selection of 'the most valuable work' within each discipline. It also implies a selection of questions, constructs and approaches within each discipline. When looking at the substantive elements of disciplinary work, multiple research programmes inevitably emerge, reflecting the diversity of perspectives through which academics formulate questions and approach the search for answers (Burawoy, 2005). For Burawoy (2005: 263), these reflect 'different types of publics and multiple ways to access them'. Especially across the social sciences but also, for example, in arts and humanities or in natural sciences such as health-related disciplines, research has also a stark public dimension. These involve addressing socially relevant issues, creating new categories, promoting and defending the value of the discipline in the eyes of society, which entail reciprocal communication between academia and its different publics:

> We should not think of publics as fixed but in flux and that we can participate in their *creation* as well as their *transformation*. Indeed, part of our business as sociologists is to define human categories – people with AIDS, women with breast cancer, women, gays – and if we do so with their collaboration we create publics. The category woman became the basis of a public – an active,

thick, visible, national nay international counter-public – because intellectuals, sociologists among them, defined women as marginalized, left out, oppressed, and silenced, that is, defined them in ways they recognized. (Burawoy, 2005: 265 – emphasis added)

From a multiple-approach/multiple-public point of view, peer assessment means also power to create or destroy publics by generating hierarchies of questions, problems, and modalities of communication. Peer assessment, from this stand, bears implications that go beyond academic motivations or the efficiency of the university organization. Rather, it impacts on the public role of academics who, through the choice of research programmes, can have an empowering (or disempowering) role for publics: for example, research that looks at academics and at their motivations in our particular case, is in fact turning academics into the specific public of their own research. Academics become a research category that constitutes the basis for recognizing and communicating the economic and social issues associated with their situations.[7]

What we suggest is that the openness of a discipline towards questions that are relevant for a multiplicity of publics can reinforce the researcher's interest by building on his/her experience and curiosity, thus contributing to renew motivational energy towards enquiry. This stand reveals a further connection between the allocation of research funds based on peer evaluation and the survival of multiple interests within each discipline, where the conservation and creation of a variety of approaches among academics contributes to discovering their motivations, as well as to discovering new publics.

2.3. Peer Support

We have argued that, since intrinsic motivations reflect the inherent interests of individuals, motivations to conduct scholarly work are favoured by the endorsement of multiple lines of enquiry. This process points to an interconnected evolutionary process that links disciplinary paradigms, academic motivations and publics across society. Think for example about the reciprocal influences between the assumptions of conventional economics (and management), its dominance in the discipline, and the way in which economic choices are taken and promoted across organizations, regions and nations in a way that stresses the particular needs and objectives of some (e.g. the elites of decision-makers across different industrial sectors) whilst denying those of others (e.g. workers, the unemployed, consumers, parents with children, young people, communities that rely on biodiversity for their survival, and so on). Much of the constructs that support conventional economic theories, for example, consider recessions as a physiological element of economies, with which a variety of affected publics has to live.

The creation of variety can benefit from a scholarly ethics that offers respectful criticism, or one that points to areas of development for the creative agent. Engagement with peers and peer support, rather than peer evaluation, is part of the process that transforms one initial intuition into a clear line of thought. This is the time during which the researcher thrives and expresses his/her 'creative intelligence' (Dewey, 1917). From this angle, peer support helps, first of all, the enquiry process and, through it, the researcher. The focus is not necessarily on the production of pre-planned results, but on discovery, understanding and search for novel opportunities and experiences (Kirzner, 1989; Bianchi, 1998; F. Sacchetti, 2009; Sacchetti and Sugden, 2009a). Commenting on his research experience at the Public Choice Center between 1976 and 1983, Brennan remembers what made the Center the right place for academic enquiry, and explicitly refers to the 'big figures' that were able to shape the 'intellectual culture' of the place (in this case Brennan talks about the economist and political theorist James Buchanan). On the other hand, in departments where peers adopt a punitive attitude (for example in terms of nasty or disrespectful comments during seminars and debates), creativity may be stifled and replaced with 'timidity and extraordinary risk aversion':

> [T]he Center was almost precisely the opposite. New ideas, even rather flaky ones, were treated hospitably. A good point at a seminar earned you more plaudits than a bad point earned you condemnation. And Buchanan had a delightful and wonderfully supportive characteristic of breaking in to say, 'Now that's interesting. Really interesting!' And the maker of said 'interesting point' would quietly glow, and think how he might be even more 'interesting' next time around. Buchanan would make such remarks not, I think, because he self-consciously set out to be supportive, but rather because he did find things 'interesting.' (Brennan, 2004: 88–9)

Similarly, Wallis et al. (2009: 125) have recently reinforced the role of leadership in 'the development of hope so that organizational members can sustain their commitments in the face of disappointments'. Similarly, reciprocal support amongst peers, open discussion, and pro-creative criticism can help creative agents to maintain their commitment towards enquiry, even in the face of disappointment, which typically arises for example after a journal rejection or when a project does not get funded. This eventuality is extremely frequent. In fact, although departments encourage publication in top journals, the acceptance rate is on average less than 10 per cent in first-tier, and 20 per cent in second-tier journals

(Day, 2011). These percentages, as Day (2011) observes, give us an indication of the scale at which academics experience rejections and, as a consequence, identity threats, reduced commitment, exclusion and dropping out, which is not, she argues, necessarily an indication of lack of skill or ability. Research universities in general fail to address the problem. Those who have a professional social network that can support them are better positioned to turn rejections into higher quality work, thus renewing their intrinsic interest in academia.

Against the uncertainty of outcomes, and particularly of research outcomes, in fact, it was Hirschman (1982) who talked about 'in-process benefits' that individuals obtain from the activity itself, rather than from the surplus gained as the difference between the final outcome and the cost of running an activity (Olson, 1965). Too much pressure to produce answers, as in the current incentive system, provides extrinsic drivers but can also prompt non-cooperative attitudes and the use of worn-out research questions, thus decreasing novelty, as well as the magnitude of in-process benefits. When cooperation deteriorates or when novelty-seeking behaviour is not supported, researchers who obtain reward from the process may withdraw their commitment and step out of the system. Hirschman (1982) warns that commitment is not a permanent feature of individual behaviour, and that rather it can be withdrawn in the face of recurring disappointment, or when the hopes for change are repeatedly challenged by events. We have suggested that disappointment and risk aversion can be mitigated by a network of peers who respectfully encourage enquiry and the development of new ideas. In this way, researchers can renew their intrinsic motivations and, as a consequence, their commitment to academic enquiry.

3   MOTIVATION AS ENERGY

We have emphasized that academic researchers are, in general, subject to peer assessment, which strongly defines individual career advancements and the distribution of research funds to both departments and individuals, as well as the extent to which different social needs receive attention. Part of the reason is that the activities of academics are often difficult to monitor, while outcomes are easier to observe and control (Geuna and Martin, 2003). This may leave some degrees of freedom to academics in the choice of specific questions within established paths, but not so much in terms of time and legitimacy to explore novel questions, methods and behavioural patterns. Peer assessment, used in this way, can be a powerful way of planning research agendas, and act as the external force that shapes research choices, with potential effects on academics' motivations, behaviour and commitment.

The current central planning of outcomes subsumes control of the aims of academics. If academics depend on pre-defined objectives, the only space left for choice is how to best fit an unchangeable context, at least in the medium run. We have suggested that a strong influence of external interests in the definition of research agenda reinforces extrinsic motivational drivers. As this happens, new populations of academics, with different desires and associated values, can be expected to emerge, in line with existing incentives and entry–exit rules. In parallel, however, where academics continue to provide peer support to each other, the process of enquiry can be stimulated thus contributing to renew inherent motivations and commitment to enquiry.

Both extrinsic and intrinsic drivers can in fact contribute to renew motivational energy. However, the aims pursued and the associated values are different in the two cases: externally defined by the research bodies or within the prevailing paradigm in the first case, rather than critically assessed by the academic in the second. The challenge is to provide a perspective that clarifies how, in particular, intrinsic motivations can be kept alive, so that academic activities continue to reflect a genuine process of enquiry and critical appraisal of research objectives. How can motivational energy of the intrinsic type last under the multiple features of the university system? What variations in the academic population will current incentives stimulate? The search for an answer requires digging into the composite nature of academic activity, focusing on the interactions amongst its different domains.

A useful analogy, although by no means exhaustive of the reality of human motivations, we think, comes from physics. Earlier applied by Georgescu-Roegen (1976) to make sense of environmental problems, the idea of thermodynamics provides motivational energy with a temporal and spatial connotation. Georgescu-Roegen (1976) was the first to identify the essence of the relationship between the economy and the natural environment. He detached economic theory from the prevailing paradigm by introducing the idea of entropy: in nature, nothing is created or destroyed, but everything is transformed. The second law of thermodynamics, otherwise called 'entropy law', opened the way to the fact that energy-matter goes from an ordered to a disordered status, making some situations irreversible.[8] The message for economists was that resources are scarce and bound to be transformed into forms that cannot be used, at the known and established state of technology. Likewise in the economy, for Georgescu-Roegen it appears simplistic to talk about circularity (or cycles) as if situations could reverse to initial conditions once disturbances have disappeared, without traces (ibid.).

Differently, and consistently with the approach of pragmatism and institutionalists, history matters and can shape the life experience of the individuals and society (Dewey, 1940; North, 1990). Likewise, motivations do not respond solely to circular self-contained flows of incentives and levels of effort. Motivations evolve, but not cyclically to go back and forth from an initial status or an optimal level of effort externally defined, but alongside a process of critical appraisal of the interactions between individual desires, actions and the environment. As Zamagni (1982) notices, the essential lesson of evolutionary dynamics is that once mutation has occurred it is impossible to go back. Processes change energy-matter, and likewise immaterial elements such as human motivation, but cumulatively rather than mechanically.[9]

By using the thermodynamics metaphor, we can think about what processes best ensure that the motivational basis of individuals, and academics in this particular case, is created and renewed. In so doing, the thermodynamics approach represents a parallel that we use for explicatory purposes, but should not be taken as an exact match of the nature of motivations, which are in their essence an immaterial aspect of individual action. We can argue that motivations, as an immaterial form of energy, can be subject to dissipation, but unlike exhaustible forms of energy-matter, they can be stimulated and renewed over the life experience of the individual and across different domains.[10] Like in thermodynamics, we focus on systems that are open to exchanges of energy with the environment, as suggested for example in Loasby (2003), Berger and Elsner (2007) and Adkisson (2010). Such a focus sheds light on the use of resources so that the individual motivational basis is not compromised, but constantly renewed through a motivational inflow. We have argued that, in academia, this is supported not so much by the promotion of some extrinsically oriented behaviour, but by the degree of openness of the disciplinary area and the research institution where the academic works. Seen from this angle, a resilient organizational system can be argued to be more efficient in preserving an adequate level of motivations than a non-resilient system (although, as suggested in the following section, the resilience of the system does not provide a sufficient condition for its population to reproduce).

4   THE EVOLUTION OF MOTIVATIONAL ENERGY

Figure 8.1 illustrates the cumulative causational cycle that explains the evolution of motivations by means of contextual interactions. Following Dewey

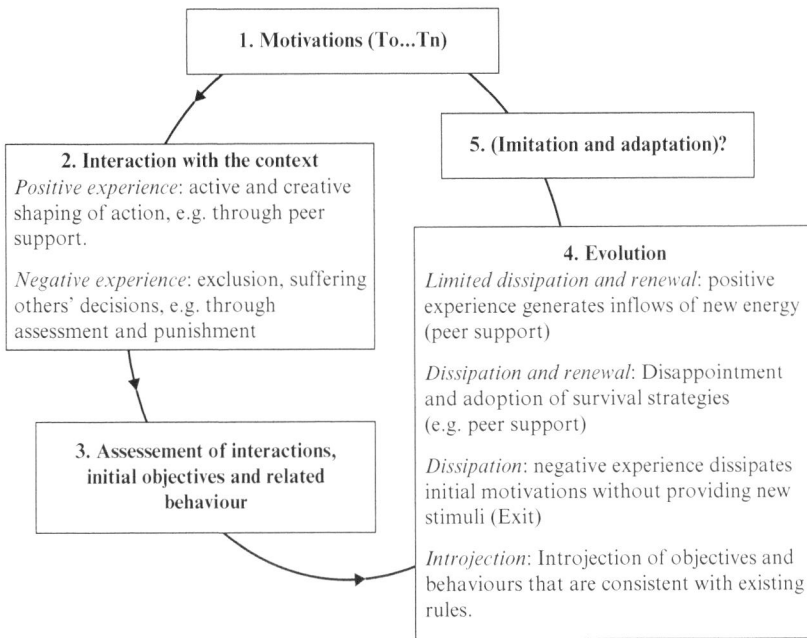

Figure 8.1   Motivational thermodynamic and resilience

(1934), it is experience that entails the whole complex set of interactions between the individual and the environment. Experience is either suffering or enjoying something happening within a context of which the individual is part (Kennedy, 1959). In particular, for Dewey the evolution of individual objectives, means and values is an elaboration of experience, including conscious reflection and interaction with others (Dewey, 1934). As valued objectives are the result of intrinsic determination, the energy that matters is the one that allows individuals to engage constantly with this learning process, which is, as a matter of fact, a process of enquiry involving the (life) objectives of the individual. We focus, therefore, on the renovation of intrinsic motivation. In striving and achieving the individual dissipates and renews this energy, learning about the importance of contextual elements and how these interact with his or her motivations and objectives (Dewey, 1917).

To apply the idea of experience to the dissipation and renewal of intrinsic motivations in academia, consider the following:

1. An academic is an actor within a population of agents occupying a specific niche defined by the subject area, the department/university, and the rules defined at policy level.

2. Motivation, like energy, dissipates through interaction with the context at each period *i*.
3. Motivational dissipation (outflows of energy) and the behavioural patterns of some actors (cooperation vs competition) in period *i* + 1 can be considered to be influenced by some actor's motivations and actions in period *i* (e.g. an esteemed senior colleague), by the 'intellectual culture' shared by the population in that niche, and by the actor's previous history (Cf. McKenzie and Galar, 2004).
4. Intrinsic motivation is renewed when inherent interests and objectives enter directly into the making of individual choices.
5. Those niches where the population of actors offers respectful peer support (rather than assessment and punishment) and promote an intellectual culture of engagement and creativity are those where actors can shape objectives, where disappointment is minimized and intrinsic motivations renewed (inflows of energy).
6. Those niches where peer evaluation tends to reproduce existing ways of doing things (objectives and means are predefined), and promote a culture of instrumental enquiry, select actors that can introject external rules and shape their objectives accordingly (inflow of energy and selection of different objectives and behavioural patterns). The balance moves towards extrinsic motivation.
7. Conditions and behaviours that are successful in injecting new intrinsic motivational energy into actors may not be acknowledged and imitated if they conflict with the established system (path dependence and power asymmetries).

By experiencing diverse situations, more or less habitual, more or less uncertain and indeterminate, the individual can reassess valued objectives and discover what elements dissipate or renew his or her motivations. The enquiring mind, in particular, strives for discovery and would value a domain that allows for such a process to occur constantly (Kirzner, 1989; Bianchi, 1998). From this perspective, it is the possibility of exerting one's creativity, or to look constantly for novelty, that helps to renew intrinsic motivations. On the contrary, when there is no opportunity for reassessing the existent (in terms of research questions, methods, or rules incentivizing specific behaviours), motivation is destined to dissipation.

In academia positive experiences occur when the context allows the creative actor to explore novelty and shape activities, involving aspects of research, teaching and relations with colleagues.[11] On the other hand, if activities are determined externally, the individual would experience exclusion from the definition of such aims, which may then erode the motivational basis for action. In both cases the individual can critically assess and learn about the impacts of contextual elements on his or her objectives and motivations and take further action, albeit with different implications with respect to the evolution of his/her motivational basis (Figure 8.1, box 4).

The worst-case scenario would be when no critical reassessment of the interactions and implications that derive from one's actions can be done (the cycle in Figure 8.1 would stop at box 2). When the individual lacks the opportunity, for whatever reasons (individual or contextual), to appreciate the implications of actions and events over his/her aims, then there can be no learning and no experience. This eventuality would be even more paradoxical in academia, where, *in principle*, enquiry is at the heart of what is valued, underpinning behaviours and activities.

5   THE UNIVERSITY CONTEXT: DECOMPOSITION OF A COMPLEX DOMAIN

We can now associate the reproduction (or 'stability' in the language of biology) of a population of individuals, such as academics, with the mutating status of the motivational basis, whose qualities (the balance between intrinsic and extrinsic drivers) change over time in response to interaction with the context. We refer to the process of evolution and adaptation that occurs in individuals to ensure the preservation of the necessary level of immaterial energy, or desire to carry out activities consistently with the enquiry principle.

We take now a step back and look at the context where the population of individuals carries out its experiences. Such a context would have in the first place to be resilient, that is, to maintain some order in the structure, or to absorb the stress coming from the inside and outside, through the selection of multiple optimal operating points within a complex environment.[12] Among the features that reveal the degree of complexity of a system, as Simon (1973) observed, are several components that form the system, their diversity and their degree of interdependence.

In explaining the architecture of complex systems such as organizations, Simon (1973) focused on the advantages of their 'near decomposability', on the fact that the division of labour within the organization is such that activities that require faster and frequent coordination are grouped under the same subsystem, and that each subsystem, internally, carries out activities that require high levels of coordination, but relatively independently from other subsystems. This principle is recurrent in organizations as it ensures control and keeps costs at bay. Complementary, decomposable systems can adapt more effectively to contextual changes, as the crisis of an individual subunit is less likely to affect the fitness of the other units. At

Motivations

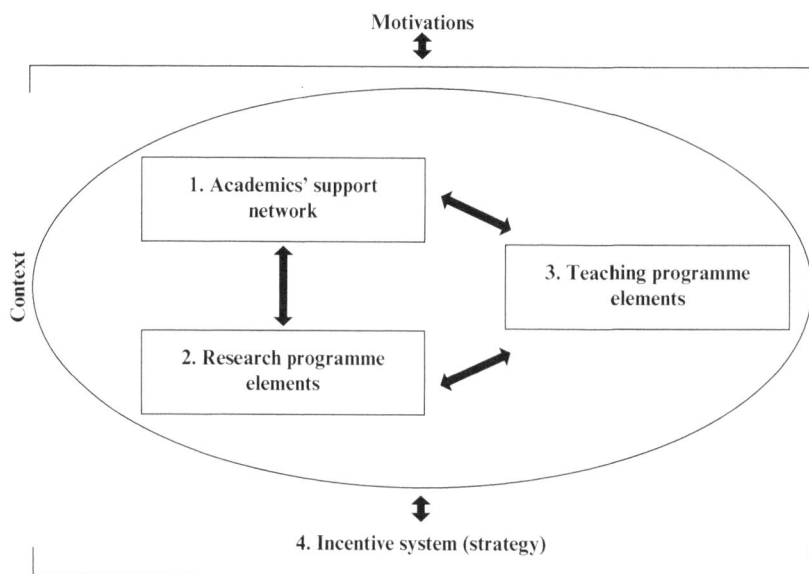

Figure 8.2 Near-decomposition of complex context

the same time, having relatively independent subsystems makes it easier to isolate and identify elements that may eventually touch the organization as a whole, favourably or unfavourably (Simon, 1973).

Following this line of reasoning, system resilience improves if there is not a single integral system but multiple subsystems, which can eventually temporarily supplement a dysfunctional subsystem. Academics in particular interact with a composite organizational and disciplinary context, which can be seen as the result of division of labour and power spheres within and across disciplines (Burawoy, 2005; Elsner and Lee, 2010; Smith, 2012). Within each subsystem academics carry out a different function. This set of functions originates, in turn, multiple motivational flows.

Following our analysis, we decompose the academic context into four fundamental domains: (1) the academics' support network, (2) research programme elements, (3) teaching programme elements, (4) incentives. Each of these domains needs to find an operating point in conjunction with all the others so that, overall, the system is sustainable (Figure 8.2). In doing so, each of the subsystems interacts with the academic's motivational basis.

The resilience of the university system, however, does not imply the stability of the population. Like in ecosystems, the university system may achieve resilience at the expense of the existing population's ability to

Table 8.1 Matrix of relationships

	1	2	3	4
1	x	M	W	W
2	M	x	W	–
3	W	W	x	–
4	M	S	W	x

Notes:
Subsystems: 1 = peer support network; 2 = research programme elements; 3 = teaching programme elements; 4 = incentives.
Interactions: S = strong; M = moderate; W = weak; – = undetermined.

reproduce its own motivations. We have discussed, in these respects, some possible implications of performance evaluation practices.

Still, decomposing the organization has the advantage of showing where academics can in fact exert their critical action to counterbalance elements that, from other subsystems, may jeopardize their motivations. In line with Simon (1973), the intensity of interaction between pairs of academic domains clusters around strong, moderate and weak interactions. If we then look at the intensity of interactions across each individual pair we can understand with more clarity the extent to which each domain can impact on intrinsic motivation.

In Table 8.1 we suggest that strong to moderate interaction occur only between elements 4&1, 4&2, 2&1 and 1&2, that is, between the domains of peer support, research, and incentives. All the others are suggested as being of weak intensity. In general, we would argue that peer support can influence the nature of the research programme to some extent, by means of collaboration on common interests, shared values and approaches (Brennan, 2004; McKenzie and Galar, 2004; Sacchetti and Sugden, 2009b). However, the extent to which collaborative work is possible depends also on the system of incentives, and despite traditional ideas of academic self-management, these are decided as part of a strategy-making process that not all academics can access.

Looking at the impact of the interaction between these three subsystems on intrinsic motivations, we have argued that peer support could contribute significantly to fulfilling needs of competence, autonomy and relatedness, to some extent balancing the potentially negative effects of a research system based on the ex-post evaluation of outcomes and monetary input from, for example, research grants. Here cooperation and support amongst peers go beyond the incentive system, and call directly for in-process benefits that can renew intrinsic motivations.

In parallel, academics face pressures to innovate and deliver on teaching programmes that meet the demand of prospective students. Teaching elements may or may not overlap with the academic's research interests. In research institutions, moreover, external incentives prioritize research outcomes. It follows, as observed, that the process of selection within universities promotes those who have already established research competences. The allocation of teaching and related activities, then, is likely to follow a comparative advantage principle, by which academics who have less experience in attracting research funds are mostly allocated teaching responsibilities, thus leaving less time and attention for research.

This is expected to activate a cumulative causation process that may have a detrimental effect on those who have entered academia with research aspirations. On the other hand however, it could renew the energy sources of academics whose aims are accomplished mostly through teaching-related activities. Still, teaching programmes can support research activities when academics can teach on their research interests and expertise, discuss ideas with students (some of whom may be future academics) and collaborate with colleagues on the substance of curricula, therefore possibly reinforcing the peer support system as well.

6   CONCLUSIONS

Solutions that have been thought to ensure the resilience of universities as organizations have prioritized, at a growing rate across national systems, an incentive system that serves the aim of revenue increase. However, we have argued that the individual adaptation to these contextual elements may endanger the stability of the population of academics and, in particular, of those whose motivations are consistent with the in-process benefits of enquiry.

Given this analysis, our framework has aimed at providing a way of understanding whether enquiry-led academics are an endangered species and how motivations can be kept alive. By taking a complex-system approach to motivational resilience we have suggested that renewal depends also on the capacity of subsystems to compensate each other's functioning, and to learn from each subsystem's experience what elements support or do not support system resilience and population survival. We have hypothesized that the incentive strategy has the power to change attitudes and select motivations across the academic population. At the same time, the dissipation of inner motivations is going to be affected by the triangulation between incentives, the peer support network and research programme elements within their institution. The key to some degree of renewal could be in the strength of the support networks amongst peers, which in particular senior staff would have the responsibility to perpetuate as part of the core values of academic activity, not only through leading by example, but by providing the conditions, by means of strategic choices, for others to do the same.

The basic conclusion is that motivational dissipation is a negative function of the degree of articulation and openness of the academic system. Openness is reflected in the support given to the emergence and development of new ideas, and in the ability of the system to internalize emerging means and objectives by means of appropriate rules.

Whether our hypothesized interactions are reflected in general in the academic population requires empirical investigation. It demands further decomposition of each domain, an analysis of organizational characteristics on a case-by-case basis and their functionality or dis-functionality with respect to motivational resilience. This includes a consideration of the objectives, strategies and incentives put in place by the organization. What academia will be in the very long term also depends on the extent to which academics will perceive a shift in the locus that controls the formation of their aims. Multiple equilibria are likely to form, encompassing variety of objectives and motivational energy in the population of academics. Variety may be supported if universities depart from strategy isomorphism towards research, teaching and peer relationships. The quality of motivations and their resilience, more generally, will depend on the degree of flexibility with which academics, through their institutions, will be able to recognize multiple interests and attitudes, and to give themselves rules and implement strategies that leave space for the creative agent to engage in academic enquiry.

ACKNOWLEDGEMENTS

I would like to thank Francesco Sacchetti, Roger Sugden, Ermanno Tortia and the anonymous reviewers who have commented on a previous version of this work and to whom I am obliged for developments in the discussion on complex organizational systems. Thanks also to the participants in the 2009 Eunip Workshop on 'The role of academic research in territorial economic development processes' (Basque Institute for Competitiveness and University of Deusto, San Sebastian, Spain), where earlier reflections were discussed.

NOTES

1. See Brennan (2004) for an analysis of esteem needs in academia.
2. An illustrative case of policy is provided by the ex-post performance measurement system in the UK (Geuna and Martin 2003). The normative purpose of the research assessment is defined by the UK higher education funding bodies of England, Northern Ireland, Scotland and Wales. The first assessment was completed in 1986 to attach the distribution of public funding to the performance of universities. In particular, the 2014 evaluation is principally related to measures of research outputs (65 per cent), alongside considerations of socio-economic impact (20 per cent) and environment (15 per cent) (HEFCE, 2009).
3. From a study of submissions and publication to the journal *Science*, Franzoni et al (2011) have found that although institutional incentives are correlated with the number of submissions, they are not significantly correlated with the number of publications. On the other hand, individual incentives in the form of career advancements are positively related to the publications and acceptance rate of submissions. These results point out that researchers submit their best work for publication when stimulated by a long-term recognition from peers, in the form of promotion, which includes clear monetary aspects too. *Una tantum* monetary incentives, like bonuses, on the other hand, crowd out quality for quantity and are detached from peer recognition. We could perhaps push the argument further and suggest that these findings would seem to be consistent with researchers obtaining satisfaction from peers' recognition, paired with stable monetary rewards. Higher levels of commitment and effort would follow, although competition for funding and recognition could reduce cooperation levels amongst academics.
4. Whereas New Zealand's institutional incentives would recognize everybody's work and give support to academic research at all levels (Meyer, 2012).
5. Challenges within disciplinary areas come also from the role of policy in identifying elements of research programmes. In exploring the field of health inequalities, Smith (2012), in particular, emphasizes the existence of multiple identities amongst academics, which reflect attitudes that attach value to research programmes defined in collaboration with policy makers on the one hand, and critical and challenging attitudes with respect to dominant discourses on the other. In this respect, the appeal of research programmes to policy makers is a way of attracting research grants, access career advancements or maintain tenure.
6. In exploring the field of health inequalities, in particular, Smith (2012), emphasizes the existence of multiple academic identities: those that value the collaboration with policy-makers in the definition of research priorities, as opposed to those who adopt critical and challenging attitudes with respect to dominant discourses on the other.
7. See Dewey (1927) on the meaning of publics.
8. Jevons (1888) defines economics in terms of the mechanics of utility and individual interest. The irreversibility of the 'entropic arrow' is in clear contrast with the principles of mechanics that characterize the prevailing economic approach, defined by the rational maximizer who makes choices at the margin on the ground of pre-ranked preferences. Collectively, Pareto efficiency represents the economic criterion: a situation is optimal when it is impossible to augment the satisfaction of one individual without worsening that of somebody else. However, critical voices and policy action have emphasized that the maximization of individual self-interest through the market cannot ensure the preservation of natural resources over time, and have argued for the introduction of extra-market mechanisms which are better positioned to deal with the idea of limit that is attached to entropy.
9. Cf. Myrdal (1957), on the principle of circular cumulative causation.
10. In analysing the metaphors of motivations, Weiner (1991) addresses the idea of energy distribution in Freudian psychoanalytic theory. He suggests that Freud's approach to motivations assimilates men to machines, where power is needed to carry out the desired actions. From this point of view, the principles of energy preservation have

been applied to explain the negative impacts of inhibitory forces on psychological equilibrium.

11. Complementary to an understanding of environing elements, the learning experience pertains also to the discovery of personal characteristics, such as the value attached to specific desires, but also elements such as tenacity and the capacity to maintain attention and focus, which can contribute to renew one's motivational basis successfully (Wallis et al., 2009).

12. In biology, resilience is measured as the capability of the system to maintain some order in the structure, or to absorb the stress coming from the outside, through the selection of multiple optimal operating points within a complex thermodynamic context (Common and Perrings, 1992).

BIBLIOGRAPHY

Adkisson, R. V. (2010), 'The economy as an open system', in T. Natarajan, W. Elsner and S. Fullwiler (eds), *Institutional Analysis and Practice*, New York: Springer, pp. 25–38.

Adler, R., J. Ewing and P. Taylor (2008), 'Citation statistics'. A Report from the International Mathematical Union in Cooperation with the International Council of Industrial and Applied Mathematics and the Institute of Mathematical Statistics, online at http://www.mathunion.org/fileadmin/IMU/Report/CitationStatistics.pdf (accessed 30 September 2012).

Berger, S., and W. Elsner (2007), 'European contributions to evolutionary institutional economics: the cases of "cumulative circular causation" and "open systems approach". Some methodological and policy implications', *Journal of Economic Issues*, **41**: 529–37.

Bianchi, M. (ed.) (1998), *The Active Consumer. Novelty and Surprise in Consumer Choice*. London: Routledge.

Brennan, G. (2004), Life in the putty-knife factory, *American Journal of Economics and Sociology*, **63** (1): 79–104.

Burawoy, M. (2005), 2004 American Sociological Association presidential address: for public sociology. *British Journal of Sociology*, **56** (2): 259–94.

Common M. and C. Perrings (1992), 'Towards an ecological economics of sustainability', *Ecological Economics*, **6**: 7–34.

Day, N. E. (2011), 'The silent majority: manuscript rejection and its impact on scholars', *Academy of Management Learning and Education*, **10** (4): 704–18.

Deci, E. L. and R. M. Ryan (1985), *Intrinsic Motivation and Self-determination in Human Behavior*, New York: Springer.

Deci, E. L. and Ryan, R.M. (2000), Self-determination theory and the facilitation of intrinsic motivation, social development and well-being. *American Psychologist*, **55** (1): 68–78.

Dewey, J. (1917), *Creative Intelligence: Essays in the Pragmatic Attitude*. Reproduced in D. Sidorsky (ed.) (1977) *John Dewey*, New York: Harper.

Dewey, J. (1927), *The Public and its Problems*, Denver, CO: Holt. Reproduced in J. A. Boydston (eds) (1988) *John Dewey. The Later Works Volume 2: 1925–1927*, Carbondale and Edwardsville, IL: Southern Illinois University Press.

Dewey, J. (2005), *Art as Experience*, New York: Penguin, (originally published 1934).

Dewey, J. (1940), 'Time and individuality', reproduced in L. A. Hickman and

T. M. Alexander (eds) (1998), *The Essential Dewey*, 1, Bloomington, IN: Indiana University Press, pp. 217–26.

Elsner, W. and F. S. Lee (2010), 'Editors' introduction', *American Journal of Economics and Sociology*, **69** (5): 1333–4.

Franzoni, C., G. Scellato and P. Stephan (2011), 'Changing incentives to publish', *Science*, **333** (August): 702–3.

Frey, B. and K. Rost. (2008), Do rankings reflect research quality? *Institute for Empirical Research in Economics*, working paper no. 390, University of Zurich. http://www.iew.uzh.ch/wp/iewwp390.pdf (accessed 30 September 2012).

Georgescu-Roegen, N. (1976), *Energy and Economic Myths*, New York: Pergamon Press.

Geuna, A. and B. R. Martin (2003), 'University research evaluation and funding: an international comparison', *Minerva*, **41**: 277–304.

Grönblom, S. and Willner, J. (2009), Destroying creativity? Universities and the new public management. In S. Sacchetti and R. Sugden (eds), *Knowledge in the Development of Economies: Institutional Choices under Globalization*. Cheltenham: Edward Elgar.

HEFCE (Higher Education Funding Council for England) (2009), 'Research excellence framework. Second consultation on the assessment and funding of research'. Policy development consultation, September 2009/38.

Hirschman, A. O. (1982), *Shifting Involvements: Private Interests and Public Action*, Princeton, NJ: Princeton University Press.

Jevons, W. S. (1888), *The Theory of Political Economy*. Library of Economics and Liberty. online at http://www.econlib.org/library/YPDBooks/Jevons/jvnpe.html (accessed 4 August 2011).

Kennedy, G. (1959), 'Dewey's concept of experience: determinate, indeterminate, and problematic', *Journal of Philosophy*, **56** (21): 801–14.

Kirzner I. M. (1989), *Discovery, Capitalism, and Distributive Justice*. Oxford: Basil Blackwell.

Larkin, M. J. (1999), 'Pressure to publish stifles young talent', *Nature*, **397** (6719): 467.

Loasby, B. J. (2003), 'Closed models and open systems', *Journal of Economic Methodology*, **10** (3): 285–306.

McKenzie, R. B. and R. Galar (2004), 'The importance of deviance in intellectual development', *American Journal of Economics and Sociology*, **63** (1): 19–49.

Meyer, L. H. (2012), 'Negotiating academic values, professional responsibilities and expectations for accountability in today's university', *Higher Education Quarterly*, **66** (2): 207–17.

North, D. C. (1990), *Institutions, Institutional Change and Economic Performance*. Cambridge: Cambridge University Press.

Olson, M. (1965), *The Logic of Collective Action*. Cambridge: Harvard University Press.

Parker, L. (2011), University corporatisation. Driving redefinition, *Critical Perspectives on Accounting*, **22** (4): 434–50.

Sacchetti, F. (2009), 'Quantity, quality and creativity' in S. Sacchetti and R. Sugden (eds), *Knowledge in the Development of Economies: Institutional Choices Under Globalisation*, Edward Elgar Publishing, pp. 249–65.

Sacchetti, S. and R. Sugden (2009a), 'Positioning order, disorder and creativity in research choices on local development', in S. Sacchetti and R. Sugden (eds) *Knowledge in the Development of Economies. Institutional Choices under Globalisation*, Cheltenham: Edward Elgar, pp. 269–88.

Sacchetti, S. and R. Sugden (2009b), 'The organization of production and its publics: mental proximity, market and hierarchies', *Review of Social Economy*, **67** (3): 289–311.

Simon, H. A. (1973), 'How complex are complex systems?' *Proceedings of the Biennial Meeting of the Philosophy of Science Association*, Vol. 1976/2: Symposia and invited papers, pp. 507–22.

Smith, K. (2012), 'Fools, facilitators and flexions: academic identities in marketised environments', *Higher Education Quarterly*, **66** (2): 155–73.

Sugden, R. (2004), 'A small firm approach to the internationalization of universities: a multinational perspective', *Higher Education Quarterly*, **58** (2–3): 114–35.

Wallis, J., B. Dollery and L. Crase (2009), 'Political economy and organizational leadership: a hope-based theory', *Review of Political Economy*, **21** (1): 123–43.

Wedlin, L. (2008), 'University marketisation: the process and its limits', in L. Engwall and D. Weaire (eds), *The University in the Market*. Colchester: Portland Press, pp. 143–53.

Weiner, B. (1991), 'Metaphors in motivation and attribution', *American Psychologist*, **46** (9): 921–30.

Wilson, J. (2009), 'Higher education and economic development: do we face an intertemporal trade-off?', in S. Sacchetti and R. Sugden (eds), *Knowledge in the Development of Economies: Institutional Choices under Globalization*. Cheltenham: Edward Elgar.

Zamagni, S. (1982), 'Introduzione', in Georgescu-Roegen, *Energia e miti economici*, Turin, Italy: Boringheri.

9.   Peer review: the academic guild's last stand or key to knowledge as a public good?

Steve Fuller

INTRODUCTION AND OVERVIEW OF THE ARGUMENT

Amidst the variously lodged calls for academic inquiry to be more 'open sourced' and 'publicly oriented', it has been common for academics who either uphold or oppose the neo-liberal mode of knowledge production to agree on the inviolability of 'peer review' as a core academic value. Indeed, nowadays the tendency especially amongst the critics of neo-liberalism is to portray peer review, under the guise of 'mutual accountability', as a mark of solidarity and collective resistance against larger forces in the political economy that threaten to compromise academic freedom (Boden and Epstein 2011). From the standpoint pursued in this chapter, such an overestimation of peer review may be seen as sounding the death rattle of the academic guild mentality. As a matter of fact, the value of peer review in the larger political economy of knowledge production is rather circumscribed and typically conservative in effect. Insofar as peer review can be harnessed to some sort of progressive ends in the neo-liberal academy, it should be in full cognizance of its limitations.

Peer review serves both an epistemic and a moral function, which are quite distinct but easily confused in ways that mystify its significance in academic inquiry (or 'science', as I shall subsequently refer to it). Epistemically, peer review 'validates' in the sense of granting a licence to a scientist to draw on a discipline's body of knowledge to advance her own knowledge claims. Ethically, peer review signals to the larger public the discipline's trust that the scientist did what she claims to have done. Thus, fraud is seen as the biggest offence against the peer review process. Nevertheless, the history of science reveals that fraud has a complicated – sometimes quite positive – relationship to the advancement of knowledge. There is an equally complicated relationship between the classical sociological model of peer review – namely, the self-organizing Royal Society – and the advancement of knowledge. In particular, this model works better for retrospective than prospective epistemic judgements. It is easier to tell whether new research carries on than breaks with old research effectively. Not surprisingly, journalists (and suspicious scientists) see groupthink lying behind peer review judgements. Interestingly, commercial publishers – always in the lookout for new markets – are generally motivated to find new domains of knowledge that break peer review monopolies. In short, peer review works very well as a definer of a discipline's mainstream and frontier – but less so as a medium for disposing of particular pieces of research. In conclusion I suggest how academic leaders might incorporate both the entrepreneurial instinct of publishers and the enlightenment instinct of academics in complementary forms of 'creative destruction' of knowledge markets. Overall my argument accepts much of the logic of neo-liberalism but in a way designed to shore up the distinctiveness of the university as an epistemic institution.

1   IS PEER REVIEW ABOUT THE EPISTEMICS OR THE ETHICS OF SCIENCE?

A philosophically flattering way of defining the function of peer review in the knowledge system is as the means by which research, regardless of origin, comes to be incorporated within a collective body of knowledge, typically an academic discipline. Thus, in the jargon of the philosophy of science, peer review marks the point at which the 'context of justification' takes over from the 'context of discovery'. Idiosyncrasies relating to the discovery process are ironed out or ignored in the peer-reviewed publication, such that readers with the requisite background knowledge and skills – but not intimate knowledge of the author – can build upon the research in question. This helps to explain the specifically *epistemic* premium placed on the 'blindness' of the peer review process – in particular, the reviewers' blindness to the author's identity. It isn't simply a matter of 'fairness' in the ordinary ethical sense of the term. The ideal reader of a peer-reviewed publication is concerned exclusively with the explicit knowledge claims, the content of which (including their larger contextualization in the literature) could have been made by any relevantly competent inquirer.

In that case, peer review literally *validates* the research in question. I say 'literally' because we need to think of this process in the spirit of the original sense of 'validation', which lingers in the idea of 'valid legal tender' in banking. When a journal publishes a peer-reviewed article, it does not claim that the article is true but rather that it draws on a common stock of knowledge by appropriate methods to draw conclusions that aim to preserve and, if possible, increase that stock. This is basically a concrete way of stating what 'validity' means in logic. In enforcing peer review, the journal's primary concern is to ensure that the common stock of knowledge that it claims as its own is whenever possible enhanced but certainly not debased. In this context, 'deduction' names a safe and 'induction' a risky epistemic investment in that stock. Again placed in a philosophically flattering light, the peer review process insures against the risk of induction that accompanies all genuinely new knowledge by requiring that authors embed their research in larger, mutually reinforcing theoretical and methodological frameworks from which an author's specific contribution can be (more or less) deduced as the logical next step of this (manufactured) collective investigation.

To be sure, most peer-reviewed publications end up yielding little palpable 'added value' for the disciplines to which they purport to contribute: The average article is rarely cited by later publications or, if cited, it is often for purposes of highlighting its shortcomings. One might look on the bright side and say that all of this unread literature constitutes a stock of 'undiscovered public knowledge' (Swanson 1986), an epistemic potential waiting to be exploited by public or private bodies with the courage to fund scholars to resurrect work that had originally fallen stillborn from the presses, to recall David Hume's memorable account of his first book's reception. (I say 'courage' because basically people would be paid for reading and synthesizing other people's work – a classically 'humanist' activity. I actually think that this would be a very good idea.) Indeed, one might metaphysically dignify this 'data mining' task by referring to Karl Popper's (1972) 'third world' of objective knowledge that is an ongoing by-product of human attempts to impose intelligent design on matter – effectively, a 'rolling news feed' from the ontological frontline.

But ultimately peer review is less concerned with the epistemic than the moral justification of the research that is published. The true enemy of the peer review process is *fraud*, the false pretence of having carried out the research that the journal's peers have credited the author through publication. Fraud is tantamount to depositing forged currency in a bank that is then circulated through the economy, contaminating all subsequent business transactions. Thus, it is claimed that fraud that goes undetected until only much later may have catastrophic consequences for the entire body of authorized knowledge. However, counterbalancing these fears is a touching faith in the policing powers of peer review. Both philosophers and sociologists tend to believe that the scientific knowledge system has a remarkable capacity for self-correction, such that the relative rarity of detected fraud corresponds to a genuine lack of frequency in the occurrence of fraud rather than simply a lack of incentive to detect it.

In this context, the concept of 'trust' can be made to do heroic work to justify the relationship between a journal's peer reviewers and authors seeking publication: a classic case of the absence of evidence being taken as evidence for absence – in this case, of fraud. Under normal circumstances, such an inference would be dismissed as fallacious – but in science, it is simply miraculous. This strange combination of scientists being both fearful of fraud and confident in its detection was epitomized in the issue on 1 June 1990 of the leading US general science magazine, *Science*, which reported a resolution passed by the governing board of the American Association for the Advancement of Science calling for the US government to grant peer-reviewed journals immunity from prosecution if they display diligence in catching and reporting fraud in their pages. The proposal went nowhere, but it was meant to perpetuate the idea that the welfare of the public was at risk through the unscrupulous reporting of scientific research – and, conversely, that peer review provided adequate insurance against that risk.

But to what extent are such claims true – or even relevant to the issue of 'fraud'? After all, fraud commits the sin of misrepresentation, which is a moral and not an epistemic fault. Thus, the *Science* editorial attempted to read the undoubted cleverness of the elusive scientific fraudster as a manifestation of unspeakable evil. Nevertheless, a fraudulent piece of work – be it bullshit or plagiarism – may correspond to how the world is, albeit it would take someone else's work to make the case properly: in the case of plagiarism, that work has been already done but has gone unrecognized; in the case of bullshit, that work will be eventually done and the 'fraud' may come to be seen as its anticipation (Fuller 2009: chapter 4). Indeed, the bullshit side of the argument has been quite significant in the history of science, with Galileo and Mendel being just two of the most adept data massagers, if not outright fabricators, who made important knowledge claims that turned out to be largely true but very likely were not quite within their epistemic reach (Fuller 2007: chapter 5).

Of course, it is somewhat – but only somewhat – anachronistic to attribute 'research fraud' to scientists who lived long before the phrase acquired a clear legal definition. I say 'only somewhat' because sufficient doubts were attached to Galileo's and Mendel's research findings to lead others to shun or persecute them in their own lifetimes. As it turned out, each suffered only a relative short-term loss of status, though that period did extend beyond their lifetimes. Though no one would dare raise the prospect now, a similar vindication may lie in store for Hwang Woo-Suk, the once celebrated South Korean biotechnologist (pictured on the cover of *Time* magazine in 2004) who falsely claimed to have cloned human stem cells. As the controversy over his actions unfolded, greater emphasis was placed on his failure to follow globally agreed ethical guidelines for securing consent from subjects than whether it might be possible to clone human stem cells by techniques akin to those that he allegedly used. Faith in that possibility has inspired hundreds of South Korean women to donate their eggs in solidarity with Hwang, even after he was indicted for fraud.

In the cases of unscrupulously reported research past and present, it has never been shown that the public welfare was at risk – at least any more so than from actions taken on the back of scrupulously reported research. Nevertheless, the willingness of scientists to associate non-peer reviewed research and risk to public welfare goes unabated. A cautionary tale in this vein concerns the fate of the UK-based journal *Medical Hypotheses*. As the title suggests, this periodical is devoted to intellectually interesting but untested speculations in the biomedical sciences. The journal was founded by the maverick physiologist David Horrobin in 1975 specifically to provide a safe haven for what he called 'revolutionary science', which by definition would be rejected by ordinary peer review. (John Ziman was an avowed inspiration and supporter.) Horrobin took all editorial decisions himself, with occasional consultation of an advisory board. A piece would be published simply on the basis of its logical coherence and scientific plausibility. The paper would not need to present any original research, nor would it need to be compatible with the dominant tendencies in the relevant fields. In regular editorials, Horrobin took aim at the peer review practices of other journals, as well as the use of random critical trials and animal-based experiments in biomedical research. He also promoted his own pet theories, including a common physiological basis for schizophrenia and creativity, and an all-purpose account of disease resulting from a failure to metabolize fatty acids. Although *Medical Hypotheses* was criticized and sometimes ridiculed for its editorial policy, the journal's articles were widely read and highly cited. Indeed, no serious attempt was made to change the journal's explicitly anti-peer review stance even after the Dutch mega-publisher Elsevier acquired the title in 2002.

But all of this changed in 2009, when Horrobin's successor Bruce Charlton accepted an article by Peter Duesberg, the distinguished Berkeley virologist, who for the past quarter-century has contested the HIV-basis of AIDS. Duesberg's article argued that the South African government was probably right to follow his advice not to administer anti-retroviral drugs to that country's AIDS sufferers because the HIV-AIDS link remains unproven and the subsequent AIDS-related deaths in that country can be more plausibly explained by other factors. This led scientists associated with the US National Institutes of Health (NIH) to threaten to have all subscriptions to Elsevier titles removed from the National Library of Medicine if the publisher did not withdraw the offending article from publication and henceforth institute peer review at *Medical Hypotheses*, since articles such as Duesberg's have 'potentially negative consequences for public health and the goals of the NIH' (Lindberg et al. 2009). Elsevier agreed to all the demands, which eventually meant the sacking of Charlton, who refused to budge as a matter of commitment to Horrobin's editorial principles (Corbyn 2010).

However, lawyers may turn out to be the main beneficiaries of this sorry tale, since Elsevier effectively conceded that publishing only peer-reviewed science constitutes a safeguard to public health. One now waits with incipient *schadenfreude* for a city or state to sue a publisher precisely because its adherence to findings from peer-reviewed science in its journals made for detrimental public health policies. Over a decade ago, I suggested that if universities wished to encourage its faculty to be 'socially relevant' in its pronouncements, then – in the spirit of 'put your money where your mouth is' – they should set aside a fund for paying damages when the advice goes horribly wrong, *especially* when the pronouncements are based on peer-reviewed publications from which no self-respecting university could distance itself (Fuller 2000: chapter 8).

2 THE EPISTEMIC DIMENSION OF PEER REVIEW: BACKWARD OR FORWARD LOOKING?

Setting aside the motives of research fraudsters and other peer review desperados, a cold 'epistemic' look at the situation reveals that peer reviewers have no choice but to expose themselves to potential fraud. Any article submitted for peer review is an invitation for the peers to assume a risk that effectively lays their collective reputation on the line by validating the author's work as living up to the same standard as the other work they have already validated. To be sure, as disciplinary gatekeepers, the peers understand that they must be always investing in innovative research to signal their field's epistemic growth potential in a crowded market that seeks the same pot of intellectual, political and financial capital. As commercial publishers often see more clearly than the peer reviewers they underwrite, the underlying strategy is 'grow or die'. I shall return to the proactive character of commercial publishers vis-à-vis peer review below.

In stressing the moral over the epistemic dimension of the peer review process, I do not wish to imply that peer review as normally practised is completely devoid of epistemic character. However, that character is distinctly *backward looking*. In other words, peer review aims to reward work that has already been done, and for that reason it is important that the work has been, indeed, done. Moreover, peer review's backward-looking character has come to colonize more of the organized knowledge system, as research capacity – the forms of capital required from produc-ing candidate publications for peer review –depends increasingly on prior funding, which is itself judged increasingly on the basis of the track record or pedigree of the researchers involved. Peer review's backward look has been further promoted by the absorption of the academic knowledge system into the larger political economy of intellectual property. To be sure, a journal publication does not carry the same promise of legal enforcement of credit acknowledgement as a patent, but the entitlement to credit in both cases is similar and increasingly salient in the evaluation of the knowledge system, ranging from judgements of individual impact based on citation counts to the rank-ordering of university departments based on the number of high-impact publications.

Lost in all this backwardness is the idea of peer review as a *proactive* process. This problem is especially pronounced nowadays in the case of academic journals. The maturity of an academic field is often signalled by the tendency of the author pool of the field's main jour-nals to constitute a self-organizing market. In that case, journal editors can simply select the best material that passes through the peer review process with minimal prompting on their own part. This *laissez faire* approach is a far cry from the origins of modern publishing, in which today's clearly distinguished roles for 'publisher', 'editor' and 'author' were absent. Until copyright legislation began to separate these roles in the eighteenth century, the 'author' was the person who stamped his authority on a body of work by commissioning the writers, editing and organizing their works, and then producing and distributing the finished product – typically with considerable content input of his own (Fuller 2002: chapter 2). Such an 'author' was proactive in the manner of an entrepreneur or impresario, in which 'peerage' was effectively conferred on others through extended collaboration, 'participatory peerage', if you will. The last generation of this heroic moment in proactive pub-lishing was epitomized in the career of Benjamin Franklin in colonial America, but its scaled-up fruits also included Ephraim Chambers' London-based *Cyclopaedia*, the prototype for Denis Diderot and Jean D'Alembert's *L'Encyclopédie*, which in turn was emulated – albeit in the politically muted tones characteristic of the Scottish Enlightenment – by the *Encyclopaedia Britannica*.

To be sure, remnants of this old heroic proactive ideal can be found in the years since 1800. A clear case in point is the late nineteenth/early twentieth century deployment of the academic journal as a discipline-building device attached to a specific university department and a founding editor with a strong intellectual vision. Here one might cite the role of *L'Année Sociologique* under Emile Durkheim at the Sorbonne, *Philosophical Review* founded by Cornell University President Jacob Schurman, and *Isis*, the history of science journal founded at Harvard by George Sarton. A similar strategy was adopted, albeit more fitfully, by the logical positivists in their various vehicles: first, the journals *Erkenntnis* and *Synthese*, while based in Vienna, and then the *International Encyclopedia of Unified Science*, once based in Chicago. In all these cases, editors actively solicited those whom they had identified as fellow-travellers. For example, in their Viennese incarnation, the logical positivists launched a manifesto as a market signal to prospective peers who might be attracted to their idiosyncratically Austro-centric genealogy of 'the scientific version of the world'. But equally important in all these cases, the editors made a point of reviewing a wide range of literature, always in terms of its relevance to the journal's mission. That regular feature alone helped to establish a 'house style of thought' for fields that had yet to accumulate a body of original research.

Many of these originally proactive journal- and book-based movements were eventually incorporated by professional academic bodies, which offered financial security in exchange for their 'bending over backward' (in temporal horizon) by catering to the default tendencies of their clientele. Thus, a decision to run a special issue of a journal on an 'emerging tendency' within a discipline typically requires tricky editorial negotiations. Ironically perhaps, it has been left to the commissioning editors of commercial publishers to seek out nascent intellectual tendencies for purposes of establishing new journals and book series. In this context, the role of the British publishers Routledge and Sage in setting the global intellectual agenda of cultural and gender studies since the 1980s should not be underestimated. After all, academic publishing houses are historically dependent on the opinions of the resident experts in established departments. In contrast, commercial publishers presume that some sustainable intellectual perspectives have been overlooked, in which case money may be made by encouraging marginalized academics to generate markets for their own distinctive work (Fuller 2002: chapter 3). In this context, the commissioning editor functions as a matchmaker amongst those sharing common intellectual interests who might go on to seed a peer community by agreeing to join a journal's editorial board. But in the end, because commercial publishing is ultimately run as a business, these prospects are given a short run (e.g three to five years) in which to generate a target level of submissions and subscriptions.

3   PEER REVIEW AS (NOT) SEEN BY SCIENCE JOURNALISTS

So far we have seen that peer review in practice directly enforces moral rather than epistemic norms: misrepresentation of self rather than reality is of paramount concern. Moreover, insofar as peer review does enforce epistemic norms, they tend to be backward and not forward looking. Put charitably, peer review aims more to determine whether research has been done well than whether it was worth doing. Indeed, those whose overriding concern is with the value of knowledge *per se* may find problems with peer review's *modus operandi*. In particular, the main source of conflict between the scientific establishment and science journalists is that journalists take more seriously than the scientists themselves that science speaks to the larger philosophical issues concerning human existence, which in turn justifies continued public support of science.

If this claim seems strange, one may think about the conflict as a by-product of scientists' reliance on peer review as a process that not only validates scientific work but also comes to be seen – if only by the scientists themselves – as self-validating. In other words, the very fact that active researchers, often operating from vastly different theoretical orientations, can agree on the value of work for which they are then willing to take collective responsibility through authorized publication is a sign that the work was worth doing. This line of argument was already present in the charter of the Royal Society of London in 1660, which, in light of England's then-recent history with civil war, implicitly set a standard for dispute resolution that in the future might be emulated by politicians. Indeed, within 50 years, much of the model was adopted by what we now call 'the mother of all parliaments'.

However, this distinguished pedigree typically fails to sway science journalists, who are less impressed by the normative standard that peer review sets for reaching ideological consensus than the more prosaic tendency of scientists to fail to live up to those avowed standards. In fact, journalists see scientists living up to another set of standards that are only misleadingly captured by the phrase, 'peer review' but may be less misleadingly called 'mutual protection racket' (Fuller 1997: chapter 4). Three features of peer review in practice come to mind.

First, reviewer and reviewed are very often not 'peers' in the strict sense. On the whole, reviewers represent a more elite sector of the research community than the authors whose work they review. Not surprisingly, articles accepted for publication tend to have more elite authors than those rejected. Worst of all, the ideas in rejected articles often end up appearing in print a few years later under the name of a more elite author: coincidence or conspiracy? Either way, little wonder that non-elite researchers with controversial views have preferred to take their chances by going directly to the mass media with their findings. Moreover, there is little incentive (other than 'good scientific citizenship') to participate in peer review, since the process is both anonymous and time-consuming, which means unpaid labour. Although journal publishers flirt periodically with providing financial incentives for peer reviewers, these are of limited value because the peers themselves are the main beneficiaries: i.e., however costly the process is for peers, it is mainly in their own – and no one else's – interest to review the work of other researchers.

Second, peer review's validation procedure rarely involves a direct test of the knowledge claims for which the author wishes to receive credit. It is nothing like Ralph Nader's *Consumer Reports* or the US Food and Drug Administration's health and safety tests. Instead, submitted articles are judged on what psychologists call their 'face validity', to wit: Is it reasonable to suppose that a competent researcher operating within the stated theoretical framework and the specified methodological parameters would acquire data of the sort indicated and interpret them in the terms suggested by the author? Here the peer reviewer is looking to internal consistency as a sign of external validity. While such a heuristic is powerless in the face of a perfect forgery, it does provide a means of capturing such common forms of research malpractice as massaged data, sample overgeneralization, and theory misinterpretation. In the early days of the Royal Society, when those likely to submit articles to its *Proceedings* knew each other as 'Fellows', much was made of the 'trustworthiness' of the scientific reports, which alluded to the character of the reporters. However, as peer review extended its epistemic authority to all researchers in a given field, the clubby character of trustworthiness yielded to a more anonymized, forensic assessment of submitted pieces that privileges being 'correct on the page', which is to leave as little as possible to the imagination. To a science journalist, this approach still does not get much beyond biblical criticism, since the peer reviewer never actually directly encounters the empirical basis for the knowledge claims.

Peer review involves what economists call 'transaction costs' that are borne by the reviewers, unless they can be offloaded to the authors. After all, if the peer reviewers are about to take collective responsibility for an author's research, they have an interest in publishing the version with which they are most comfortable. However, instead of the reviewers themselves writing additional pieces that correct or contest in detail what an author has written, the reviewers can make publication conditional on the author's incorporation of such criticism in a revised version. Thus, the potential for displaying intellectual conflict is pre-empted – some would say 'sublimated' – through a negotiated settlement (Fuller 2000: chapter 1). At one level, this is a win–win situation. The author gets published, while the peers continue to give the impression that the field's knowledge base is subject to steady, cumulative growth. However, in this backroom deal, the journalist sees proof of what economists call 'rent-seeking' behaviour: a situation that would otherwise allow for genuine epistemic growth by forcing both sides to defend and possibly alter their positions is replaced by one in which the author agrees to depend on the peers for validation. The author's individuality is essentially bought. Thus, a common condition for publication is that the author must add references to other putatively related work that the author may not have read – let alone been influenced by – but serves to reinforce the peers' sense of the lines of epistemic descent. The author effectively yields some of her origi-nality to acquire legitimation from retrofitted precursors and fellow travel-lers whom the peers regard as 'politically correct' authorities. When these retrofitted sources have themselves published in the journal in which the author seeks publication, the author's acquiescence helps to boost what scientometricians call the journal's 'impact factor', which measures the likelihood that others will cite articles published in a given journal, which in turn perpetuates the appearance of the journal's centrality to its field.

In short, science journalists see peer review as a theory of scientific governance that has yet to find an adequate practice. Under the circum-stances, it should come as no surprise that science journalists have given significant publicity to scientific opinions that have circumvented, if not been outright condemned, by the scientific peer review process. Examples abound, including HIV–AIDS denialism, cold fusion, creationism, and climate change scepticism. As we have seen, there is perhaps good reason to distrust that peer review is capable of giving a fair hearing to exception-ally challenging views. Indeed, rather than presuming that opposing sides of a scientific issue deserve equal time, journalists typically see themselves as redressing the scientific establishment's misrepresentation of the side it has come to condemn with such apparent unanimity. To be sure, scientists are prone to condemn such journalistic attempts at 'even-handedness' as ignorant arrogance.

A more illuminating assessment of the situation would start by noting that both scientists and journalists are committed to knowledge as a 'universally available public good'. However, they interpret key terms in that phrase rather differently. The main source of this difference is that journalists believe that the sort of intelligence that separates their readers from scientists is a matter of degree, not kind. In effect, journalists espouse a vulgar logical positivism in their insistence that anything worth saying is reducible to something that anyone could judge for herself by using her senses and ordinary powers of reasoning. In that respect, 'everyman' is potentially a scientific peer capable of judging cutting edge research for herself. All that matters is perspicuous presentation – the main task for journalists. In stark contrast, scientists are inclined to believe that specialist training imparts a certain cast of mind that is qualitatively different from the sorts of judgements that even well-informed amateurs might make. It follows that science journalists would better spend their time informing the public about whose judgement they should and should not trust, based on what has and has not successfully passed the peer review process. This 'underlabouring' version of science journalism is very much alive and well in, say, Ben Goldacre, the award-winning, Oxford-trained medical scientist who writes the weekly 'Bad Science' column for the (London) *Guardian*.

4 PEER REVIEW FROM THE INSIDE: CAN ONE REMAIN UNCYNICAL?

Peer review may have many invidious features, but the one on which science journalists cast the harshest light is its capacity to generate closure on the creditworthiness of a given piece of research. Such 'inter-rater reliability', as psychologists like to call it, may be explained in several ways. If we take an uncynical view, the predominance of peer consensus simply reflects that a field possesses objective standards of assessment – that there exists a domain about which one may make demonstrably true or false claims. Indeed, the fact that interdisciplinary peer review panels at very competitive research funding agencies generally reach agreement without too much trouble suggests that academia's higher echelon is populated by those who defer to distinguished colleagues outside their sphere of expertise, while presuming that their own expertise will be respected at the appropriate time. That such mutual expectations are borne out in practice was the conclusion drawn by the most intensive participant-observation study of the peer review process at US public and private sector funders in the humanities and the social sciences, *How Professors Think* (Lamont 2009).

However, even a work as sympathetic to the peer review process as *How Professors Think* can provide ammunition for cynics, especially since it stresses the relative difficulty in securing the best grants over that of getting published in the best journals: 'Grants and fellowships are becoming important as academic signals of excellence, especially because the proliferation of journals has made the number of publications of academics a less reliable measure of their status' (Lamont 2009: 15). Scarcity of funds is less negotiable than scarcity of journal pages. After all, there is a long history of academics who faced with poor acceptance rates of their work in the established disciplinary journals have gone on to found journals devoted to their specialities, which in turn have acquired established reputations. Notwithstanding the intellectual trail-blazing qualities of such journals, from Lamont's standpoint this practice amounts to currency inflation in the academic credit market.

Against this backdrop, the mutual expectations of peer deference produces what Lamont calls 'conspicuous collegiality' the courtly discourse that accompanies it in the face-to-face peer review panels at the funding agencies. Thus, the conspicuously collegial panellists ostentatiously defend the standards of their own discipline while deferring graciously to the standards of other disciplinary practitioners. They are mindful of disciplinary boundaries to such an extent that, in their final evaluations, they readily sacrifice more reckless, typically younger colleagues whose grant proposals threaten to 'transgress' the epistemic *cordon sanitaire* defined by those boundaries. Here Lamont's reliance of Karin Knorr-Cetina's (1999) conception of disciplines as 'epistemic cultures' serves to reinforce – if not simply repeat in more abstract terms – the panellists' own tendencies to stereotype their fields for purposes of boundary maintenance. Invoked in this context is 'opportunity hoarding', a concept introduced by the historical sociologist Charles Tilly to capture how groups generate inequality by monopolizing access to the enabling conditions for certain activities (Lamont 2009: 37). All along, both Lamont and her informants presume that a good interdisciplinary project must demonstrate mastery of the constitutive disciplines, a quality that panellists appear to think they can identify with relative ease, though (Lamont admits) such projects are never discussed in sufficient detail to allow readers to reach an independent judgement on the matter.

One classic social theoretic concept that makes a fleeting appearance in *How Professors Think* is *corruption*, the identification of the public good with an exclusionary sense of self-interest, which is more accurately rendered by the concept of 'club goods' (discussed below). Put more metaphysically, the corrupt person does not allow the concerns of the spirit to transcend those of the body. For example, the trademark indignation about French academic life registered by Lamont's erstwhile mentor, Pierre Bourdieu (1990), was a response to the corruption he perceived amongst his colleagues, who collectively reproduced their society's class structure in their intellectual discriminations, or 'judgements of taste'. Bourdieu understood this phenomenon more as a function than a cause of the existing class structure. Thus, he did not anticipate the sort of corruption that Lamont's account unwittingly suggests, namely, that when it comes to allocating research funds, academic peer review panels are sites for the outright manufacture of an academic class system that might otherwise not exist, or at least not so markedly.

Here it is worth recalling that the 'peerage' implied in the phrase 'peer review' is traditionally to do with the equality of inquirers in both giving and receiving criticism. In other words, the peers are presumed to be not only equally competent for purposes of passing judgement, but also equally resilient in the face of negative judgement. This principle made sense in the early days of the Royal Society, when members were for the most part of independent means and scientific research required a greater dedication of time than money. However, once research became undoable without external funding, and peer review was used as the principle of allocation, judgements were effectively passed on not simply one's research results but on one's very capacity to do research. Corruption is a very likely – if perhaps unintended – consequence of this arrangement, since the peers are being forced to treat grant-seekers as capital investments. It becomes virtually impossible to judge proposals without considering the opportunity costs, track record and prospects of an academic field in which the judge herself is a player. Implicit realization of this fact explains why 'affirmative action' and 'diversity management' considerations matter when academic peers are allocating research funds but not journal pages. However, Lamont leaves the impression that the conspicuous collegiality of academic peer review is not an elaborate exercise in corruption simply because those who engage in it invest enormous time and effort, which (at least to her) amounts to an indirect measure of sincerity. In contrast, I am left with a renewed sense of the value of Bourdieu's demystified approach to the academic field.

But peer review's tendency to assign too much epistemic weight to what is, in effect, a glorified version of groupthink is perhaps not nearly as sinister as a by-product of that tendency – namely, the reification of academic judgement. Thus, even though a given set of peer reviewers may only somewhat overlap in their reasons for accepting or rejecting an article for publication, the common bottom line judgement is what matters, which in turn may be converted into a quantity that figures in the various knowledge-based metrics used in research evaluation, what Nicholas Rescher (2007) has recently called 'epistemetrics'. Moreover, this point applies not only to which articles get published but also which ones get cited. If the former indicators capture whether research has been done well, the latter indicators increasingly serve as a proxy for whether research was worth doing – a *de facto* 'invisible hand' of post-publication peer review tracking epistemic merit in the marketplace of academic ideas (Mirowski 2004). However, the main problems with peer review's easy reification go beyond the simple misrepresentation of academic judgement. More important is the distortion of academic motivation that it encourages. Here two issues stand out: (1) the bias towards consensus while the dynamics of inquiry favours disagreement; (2) the incentive that reification offers to 'gaming the system', by engaging in the sorts of practices that were associated above with the 'mutual protection racket' aspect of peer review.

5 CONCLUSION: 'OPEN ACCESS' OR 'OPEN SCIENCE'? LOOKING BEYOND PEER REVIEW

In conclusion, let me start by saying I do not wish to leave the impression that peer review – outside of the proactive mode promoted by publishers – is a remedy worse than the problem it is meant to address. On the contrary, it has a clear but circumscribed role in the governance of the knowledge system. In particular, peer review is a good mechanism for focusing and channelling disagreement – which is to say, providing auxiliary constraints on the flow of academic discourse. This role was immediately recognized in the first modern scientific societies and was typically performed by the society's secretary (e.g. Henry Oldenburg in England and Marin Mersenne in France). Before the establishment of academic journals, new research was sent in the form of correspondence to the secretary who then distributed it to society members. However, the secretary took care to correct obvious errors of fact, remove infelicities of expression that could lead to both personal and scientific misunderstanding among the members, query or curb overstretched inferences, and censor outright irreligious or politically inflammatory statements. But the secretary did not attempt to adjudicate on the proposed knowledge claims or even compel the author to bear a specific burden of proof. In this way, the secretary remained a peer of the author by avoiding the temptation to become a second-order critic – or, worse, inquisitor. In terms of today's standards, it also led to a wider range of intellectual starting points and endpoints being seriously entertained. Indeed, reinstating the secretarial role of peer review (although clearly it would no longer be a single individual) would allow our own scientific controversies to be played out in a more epistemically edifying fashion. As it stands, all too often the scientific establishment uses peer review to exclude radically alternative intellectual starting points. This in turn forces the mavericks to non-peer reviewed forums that are themselves ill-equipped to catch technical errors. These errors – the sort of thing that a secretarial peer would have caught – may not affect the major maverick knowledge claims, but they do provide a further pretext – incompetence – for the establishment's refusal to give a proper hearing to the mavericks' claims.

Thus it is the authoritarian appeal to peer review, so alien to the early modern science societies, that needs to be ended, and preferably replaced.

Nevertheless, journalists and other cynics of the peer review process have a point. The relatively similar training and career orientation of peers create common expectations about the qualities that should be possessed by publishable – and, as we have seen, fundable – work. This creates a sense of solidarity that is evident even in the so-called *open access* movement, which would have academics take their business away from commercial publishers, who charge increasingly high fees for academics to get access to their own work. Interestingly, the world's wealthiest university, Harvard, has attempted to spearhead this movement by exhorting its academics to migrate to self-organizing open access journals – operating on the assumption that commercial publishers are irrelevant to the maintenance of the quality control standards associated with peer review (Rosen 2012). But as we have seen, publishers are more than the parasitic rent-seekers that this image presumes. Minimally they impose a discipline that might be otherwise lacking in academics (i.e. the regular delivery of research results), but historically they have lured academics from their disciplinary comfort zones by providing opportunities to reconfigure their fields.

From this standpoint, the open access movement should be seen as nothing more – but also nothing less – than a consumer revolt, academic style. No one in this revolt is calling for what is sometimes called 'extended peer review' (whereby relevant non-academic stakeholders operate as knowledge gatekeepers), let alone the abandonment of science's normal technicality. Indeed, much of the moral suasion of the open access movement would be dissipated if it complained not only about the price of academic journals but also the elite character of the peer review process itself. After all, only the presumption of self-recognition amongst the 'peers' in the peer review process gives the appearance that publishers play a 'merely administrative' function. Put another way, the open access movement fails to see the prospecting work done by publishers that cuts against the default self-reproducing tendencies of the peer review process, when left entirely in the hands of academics. In effect, open access is limited to making research cheaper to access by those who already possess the skills to do so but are held back by such 'artificial' barriers as publishers' paywalls. Nothing in the movement bears on questions concerning how one might democratize knowledge production itself – such as how research credit might be distributed across students, informants, etc.; how one might select research topics that people find worthwhile; how access to many audiences might be made a desideratum for securing publication (Bell 2012).

In short, open access relates to what genuine democratizers of inquiry

call *open science* as *club goods* relate to *public goods* in economics (cf.
Marginson 2007). Open access is designed to ensure the smooth flow of
club goods – namely, that those who have already paid into the system
– that is, by virtue of having invested in acquiring the relevant social and
intellectual capital – are its primary, if not exclusive, beneficiaries. (Note
that this sense of 'paying into the system' runs deeper than the usual open
access claim that state-funded research, even if published commercially,
should be made freely available to taxpayers – even if they would not
know what to make of its content.) Whereas public goods are governed by
the idea that it would cost more to exclude people who do not pay into the
system than simply to include them, club goods operate on the principle
that the goods themselves would lose value if the terms of membership are
not strictly observed. Whereas defenders of science as a public good worry
about the forgone benefits that might later arise from the activities of the
'free riders', those who defend science as a club good are more concerned
that, so to speak, fully paid-up members get their money's worth, which in
this case is an entitlement to exercise a certain epistemic advantage. In this
respect, by presuming the club good model, open access campaigners take
knowledge to be a *positional good* (cf. Fuller 2005). However, there is a
difference. Whereas theorists of positional goods are normally concerned
with the depreciation of value that comes from too many people having
access to a good, in the open access case the source of depreciation is too
limited access.

Clearly, when taken as descriptors of knowledge systems, 'open' and
'public' stand in an interesting tension with each other. They are by no
means contradictory but they may be orthogonal, such that a 2×2 matrix
of possibilities would include not only 'open and public' (i.e. knowledge
as Enlightenment) and 'closed and private' (i.e. knowledge as intellectual
property) but also two other quadrants: 'open and private' and 'closed
and public'. The former corresponds to a classical free market for knowledge, the latter to a Soviet-style planned knowledge economy. These two
possibilities – perhaps especially the former – are obscured by a tendency
to confuse unboundedness with universality: openness addresses the first
concept, publicity the second. In other words, to say that knowledge is
allowed to migrate freely is not necessarily to say that it will reach everyone who might have use for it. On this basis the social democratic welfare
state could lay claim to being the sole providers of knowledge as a public
good. It is a mark of our neo-liberal political economy of knowledge production that openness and publicity are so confused.

Symptomatic of this confusion is a tendency to ignore the spontane-
ously path-dependent nature of knowledge production. In philosophical
terms, the *context of justification* is much more embedded in the *context*

of discovery than one might like to admit. (The reverse is also the case, which helps to explain the limits on the discoveries that can be made at a given time, namely, people narrowing their vision to second-guessing what will succeed.) Indeed, the normative force of the logical positivist and Popperian injunction to divorce the two contexts is itself a measure of their default historical linkage. Under normal circumstances, it is presumed that the person who originates a knowledge claim can capitalize on that initial advantage, perhaps resulting in a monopoly. Academic life in this respect is more invidious than business because, instead of having the law safeguard original advantage through copyrights and patents, which entrepreneurs are then motivated to overturn or circumvent, academics themselves have a vested interest in establishing the advantage of their predecessors as an indirect means of promoting themselves. In the end, one sees a putatively 'open' system resulting in a scheme that resembles a Mafia.

In light of the above considerations, an interesting version of the constitutional strategy of 'checks and balances' may be adopted by senior university administrators to play the natural openness of entrepreneurial publishers against the natural public-mindedness of Humboldtian scholar–teachers. Both are engaged in a sort of 'creative destruction' of somewhat different knowledge markets. On the one hand, publishers are keen to displace the hegemony of disciplinary structures by locating uncharted intellectual terrain and reconfiguring academic networks. On the other, academics keen to translate their research into classroom practice dissipate the epistemic advantage, if not monopoly, that the original researchers – possibly including oneself – have enjoyed. Indeed, that elimination of an original advantage may be organized so as to provide an incentive for academics to engage the services of publishers to move into relatively fallow fields of inquiry. In short, the savvy academic leader would enable publishers and academics to engage symbiotically in their complementary movements of creative destruction. Concretely, and perhaps most controversially, this policy might involve bringing publishers into the governing structure and staffing of the university, so as to enable it to acquire more of the proactive orientation of a proper corporate enterprise.

REFERENCES

Bell, A. (2012), 'Wider open spaces'. *Times Higher Education* (London) 19 April.
Boden, R. and D. Epstein (2011), 'A flat earth society? Imagining academic freedom'. *Sociological Review* **53**: 476–95.
Bourdieu, P. (1990), *Homo Academicus*. Originally published 1984. Cambridge: Polity.

Corbyn, Z. (2010), 'Unclear outlook for radical journal as HIV/Aids deniers evoke outrage'. *Times Higher Education* (London) 14 January.

Fuller, S. (1997), *Science*. Milton Keynes: Open University Press.

Fuller, S. (2000), *The Governance of Science*. Milton Keynes: Open University Press.

Fuller, S. (2002), *Knowledge Management Foundations*. Woburn, MA: Butterworth-Heinemann.

Fuller, S. (2005), 'Social epistemology: preserving the integrity of knowledge about knowledge', in D. Rooney, G. Hearn, A. Ninan, eds., *Handbook of the Knowledge Economy* (pp. 67–79). Cheltenham: Edward Elgar.

Fuller, S. (2007), *New Frontiers in Science and Technology Studies*. Cambridge MA: Polity Press.

Fuller, S. (2009), *The Sociology of Intellectual Life*. London: Sage.

Knorr-Cetina, K. (1999), *Epistemic Cultures: How the Sciences Make Knowledge*. Chicago, IL: University of Chicago Press.

Lamont, M. (2009), *How Professors Think: Inside the Curious World of Academic Judgement*. Cambridge, MA: Harvard University Press.

Abdool Karim, S. S., N. Bennnett, J. Bergman, P. Clayden, S. Collins, R. W. Doms, B. Foley, N. Geffen, T. Hope, S. Kalichman, S. P. Koenig, M. M. Lederman, J. McCune, J. Moore, N. Nattrass, T. Smith, M. Stevenson, M. Wainberg, R. A. Weiss and K. Witwer (2009), 'Letter from US National Library of Medicine to MEDLINE concerning the de-selection of *Medical Hypotheses*', http://www.aidstruth.org/sites/aidstruth.org/files/NLMLetter-2009.08.05.pdf (accessed 15 August 2011).

Marginson, S. (2007), 'The public/private divide in higher education: a global revision'. *Higher Education* 53: 307–33.

Mirowski, P. (2004), *The Effortless Economy of Science?*. Durham, NC: Duke University Press.

Popper, K. (1972), *Objective Knowledge*. Oxford: Oxford University Press.

Rescher, N. (2007), *Epistemetrics*. Cambridge: Cambridge University Press.

Rosen, R. (2012), 'Harvard now spending nearly $3.75 million on academic journal bundles'. *The Atlantic*. 23 May.

Swanson, D. (1986), 'Undiscovered public knowledge'. *Library Quarterly* 56 (2): 103–18.

10. Cooperation and leadership in academia: the roles of non-academics

John Rogers and Eileen Schofield

> A house divided against itself cannot stand. I believe this government cannot endure, permanently, half slave and half free. I do not expect the Union to be dissolved – I do not expect the house to fall – but I do expect it will cease to be divided.
> Abraham Lincoln, Illinois, 16 June 1858

Discussion of the roles of non-academic staff, in academic and practitioner literature and the media, has tended to emphasize and so perpetuate a deep and unhelpful divisiveness within university communities. The many functions and activities of staff within higher education institutions whose primary employment is other than in research and teaching are not generally discussed in terms of their nature, merits or contribution. Rather, they tend to be portrayed as an impediment to the pursuit of scholarship. Unless addressed, both the rhetoric and realities of such division work to the detriment of the academic endeavour, frustrate the development and achievement of shared objectives, and so inhibit the success of institutions and their constituent parts.

Fundamentally, universities are concerned with the creation and dissemination of new knowledge and ideas, placing clear responsibility on leaders within them, of every category and at every level, to ensure that all available resources and talents are directed towards those ends. Given the ever-increasing complexity of both academic work and the external environment within which it is undertaken, this responsibility presents substantial and growing challenges to leaders and managers within academia. It also offers considerable opportunities and competitive advantage, however, to those institutions that can resolve, and continue to embrace, those challenges. Such institutions will capitalize on emerging modes of operation characterized by embedded partnership, co-operative approaches, mutual professional respect and clarity in pursuit of common purposes.

Ye haue made this arte to appeare verie monstruous & detestable
King James VI of Scotland, *Daemonologie*, 1597, 1 vii

Non-academic staff in universities have many roles. These include special-ist, technical functions such as financial regulation and planning, human resource management, development and maintenance of physical assets and infrastructure; services which directly support academic activities including research management, student and academic administration, library and information resources; welfare and guidance services; support for governance and academic leadership and management, and many others. The skills and qualifications, organization and deployment, of non-academic staff reflect the work for which they are engaged. In this, only the core business differentiates universities from most other organizations, almost all of which also have a significant proportion of their employees undertaking tasks that are ancillary to, but nonetheless essential for the effective pursuit of, the primary activities of the organization. And yet, in stark contrast to most sectors and industries, universities appear to strug-gle with accepting the role and contribution of those of their employees who do not labour directly on the 'production line':

> Why would administrators choose to work in a university? The academics they work alongside often dismiss them as a lower form of life, parasites – the non-academics who drain resources. Administrators talk of the existence of apart-heid, an iron curtain, of being thrown together in an arranged and unhappy marriage in which neither party understands the other. (Mroz 2009)

It is rare to find examples outside higher education of organizations which categorize a substantial part of their workforce by reference to what they are not (non-clinical staff in the UK National Health Service is one such, but the generic distinction between skilled and unskilled labour is perhaps the closest parallel!). The idea of 'non-academic' staff, however, is one that extends well beyond issues of terminology. Whilst there is a considerable discourse about what to call members of university staff who are not primarily employed to research or teach or both (service, support, administrative, managerial and professional staff have all been attempted with varying degrees of success) ultimately this debate is the wrong one and, while it can be informative, is largely unproductive. The real issue is that any terminology applied to individuals or groups believed or perceived to be not amongst those of the first order of importance is that it marginal-izes, undervalues and, at its worst, demonizes the excluded. Interestingly, the fullest discussions of such behaviour are found in the anthropological, political and sociological, rather than the business and management lit-erature. And yet the evidence for this phenomenon litters academia, with non-academic staff regularly portrayed in a multitude of ways as unhelpful, obstructive or damaging to the effective conduct of academic pursuits.

Jesus asked him, What is thy name? And he answered, saying, My name is Legion: for we are many
The Gospel of Mark, v, 9

There is no doubt that the number of non-academic staff in Higher Education Institutions has grown substantially over the last 30 years. Discussion of this growth is illustrative of the wider debate concerning roles and functions, not least through its frequent use of pejorative language. Amongst the clearest of recent examples is *Administrative Bloat at American Universities: The Real Reason for High Costs in Higher Education* (Greene et al. 2010), which contrasts growth in students and academic staff at 'leading' universities in the US between 1993 and 2007 (15 per cent and 18 per cent respectively) with the growth in administrators (39 per cent), laying the blame for very substantial increases in the cost of tuition over the period squarely at the door of non-academic driven diseconomies of scale. Even more polemic is the commentary on the pattern of growth across the whole US sector from 1985 to 2005 by Benjamin Ginsberg. Noting a 50 per cent growth in faculty numbers but an 85 per cent rise in administrators and a 240 per cent rise in associated professional staff, Ginsberg claims:

> These numbers do not merely indicate an enormous shift of resource away from teaching and research, they also signal a continuing transfer of power from the faculty to the administration ... With ever growing legions of deanlets and deanlings at their command, senior administrators increasingly have the capacity to circumvent the faculty, seize control of programs, oversee research activities, and meddle in the curriculum. The result will be a continuing erosion of educational quality and research productivity. (Ginsberg 2011: 199)

The extremity and frequent offensiveness of Ginsberg's language and views, which would rightly be regarded as unacceptable in most work and social contexts, does not prevent them from having many echoes elsewhere in the academy.

The growth in non-academic staff volume is reflected in the increase, both in volume and range of their functions. Some would claim that the growth in numbers is actually the cause of the expansion in the range and complexity of non-academic roles, with work being created as a justification for an increase in staffing levels. That is unlikely to stand up to close scrutiny. Historically, in some higher education systems pay grades for non-academic managers were often related to the number of staff supervised, so a degree of vested interest may have been in operation. It is not credible, however, to believe that large numbers of universities, with their increasingly sophisticated governance and decision-making systems, careful scrutiny of the expenditure of largely competitively earned income and, in many cases, stringent accountability requirements for their use of public funding, would have allowed an unnecessary proliferation of staff positions not directly engaged in research and teaching.

Growth in higher education has by no means been confined to non-academic staff. By virtually every measure, higher education has expanded beyond recognition over the last 50 years. On average across OECD countries, for example, the proportion of people with degree-level qualifications has risen from 13 per cent to 37 per cent, and participation rates in higher education continue to rise (OECD 2011). The transition to a mass higher education system has fuelled the growth in non-academic staff numbers as a simple product of scale. More significantly, it has produced an expansion in the variety and complexity of the roles that are required to be undertaken in higher education institutions. It is not sufficient for universities to research and teach: in doing so they must also attend to very much broader societal and governmental expectations and norms whilst subject to a substantially enhanced level of public scrutiny. Students with a considerably widened range of socio-economic and educational backgrounds now progress to higher education, enhancing the demands placed on welfare and academic support services. The nature of learning and teaching has changed dramatically, bringing new expectations of learning resources and ICT infrastructure. Increased public and private investment in university teaching and research has been accompanied by greater requirements to demonstrate outputs, outcomes, efficiency and return on investment. Audit, accountability, ethical, legislative, regulatory and governance regimes are more complex and rigorous. Competition for resources, learners, reputation and prestige is both intense and accompanied by the pressures and realities of consumer behaviour and mass media. All this and more produces an ever more complex operating environment that undoubtedly impacts on the academic endeavour but also generates requirements for a much wider range of professional skills, tasks and roles within university communities, many of which are far removed from the core competencies of academic staff.

OH, East is East, and West is West, and never the twain shall meet
Rudyard Kipling, 'The Ballad of East and West', 1889

There are a number of contributory factors behind the seemingly entrenched division between academic and non-academic staff within higher education institutions. In part, it is based on discussions, beginning in the 1970s and 1980s, of the changing nature of staffing within universities and their professional training and development requirements. Within these, the supporting infrastructure in pre-1992 UK universities was frequently described as an 'academic civil service' or 'academic administration', while in polytechnics and their successors, the post-92 universities, the administration was designed with reference to local authority structures (Whitchurch 2007: 4). In the US and elsewhere, similar models based on governmental support structures that distinguish democratically elected representatives from permanent support staff were used. Under such classifications, members of 'the administration' were seen not only as different in type or species from academic staff, but also subservient both to them and to academic activity. The civil service model is inherently divisive, whatever its merits in emphasizing notions of public service within professional administrative training and practice, in enhancing the availability of expert technical advice to support collegial academic decision making and governance, and in facilitating institutional memory and continuity. It is, in many regards, a caste system within which members of the administration would always be denied entry to the ruling elite and so to parity of respect and esteem. Interestingly, 'the administration' has itself in many institutions become an unfavourable term amongst academic colleagues, seen as set apart from and antithetical to the pursuit of research, scholarship and teaching. This is almost certainly related to the perception, and perhaps reality, of an increasing alignment between the administration and the management, especially at senior levels, of institutions, where management is, needless to say, also seen as a hostile force. It is interesting to observe, indeed, that 'the management' or 'the administration' in universities is often used as a term which encompasses both professional service staff and senior academic staff who have been appointed to management and organizational leadership positions.

The growth of managerialism is inexorably linked in the collective experience of what is still a large proportion of the contemporary academic workforce in the UK to the 1985 Jarratt Report (CVCP 1985) which heralded the removal of academic tenure, the replacement of collegial by corporate and executive governance, and the model of universities as competitive knowledge factories:

> To my mind one of the most damaging inquiries into higher education over the last half-century was the Jarratt report published in 1985 . . . a mischievous and malevolent investigation which, *inter alia*, popularised if it did not invent the notion that students are 'customers', which foisted on the sector the delusion that factory-floor 'performance indicators' are entirely suited to a higher-education setting, and which led to the abolition of academic tenure and the concomitant triumph of managerialism in the academy. (Alderman 2009)

The Jarratt Report was, of course, commissioned by the Committee of Vice-Chancellors and Principals and so viewed by rank-and-file academics as the self fulfilling prophecy of an increasingly powerful vested interest group, working alongside a national government known to have a sceptical view of the value for public money being expended on the higher education sector.

From the mid-1980s at least, non-academic staff within higher education institutions have often been, and continue to be, viewed by academic colleagues as the agents of internal or external forces that are regarded as hostile to, or inhibitors of, the objectives of academic enquiry:

> [Non-Academic] staff may be perceived by academic colleagues to be aligned with the policies they have been charged with implementing, whether or not they have been responsible for creating them. These policies may be generated internally, such as the restructuring of departments and research groupings, or externally, such as quality audit. Professional managers may also be regarded as agents of government in imposing unwelcome requirements upon the academic community. In this they become identified as perpetrators rather than interpreters of government policies. (Whitchurch 2006)

Do we have, then, a deep and treacherous fissure through the heart of our higher education institutions, rooted in concepts of typological superiority and subservience, suspected fifth column conspiracies, fear of being outnumbered, and resentment at the wasteful consumption of resources by the lower orders? This may be hyperbole, but it does reflect the nature of the language and behaviour regularly observed throughout the academy. When looked at objectively, this is an utterly bizarre state of affairs, and highly counterproductive to the academic endeavour. Such beliefs, vocabulary and conduct surely have little place in modern organizations or professional practice, especially so within communities of colleagues typified by their intellect, eloquence and liberal democratic values. It would be entirely wrong, however, to attribute the blame solely to the academic members of those communities.

Dissertations stood in place of action; a million of reports were written every year; bureaucracy was enthroned! Records, statistics, documents, failing which France would have been ruined, circumlocution, without which there could be no advance, increased, multiplied, and grew majestic.
Honoré de Balzac, *Bureaucracy*, 1824

Many of the activities in which non-academic members of university staff engage, and many of the behaviours that they exhibit while pursuing them, regularly seem to contribute little to the pursuit of research, scholarship and education. Undoubtedly this is in part because the activities for which they are employed are often directly related to processes the purpose and value of which are not recognized by the academy. Furthermore, such processes frequently involve complex rules and regulations, and require academic time to be spent on bureaucracy, which is inevitably an additional burden and unwelcome distraction. Notorious examples from the UK are external quality assurance of learning and teaching, and the periodic national assessment of research quality, while the US has led the way in the development of legislative, financial and ethical compliance in research management. Whatever the intent behind, and (arguable) improvements arising from, such processes, guilt by association readily attaches to those paid to operate them. Such guilt also, of course, attends universities' own corporate processes and arrangements: strategic planning, performance measurement and management, and financial, technical, environmental and legislative regulations.

As has been discussed, many of these administrative, management and governance procedures are the product of external pressures for increased accountability for use of public funds, increasingly complex legislative and regulatory frameworks, or student and other 'customer' demands. To lay blame upon those whose roles are frequently to implement these policies for their impact on academic activity may seem unreasonable. What is counter-productive, however, is the way in which non-academic staff sometimes go about their business or view their academic colleagues as the major impediment to getting the job done. The point of the exercise all too often becomes focused on completing the task at hand, or enforcing the rules. Financial strategy and regulation in a university, for example, should be about optimizing the resources available for teaching and research yet often implementation is hindered by petty squabbling over control of 'discretionary' funds, over-budget surpluses and in-year savings. Strategic planning, rather than debating, building engagement around, and articulating shared goals and ambitions, becomes a statistical battleground and bun fight for a share of scarce new and replacement staff posts. The focus of human resource management is transformed from attracting, retaining and developing the required richness and diversity of talent into a tangle of grading forms, equal opportunities compliance, tightly policed selection procedures and mandatory health and safety training.

For bureaucrats, rules mean power, and in some cases non-academic staff have become experts at exacting revenge through regulation. At its worst, regulatory compliance can be used to maintain influence and control over academic colleagues through in-depth knowledge of internal and external policies, labyrinthine funding models, and guardianship of the rule book, all in the guise of advising, interpreting and supporting.

The rapid professionalization of university administration over the last 30 years, while undoubtedly delivering substantial benefits in terms of the skills, expertise and capabilities available to universities through their non-academic employees, has also served to reinforce entrenched positions. An extensive practitioner literature had been built up by the many member-ship organizations that cater for both general and specialist administra-tors, much of which is professionally valuable, but which also includes a healthy dose of self-justification. Perhaps the weakest argument of all within this apologia is that significantly larger and ever-growing numbers of non-academic staff are a necessary evil simply to enable universities to cope with the exponential rise in the external requirements with which they must comply. The administration, by this argument, stands as the bulwark between the ivory towered academic and the cruel world beyond, and so must be constantly reinforced.

Most businesses choose to respond to increasing external regulatory requirements by striving for corresponding efficiency gains: university administrations have too often used them as an excuse for diverting more resources away from their primary business activities. In evolving, out of necessity, into more business-like organizations, many universities have struggled to assimilate and adapt good business practice for their own needs. A focus on structure and function, rather than objectives and outcomes, in designing and delivering university administrations and services, has created inefficiencies, disconnects and a general ungainliness. Furthermore, universities have often tended both to attempt to overcome such deficiencies and to respond to changing external priorities through accretion rather than re-engineering, further exacerbating, rather than resolving, these weaknesses.

But there is neither East nor West, Border, nor Breed, nor Birth,
When two strong men stand face to face, tho' they come from the ends of the earth!
Rudyard Kipling, 'The Ballad of East and West', 1889

Kipling's poem is, of course, a powerful treatise on the achievement of co-operation and shared success in the face of apparently insurmount-able enmity, cultural difference, mutual misunderstanding and compet-ing interest. There is hope! The scale and pervasiveness of non-academic staffing in contemporary higher education institutions is such that it can no longer be marginalized or ignored, and no amount of vilification is going to make it disappear. Rather, it represents a rich seam of talent that, properly deployed, could and should be a highly valuable resource. This realization is producing increasingly sophisticated and interesting analysis of the roles of non-academic staff and, importantly, their changing professional engagement with academic colleagues. In their provocatively titled 'Fear and loathing in university staffing', Dobson and Conway observe that 'half or more of the staff working in and for Australian universities is treated as though it is invisible in the broad discourse about those institutions,' (Dobson and Conway 2003: 124) before going on to argue why that is no longer tenable nor appropriate. Their conclusion is salutary:

> The nature of the partnership [between academic and non-academic staff] and what it needs to be to help universities function effectively and to transform to meet the demands of the 21st century should be the focus of our effort and attention from now on. (Dobson and Conway 2003: 132)

Dobson and Conway also note that, while the impact on the academic profession and on higher education institutions of the changing policy, funding and managerial environment in which universities operate has been extensively studied, and very largely from an unfavourable academic viewpoint, 'the impact of change upon the administrative occupation has not been explored with the same vigour' (p. 125). And yet it is just such exploration that is currently providing some of the most interesting insights into the changing nature of leadership, management, agency and collective action within contemporary university communities. The UK Leadership Foundation for Higher Education, for example, has undertaken a major qualitative survey of perceptions of the changing roles and experiences of non-academic staff in universities, both from a range of such staff and their managers, and from heads of institutions. The survey sample was drawn primarily from UK institutions, supplemented with targeted comparative international perspectives from Australia and the US (Whitchurch 2006, 2008). This study was part of a wider set of research projects by the Leadership Foundation examining changing professional and leadership roles, behaviours and challenges, including at the most senior levels of university management and governance (Smith et al. 2007; Bolden et al. 2008; Kennie and Woodfield 2008). Together, these have developed discussion well beyond more traditional analyses of changing roles of non-academic staff, which were characterized by a move from 'administrative' to 'managerial' emphases accompanied by growing professional organization.

The Leadership Foundation's work has produced an interesting categorization of those members of non-academic staff it describes as 'professional staff' (defined as individuals having management roles but not an academic contract; the inadvertent implication that academic roles are not professional is a further demonstration of the challenges of terminology that permeate this whole debate), identifying bounded, cross-boundary, unbounded and blended professionals with a range of identity characteristics for each. Broadly, these categories move further away from 'bounded' professional identities that are determined by functions, regulations, resources and organizational structures as they progress. Cross-boundary and unbounded professionals are characterized by increasing degrees of flexibility, innovation and creativity. The final 'blended' category consists of individuals who occupy a range of hybrid posts spanning professional and academic work (Whitchurch 2008: 11–26). As with most such typological schemes, this is perhaps over-simplistic with its rules, in practice, proven by the many exceptions. There is also an implication that roles become more valuable the less bounded they are, although there is a recognition that each role type is effective in different work contexts. It is, nonetheless, helpfully illustrative of the degree to which non-academic roles have evolved, and continue to develop, and provides a useful framework against which to appraise the varied contemporary working practices and contributions of non-academic staff. Most interestingly, however, the study goes on to identify the emergence of what it calls a 'third space' in universities, between academic and professional domains, across and outwith boundaries and hierarchies. It also considers the legitimization of work in this space, contrasting it with the justice, service, performance and negotiation legitimacies of more conventional 'hard' and 'soft' administrative and managerial activities. Third space working, which is characterized by project orientation, team working (involving both academic and non-academic colleagues), partnership, creativity, adaption, uncertainty and complexity, is legitimated by institutional development and capacity building (Whitchurch 2008: 27–31). In other words, the non-academic contribution becomes directly aligned with pursuit and achievement of the core academic purposes of universities.

This analysis points to exciting possibilities. Although it describes third space working as an as yet atypical, emerging characteristic of professional work in universities largely confined to a small number of relatively new areas of activity (including 'hybrid' areas spanning academic and professional activity), it surely points the way to a much more rewarding and effective mode of interaction and shared endeavour between academic and non-academic colleagues. The legitimacy found in organizational success, in particular, may readily be extrapolated into a model of collective ambition and enterprise capable of being deployed successfully both at the institutional level and within specific projects (and, indeed, at all points of scale between and beyond these). The unifying force is the intended or desired outcome or achievement, towards which the full range and diversity of talents, skills and inventiveness available within groups of colleagues unfettered by their 'class description' may be utilized.

Regard the Franj! Behold with what obstinacy they fight for their religion, while we, the Muslims, show no enthusiasm for waging holy war
Ṣalāḥ ad-Dīn Yūsuf ibn Ayyūb, 1187

Discord between the roles of academic and non-academic staff may be a peculiarly Anglophone perspective. The phenomenon, and more recent attempts to address and overcome it, is played out principally within the context of the UK, North American and Australasian higher education systems. The situation in other national systems is often radically different and much more appreciative of the professional contributions of all colleagues.

The area of research management and administration provides an example. In a prescient commentary from 1987, the profound challenges being presented to established models of both research and research management and administration in the US by growing global competition in science and technology development, often backed by aggressive national policies and funding regimes, were noted:

> Research programs in Europe and Japan often contain significant direct public funding. They also increasingly involve cooperative forms of research management, typically involving a number of industrial corporations, and often including public or university research laboratories. These new programs have structures that may prove to be incompatible with traditional methods of research management, especially the single enterprise and university-based models. As a result, the field of research management is experiencing dramatic pressures for change in many of its fundamental dimensions. (Davidson 1989)

Universities in the US were ill equipped to respond to the rapidly advancing success of research systems elsewhere in the world, which were characterized by a focus on targeted outcomes and collaborative modes of operation. Many more national systems have emerged since then, and tend towards these same characteristics. Furthermore, they display a very different attitude towards academic and non-academic roles, seeing both as essential contributors to the achievement of the desired objectives, each requiring development and support to operate effectively. This is, in part, because non-academic roles are often developed within the remit of academic staff rather than through a separate set of employees. A survey of research management practice in the African and Caribbean regions in 2010 found that over half of academic staff in universities spend between 10 per cent and 40 per cent of their time on research management and administration, while the majority of staff classing themselves as research managers are also engaged in academic work (Falk 2011). It is also, however, because the development of capacity and expertise in professional, non-academic functions, is seen as a means to an end; the end being the economic and social outcomes that are the drivers of national research policy and funding.

The vision of the Society of Research Administrators International (which, despite its name, is one of the two major professional organizations for North American research managers and administrators) is 'Fostering excellence in research administration' and its mission 'is dedicated to the education and professional development of research administrators working in varied organizational settings as well as the advancement of research administration as a profession around the world' (SRA International 2012). This is fundamentally an organization concerned with the professional welfare of a discrete sub-set of the higher education workforce for its own sake. The mission and objectives of the South African Research and Innovation Management Association stand in sharp contrast:

1. Professional development and capacity building of those involved in managing research and/or innovation.
2. Promotion of best practice in the management, administration and support of research and innovation to create value for education, public benefit and economic development.
3. Creation of awareness in academic and public forums of the value of a stronger research and innovation system and the contribution it can make to economic and social development.
4. Advocacy of appropriate national and institutional policy in support of research and innovation and participation in the development and testing of policy.
5. Taking the lead in research and innovation management improvement within Southern Africa, incorporating guidelines for the various components of the research and innovation cycle.
6. Advancement of science, technology and innovation, including addressing the asymmetries in access to, and diffusion of, knowledge between 'North' and 'South'. (SARIMA 2012)

The concerns of SARIMA are with the societal benefit created by successful research, addressing global inequalities, and the welfare of 'those involved' in this endeavour rather than creating a separate professional identity for them. The perspective from national systems outside the Anglophone tradition exemplifies the primacy of purpose and the collective endeavour over the narrow concerns of separate academic and non-academic factions.

One love, One heart, Let's get together and feel all right
Bob Marley, 'One Love/People Get Ready', 1977

The roles of non-academic staff in modern universities, then, whatever their functional details, are to achieve the aspirations and objectives of those universities. In this they find common cause with their academic colleagues. Those aspirations and objectives, of course, are complex and the product of ongoing debate, reflection, discussion and consensus within the community of each university as it continues to develop, grow and evolve in response to emerging academic interests and the concerns of students, governments, research funders and partners, and others. If members of either, or both, groups of colleagues cannot align themselves to this collective endeavour, and display the professional behaviours and skills necessary to its success, then either they are in the wrong jobs or this must be regarded as a failure of leadership. For the task of ensuring that all of the talents available within a university are engaged effectively in pursuit of shared goals defines the role of leaders in higher education institutions. That leadership challenge does not rest only with the top management teams of universities: it is a responsibility of every member of the community with a leadership role, whether formally determined or not, non-academic or otherwise.

REFERENCES

Alderman, G. (2009), Higher Education in the United Kingdom since 1945 (Review Article). *Times Higher Education*, 30 July.

Bolden, R., G. Petrov and J. Gosling (2008), *Developing Collective Leadership in Higher Education*. Exeter: Centre for Leadership Studies, University of Exeter.

Committee of Vice-Chancellors and Principals (CVCP) (1985), *Steering Committee for Efficiency Studies in Universities (Chairman Sir Alex Jarratt) Report*; London.

Davidson, W. H. (1989), The global research race: new models of research management. Research management review: *Journal of the National Council of Research Administrators*, **3** (1) (Spring), pp. 7–16.

Dobson, I. and Conway, M. (2003), Fear and loathing in university staffing: the case of Australian academic and general staff. *Higher Education Management and Policy*, **15** (3) (November), pp. 139–52.

Falk, E. (2011), *Survey of Current Research Management Practice within the Africa and Carribean Regions*. London: Association of Commonwealth Universities.

Ginsberg, B. (2011), *The Fall of the Faculty: The Rise of the All-Administrative University and Why It Matters*. Oxford: Oxford University Press.

Greene, J. P., B. Kisida and J. Mills (2010), *Administrative Bloat at American*

Universities: The Real Reason for High Costs in Higher Education. Phoenix, AZ: Goldwater Institute policy report no. 239, August.

Kennie, T. and S. Woodfield (2008), *Top Team Structures in UK Higher Education Institutions: Composition, Challenges and Changes.* London: Leadership Foundation for Higher Education.

Mroz, A. (2009), Different players, same side. Leader, *Times Higher Education,* 9 April.

OECD (2011), Centre for Educational Research and Innovation; *Education at a Glance 2011: OECD Indicators.* Paris: OECD Publishing.

Smith, D., J. Adams, and D. Mount (2007), *UK Universities and their Executive Officers: the Changing Role of Pro-Vice-Chancellors.* London: Leadership Foundation for Higher Education.

Society of Research Administrators (SRA) International (2012), *Vision and Mission Statement,* http://www.srainternational.org/sra03/template/tntbAB.cfm?id=557 (accessed 30 September 2012). Falls Church, VA: SRA International.

South African Research and Innovation Management Association (SARIMA) (2012), *Mission Statement.* http://www.sarima.co.za/about-us/ (accessed 30 September 2012), Pretoria, South Africa: SARIMA.

Whitchurch, C. (2006), *Professional Managers in UK Higher Education: Preparing for Complex Futures*; Interim Report. London: Leadership Foundation for Higher Education.

Whitchurch, C. (2007), The changing roles and identities of professional managers in UK higher education. *Perspectives: Policy and Practice in Higher Education,* **11** (2), 53–60.

Whitchurch, C. (2008), *Professional Managers in UK Higher Education: Preparing for Complex Futures,* final report. London: Leadership Foundation for Higher Education.

11. The global reach of universities: leading and engaging academic and support staff in the internationalization of higher education

Elspeth Jones

1 INTRODUCTION

Universities today must reach across national boundaries beyond traditional approaches to the dissemination of knowledge and ideas. Globalization, intensifying competition in international education, mobile students, institutional rankings and stakeholder demand are just some of the compelling drivers for international engagement. These distinct economic and stakeholder pressures are becoming progressively more powerful, with the result that the concept of internationalization has 'moved from the fringe of institutional interest to the very core' (Brandenburg and de Wit 2010: 31) and it is now an 'institutional imperative, not just a desirable possibility' (Hudzik 2011: 7).

The field of internationalization practice and research is emerging as a meta-discipline, with its literature informing differing levels and types of strategy and engagement both at institutional level and within individual subject disciplines. It is no longer sufficient for university leaders to frame their international engagement through uni-dimensional interpretations of internationalization such as student mobility, international recruitment or research partnerships. Nor are simplistic measurements of internationalization appropriate, such as the number of students on exchange programmes, the number of staff involved in collaborative international research, international student percentages or programmes delivered overseas or, for institutions in non-English-speaking countries, the number of programmes delivered in English. A more qualitative evaluation of the impact of internationalization practice, according to institutional mission, is also required in order for the real benefit of such engagement to be understood and valued in its own right.

Yet internationalization is a vehicle for achieving wider goals not an objective in its own right. Internationalization facilitates an inclusive, intercultural dimension to the teaching, research, service, and the commercial and entrepreneurial pursuits of a contemporary university. As a consequence, 'global reach' involves not only international undertakings but also local, regional, national and, crucially, internal systems, processes and organizational culture. Central to this is the engagement of staff across the institution, both academic faculty and professional support staff and, in order to achieve this, engaged and encouraging leadership will be required at a range of levels.

Integrating internationalization means developing the culture, attitudes and practices that enable international and cross-cultural perspectives and approaches to permeate all aspects of university life. This chapter considers how such a definition of integrated internationalization might be reflected at the institutional level. It offers a number of indicators of successful achievement and considers a model for evaluating progress, while taking account of the leadership and staff development issues that arise.

2   THE 'GLOBAL REACH' OF UNIVERSITIES AND DRIVERS FOR INTERNATIONALIZATION

Internationalization as a process is evolving 'as the complexities and nuances of internationalization become apparent' (Luker 2008: 11). Our enhanced understanding of internationalization in all its forms has developed, in part, as a consequence of its implementation not only in western countries but also in emerging contexts across Asia, Africa and Latin America. Jones and de Wit (2012) discuss the different thematic and geographical interpretations of internationalization and identify eight key priorities for the next phase, as the concept of internationalization itself becomes 'globalized'.

The many dimensions of 'global reach' result in each institution rightly adapting the concept for their own purposes, and thus the term 'internationalization' varies according to university mission, aims and strategies. Some universities take it to mean establishing and enhancing their position among the global elite as measured by quality rankings. In pursuit of this they seek internationally renowned academics, to attract the highest performing students who will add value to what may be long-established traditions of excellence in research and teaching, as well as partnerships with universities of similar prestige. For others, the focus of internationalization is how this will enhance the student experience, whether through staff and student mobility or other forms of international and intercultural engagement. Turner and Robson (2008) argue that university approaches to internationalization range from 'symbolic' to 'transformational', and it is through the transformational end of the spectrum that universities can offer students new insights and perspectives.

For other universities, the driver is largely economic in that international student fees in many countries assist financial stability. As financial pressures and student demand have led to market growth in international education, the competition for students has increased, and institutions with similar histories, missions and programmes now vie to recruit ever-higher numbers of international students onto home campuses or to collaborative programmes with international partners and other forms of trans-national education overseas. Australian higher education recently celebrated 25 years of entrepreneurial international activity, an event marked by the publication of a wide-reaching volume (Davis and Mackintosh 2011), indicating that Australia 'has become a world leader in international education through innovative promotion and marketing; pathway programs; offshore delivery of courses; teaching and learning; outbound mobility; strong quality assurance, student support and consumer protection arrangements; linkages with migration and employment, and an entrepreneurial business focus' (Thompson and Connelly 2011: 5).

Although international recruitment may take place as part of a wider internationalization strategy, there can be dangers in a purely commercial approach, not least when it is seen as synonymous with internationalization rather than one element of it. Archer et al. suggest that the pace of growth in the number of internationally mobile students has not always been matched by equally high levels of support for these students (2010). Nevertheless it is widely accepted that there are clear benefits to universities of managed international engagement and a report for the Observatory on Borderless Higher Education offers three models as a basis for this (Gore 2012). The International Association of Universities offers a word of caution, noting the potential disadvantages of internationalization as well as the benefits, and encouraging universities to take these into account as they progress their global efforts (IAU 2012).

A further key driver for internationalization relates to graduate employability. Universities, particularly in the global north, seek a distinctive niche for themselves in comparison with others in the same market segment and internationalization may be one means of achieving this. Claims of preparing graduates to 'meet the challenge of a globally interconnected world', 'to be workforce-ready global citizens' or 'ready for a global career trajectory' are readily found on the websites of universities aiming to distinguish themselves from competitors. Yet it seems indisputable that unless we offer global perspectives within our curricula, we are not preparing students effectively for the world they will face after their studies. Zimitat (2008: 136) argues that 'even if domestic graduates never leave their own country, on graduation they will be forced to compete in international, or multi-national, work and discovery environments'. Webb takes this further:

> As part of their preparation to live and work in a globalising world, graduates need increasingly well-developed lifelong learning skills and attitudes, including an international perspective. They need to interpret local problems within a wider and global framework and to judge the importance of global phenomena for their own lives and work. Internationalisation of the curriculum therefore incorporates a range of values, including openness, tolerance and culturally inclusive behaviour, which are necessary to ensure that cultural differences are heard and explored. (Webb 2005: 10)

Press reports around the world suggest that employers are seeking graduates with first-hand experience of living and working in other countries and cultural contexts as a response to an increasingly global workplace. With the employability skills gained through international experiences potentially distinguishing one job applicant from another (Jones 2010), student demand is increasing. Recognizing that not all students have the opportunity to study, work or volunteer overseas, many universities are responding by striving to offer global perspectives and an internationalized curriculum for all students (Leask 2012), not simply those who are willing and able to travel (Fielden et al. 2007).

Leggott and Stapleford (2007) demonstrate that international experiences enhance the employability skills of students and note that employers are seeking the kinds of communication, negotiation skills, self-sufficiency and self-efficacy skills that are developed through such experiences. Equivalent results from international volunteering programmes have been reported (Jones 2010) and there is emerging evidence of internationalization on the home campus having similar benefits (e.g. Leask 2010). Emphasizing the transformational power of internationalization (Turner and Robson 2008), Jones and Brown (2007) call for a values-based approach that sees internationalization as a fundamental part of higher education. Bennett (2008) argues for the development of the 'Global Soul', further illustrated in this view from Iran:

> The concept of intercultural learning and dialogue lays the foundation for a shifting sense of one's place in the global arena, from the egocentric and individualist to the concept of integral global diversity, which privileges tolerance, solidarity and a mutual sense of understanding. (Jassbi 2004)

According to these drivers – globally mobile students and programmes, demands of employers and the development of global perspectives for all students – it seems undeniable that universities have a critical role to play in supporting the development of knowledge, skills and attributes that will contribute to enhancing global society (Rammell 2008). Embracing internationalization as a powerful force for change (Taylor 2004) can thus enrich the learning experience for home and international students, enhance employability skills and provide opportunities to develop global citizenship and cross-cultural capability for both personal development and the world of work (Jones 2009).

While stakeholder demand may place students at the heart of the internationalization enterprise, there are clear benefits for academic and support staff from the activities and methodologies that are required of them in order to achieve these student outcomes. Whether researching, supporting international students or delivering programmes overseas, an integrated approach to internationalization extends the advantages of international activity to staff as well as students. Hudzik advocates 'comprehensive internationalization', which he argues, 'shapes institutional ethos and values and touches the entire higher education enterprise' (Hudzik 2011: 6). In seeking to achieve diverse goals, the key to success lies with the individuals delivering the strategy, i.e. the academic and support staff across the institution. An internationalization strategy that does not give sufficient attention to the leadership and development of staff is unlikely to achieve its aims.

3   INTEGRATING INTERNATIONALIZATION

As we have seen so far, the activities, opportunities and issues encompassed by 'global reach' present many and varied leadership challenges, particularly in leading institutional change. Middlehurst (2008) notes that leadership for internationalization occurs at many levels across an institution, and identifies a number of potential pitfalls including lack of co-ordination, lack of clarity over roles and responsibilities and failure to gain internal support from faculties, departments or the governing body.

Given such a wide range of factors potentially involved in achieving internationalization goals, an equally broad set of leadership and staff development questions will follow. However if a university has as its goal an integrated strategic approach that is 'transformational' for students, staff and the institution rather than merely 'symbolic' (Turner and Robson 2008), what are the internal, organizational issues to be considered? It might be argued that an institution of this kind would see students

5. Student diversity

6. Guidance and support for students outside the classroom

4. International campus culture and informal curriculum

7. Staff development, recognition and reward – all staff

3. Internationalization of the formal curriculum for all students

Globally competent graduates

8. Broad and deep international partnerships

9. Resources follow strategy

2. Governance, leadership and management

1. Rationale and strategy for internationalization

10. Monitoring, reflection, evaluation and review

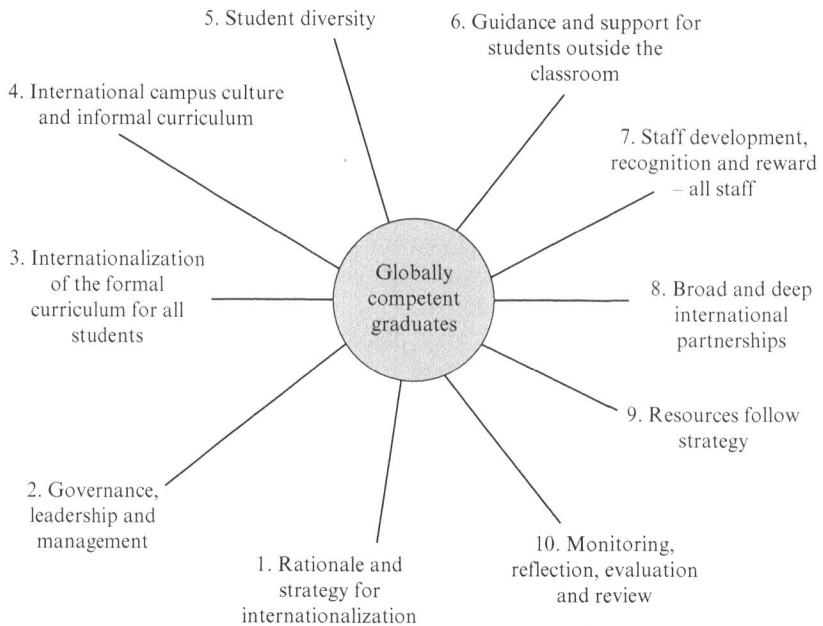

Figure 11.1   Ten key elements of integrated internationalization

at the heart of the internationalization effort and its ultimate beneficiaries, so what are the key elements that will help to bring this about? Figure 11.1 offers ten key indicators as a benchmark. Each indicator is explored in more detail below.

3.1   Rationale and Policy or Strategy for Internationalization

Indicator
An effective and comprehensive policy or strategy for internationalization linked to the university's vision and values is clearly communicated to and understood by academic and support staff at all levels across the institution as well as academic committees, the governing body and external stakeholders.

Explanation
Clarity of purpose and sharing of vision is generally seen as the starting point for any strategy, but assumes greater importance when it comes to 'global reach'. Given the many and diverse interpretations of internationalization, depending on institutional mission, it is crucial that all

staff understand what their own university means by this term. Is the university planning to engage in new international partnerships and networks? Will trans-national delivery follow and what does that mean for curriculum and pedagogy? Is recruitment of students the primary focus? How will internationalization for home students tie in with the university's approach to multiculturalism? What international opportunities will there be for students? Is there a plan to engage employers and other stakeholders in this global reach? Will an 'international outlook' be expected of students on graduation? What of international staff – does the university aim to harness their experience and expertise? The rationale for internationalization will be accepted most readily if it ties in with the existing vision for the institution and with its values, and it is made clear how the term is to be understood in the context of the individual institution.

Differing interpretations of the term 'internationalization', combined with what may be limited international experience, could lead staff to develop their own expectations and understandings unless the goals are made clear. Engaging staff in making the rationale explicit, consulting widely on the development of the internationalization strategy, ensuring effective debate and appropriate staff development can encourage support for the resulting plans. This will only be effective, however, if the strategy is real and part of everyday life, with milestones indicating achievement, not merely a paper exercise subject to annual review by university committees. The 'message' in the strategy and the encouragement of all staff in achieving the strategic objectives needs regular reinforcement, including through departmental and faculty plans.

Internationalization is most successful when seen as an enabling factor in the achievement of wider corporate goals rather than as an aim in itself. When it is part of institutional language and culture rather than a separate objective, it can become embedded as one aspect of everything the university does. Thus, consideration of how internationalization can support and enrich learning, teaching, research or curriculum development or how it can enhance employability is more likely to engage staff interest than asking how we can change our approach in order to deliver internationalization. The means by which the rationale and strategy are developed and communicated will depend on organizational culture, but governing bodies and stakeholders, such as employers, as well as academic and support staff all have contributions to make. Integrated or comprehensive internationalization involves every aspect of university life and consequently all staff. One means by which culture change for internationalization was achieved at Leeds Metropolitan University was through daily 'International Reflections' by staff and students (Jones 2007), illustrating different aspects of internationalization as experienced by those involved.

In its seven years, over 1600 articles of 200 words reflected progress and encouraged students and staff to participate.

3.2 Governance, Leadership and Management

Indicator
The importance and relevance of internationalization is recognized by senior leaders and communicated as such across the institution. It is explicit in all key university policies and strategies, incorporated into planning processes, delivered through normal line management routes across academic and corporate services and reported on annually to Governors and/or Senate. Amongst other strategies this includes policies for assessment, learning, and teaching, research strategies, a human resources policy, library resourcing and operations, and food and accommodation policies.

Explanation
By engaging staff and stakeholders, the message is reinforced that internationalization is important and relevant to all university activities as one aspect of debate. As a matter of course it can be incorporated into key university policies and strategies and as a regular function of planning processes. For example, it might be expected that the human resources policy take account of staff recruited from other countries, their specific support needs on arrival and how they may be engaged to support the inter-cultural competence development of staff with more limited international and/or intercultural experience. The research strategy could be specific about how to facilitate international collaboration for early career researchers and how these experiences will support curriculum development. Staff development and appraisal policies might incorporate opportunities for staff exchange and international volunteering. The learning, teaching and assessment policy may include strategies to promote intercultural learning. Library policy could mean specific support for those who do not speak English as a first language and group learning spaces with tutorials facilitated by an English language specialist. University accommodation policies could take account of students who need family accommodation or who do not feel comfortable sharing flats with younger students making the most of living away from home for the first time. Food services might offer choices reflecting religious and cultural diversity, such as meat-free, halal or kosher food.

Incorporating internationalization into all aspects of university policy in this way means that delivering and evaluating the internationalization strategy, along with relevant staff development, can be embedded into normal line management and appraisal routes across academic and corporate services.

3.3   Internationalization of the Formal Curriculum for All Students

Indicator
Internationalized curricula across the institution – in terms of content, pedagogy, assessment processes and graduate outcomes – demonstrate the impact of global issues on a given discipline and related professions along with the role and impact of that discipline in the global context. Curricula are accessible to and appropriate for international students and those from diverse cultural backgrounds. Varied international mobility opportunities support the internationalized curriculum. These may include academic study abroad, work placements, group study tours, international volunteering and service learning. Intercultural learning opportunities are available within the local community for those unable or unwilling to travel.

Explanation
According to Leask:

> Internationalisation of the curriculum is the incorporation of an international and inter-cultural dimension into the content of the curriculum as well as the teaching and learning processes and support services of a program of study. An internationalised curriculum will engage students with internationally informed research and cultural and linguistic diversity. It will purposefully develop their international and intercultural perspectives as global professionals and citizens. (Leask 2009: 209)

Leask's emphasis on pedagogy is supported elsewhere. 'Internationalising curricula is not just about content, it also requires changes in pedagogy to encourage students to develop critical skills to understand forces shaping their discipline and challenge accepted viewpoints' (Zimitat 2008: 143), while Aulakh et al. argue that:

> internationalisation includes teachers and students learning from each other, meeting the needs of overseas, offshore [i.e. those studying on programmes overseas] and local students, creating interdependence between students, viewing our professional practice from diverse perspectives, using culturally inclusive teaching practices, accessing teaching and learning resources which reflect diversity, and offering high quality courses which are internationally relevant. (Aulakh et al. 1997: 15)

Internationalization of the formal curriculum can offer creative assessment, learning and teaching approaches for staff willing to engage seriously with the multicultural dimensions of their classrooms. It can facilitate the extension of comfort zones in a controlled manner by challenging cultural assumptions and extending knowledge and experience through the responses of fellow students (Jones and Caruana 2010). Killick (2006) articulates a strategic framework to support the delivery of cross-cultural capability and global perspectives across the curriculum within individual discipline areas, with the help of a series of enabling questions. Internationalization has since been embedded further (Leeds Metropolitan University 2011), with a 'Global Outlook' identified as one of three graduate attributes. Leask (2012) offers an extensive range of ideas for curriculum internationalization, along with a range of resources including discipline-specific literature. Work within the disciplines is a key aspect of embedding an internationalized formal curriculum and engaging staff within their subject disciplines will be crucial to success.

Internationalizing the formal curriculum is likely to entail development and training for staff with limited experience and is a prime example of the need for leadership at a range of levels, as noted above (Middlehurst, 2008). Figure 11.2 illustrates a possible model for assimilating curriculum internationalization into an existing university framework. Starting with the overarching leadership of internationalization at

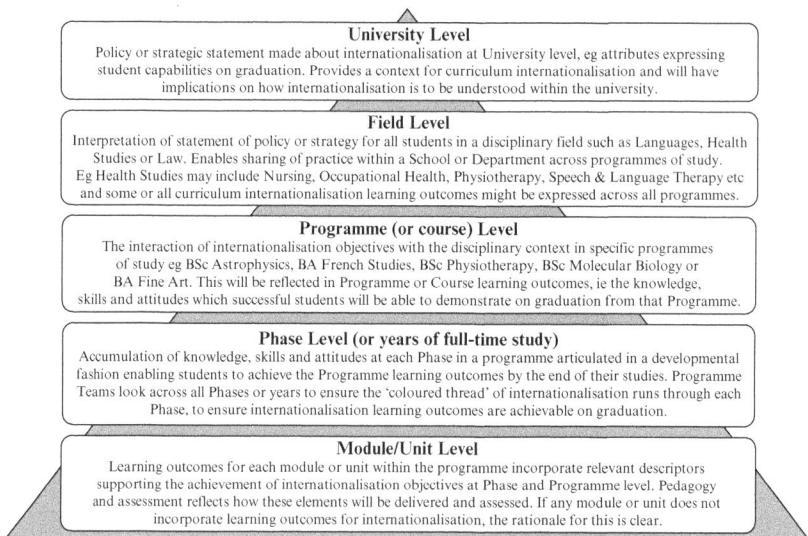

University Level
Policy or strategic statement made about internationalisation at University level, eg attributes expressing student capabilities on graduation. Provides a context for curriculum internationalisation and will have implications on how internationalisation is to be understood within the university.

Field Level
Interpretation of statement of policy or strategy for all students in a disciplinary field such as Languages, Health Studies or Law. Enables sharing of practice within a School or Department across programmes of study. Eg Health Studies may include Nursing, Occupational Health, Physiotherapy, Speech & Language Therapy etc and some or all curriculum internationalisation learning outcomes might be expressed across all programmes.

Programme (or course) Level
The interaction of internationalisation objectives with the disciplinary context in specific programmes of study eg BSc Astrophysics, BA French Studies, BSc Physiotherapy, BSc Molecular Biology or BA Fine Art. This will be reflected in Programme or Course learning outcomes, ie the knowledge, skills and attitudes which successful students will be able to demonstrate on graduation from that Programme.

Phase Level (or years of full-time study)
Accumulation of knowledge, skills and attitudes at each Phase in a programme articulated in a developmental fashion enabling students to achieve the Programme learning outcomes by the end of their studies. Programme Teams look across all Phases or years to ensure the 'coloured thread' of internationalisation runs through each Phase, to ensure internationalisation learning outcomes are achievable on graduation.

Module/Unit Level
Learning outcomes for each module or unit within the programme incorporate relevant descriptors supporting the achievement of internationalisation objectives at Phase and Programme level. Pedagogy and assessment reflects how these elements will be delivered and assessed. If any module or unit does not incorporate learning outcomes for internationalisation, the rationale for this is clear.

Figure 11.2 The Curriculum Pyramid: internationalization of the curriculum within the university framework

university level, which is a critical success factor, as noted in section 3.1, at the next level (Field), leadership for curriculum internationalization might be provided by deans or heads of school. At programme level, programme or course leaders provide curriculum leadership for each programme and there may be other organizational leadership for larger cohorts, e.g. phase or year-group leaders who are responsible for curriculum internationalization in each year or stage of the programme. Module or unit tutors responsible for the 'building blocks' of programmes may work with other tutors on that module/unit and provide leadership to ensure that internationalized learning outcomes effectively permeate the programme of study.

3.4   International Campus Culture and Informal Curriculum

Indicator
An international and multicultural campus culture is evident, including Student Union clubs and societies, and forms the basis of the informal curriculum for all students. The international aspects of university life are celebrated regularly through events, displays and activities that support internationalization at home, and are widely communicated using standard information channels.

Explanation
Going beyond the traditional programme of study, Webb encourages us to 'normalise internationalisation of the curriculum' and offers strategies for doing so that extend beyond the narrow interpretation of curriculum into the student experience as a whole. He defines such normalization as 'turning the ad hoc and uneven efforts of a few enthusiasts into the normal expectations and requirements of the organisation' (2005: 117). Thus, in addition to internationalizing the formal curriculum, opportunities for transformational learning can be offered by the 'informal' curriculum: 'that element of the student experience that is provided by the university beyond the formal programme of study but not assessed within the course' (Jones 2011: 33).

Such learning may indeed be accredited beyond the student's main programme, for example through a Global Leadership Programme (Macquarie University; University of South Australia) or Global Citizen Award (Leeds Metropolitan University), which recognize the informal curriculum in a stand-alone award alongside the formal programme. Examples abound of creative ideas to support intercultural development by this means and these may be based on the home campus or overseas. Examples include international photo competitions or exhibitions (for example, at Brock University, Ontario, Canada's annual 'This is my home' exhibition); festivals (for example, the University of Warwick's support for the student-led One World Week); international/intercultural buddying programmes (Leask 2010); international students or domestic students returning from study abroad visiting local primary or secondary schools to talk of their experiences and support cultural learning (as in Bellarmine University, Louisville, KY); and international volunteering (Jones 2010). Other examples include tandem culture learning, clubs and societies appealing to home and international students, celebrations of international culture and the international dimensions of all aspects of university life.

'Campus internationalization' is a term used in many North American institutions to reflect the process of internationalization becoming part of the fabric and expectations of university life on the home campus. This can be as simple as celebrating the national days of different countries through the menus of campus restaurants, exhibiting the country flags of all international students, promoting study abroad through displays and recruitment events, or showing world maps of all the countries in which the university has partnerships or other activities. Visibly celebrating and engaging students in everyday internationalization sends the message that the university sees it as important.

3.5 Student Diversity

Indicator
Effective processes and actions result in a vibrant, diverse international and multicultural student community as active participants in campus life, and with students being valued for the way in which they enrich class-room and campus culture.

Explanation
The intercultural competence required to operate effectively in global contexts is equally important for living in today's local multicultural and increasingly diverse communities. By treating internationalization as one aspect of student diversity, universities have the potential to exploit the opportunities offered by the wider multicultural context. Bone (2008) emphasizes the importance of a multilateral approach to internationalization as a framework to support international student recruitment. At the same time a multicultural and/or international campus culture is a key element in assisting the internationalization of domestic students and in building 'bridges of tolerance and respect for other cultures' (Kramsch 2002: 272, quoted in Leask 2009).

Recruiting international students to home campuses is an important part of an integrated approach to internationalization. International students have a crucial role 'at the heart of the university as a source of cultural capital and intentional diversity, enriching the learning experience both for home students and for one another, expanding staff horizons, building a more powerful learning community and thus deepening the HE experience as a whole' (Brown and Jones 2007: 2). But it is essential to be aware that merely co-locating students from different cultural backgrounds will not result in intercultural competence development without intervention. Several studies have found that universities are failing to capitalize on the opportunities presented by international and intercultural diversity on campus (Harrison and Peacock 2010a, 2010b; Leask 2009; Montgomery 2010; Summers and Volet 2008; Thom 2010; Volet and Ang 1998, among others). Engagement and integration of students from all cultural and national backgrounds requires effort within the classroom in terms of content and pedagogy, and beyond it through informal curriculum activities. Staff development for internationalization intersects here with broader policies on equality (or equity) and diversity as part of the move towards increasing participation rates in higher education. Indeed, in their study of six UK and Australian universities, Caruana and Ploner (2010), argue that the 'at home' element of internationalization is synonymous with Equality and Diversity.

3.6 Guidance and Support for Students Outside the Classroom

Indicator
Effective systems and services are in place to provide support for incoming international students as well as promoting and encouraging internationalization for all students. As a minimum there will be language, cross-cultural capability, academic and pastoral support and relevant advisory and counselling services.

Explanation
Many universities nowadays provide a range of services for international students that begin from their first point of contact with the university (Ziguras and Harwood 2011). Nevertheless, it is argued that such services can often be improved further, in particular employment and career counselling (Archer et al. 2010).

Support and guidance to enhance internationalization for domestic students has been seen as less of a priority. Counselling of students planning to study abroad is a service that may already be provided. Equally, some universities offer placement services for students wishing to work overseas as part of an accredited programme of study. Others, including Liverpool Hope and Leeds Metropolitan universities offer another form of mobility, and support for this, through international volunteering programmes. However, all the above merely scratch the surface and reach the small percentage of students who choose to work, study or volunteer overseas as part of their university experience. Integrated internationalization calls for a broader range of services for all students, including language learning and opportunities or programmes to develop inter-cultural competence and global perspectives on the home campus or in the local environment. For the kind of activities mentioned in section 3.4 to be effective, there must be appropriate systems of support and advice as well as promotional activity. The Library and various student support services have a significant role to play. This is a key example of why professional support staff need to be engaged in the internationalization effort.

3.7   Staff Development, Recognition and Reward

Indicator
There is a wide-ranging staff development programme to support internationalization, including language and inter-cultural competence development. Identification of need, along with recognition and reward for engaging in any aspect of the international dimension of university life, is offered systematically for all staff through performance review or appraisal and may form part of the promotion and/or salary policies of the institution.

Explanation
As noted elsewhere in the chapter, staff development considerations permeate the indicators outlined here. A separate indicator is used both to emphasize the centrality of staff to the achievement of internationalization aims and also to ensure that consideration is given to all potential development needs for internationalization, not only for academic staff.

Those universities engaging in trans-national delivery of programmes may recognize and provide for the intercultural and/or linguistic needs of staff involved in teaching or supporting those programmes. Equally, appropriate funding for collaborative research overseas or to attend international conferences may already be in place. When it comes to curriculum development and appropriate pedagogy to deliver an internationalized curriculum, alternative approaches may be needed if staff are to help students develop globally informed knowledge, skills and attitudes. The importance of discipline teams or subject groups cannot be underestimated. It is to these that academics will feel greatest loyalty and commitment and the promotion and achievement of internationalization goals will depend on the contributions of the disciplines. Logically, staff development within and for individual disciplines may have a greater likelihood of success. Leask (2012) includes examples of subject-based curriculum internationalization projects along with a number of publications at disciplinary level.

If internationalization is to be viewed as a normal aspect of university life, a system of recognition and reward also needs to be normalized. Embedding this within standard processes of performance review or appraisal will encourage the notion that internationalization is for all staff, whether they be academics or providing professional support. A number of institutions already reward the international activity of staff as a means of encouraging others to take part. Some universities, for example in Australia, require academic staff to participate in at least one international conference a year to ensure that their work is benchmarked internationally. Some staff see the opportunity for international travel as reward in itself.

Staff responsible for leading internationalization at different levels across the institution may well need specific support and development in order to fulfil their role, as may those who are required to teach overseas as part of an offshore programme. However, international and intercultural development opportunities available to all staff, professional support staff as well as academics, may yield unexpected institutional benefits, including renewed commitment to their work and to the internationalization of the university (Jones 2012). Some examples of such programmes include language lessons, workshops on developing cross-cultural capability, learning how to modify language for effective communication with non-native speakers, or inter-cultural volunteering in the local community. Further afield, it may be possible to arrange for staff exchange or attachment with an international partner university, or even the sharing of good practice with equivalent colleagues overseas via video conferencing. Clearly the role of line managers is key to helping identify development needs or opportunities and those managers will require effective support and development if they have insufficient experience themselves. Academic staff may have their own international contacts or research projects and, again, line managers are key in encouraging international engagement among early career academics or those with fewer overseas contacts.

3.8 Broad and Deep International Partnerships

Indicator
Strong and well-maintained international partnerships provide global opportunities for student and staff engagement through research, staff

and student exchange or placement, benchmarking of performance and a bilateral programme of visiting academic and support staff.

Explanation

For some universities success in international partnership is measured by the number of collaborative agreements that have been signed. This may well be at the expense of working with some of those partners to explore a range of opportunities to enhance integrated internationalization. Obvious examples of such learning partnerships include collaborative research or staff and student exchange. Consideration is given less frequently to mutual learning through the benchmarking of practice. This is as likely to involve professional support staff as it does academics. Sharing approaches across national boundaries to governance, leadership, financial or human resource management, student recruitment and information systems, support services or library provision can offer new insights and challenge received wisdom. It also helps to engage support staff in the wider internationalization process (Jones 2012).

3.9   Resources Follow Strategy

Indicator

Resource allocation and the engagement of senior leadership ensure that the commitment to integrated internationalization can be delivered. Travel and human resources policies support international activities and collaborative research.

Explanation

Financial backing for integrated internationalization is required through the resource allocation process. This is one means by which senior leaders and governing bodies can indicate commitment to the activities and processes involved and confirm that these are indeed valued. Appropriate financing of staff development as well as activities aimed at internationalizing the campus and supporting overseas and domestic initiatives for students give clear assurances of dedication to integrated internationalization going beyond mere lip service.

3.10   Monitoring, Reflection, Evaluation and Review

Indicator

A body or individual with over-arching responsibility for internationalization is incorporated within management structures, and active sub-groups report regularly on progress. Continuous enhancement of internationalization activities and strategy is undertaken through feedback, reflection and evaluation processes that inform revisions to policy and practice.

Explanation
In order to ensure the effective delivery of an integrated internationalization strategy, built-in mechanisms can evaluate success and impact, enabling continuous improvement of the approach. While leadership of internationalization needs to be incorporated at different levels across the institution, a critical factor in successful implementation is that a senior leader takes overall responsibility, working with an appropriate overarching body to monitor and evaluate progress, and to effect changes as required.

Figure 11.3 offers a model for evaluating integrated internationalization within an institution, making it clear that Report (quantitative) data must be supported by Return (qualitative) indicators if the impact of initiatives is to be understood. It also stresses the importance of Reflection to effect Revisions to Rationale, Route and Realization.

4   FIVE KEY LEADERSHIP MESSAGES FOR LEADING AND ENGAGING ACADEMIC AND SUPPORT STAFF IN THE INTERNATIONALIZATION OF HIGHER EDUCATION

On the basis of the ten indicators outlined in section 3, a number of leadership lessons for success may be postulated. *The first key message is that the rationale and purpose for internationalization needs to be supported by senior leaders and articulated clearly as a context for the institution's international engagement.* Development for academic and support staff can both assist in achieving the university's objectives and provide a framework for evaluation of progress.

Some academics will feel that they are already engaged in internationalization, while others will not. In positive terms this means that a group of internationalization 'champions' may be available to support institutional goals. The negative side is that certain academics feel that their subject is by definition international, meaning they do not need to work at it. Others may have the sense that they lack experience and do not know how to address the opportunities afforded by internationalization. Others again may be unwilling to 'share' contacts in a country or region where they have worked hard to make inroads. Largely speaking, the staff body can be divided into those who are champions, potential supporters

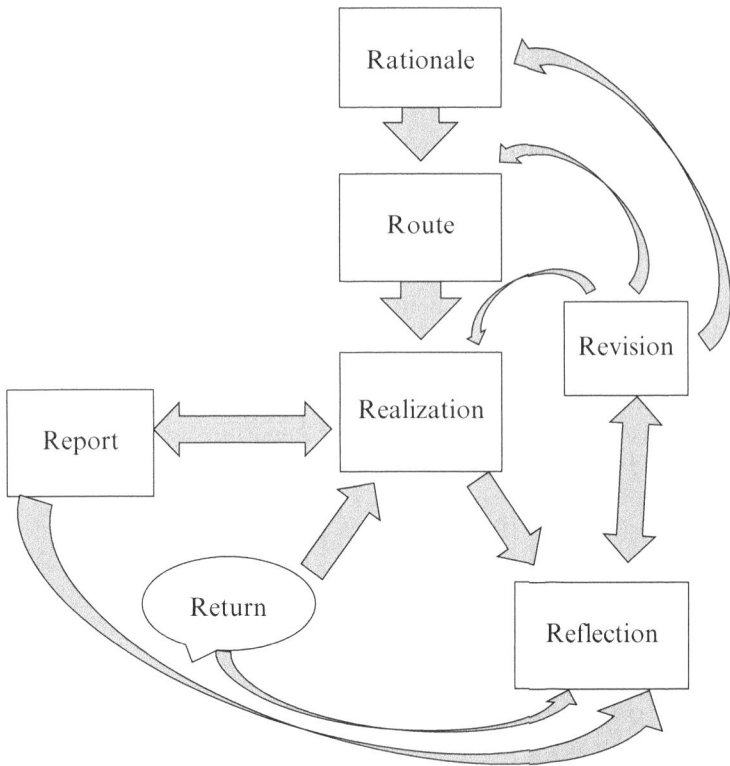

*Figure 11.3   A model for evaluating holistic internationalization. The
University's Rationale or policy for internationalization
is agreed, and a Route (strategy) for delivering this is
chosen. As the various elements of strategy are delivered
(Realization) they generate quantitative Reports to measure
achievement. There may also be qualitative evaluation
(Return), which measures the value of the activity instead
of mere quantitative Reports. Both Report and Return
feed back into Realization, which results in Reflection
on the efficacy of this means of delivering the strategy.
This may or may not result in Revision of either the
Realization (delivery of strategy) or the Route (strategy
for delivering policy objectives) or even the Rationale for
internationalization itself. Either the Report or Return can
also lead directly to Reflection, which may result in similar
Revisions*

or opponents of internationalization. Champions need no convincing, while opponents are unlikely to be won over and the best return on effort may be expected by focusing on the potential supporters. Childress (2010: 140) identifies 'five I's of faculty engagement in internationalization' (Intentionality, Investments, Infrastructure, Institutional Networks, and Individual Support) and a 'typology of strategies' to achieve this (Childress 2010: 143).

However, it is not only academics who create the culture of an internationalized university, but all staff who support the student experience. Indeed, as has been argued in this chapter, in the kind of integrated approach outlined above, no aspect of university life is untouched by internationalization and staff across the university community are crucial to its success: 'the enthusiasm of students, staff, alumni and partner organizations provides the momentum which will sustain enduring institutional change' (Jones and Lee 2008). *The second key leadership message, then, is that internationalization is for all staff, whether in teaching, research, senior administration or support roles.*

Leadership message three is to embed staff development for internationalization into review, recognition and reward processes for academic and professional support staff to make it clear that such engagement is valued. This is the most effective means of ensuring that international and intercultural development opportunities are open to all, whether through appraisal, performance review or staff development processes. It is also a route to ensuring that recognition and reward for furthering the university's internationalization objectives become valued as standard practice in university life, thus encouraging greater participation in the achievement of those goals.

Leadership message four is that resources need to follow commitment to internationalization, whether for staff development, overseas initiatives or to support curriculum internationalization for all, consideration needs to be given to appropriate funding and staffing resources.

Leadership message five is monitor, evaluate and review. Clear indications of progress can provide encouragement to those involved, as well as suggest ideas for future direction and initiatives. Evaluation can also highlight less successful ideas and activities that it is time to alter or bring to an end. Simply reporting quantitative measures such as the number of mobile students each year does not indicate what students have learned from the experience or support an understanding of the kind of overseas or domestically based activities that are the most effective in developing cross-cultural capability or 'intercultural confidence' (Kimmel and Volet 2010).

SUMMARY

This chapter has outlined some aspects of the global reach of universities. It has suggested a definition of integrated internationalization and identified ten indicators of effective implementation. A model for assimilating curriculum internationalization into the existing university framework has been proposed in order to illustrate the need for leadership across the institution at various levels of seniority. It has offered five key leadership messages and proposed a model for evaluating integrated internationalization based on 7Rs – Rationale, Route, Realization, Report, Return, Review, Revise.

Whatever approach to internationalization is adopted within a given university, the key to achieving objectives successfully lies with the academic and support staff throughout the institution. They have the means to ensure that plans are realized and are the crucial contact point with students, who can reap the benefits of the university's internationalization endeavours. If internationalization is to realize its potential as 'one of the most powerful forces for change in contemporary higher education' (Taylor 2004), it is vital that leaders across the university recognize the important contribution to be made by staff and engage them appropriately in this enterprise.

BIBLIOGRAPHY

Archer, W., E. Jones and J. Davison (2010), A UK guide to enhancing the international student experience. UK Higher Education International Unit Research Series/6. London: International Unit. Available at http://www.international. ac.uk/our_research_and_publications/index.cfm (accessed May 2012).

Aulakh, G., P. Brady, K. Dunwoodie, J. Perry, G. Roff and M. Stewart, (1997), *Internationalizing the Curriculum across RMIT University.* RMIT University: Commonwealth Staff Development Fund Internationalization Project Report.

Bennett, J. M. (2008), On becoming a global soul, in V. Savicki (ed.) (2008), *Developing Intercultural Competence and Transformation: Theory, Research and Application in International Education.* Sterling, VA: Stylus.

Bone, D. (2008), Internationalisation of HE: a ten year view. Available at http:// webarchive.nationalarchives.gov.uk/+/http:/www.dius.gov.uk/policy/int_issues _in_ HE.html (accessed May 2012).

Brandenburg, U. and H. de Wit (2010), The end of internationalisation. *EAIE Forum Winter 2010*, pp 30–33 ISSN: 1389-0808. Available at http://issuu.com/ eaie/docs/winterforum2010?mode=embed&layout=http%3A%2F%2Fskin. issuu.com%2Fv%2Flight%2Flayout.xml&showFlipBtn=true&pageNumber=30 (accessed May 2012).

Brown, S. and E. Jones (2007), Values, valuing and value in an internationalised higher education context. In E. Jones and S. Brown (eds) (2007), *Internationalising Higher Education*. London: Routledge.

Caruana, V. and J. Ploner (2010), *Internationalisation and equality and diversity in HE: merging identities*. London: Equality Challenge Unit. Available at http://www.ecu.ac.uk/publications/internationalisation-and-equality-and-diversity-in-he- merging-identities (accessed May 2012).

Childress, L. K. (2010), *The Twenty-first Century University: Developing Faculty Engagement in Internationalization*. New York: Peter Lang.

Davis, D. and B. Mackintosh (for the International Education Association of Australia) (eds) (2011), *Making a Difference: Australian International Education*. Sydney: UNSW Press.

Fielden, J., R. Middlehurst and S. Woodfield, (2007), *Global Horizons for UK Students. A Guide for Universities*. London: Council for Industry and Higher Education. Available at http://www.international.ac.uk/resources/GLOBAL%20horizons.pdf (accessed May 2012).

Gore, T. (2012), Higher education across borders: models of engagement and lessons from corporate strategy. Report for the Observatory on Borderless Higher Education. Available at http://www.obhe.ac.uk/documents/view_details?id=895 (accessed May 2012).

Harrison, N. and N. Peacock (2010a), Interactions in the international classroom – the UK perspective, in: E. Jones (ed.) *Internationalisation and the Student Voice. Higher Education Perspectives*. London: Routledge.

Harrison, N. and N. Peacock (2010b), Cultural distance, mindfulness and passive xenophobia: using Integrated Threat Theory to explore home higher education students' perspectives on 'internationalisation at home'. *British Educational Research Journal* **36** (6), 877–902. Available at http://www.informaworld.com/smpp/content~db=all~content=a914207566 (accessed May 2012).

Hudzik, J. (2011), *Comprehensive Internationalization: From Concept to Action*. NAFSA E-Publications. Available at http://www.nafsa.org/resourcelibrary/Default.aspx?id=24045 (accessed May 2012).

IAU (2012), *Affirming Academic Values in Internationalization of Higher Education: A Call for Action*. International Association of Universities. Available at http://www.iau-aiu.net/sites/all/files/Affirming_Academic_Values_in_Internationalization_of_Higher_Education.pdf (accessed May 2012).

Jassbi, A. J. (2004), *Intercultural Learning and Dialogue: Practical Approaches, Iran*. Available at http://www.iau-aiu.net/id/id_case_studies.html (accessed May 2012).

Jones, E. (2007), International reflections and culture change. In E. Jones and S. Brown (eds) (2007) *Internationalising Higher Education*. London: Routledge.

Jones, E. (2009), Shouldn't all faculties be international? The international faculty at Leeds Metropolitan University, in *Enhancing Learning in the Social Sciences* **2** (1). Available at http://www.eliss.org.uk/CurrentIssueVol21/Commissionedpapers/tabid/249/Default.aspx (accessed May 2012).

Jones, E. (2010), Don't worry about the worries. Transforming lives through international volunteering, in: E. Jones (ed.) *Internationalisation and the Student Voice. Higher Education Perspectives*. London: Routledge.

Jones, E. (2011), Internationalisation, multiculturalism, a global outlook and employability. *Assessment, Teaching and Learning Journal (Leeds Metropolitan University)* **11** (Summer), pp. 21–49. Available at http://repository-intralibrary.leedsmet.ac.uk/open_virtual_file_path/i5747n401688t/Internationalisation,%20 multiculturalism,%20a%20global%20outlook%20and%20employability.pdf (accessed May 2012).

Jones, E. (2012), Challenging received wisdom – personal transformation through short-term international programmes, in J. Beelen and H. de Wit (eds) *Internationalisation Revisited: New Dimensions in the Internationalisation of Higher Education.* Amsterdam: Centre For Applied Research on Economics and Management. Available at http://www.carem.hva.nl/wp-content/uploads/2012/07/Internationalisation-Revisited-CAREM-2012. pdf#page=40 (accessed July 2012).

Jones, E. and S. Brown (eds) (2007), *Internationalising Higher Education.* London: Routledge.

Jones, E. and V. Caruana (2010), Nurturing the global graduate for the 21st century: Learning from the student voice on internationalisation. In E. Jones (ed.) (2010) *Internationalisation and the Student Voice: Higher Education Perspectives.* London: Routledge.

Jones, E. and H. de Wit (2012), Globalization of Internationalization: thematic and regional reflections on a traditional concept, in *Special Edition on Rethinking Internationalization, International Journal of Higher Education and Democracy.* AUDEM.

Jones, E. and Lee, S. (2008), Perspectives and policy and institutional cultures, in C. Shiel and A. McKenzie (eds), *The Global University: The Role of Senior Managers.* DEA publications. Also available online at http://www.think-global. org.uk/resources/item.asp?d=907 (accessed May 2012).

Killick, D. (2006), *Cross-Cultural Capability and Global Perspectives: Guidelines for Curriculum Review.* Leeds: Leeds Metropolitan University. Available at http:// www.leedsmet.ac.uk/Cross_Cultural_Capability_Guidelines.pdf (accessed May 2012).

Kimmel, K. and S. Volet (2010), University students' perceptions of and attitudes towards culturally diverse group work: does context matter? *Journal of Studies in International Education.* Online first July 2010 http://jsi.sagepub.com/content/ early/2010/06/29/1028315310373833.full.pdf+html (accessed May 2012).

Kramsch, C. (2002), In search of the intercultural. *Journal of Sociolinguistics,* **6**, 275–85.

Leask, B. (2009), Using formal and informal curricula to improve interactions between home and international students. *Journal of Studies in International Education* **13** (2), 205–21.

Leask, B. (2010), 'Beside me is an empty chair'. The student experience of internationalism, in: E. Jones (ed.) *Internationalisation and the Student Voice. Higher education perspectives.* London: Routledge, 3–17.

Leask, B. (2012), Internationalisation of the curriculum in action. Australian Learning and Teaching Council National Teaching Fellowship. Available at http://www.ioc.net.au (accessed May 2012).

Leeds Metropolitan University (2011), *Embedding A Global Outlook As A Graduate Attribute At Leeds Metropolitan University.* Available at http://www.leedsmet. ac.uk/A_Global_Outlook_final.pdf (accessed May 2012).

Leggott, D. and J. Stapleford (2007), Internationalisation and employability. In: E. Jones and S. Brown (eds) (2007), *Internationalising Higher Education.* London: Routledge.

Luker, P. (2008), The internationalisation of higher education: shifting the paradigm, in C. Shiel and A. McKenzie (eds) *The Global University: The Role of*

Senior Managers (DEA publications). Also available online at http://www. think-global.org.uk/resources/item.asp?d=907 (accessed May 2012).

Middlehurst, Robin (2008), Not enough science or not enough learning? Exploring the gaps between leadership theory and practice. *Higher Education Quarterly* **62** (4), 322–39.

Montgomery, C. (2010), *Understanding the International Student Experience*. Basingstoke: Palgrave Macmillan.

Rammell, B. (2008), Preface, in C. Shiel and A. McKenzie (eds) *The Global University: the Role of Senior Managers*. DEA publications. Also available online at http://www.think-global.org.uk/resources/item.asp?d=907 (accessed May 2012).

Summers, M. and S. Volet (2008), Students' attitudes towards culturally mixed groups on international campuses: impact of participation in diverse and non-diverse groups. *Studies in Higher Education* **33** (4), 357–70.

Taylor, J. (2004), Toward a strategy for internationalisation: lessons and practice from four universities, *Journal of Studies in International Education* **8** (2), 149–71.

Thom, V. (2010), Mutual cultures: engaging with interculturalism in higher education, in: E. Jones (ed.) *Internationalisation and the Student Voice. Higher Education Perspectives*. London: Routledge.

Thompson, D. and A. Connelly (2011), Programme welcome, in *International Education: The Next 25 Years?*, Australian International Education Conference Programme 2011. Available at http://www.aiec.idp.com/pdf/AIEC2011Program_Web.pdf (accessed May 2012).

Turner, Y. and S. Robson (2008), *Internationalizing the University: an Introduction for University Teachers and Managers*. London: Continuum.

Volet, S. and G. Ang (1998), Culturally mixed groups on international campuses: an opportunity for inter-cultural learning. *Higher Education Research & Development* **17** (1), 5–23. Available at http://www.informaworld.com/smpp/content~db=all~content=a758496236 (accessed May 2012).

Webb, G. (2005), Internationalisation of curriculum: an institutional approach, in: Carroll, J. and J. Ryan (eds) *Teaching International Students, Improving Learning for All*. London: Routledge.

Ziguras, C. and Harwood, A. (2011), Principles of good practice for enhancing international student experience outside the classroom. Report prepared for ISANA, International Education Association. Available at http://www.isana.org.au/index.php?option=com_content&view=article&id=354&Itemid=120 (accessed May 2012).

Zimitat, C. (2008), Internationalisation of the undergraduate curriculum, in: L. Dunn and M. Wallace (eds) *Teaching in Transnational Higher Education*. London: Routledge.

12. Funding higher education in the great recession: an international perspective

David Bell

INTRODUCTION

This chapter focuses on the funding of higher education (HE) during a period of almost unprecedented fiscal austerity. The financial crisis of 2007 and the associated problems of sovereign debt have placed governments, particularly those in Europe and the United States, under huge fiscal pressure. Many have responded, probably unwisely, by introducing fiscal packages comprising a mixture of higher taxes and lower government spending. This strategy is being followed even though the evidence that fiscal austerity will reduce government indebtedness in the short run is very limited.

In some countries, lower public spending has led to reduced government support for HE. Stakeholders are now struggling to respond. There is now greater pressure for 'cost sharing', where the costs of HE do not entirely fall on the taxpayer, but are shared with other stakeholders including students and alumni.

Fiscal decentralization also affects HE funding. In states where many tax and spending decisions are devolved to lower layers of government, there may be widely different pressures on HE budgets across the nation. In the USA, where many of the decisions on HE funding are made at the state level, the differential impact of the Great Recession across states has led to markedly different effects on the funding of state universities.

Relationships between government and HE have typically been uneasy. This is as it should be within a democratic state. But the new financial pressures are leading to realignments of these relationships and a consequent redistribution of power that will affect both higher education itself and, through it, society in general.

There are several competing pressures. First, governments wishing to cut budgets inevitably look at the rationale for retaining each component of state spending. The more immediate the pressure for cuts, the more these are likely to be aimed at programmes of government investment because they carry less political cost. Thus budgets that are most susceptible to cuts are often those that focus on human and physical capital. Second, one way to improve competitiveness is to produce highly skilled graduates. In turn, this is likely to stimulate growth. While these benefits may only become apparent in the medium to long run, this logic argues against the application of cuts in the HE sector. Third, demand for HE rises during economic downturns. This is because during a recession young people have more difficulty finding jobs, and wages are more likely to be depressed, making remaining in, or rejoining, the educational system more attractive.

There is also strong empirical evidence that entry to the labour market during a period of depressed economic activity can have long lasting negative effects on labour market outcomes. Young people are more likely to experience later spells of unemployment and depressed wages, if they join the labour market when it is depressed. They also are more likely to suffer adverse health and well-being outcomes.

This chapter looks at HE funding during a period of fiscal austerity, considering how funding changes might influence the behaviour of potential students, students themselves, graduates and universities. It first considers the policy responses by governments and how these have affected HE. It then considers the reaction of other stakeholders to this new policy environment. Its geographic focus is the US, mainland Europe and the United Kingdom, each of which has been confronted by severe fiscal problems, to which the policy responses have been diverse.

POLICY ENVIRONMENT

This section examines the pressures on HE funding since the onset of recession in 2008. As indicated above, these have varied widely. However, it is worth establishing the baseline from which to compare recent changes in funding for HE. Spending commitments to HE varied widely before the recession. Figure 12.1 shows OECD estimates of the share of GDP spent on HE by its membership. The USA leads the pack, spending more than double the share allocated by several major European economies – Germany, Italy, Spain and the UK. Within Europe, the Scandinavian economies devote more resources to HE. These countries tend to have a strong commitment to the growth-enhancing potential of intellectual capital.

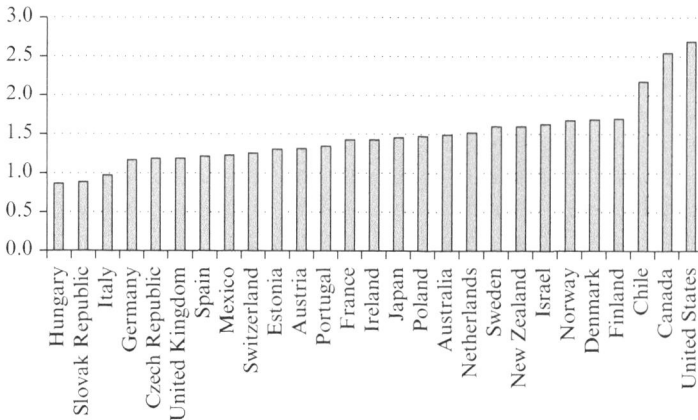

Source: 'Education at a glance', OECD (2012).

Figure 12.1   Spending on higher education as a share of GDP, 2008

THE US

Higher education in the US has been subject to unprecedented pressures during the Great Recession. Key to this has been the collapse in state budgets. Recession was accompanied by a significant fall in tax revenues. Rapid increases in unemployment led to reductions in income tax and other taxes on the payroll. In states where there had been a significant property bubble, such as California and Florida, there were also pressures on state budgets due to falls in property and business taxes.

States on average devote 10.2 per cent of their budgets to HE. This is a very significant share of their budget, and the states' commitment to HE partly explains why the US comes at the top of the international league in the share of its GDP that is devoted to HE. Nevertheless, such a high share is vulnerable when budget cuts are being made.

US states have limited borrowing powers. They were generally unable to raise commercial funding after the onset of recession. During 2008, their financial position continued to worsen. As of the 2011 Q3, state revenues were still 7 per cent below their pre-recession levels. The combined state revenue shortfall between 2009 and 2012 was more than $530 billion. In these circumstances, it was inevitable that institutions would closely examine their commitments to fund HE.

In February 2009, following the election of President Obama, the American Recovery and Reinvestment Act (ARRA) was passed. This

$790 billion stimulus package included $140 billion for states to offset their fiscal deficits. Yet the cash injection typically only covered a share of the shortfall. For example, federal funds only closed 37 per cent of Virginia's 2010 budget deficit and 31 per cent of New York's (Oliff et al. 2009). Not surprisingly, cuts to HE have been implemented by a substantial majority of states because the ARRA package did not fully close their deficit shortfall.

One of the most dramatic contractions in HE spending occurred in California. The state contribution to the budget of the University of California fell by $813 million in 2009–10. Around 1900 employees were laid off and classes were cut. In response, and for the first time, the University of California and the California state university (both of which receive state funding) have restricted enrolment. And the state of Pennsylvania proposed to cut 25 per cent of its state university funding in 2012. By any measure, these are draconian cuts.

Around 75 per cent of students in the US attend state-funded institutions. Given that the recession has reduced the range of alternative opportunities, it is not surprising that the number of students wishing to attend HE has continued to rise since 2008. Between 2007 and 2013, the number of students in public colleges and universities is expected to rise by 1.7 million, putting further strain on the already overextended state university system.

Figure 12.2 shows the number of full-time equivalent students attending state HE institutions between 1986 and 2011. It follows a relentless upward trend from around 7 million in 1986 to almost 12 million in 2011. This is partly the result of population growth, and partly a result of the continuing observable success of graduates in the US labour market.

Figure 12.2 also shows the value of student support per student FTE coming from both the state and the individual on the right-hand axis. The state contribution is shown in dark grey, while the net contribution from tuition fees is shown in light grey. The values are in constant 2011 dollars and show how state contributions have substantially declined since 2000. Increasing contributions from students have partly made up the shortfall, so that in 2011, the overall real value of student support per FTE was only 6 per cent lower than it had been in 2000, given that state support had fallen by 24 per cent over the same period. In 1986, state support comprised 77 per cent of total tuition costs; by 2000 the state share had fallen to 71 per cent and since 2000, it has fallen to 57 per cent. Thus, the size of state contribution to state universities has been in long-run decline. This has accelerated since the start of the recession in 2008 and shows no sign of stopping, given the fiscal difficulties in which states find themselves.

Kane et al. (2003) argue that there are a number of long-term factors affecting the decline in state appropriations for HE. All of these are related

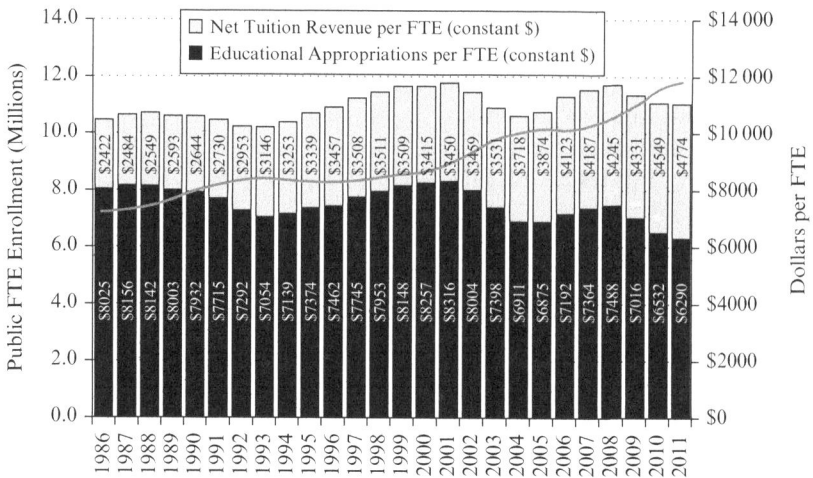

Note: Constant 2011 dollars adjusted by SHEEO Higher Education Cost Adjustment. Education appropriations include ARRA funds.

Source: State Higher Education Executive Officers (SHEEO).

Figure 12.2 Public FTE enrolment, educational appropriations and total educational revenue per FTE, US, fiscal years 1986–2011

to increasing commitments by states to provide health care. First, there was an increase in eligibility for Medicaid during the late 1980s and 1990s. Eligibility was extended to include disabled children. Second, during the 1990s, states were required to extend their Medicaid programmes to cover low-income children and pregnant women. Third, states are required to extend Medicaid to cover low-income beneficiaries of Medicare, the federal health insurance programme. The number of recipients of Medicaid is likely to increase in the future due to demographic change, making it even more difficult for states to provide generous funding to HE. Thus, both the short-term and long-term outlook for US state universities is problematic. Unless there is a return to rapid growth, with associated increases in state revenues, the outlook for the state universities is bleak.

The private universities are perhaps less threatened. Their endowments may have suffered somewhat during the recession, but these may recover even if the economy does not grow substantially. They charge higher tuition fees than the state institutions, and in consequence have a broader funding base.

Reducing budgets for state institutions may have an adverse effect on socio-economic mobility within the US. Grants to students have been indexed on the rate of inflation. Tuition fees have increased much more rapidly than inflation in recent years both in state and private institutions. The real cost of college education has been rising. The average debt of 2009 graduates was $25 000 (debts of black students were, on average, $4000 greater than those of white students). Between March 2001 and March 2011, student debt more than quadrupled to more than $920 billion. Student debt now exceeds the value of credit card debt in the US, and is a potential source of financial instability if unemployment rates continue at historically high levels and increasing numbers graduates default on their college debts.

Even though many students are using debt to access HE, it is now the case that parental background is a better predictor of outcomes for children in the US than in Europe. This contradicts the notion that in comparison with Europe, the US provides a much greater breadth of opportunities in which success can be achieved through one's own efforts.

EUROPE

The Great Recession has had widely differing macroeconomic effects across Europe. Differences in fiscal deficits, public debt and instabilities of the banking system have provoked a variety of fiscal responses. These include dramatic cuts in spending in countries such as Ireland, Greece, Italy, Spain and the UK. Inevitably, this has had consequent effects on HE funding. In others, where the pressures on public spending have been less intense, HE has emerged almost unscathed. Finally, some countries have seen little need for fiscal adjustment and have made a strategic decision to expand HE to promote longer-term economic growth and stability.

The European Union has followed the argument that cuts in HE spending may be counter-productive. José Manuel Barroso, President of the European Commission argued that education had to be a priority if the European Union was to 'emerge stronger and more competitive'. He suggested that with downward pressure on university funding being exerted by deficit-cutting governments, it was 'important to look at alternative and innovative effective governance and funding mechanisms for the higher education sector' Barroso (2011). It is perhaps the UK (specifically England) that has followed this advice most closely by increasing tuition fees well above those charged in the rest of Europe.

The European Commission itself proposes to invest €15.2 billion in education and training and €80 billion in research and innovation between 2014 and 2020 – increases of 68 per cent and 46 per cent respectively compared with the previous seven-year funding period. The objective is to create 'the jobs and ideas of tomorrow' (Barroso 2011). However, as we shall see, institutions in those countries where HE budgets are being cut may find it difficult to compete successfully for this additional funding. This initiative may have the unintended consequence of reinforcing the relative strength of universities in northern Europe relative to those in the south.

We now list alphabetically a number of European countries, describing in each case recent pressures on their HE budget.

France

Prior to the recession, France planned to increase funding for HE. Rather than cutting back, the Sarkozy government planned to increase investment in HE, irrespective of the debt consequences. President Hollande's lack of enthusiasm for austerity measures might suggest that he will follow a similar course to his predecessor. France faces fiscal pressures much less extreme than those facing the UK, Ireland or Spain. Nevertheless, to continue investing in HE in these circumstances is a relatively courageous decision.

Germany

As in the United States, much of the funding for German universities comes not from the federal authorities, but from the *länder* (states). Unlike most European economies, the German economy has few fiscal worries and in consequence has been able to grow its HE sector. For example, it has recently moved towards full-cost research funding.[1] The federal government has also progressed an *Exzellenzinitiative* ('excellence initiative'), which will result in funding being much more concentrated in a group of elite institutions. This has particularly upset the *länder*, whose control over HE is being diluted by this policy. This policy of targeting research excellence suggests that Germany wishes to become perhaps the pre-eminent provider of HE in Europe, a role that has traditionally been the domain of the UK.

Italy

Fiscal pressure has been intense in Italy. Previously moderate cuts in spending for universities have been replaced by a more Draconian regime that will see funding reduced by around 20 per cent by 2013. A crippling public sector debt and an extremely sluggish economy mean that continuing downward pressure on HE funding in Italy is almost inevitable.

Ireland

The Irish government has had to bail out one of its banking institutions at a cost of around €50 billion. To effect this bailout, it had to take loans from the IMF and European Central Bank. Repayment will be staged over the next 15 years and will prove a significant drain on tax revenues. In these circumstances, it is not surprising that Irish universities were forced to cut their staff headcount by 3 per cent in 2009 and a further 3 per cent in 2010 even though demand for places was still rising. A further cut in funding of 5 per cent was imposed in 2012. Interestingly, the cuts to HE have been larger than the cuts applied to the rest of the education budget. This is partly being offset by the student contribution towards tuition, which is scheduled to rise by 12.5 per cent to €2250. Eligibility rules for student maintenance grants are also being tightened. Extreme fiscal pressure on the state will mean that Irish HE is facing a difficult future in the short, medium and long term unless alternative sources of funding can be found (THE 2012).

Netherlands

In comparison with the rest of Europe, fiscal pressures in the Netherlands have been mild. Nevertheless, it has adopted a very tight fiscal stance and argued strongly in favour for the adoption of tighter fiscal rules across Europe. One consequence has been the decision of the Dutch government to end student grants and to replace them with the loans.

The coalition government has also announced cuts of up to €500 million (US$681 million) per annum for HE, penalties for students and universities if they fail to complete their degree after four years, and the abolition of grants for masters students. Not surprisingly, there has been a political backlash. University rectors and the mayors of university cities warned that the cuts would 'push the Netherlands out of the world's top 10 knowledge economies'. Clearly, the current Dutch government takes a different perspective from those in France, Germany and, as we shall see, Sweden.

Spain

Spain, like Italy, endured severe fiscal pressures during the Great Recession. These culminated in extreme market pressure in 2011 and 2012, when the cost of debt rose to almost unsustainable levels. The Spanish government embarked on an austerity programme, one consequence of which was a collapse in growth, which in turn led to a further loss of confidence by the markets.

The HE budget in Spain was cut by €300 million in 2011, contributing to a 20 per cent budget reduction over the past three years. A further €485 million was cut from the overall education budget in 2012.

As in Germany and the US, fiscal decentralization plays an important role in the funding of HE in Spain. The 'autonomous communities' (such as Catalonia, the Canary Islands, the Basque Country, Castile–La Mancha, and so on) are responsible for much of HE spending in Spain. Some of these communities themselves experienced serious fiscal difficulties during the Great Recession, particularly those that experienced a significant construction boom, and have found it difficult to finance their own debt. Federal funding to these communities is to be reduced by just over €1 billion in 2012/13. Again, this is likely to adversely affect HE budgets. Either the universities find other sources of funding, which is unlikely, given that the rate of unemployment exceeds 20 per cent, or they experience further decline.

Sweden

Sweden has emerged relatively unscathed from the financial crisis, though it has a high level of youth unemployment. It has been able to increase spending on HE. For example, in 2011, the Swedish government announced a plan to increase spending on HE by $1 billion over the next four years with the specific objectives of improving the quality of teacher training, and of increasing the number of civil engineering places. These increases are being portrayed as a means of enhancing Sweden's long-term growth potential through increased productivity.

Consistency of funding has enabled some Swedish institutions to thrive. For example, the University of Lund hired 471 new staff in 2011, a 9 per cent increase. It now has 47000 students, an operating budget of $890 million. It was involved in 110 research projects under the EU Framework 6 funding stream.

These developments are consistent with the Swedish view that in order to maintain international competitiveness and so be able to pay for a relatively generous welfare system, Sweden needs to outperform its competitors in the production of intellectual capital. There is evidence to suggest that Sweden is among the most efficient states in producing academic excellence, given the size of its population.

UNITED KINGDOM

At over 10 per cent of GDP, the UK had one of the highest budget deficits at the onset of the Great Recession. The UK Treasury conducted a public spending review in 2010, and concluded that the HE budget should be reduced from £7.1 billion in 2010 to £4.2 billion by 2014. The cuts are particularly focused on teaching rather than research. Research funding has been largely protected, again based on the argument that competitiveness in research will provide part of the solution to the need to rebalance the UK economy.

The UK government argument is that there are considerable private returns to a university education and therefore that the beneficiaries of these returns should contribute more. Specifically, students should be asked to make a contribution of up to £9000 per annum towards the cost of their tuition. The fees will be paid to HE institutions by the UK Government and then repaid by students to the government after graduation. Repayments will only be required from graduates earning more than £21 000. Alongside a loan to cover their fees, students also receive a loan of up to £5500 to cover accommodation and study costs if living away from home and studying outside London. Different rates apply for study in London and/or living at the parental home. Repayments will be made at the rate of 9 per cent of income above the £21 000 threshold. Poorer students will also receive grants of up to £3250. Loan repayment is deducted from salary, normally through the tax system. And if loans are not repaid after 30 years they are to be written off.

This is one of the most dramatic withdrawals of state support for university teaching that has ever occurred in Europe. Not only will there be a substantial reduction in overall funding to support teaching, there will also be a significant change in its composition. Hardest hit will be arts and humanities where government funding support for teaching is being entirely removed. Funding for the sciences and engineering will be maintained. HE institutions that specialize in the arts and humanities are therefore disproportionately adversely affected by the spending cuts. Therefore, a consequence of the recession in the UK has been an acceleration in the realignment of funding towards technical subjects, presumably based on the instrumental argument that these subjects are more likely to produce the skills required to help rebalance the UK economy.

Interestingly, the increase in tuition fees has been applied in England and Northern Ireland. Wales and, particularly, Scotland have adopted different strategies. Scotland has continued to offer free university tuition funded by savings elsewhere in its budget. However, students from the rest of the UK (though not from the rest of the EU excluding the UK) will have to contribute fees at broadly equivalent rates to those charged in England. In Wales, students will receive a non-means-tested tuition fee *loan* up to £3465; and a non means-tested tuition fee *grant* to cover the difference between the maximum tuition fee loan available and the tuition fee actually charged by the UK university. This means that Welsh students will not be affected by the increase in tuition fees, but will have to repay the loan on the much lower charge that was levied prior to 2012/13.

Thus the conjunction of the Great Recession and fiscal decentralization in the UK has resulted in quite different outcomes for students across the nations that comprise the UK. These reflect differences in the political perception of how the costs of HE should be distributed between taxpayers and students.

A final remark: international evidence suggests that in terms of world rankings, UK universities are second only to those in the US. However, the effects of the Great Recession may cause significant threats to this position to emerge. The Times Higher Education world ranking of universities shows 44 US universities in the top 100, while the UK has 10. Most of the UK institutions are slipping down the ranking, with the LSE being the main exception. Meanwhile all the leading Asian universities increased their ranking, partly as a result of increased investment by their respective governments. In particular, the Chinese government is making significant investments aimed at improving the performance of China's top 10 universities. The number of university places available in China is also growing rapidly. Between 1997 and 2007 college enrolments increased from around 1 million to 5.5 million. It has been estimated that 6.5 million students will graduate from Chinese universities in academic year 2011/12. It is focusing its research effort on applied research but aims to increase overall spending on research and development to 2.5 per cent of GDP.

CONCLUSIONS

The Great Recession and its aftermath will have a long-lasting impact on HE funding and consequently on the performance and reputation of institutions both within and across countries. However, the effects will be varied. They partly depend on the overall fiscal stance adopted by countries in response to events. Some countries have decided to cut back on national education budgets quite severely, with direct effects on HE institutions. On the other hand, where states have some degree of fiscal decentralization, it is HE institutions in those territories worst affected by the recession that are likely to suffer most. Often these are areas that have been subject to a severe construction bubble.

Some countries have sought to protect HE, particularly research, even while other budgets are being cut. The rationale is that to weaken HE, and particularly its innovative aspects, may reduce the future productive capacity of the economy. Thus, for example, France and the UK are currently striving to maintain or expand HE spending on research.

Another major development is the attempt to shift the costs of HE on to students, who are the most obvious direct beneficiaries of state-funded HE provision. While the UK is an extreme example within Europe, increases in tuition fees at US state universities have been taking place for some time and are likely to accelerate in states facing serious fiscal deficits. Many European states still try to provide free state-funded HE, which is made easier where a relatively small proportion of the youth cohort is admitted to HE.

Changes in funding will affect the relative strength of institutions. At present, within Europe, it appears that those in northern Europe, particularly those with a strong research capability, are more likely to prosper than those in southern Europe. And in the wider world of HE, the effects of the recession are likely to accelerate the growing relative strength of institutions in Asia. In the US, the private institutions that are not reliant on state funding will gather strength relative to publicly funded institutions. This may have adverse effects on social mobility within the US, although some of the US private institutions have 'needs-blind' admission policies.

More speculatively, the recession may promote a drift towards 'vocational' subjects and applied research. Governments, keen to demonstrate to their public that the decision to continue investment in HE is paying off, will want to be able to demonstrate immediate benefits, such as increased numbers of engineers or some new commercial development. Financial support for 'blue skies thinking' and non-commercial subjects may weaken.

Governments may also use the recession as an opportunity to strengthen their control of HE. This will be particularly the case if HE institutions are seen to be failing to promote wider government aspirations, such as promoting economic growth or encouraging social mobility. This is likely to result in an extension of the 'managerial' model of HE. Compared with the 'collegiate' model, the managerial approach may be more likely to deliver governments' short-term objectives. Ultimately this approach may be damaging to the freedom of HE to innovate, develop and make a more substantial contribution to national well-being.

Where tuition charges are increased, one would expect students to take a more strongly consumerist approach to HE. They may wish to exert more control over teaching, its delivery and its outcomes. On most grounds, this is probably desirable, but there are also inherent dangers for standards and therefore the ultimate credibility of the system in allowing this process to go too far.

The Great Recession will bring about many significant changes in HE worldwide. These have only begun to emerge. Some of the consequences will be far-reaching, affecting the fate of HE institutions and the students whom they teach for decades to come. In some sense, these changes provide an opportunity for those who can use a time of significant change to effect improvements in the system. But in many instances, improvements will have to be made against a background of diminishing resources.

NOTE

1. http://www.research-in-germany.de/main/2868/research-funding.html   (accessed   30 September 2012).

REFERENCES

Barroso, J. (2011), 'European higher education – an engine for growth and jobs', European Commission, Speech/11/749.

Kane, T. J., P. R. Orszag and D. L. Gunter (2003, May), 'State fiscal constraints and higher education spending: The role of Medicaid and business cycles', discussion paper no. 11, Washington, DC: Urban Institute. Accessed, May 2012.

Oliff, P., J. Shure and N. Johnson (2009), 'Federal fiscal relief is working as intended', Center on Budget and Policy Priorities, June 29.Times Higher Education (2012) February, accessed at: http://www.timeshighereducation.co.uk/story.asp?storycode=418954, May 2012.

13. Developing the 'third place': the collaborative roles of universities in territorial knowledge creation

Roger Normann and
Hans Chr Garmann Johnsen

INTRODUCTION[1]

Universities are supposed to play a major role in the knowledge economy. This was already outlined by Daniel Bell in his 1973 book on the post-industrial society (Bell 1973). One could argue that the role of knowledge and the role of knowledge institutions in society since then have gained importance. Over the last two decades, there has been a large literature that addresses this. Most of this literature sees universities as knowledge developing institutions that can fuel the economy with knowledge inputs (Trani and Holsworth 2010). Although knowledge, like so many other general concepts, covers many meanings, and refers to many different understandings, knowledge development and transfer has become an important topic in discussions of economic development. Likewise, the discussion of university policy, at least in Norway, is increasingly framed in terms of economic policy; that is how universities can support innovation and collaborate for business development.

In this chapter we argue that in spite of this increased interest and relevance of university–society collaboration, the topic of understanding what happens when the two meet is underdeveloped. The reason for this is that this meeting is not of one type only, but rather represents a plurality of interaction forms. Generic statements about university–society relations therefore tend to be too abstract. University–society collaboration can be very context-specific, and these meetings can put many different role dimensions into play, such as institutional, communicative, power, identity and culture, as well as more formal and structural elements. We call this plurality, the 'third place'. We try to argue, by using data from the Agder region in the southernmost part of Norway, that there is a need to develop a better understanding of what happens at this 'third place', how is it organized, how is it managed, and what knowledge development and learning takes place there.

The 'Third Place'

There are many 'trends' in innovation policy that are in line with the collaborative mode of thinking. For example: universities becoming more engaged and active in supporting their regions; changes in industrial policy away from 'direct public support' towards indirect measures like promoting networking; normative 'prescriptions' for development work, through concepts such as triple-helix, regional clusters, regional innovation systems, etc.; understanding the region as a development unit (regionalization); increased focus on regional (local) competitive advantage, and the growth of the knowledge economy that presupposes 'people's climate', not only 'business climate'; and increased network steering and use of partnerships (regional network governance).

Subsequently the collaboration with universities over innovation and knowledge creation in territorial development has become an important issue. In 1994, Gibbons et al., in their book *The New Production of Knowledge*, introduced the term Mode-2 (Gibbons et al. 1994). By this they meant a new field of knowledge development that was neither purely academic, nor purely business-related. What they had in mind was a meeting of the two that would produce a new kind of knowledge, more practical, but still based on academic research. They write:

> In transdisciplinary contexts, disciplinary boundaries, distinctions between pure and applied research, and institutional differences between, say, universities and industry, seem to be less and less relevant. Indeed, attention is focused primarily on the problem area, or the hot topic, preference given to collaborative rather than individual performance and excellence judged by the ability of individuals to make a sustained contribution in open, flexible types of organization in which they may only work temporarily. (Gibbons et al. 1994: 30)

Later the same authors introduced the term 'Agora', known from Plato's work as a meeting place for public discourses, in order to indicate that Mode 2 happens in a specific kind of arena (Gibbons et al. 1994; Nowotny et al. 2001). In this chapter it is some of the dynamic of the Agora that we will discuss. We use the sociological term 'third place' (Oldenburg 2000; Putnam 2000) and we will explain what we understand by this term. In particular, we will not refer to the 'third place' in its original meaning, but rather give it a specific meaning, namely as a general description of the seemingly complex and messy intersection between academia, public administration and business. We ask what are the main challenges for governing and developing knowledge in this 'third place'?

The rest of the chapter is organized as a discussion of the 'third place' from two sides/perspectives; from the university and from the business community/the region. Thereafter we try to develop some principles for how the 'third place' can be organized. Finally, we present some empirical examples, using our own region, Agder of Norway, as a case.

The University Perspective: Transferring Knowledge and the Third Mission

Universities all around the world have over the last two decades been increasingly encouraged to take an active role in economic and social development. One concrete example and manifestation of this is the so-called 'Bayh–Dole Act' that was passed by the US House of Representatives Congress and Senate in 1980. The legislation dealt with intellectual property arising from federal government-funded research, and permits a university to choose to pursue ownership of an invention. The basis of this model, which means that the professor's privilege system to property rights was abolished, was adopted in Denmark in 1999 and in Norway in 2003. It has become the standard model across Europe, with the exception of Sweden and Italy. The organizational consequence of the model is that universities have established Technology Transfer Offices (TTOs) that handle IPR, patenting, copyright and licensing issues on behalf of employees at the University.

In the US there was a radical increase in US academic patents after the enactment, leading academics and policymakers alike to interpret the law as a success. Critics of this interpretation have pointed out that the changes have little to do with the legislation as such. Instead, the changes are different across the spectrum of technologies, and mostly tied to the rise of patents in the field of drugs, medicine and biotechnology as an important academic and highly commercial field (Henderson et al. 1998; Klitkou and Gulbrandsen 2006; Mowery et al. 2004).

This transfer perspective inherent in the TTO initiative has however increasingly been replaced by a more interactive perspective where the core idea is not how university knowledge can be transferred but how universities can contribute to develop knowledge in collaboration with others. This change of focus means that we need to understand the process of developing knowledge (Amin and Roberts 2008; Arbnor and Bjerke 2005; Fuller 2001; Knorr Cetina 1999). One might argue that this question is complex since knowledge is many things and is developed in different ways. Table 13.1 tries to indicate some different types of knowledge and processes of knowledge development and their organizational implications.

Table 13.1   Different types of knowledge and organizational implications

Knowledge	Organizational implication:		
	Leadership	Organizing	Relevance/example
Subjective and personal	Supportive and dialogic	Autonomy	Service encounters, personal meetings
Unique and local	Divisions and decentralized leadership	Decentralized and diversified	Time and place specific knowledge
Collective knowledge	Collegiate and distributed leadership	Networking missionary organization	Learning and collaboration communities as a solution
'Professional' knowledge/ discipline based	'Everyone their own leader'	'Uniform' expert network	Specialist knowledge
Experience-based and transferable knowledge	Team based	Working together and common problem solving	Learning through best practice
Expert system	Guidance – 'weak leadership'	Loosely bounded network	Very specialized problem solving
Objective and codified	Authoritarian	Hierarchy	Rules and controls

All these knowledge forms are relevant when we talk about 'the third mission' of the university. However, they imply very different organizational forms. Also it is important to note that these forms might differ between institutions. Universities might emphasize forms different from those that industry emphasizes.

Recent studies (Bruneel et al. 2010; Muscio 2010; Nilsson et al. 2010) discuss what might reduce the barriers between university and business in knowledge development and argue that university and market represent very different cultures (paradigms), and this might explain why this type of co-operation is so hard to develop. Subsequently, Venditti et al. (2011) write:

> In our opinion, one should not at forehand narrow the 'third mission' to best-practices and private demand for innovation as articulated by industry.

In a knowledge-based economy, variation on the demand side is as important as variation on the supply side ... Before one focuses on success stories of 'building bridges,' the rich varieties on both banks of the river could be made visible so that more options for relating demand and supply in innovations can be explored. One should keep in mind that only 10% of the innovative ideas lead eventually to successful innovations. Leaving the pre-selection in this process only to private (consumer or industrial) demand thus seems counter-productive. The notion of 'government' in university-industry-government relations provides room for additional democratisation in terms of access to research capacities.

Our reflection is that research into this field shows that what we are facing here is more than knowledge transfer. It is the rather complex and 'messy' field of interrelation between different social institutions. When trying to reduce this complexity, one conceals the reality of this field. This is often what happens when references is given to concepts like 'third mission' or 'entrepreneurial university'.

The Regional Perspective: Enhancing Innovation in a Collaborative Economy

A second perspective we would like to emphasize with regards to the collaboration between university, public administration and business is the innovation policy perspective, in particular in its regional form. Some of the most influential concepts and theories addressing these issues are related to Michael Porter's concept of 'business or regional clusters' (1998a, 1998b, 2003), Henry Etzkowitz and Loet Leydesdorff's concept of a 'triple-helix' emphasizing the importance of institutional collaboration between universities, government, and industry (Etzkowitz and Leydesdorff 1997), Richard Florida's concept of 'creative class' and 'creative regions' (Florida 2002, 2005), the development of the concept of 'learning regions' as a way of further conceptualizing an interactive learning economy (Asheim 1996; Florida 1995; Morgan 1997; Storper 1993), and the concept of 'regional innovation systems' (Asheim and Isaksen, 1997; Cooke 1992). The sum of technological change, shifts in industrial structure and influential academic concepts and theories has proved to be a very potent recipe for the development of new policies towards regions. It has been transformed into agenda for regionalizing industrial policy and economic development in many countries in Europe since the 1990s (OECD 2001). Moreover, a common feature of the concepts of innovation system and clusters are that they see business development as part of knowledge development between different businesses and knowledge institutions.

When we focus on what we could describe loosely as the regional level, the emerging collaborative perspective on development can be explained with changes in dominant understandings of the role of territory itself, what geographers refer to as the spatial dimension. From this it follows that the region is something more than a vague context for industrial and societal developments. The region is now a subject, something that we work with, compare to others, and systematically try to develop. In one sense one could argue that the region in recent years has moved up our 'ladder of attention', and is now 'competing for interest' as the central development unit, together with the nation state, the city, the municipality and the firm: a role that the region in countries such as Norway did not have 20 years ago. This we could argue is a change of direction, which has been termed 'new regionalism' (Keating 1998).

A common denominator for concepts such as regional innovation systems, triple-helix, regional clusters, creative class, mode 2, new economy and knowledge economy, is that they describe challenges, practices and solutions, but in general do not address issues such as organization, leadership, politics and institutions (Uyarra 2011); notable exceptions including the work of Markku Sotarauta (Sotarauta 2005, 2009, 2010; Sotarauta and Kautonen 2007). Stringent academic disciplinary boundaries are part of the explanation why discourses related to power and institutional theory are seldom explicitly discussed directly in relation to, for instance, regional innovation system studies. In fact, as noted in Table 13.2, there are many separate and different explanations and theories that address issues on collaboration.

The list in Table 13.2 is meant to illustrate how one might look conceptually at collaborative activities between industry and public institutions. One can choose to see these activities as concerning mainly economic development, or as concerning mainly social and cultural development. One can also choose to see them form different innovation perspectives and subsequently the policy (and managerial) implications will differ. Our view is that these different approaches do not communicate well with each other.

So we argue that the collaborative dimension in regional innovation and development theory can in general be characterized by its absence. The concepts associated with regional turn, such as Regional Innovation Systems, Triple Helix and Mode 2, give us a better understanding of the systemic mechanisms of knowledge creation and dispersion within different industries, and how innovative activities could and should be structured. As discussed, little attention has been given to the institutional, organizational and political implications, and to how new structures become intertwined and merge with old institutions. Nevertheless the new

Table 13.2   What creates collaborative advantage? Some initial positions

	Collaboration within firms	Collaboration between firms	Collaboration between firms and the public sector
Economic, non-context specific explanations	Transaction cost	Externalities, economics of scope	Rent seeking, public choice, monopoly competition
Cultural, context specific and non-economic explanations	Trust, relations, social capital	Networks, social capital, path dependencies, cultural cohesion	Social cohesion, partnership and network steering, public administrative reforms
Type of innovation/development dynamics	Participatory processes, incremental innovation, process improvements	Diffusion of ideas, new collaborative solutions, open innovations	New policies, public support for innovation in initiatives, public goods
Policy implications	Promoting innovative organizational forms	Stimulate networking, collaboration between firms	Organize partnerships, public dialogue, create connectedness

Source: Adapted from Johnsen and Ennals (2012).

concepts and policies for development, not least economic development, increasingly talk about partnership and collaboration in order to meet challenges. Networks are seen as an important part of enterprise strategies, with 'open innovation' as a relatively new way of utilizing external resources (Chesbrough 2003). The point to be made here is that the social field that these initiatives refer to comprises neither purely markets, nor purely organizations. They are rather *ad hoc* initiatives, often based on relations and connections that are somewhat 'loose' and often refer to many different and conflicting organizational forms.

DISCUSSION OF SOME OF THE DYNAMICS OF THE 'THIRD PLACE'

Having thus presented the two perspectives; collaboration as seen from the university and collaboration as seen from the region (including industry), we conclude that it is a complex task to match the two. The reasons are that knowledge is complex, that knowledge development thus happens within many different organizational forms, that university and region have different intentions in collaborating and that there is a multitude of motives, structural dimensions (power relations) and interests when the two meet in the 'third place'. Managing these complex processes is thus a challenge beyond traditional leadership thinking. Thus the concept of network governance has increasingly been adopted.

There is much contemporary disciplinary literature that deals with issues relating to regional governance networks and regional development concepts. There are also important contributions yet to be made to current understandings and practices. These contributions might come from insights stemming from trans-disciplinary work, dialogue between research and practice and international collaboration. It is possible to establish some structure for this field; what happens here, what are reasonable relations between input and output, how instrumental can it be made, and what rational expectations might we have with respect to what it produces in terms of outcome. In short, how does it work?

The 'third place' is a meeting place between different 'logics' or social institutions, such as market (business), public (government) and research (academia). It is also a functional meeting place. Something is supposed to be exchanged or to develop, and at least some agents (perhaps all) at some point in time are supposed to benefit from the exchange. However, it is not obvious that all actors in this exchange have the same motives and objectives. Rather, it is likely that they do not.

The 'third place' can be conceptualized in different ways. Gibbons, et al. (1994) discuss it as follows: 'The field we will try to approach is an interrelated field between different spheres of social open, flexible types of organization in which [university and industry] may only work temporarily'. In order to go deeper into what this might imply, or how it might look in real situations, we will look first at some alternative theories of the 'third place', and second at how these theories describe the processes in the 'third place'.

What is the logic of this new, interrelated field of different institutions? Has it developed its own basic rules or structures? What are they and why are they so complex and difficult to overview? Walter W. Powell (1990) identified some ideal types of approaches to innovation policies in a region, and from what point the network of economic organization can be viewed as a distinct form, separate from the market and public hierarchy.

The totality such networks generate collectively within the framework of a region could be described as a *regional governance system* (Normann 2012). A region is in this sense not necessarily the same as an administrative structure. We therefore end up with what has been described as a pragmatic notion of a region – 'regions of meaning' are something that local actors experience as meaningful when discussing development processes (Gustavsen and Ennals 2007).

Literature that addresses the governance network phenomenon at various systemic levels does not represent a uniform body of thought with regards the role and emphasis on central concepts such as trust, power and collaboration (Gustavsen 1992; Lave and Wenger 1991). Some of the new institutional theories that have addressed the governance network phenomenon are probably among those that have made the role of collaboration most explicit in their writing. James March and Johan P. Olsen (1989, 1995) have for instance made the development of robust and democratic institutions, norms and rules an explicit normative goal of their institutional theory on politics and governance. Others (Burchell et al. 1991; Dean 1999), can be interpreted as viewing governance structures and their adjacent institutions as power structures that exert specific views and ideas about society (Sørensen and Torfing 2007). In such perspectives collaboration and trust are not the core of development, or even a goal. Collaboration and trust play the role of being a veil, a rhetoric, which hides other more instrumental agendas (Normann 2007). A third notable path within governance network theory, which in part builds on more 'rational choice' inspired approaches to governance, views collaborative features such as trust as either necessary or unnecessary for achieving co-ordinated actions, depending on whether rational governance network actors are viewed as autonomous or interdependent of each other. If they are viewed as autonomous then co-ordinated action through networks requires a co-ordinating mechanism on a higher systemic level, a form of meta-governance (Kickert et al. 1997; Kooiman 1993; Mayntz 1991; Scharpf 1994).

EXAMPLE OF A 'THIRD PLACE' PROCESS

These different conceptualizations of the organization of the 'third place' are represented in findings that we have made by following the process of university/region development in the Agder region in Norway. Few processes demand clarification of the role of a University in the 'third place' as much as deciding upon how to organize a Technology Transfer Office. The University of Agder has been working since its establishment in 2007 with different policies and strategies relating to how it should organize this function. Until 2011 an external consultancy had attended to this function on behalf of the University (Model C in the Table 13.3). In 2011 the University of Agder commenced a feasibility study in order to explore

Table 13.3   Models for handling the TTO function of the university

	Model A: Institutional model *(develop the activity by the university)*	Model B: The network model *(contract/ organizational cooperation between institutions)*	Model C: Market model *(outsourcing of operations to another institution)*
Perspective	Commercialization of research-based knowledge is a core activity for the university in line with research and teaching. There is a large untapped potential that can be exploited by targeted investment by the university.	The university can help to establish a larger and more robust academic environment by initiating cooperation, and create a neutral platform for knowledge exchange. Separate development of ideas from investment and commerciali-zation activities.	In the case that the potential for commercialization of knowledge is small. It is important for the university to focus on research and teaching. External actors can manage statutory duties on behalf of the university.
Institutional changes regionally	Regional competition for share of renewable contracts, and purchase of consultancy services.	A network structure must be developed and contracts negotiated.	A system of legal tender must be established. Possible need for an agreement to limit time/ roles between actors.
Implications for leadership	Incorporate these activities in line with research and teaching. Avoid conflict between the applied and the more pure research.	The university must take the role of designer, exercise strategic leadership on behalf of several institutions.	Requires no legal resources to develop specifications and monitoring of external contractors.

Table 13.3 (continued)

	Model A: Institutional model *(develop the activity by the university)*	Model B: The network model *(contract/ organizational cooperation between institutions)*	Model C: Market model *(outsourcing of operations to another institution)*
Benefits	The university retains a high degree of autonomy and control over its own knowledge development.	In the regional network, there will be a development of strong regional specialists.	University leadership can focus on the needs of the university.
Disadvantages	The university does not contribute to the development of cooperation and coordination between institutions and experts in the region.	The most demanding leadership model for the university	Does not necessarily contribute to the development environment in the region beyond the current level.
Adaptation to regional characteristics	Best adapted to the commercialization and collaboration/ knowledge exchange with a research-based industry.	Ability to draw on the expertise of many organizations, providing opportunities for knowledge exchange with businesses that innovate based on experience.	Limited assistance with commercialization and knowledge exchange with all types of businesses.

alternatives (Normann and Johnsen 2011). The following models were considered:

In considering these models, the university was well aware that the challenge of 'transferring technology' was actually part of a much larger issue of developing knowledge in the region and seeking to be relevant for regional and social development at large. There was an expressed desire for more knowledge, meaning more disciplines, to be engaged in regional practices. As such the concept of a '*knowledge exchange platform*' was launched as an alternative to the 'TTO office model'.

As the University of Agder is very highly aware of the perspectives discussed in this article, they have started to develop strategies along the lines of all three models described above. They have expressed a clear intention to take a role in regional development together with regional authorities, so model B is an intended strategy. At the same time they acknowledge the need to develop their own organization and knowledge production, so they will try to develop model A. Finally they see the need for a dynamic and competitive milieu in the region that can be creative, and for an open innovation type of business environment.

This multi-strategy choice is a clear indication of the issue discussed in this chapter: first, that different organizational forms are related to different types of knowledge development and learning, and second, that in the interaction between university and region, the 'third place', we find a multitude of these forms. The multitude of forms represents a particular challenge for institutions that operate in this 'third place'. They need to be able to combine different organizational forms that require different competencies in management, even if they have been able to identify certain specific strategies.

THE 'THIRD PLACE' AS A MULTI-LEVEL FIELD

Thus within the different conceptualizations of the third place we find arguments at different levels; from the individual entrepreneurial perspective to perspectives emphasizing social structures and systems. The argument that there are collaborative arenas that are neither hierarchy (organizations), nor market, has therefore been put forward by many observers from different viewpoints. Thus concepts such as *social field* (Bourdieu 1977), *public sphere* (Habermas 1981), *the clan* (Ouchi 1980), *the network* (Powell 1990), or *community of practice* (Lave and Wenger 1991) are all terms that catch elements of the third place. This again implies that what we understand as collaboration and learning in these concepts refers to many different levels and types of learning, and also to different understandings of knowledge (Amin and Roberts 2008; Arbnor and Bjerke 2005; Fuller 2001).

Learning and knowledge development can be understood on different levels, and indeed the concept of learning changes meaning when we walk

Table 13.4   Learning at different levels of tension between process and structure

	Learning understood as a human/social process	Learning understood as a structural/technological process
Learning at the individual level	*Learning type 1*: Personal experience, cognitive development	*Learning type 2*: External, relational conditions for learning
Learning at an organizational level	*Learning type 3*: Social conditions for learning	*Learning type 4*: Procedures, technology, functional framework for learning
Learning at the system level	*Learning type 5*: Change in the legitimacy of understanding	*Learning type 6*: Changes in functional requirements

from one level to another, in turn 'producing' different kinds of knowledge. The idea of the university as an institution for developing a Humboldtian concept of social development is for example very different from a technology transfer (TTO) perspective. We are simply not talking about the same thing when we speak of learning as a personal, private and individual, as when we say that organizations learn, or that learning is an integral part of social development – a point that is further illustrated in Table 13.4.

The 'third place' and the Agora has features of all this. It is a meeting point where both the larger objective of the university and its more practical issues are handled. Because of this multi-dimensional aspect of the 'third place', it is seemingly unplanned. However, still something brings it together, although no one 'owns' it. It is a field of mutual dialogue, adjustment and relations. This is exemplified in the term learning. Learning can be instrumental, but also systemic. If society wants universities to enhance learning, it might imply both to increase factual knowledge (learning type 2), but also to enhance cultural development (learning type 3). The German word *Bildung* is often referred to in the Norwegian debate about how to enhance learning type 1, while much of the innovation literature and TTO thinking often refers to learning in the understanding of learning type 4. The role of the university is thus different in these different learning forms, and so is the relevant organizational forms and managerial implications. As for learning at a system level, it is questionable if managerial strategies have any meaning at all. Learning at the system level is often an unintended consequence of intended actions. However, with insight into systemic mechanisms in society, some way of orchestrating the role of the university might be possible.

Using the term 'field' implies a reference to Bourdieu (1977), among others. We see his analysis of social fields as relevant to the argument we develop here. This also implies that a term such as 'social capital' is central to the discussion. However, the approach we should like to take is not merely to define the structure of the social field of the 'third place' or Agora, but to try to understand what it implies to work in this field. A related approach to Bourdieu is captured in the term 'post-modern organisations'. Post-modern organizations (Hatch 1997) are something between organizations and anti-organizations. They are less fixed in relation to rules than formal organizations; in fact, they to a large extent create their own rules as they develop. This might for instance be a group of designers that work together in a collegial partnership, or a group of researchers that work as a community of practice. They might even form a group across organizations. Post-modern organization emphasizes the self-organizational structure of organizing that allows particular issues of power to be played out. Instead of fixed structures, the more open, fluid feature of the post-modern organization allows actors to form and rearrange alliances and play out their power, not only within a structure, but also by constantly rearranging structure.

So although we acknowledge this complexity of the 'third place', we might also be able identify some different organizational forms (arenas) within this complexity. Table 13.5 indicates four types.

*Table 13.5	Perspectives on organization (type of arena) in the 'third place'*

	Transaction perspective; economic focus	Learning, development perspective; social and democratic focus
Short-term utility	(A) The arena is about negotiating specific solutions to current challenges. Business sees universities as a 'free resource' that can support their activity. The arena is like a negotiation place, clarifying terms of engagement	(C) The arena is here seen as important for giving institutions insight into what goes on in the other institutions in the region, creating coherence and supporting policy development
Long-term advantages	(B) The perspective here is that the arena and collaboration will support the development of new ideas that over time can become businesses. The arena is like a 'development organization'	(D) The arena is here seen as an experiment in developing dialogue between institutions and in the region on long term issues; identity, legitimacy, etc.

Type (A) is likely to appear when developing interaction in the region among many small businesses and business networks, but is likely also to be used by the university leadership in order to promote the university and to get support for the university in the region. The organizational reference here would be a new, intermediate organization, or a joint venture. Linking this to our Agder case, the original TTO solution (Model C) should correspond with this perspective.

Type (B) becomes relevant as the business community organizes and develops professional network organizations, as well as when the university develops a similar function. The organizational reference here could be a network organization, where equal partners meet with a common agenda. At Agder, this resembles partnerships where the university has an educational role towards public administration. The form here is often projects or collaborative agreement where university researchers assess developments in administrative fields.

Type (C) is likely to be the form that develops in interaction with the public administration in the region. The call here is to develop legitimacy and recognition. The organizational reference to this is perhaps a campaign, or political mobilization/organization.

Type (D) is likely to be the reference for regional authorities as they develop their strategic function in the region. The organizational reference here is a looser connection between parties, meeting each other for discussion and dialogue, creating mutual understanding and trust over time with no specific agenda. It is a form where there is discussion, dialogue and interaction, but with clearly defined mutual respect and independence. At Agder some of the voices that have warned against the university becoming too involved with business, and arguing for intellectual freedom and independence of research, argue along these lines.

Again, these different arena forms and organizational forms in the 'third place' will be able to handle different aspects of universities' objectives, provide different types of learning and 'produce' different types of knowledge.

CONCLUSION

In this chapter we have argued that in spite of the increased interest and relevance of university–society collaboration, the intersection between universities and regions creates a new space that is difficult to capture and conceptualize. The reason for this, we have argued, is that this meeting is not of one type only, but rather represents a plurality of interaction forms. We call this plurality the 'third place'. Subsequently we have argued that an understanding of what happens in the 'third place', how it is organized, how it is managed and what forces it operates, is poorly developed.

This, if true, questions some of the assumptions in development theories and concepts that presuppose some sort of instrumentality in this relation. The reason for this messiness is related to the complexity and inconsistency in what is referred to when discussing this 'third place'. There are different perspectives on collaboration, different ideas on knowledge development, different ideas on learning and different ideas on organization. We have tried to present some typologies that could help structure this field. However, our general conclusion is that there is more to be done in developing a set of concepts and types that can operate as a general reference in the further discourse on the 'third place'.

If we were to formulate some thesis based on our argument, it would be that interaction between university and society (region) takes many forms and that these are organized in different ways. There is not, and neither should there be, only one way of organizing this interaction, whether it is called Agora, Mode 2, a regional innovation system, triple-helix or an intermediate organization.

For academics and university managers seeking to undertake their day-to-day work in the context of this plurality of interaction forms, this poses a challenge. Although we have, based on our own case, argued that the different strategies employed in Agder characterizes this plurality very nicely, it does not imply that it is unproblematic. Although we find examples of good ways of handling this plurality, we also have examples of faults, confusion and tension related to decisions in this area. So, although we argue that universities are far too complex and society's needs are far too manifold for there to be only one way to interact we also argue that it would be useful to see a better conceptualization of the different interaction forms. A mixed strategy, which is a likely position to take, is at the same time difficult to manage because it is difficult to communicate. At the same time universities are to some extent loosely coupled institutions. That is perhaps why the tension has not become more exposed than it actually has.

NOTE

1. An earlier version of this chapter has been presented at: European network on industrial policy (EUNIP) workshop on the role of academic research in territorial economic development processes. University of Deusto campus, San Sebastián, Spain, 26–27 November 2009, and the HSS11 conference, 4 and 5 May 2011, Høgskolen i Ålesund, Norway.

REFERENCES

Amin, A. and J. Roberts (2008), *Community, Economic Creativity, and Organization.* Oxford: Oxford University Press.

Arbnor, I. and B. Bjerke (2005), *Methodology for Creating Business Knowledge.* Thousand Oaks, CA: Sage.

Asheim, B. T. (1996), Industrial districts as 'learning regions': a condition for prosperity. *European Planning Studies*, **4**(4), 379–400.

Asheim, B. T. and A. Isaksen (1997), Location, agglomeration and innovation: towards regional innovation systems in Norway? *European Planning Studies*, **5**, 299–330.

Bell, D. (1973), *The Coming of Post-industrial Society: A Venture in Social Forecasting.* New York: Basic Books.

Bourdieu, P. (1977), *Outline of a Theory of Practice* (translation by R. Nice). Cambridge: Cambridge University Press.

Bruneel, J., P. D'Este and A. Salter (2010), Investigating the factors that diminish the barriers to university–industry collaboration. *Research Policy*, **39**(7), 858–68.

Burchell, G., C. Gordon and P. Miller (eds) (1991), *The Foucault Effect: Studies in Governmentality; With Two Lectures by and an Interview with Michel Foucault.* Chicago, IL: University of Chicago Press.

Chesbrough, H. (2003), *Open Innovation: The New Imperative for Creating and Profiting from Technology.* Boston MA.: Harvard Business School Press.

Cooke, P. (1992), Regional innovation systems: competitive regulations in the new Europe. *Geoforum*, **23**, 365–82.

Dean, M. (1999), *Governmentality. Power and Rule in Modern Society.* London: Sage.

Etzkowitz, H. and L. Leydesdorff (eds) (1997), *Universities and the Global Knowledge Economy: A Triple Helix of University-Industry-Government Relations.* London: Continuum.

Florida, R. (1995), Toward the learning region. *Futures*, **27**(5), 527–36.

Florida, R. (2002), *The Rise of the Creative Class: And How It's Transforming Work, Leisure, Community and Everyday Life.* New York: Basic Books.

Florida, R. (2005), *The Flight of the Creative Class: The New Global Competition for Talent.* New York: Harper Business.

Fuller, S. (2001), *Knowledge Management Foundations.* Woburn, MA: Butterworth Heinemann.

Gibbons, M., C. Limoges, H. Nowotny, S. Schwartzman, P. Scott and M. Trow (1994), *The New Production of Knowledge. The Dynamics of Science and Research in Contemporary Societies.* London: Sage.

Gustavsen, B. (1992), *Dialogue and Development: Theory of Communication, Action Research and the Restructuring of Working Life.* Assen, Netherlands: Van Gorcum.

Gustavsen, B. and J. R. Ennals (2007), Designing a European project on learning for local innovation. In B. Gustavsen, B. Nyhan and J. R. Ennals (eds), *Learning Together for Local Innovation Promoting Learning Regions* (pp. 35–45). Luxembourg: Cedefop.

Habermas, J. (1981), *The Theory of Communicative Action: Reason and Rationalization of Society.* Boston, MA: Beacon Press.

Hatch, M. J. (1997), *Organization Theory: Modern, Symbolic and Postmodern Perspectives*. Oxford: Oxford University Press.

Henderson, R., A. B. Jaffe and M. Trajtenberg (1998), Universities as a source of commercial technology: a detailed analysis of university patenting, 1965–1988. *Review of Economics and Statistics*, **80**(1), 119–27.

Johnsen, H. C. G. and J. R. Ennals (2012), Introduction: collaborative advantage in regional economies. In J. R. Ennals and H. C. G. Johnsen (eds), *Creating Collaborative Advantage: Innovation and Knowledge Creation in Regional Economies* (pp. 1–24). Farnham: Gower.

Keating, M. (1998), *The New Regionalism in Western Europe: Territorial Restructuring and Political Change*. Cheltenham: Edward Elgar.

Kickert, W. J. M., E. H. Klijn and J. F. M. Koppenjan (1997), *Managing Complex Networks: Strategies for the Public Sector*. London: Sage.

Klitkou, A. and M. Gulbrandsen (2006), Academic patenting and university research in Norway. Paper presented at the SPRU 40th Anniversary Conference – The Future of Science, Technology and Innovation Policy.

Knorr Cetina, K. (1999), *Epistemic Cultures: How the Sciences Make Knowledge*. Cambridge, MA.: Harvard University Press.

Kooiman, J. (1993), *Modern Governance: New Government–Society Interactions*. London: Sage.

Lave, J. and E. Wenger (1991), *Situated Learning*. Cambridge: Cambridge University Press.

March, J. G. and J. P. Olsen (1989), *Rediscovering Institutions: The Organizational Basis of Politics*. New York: Free Press.

March, J. G. and J. P. Olsen (1995), *Democratic Governance*. New York: Free Press.

Mayntz, R. (1991), *Modernization and the Logic of Interorganizational Networks* (MPFIG discussion paper no. 8): Max Planck Institute für Gesellschaftsforschung.

Morgan, K. (1997), The learning region: institutions, innovation and regional renewal. *Regional Studies*, **31**(5), 491–503.

Mowery, D. C., R. R. Nelson, B. N. Sampat and A. A. Ziedonis (2004), *Ivory Tower and Industrial Innovation: University–industry Technology Transfer Before and After the Bayh–Dole Act in the United States*. Stanford: Stanford University Press.

Muscio, A. (2010), What drives the university use of technology transfer offices? Evidence from Italy. *Journal of Technology Transfer*, **35**(2), 181–202.

Nilsson, A. S., A. Rickne and L. Bengtsson (2010), Transfer of academic research: uncovering the grey zone. *Journal of Technology Transfer*, **35**(6), 617–36.

Normann, R. H. (2007), *Democracy in Development – A Critical View on Regional Governance, Theses at NTNU nr. 88*. Trondheim: Norwegian University of Science and Technology.

Normann, R. H. (2012), The collaborative steering dilemma of network-based development. In J. R. Ennals and H. C. G. Johnsen (eds), *Creating Collaborative Advantage: Innovation and Knowledge Creation in Regional Economies* (pp. 91–101). Farnham: Gower.

Normann, R. H. and H. C. G. Johnsen (2011), *Mulighetsstudie for 'Technology Transfer Office'-funksjonen ved Universitetet i Agder – En utredning for Universitetet i Agder* (No. FoU rapport nr. 3/2011). Kristiansand: Agderforskning.

Nowotny, H., P. Scott and M. Gibbons (2001), *Rethinking Science: Knowledge Production and the Public in an Age of Uncertainty*. Oxford: Polity Press.

OECD (2001), *Innovative Clusters: Drivers of National Innovation Systems*. Paris: OECD publication.

Oldenburg, R. (2000), *Celebrating the Third Place: Inspiring Stories about the 'Great Good Places' at the Heart of Our Communities*. New York: Marlowe & Company.

Ouchi, W. G. (1980), Markets, bureaucracies, and clans. *Administrative Science Quarterly*, **25**(1), 129–41.

Porter, M. E. (1998a), *The Competitive Advantage of Nations* (with a new introduction). Basingstoke: Macmillan Business.

Porter, M. E. (1998b), *On Competition*. Boston, MA: Harvard Businesss School.

Porter, M. E. (2003), The economic performance of regions. *Regional Studies*, **37**(6/7), 549–78.

Powell, W. W. (1990), Neither market nor hierarchy: network forms of organization. *Research in Organizational Behavior*, **12**, 295–336.

Putnam, R. D. (2000), *Bowling Alone: The Collapse and Revival of American Community*. New York: Simon & Schuster.

Scharpf, F. W. (1994), Games real actors could play: positive and negative coordination in embedded negotiations. *Journal of Theoretical Politics*, **6**(1), 27–53.

Sotarauta, M. (2005), Shared leadership and dynamic capabilities in regional development. In I. Sagan and H. Halkier (eds), *Regionalism Contested: Institution, Society and Governance* (pp. 53–72). Cornwall: Ashgate.

Sotarauta, M. (2009), Power and influence tactics in the promotion of regional development: an empirical analysis of the work of Finnish regional development officers *Geoforum*, **40**(5), 895–905.

Sotarauta, M. (2010), Regional development and regional networks: the role of regional development officers in Finland. *European Urban and Regional Studies*, **17**(4), 387–400.

Sotarauta, M. and M. Kautonen (2007), Co-evolution of the Finnish national and local innovation and science arenas: towards a dynamic understanding of multilevel governance. *Regional Studies*, **41**(8), 1085–98.

Storper, M. (1993), Regional 'worlds' of production: learning and innovation in the technology districts of France, Italy and the USA. *Regional Studies*, **27**(5), 433–55.

Sørensen, E. and J. Torfing (eds) (2007), *Theories of Democratic Network Governance*. Basingstoke: Palgrave Macmillian.

Trani, E. and R. Holsworth (2010), *The Indispensable University – Higher Education, Economic Development and the Knowledge Economy*. Lanham, MD: Rowman & Littlefield Publishers, Inc.

Uyarra, E. (2011), Regional innovation systems revisited: networks, institutions, policy and complexity. In T. Herrschel and P. Tallberg (eds), *The Role of Regions? Networks, Scale, Territory*. Kristianstad: Kristianstads Boktryckeri.

Venditti, M., E. Reale and L. Leydesdorff (2011), The disclosure of university research for societal demand: a non-market perspective on the Third Mission. Unpublished paper proposal.

14. The development of action research processes and their impacts on socio-economic development in the Basque Country

Mari Jose Aranguren, James Karlsen, Miren Larrea and James R. Wilson

1 INTRODUCTION

As reflected in several other contributions to this volume, there is strong debate around the role that universities and their academics should play in the societies in which they are situated, with respect to both their teaching and their research activities. In particular, academia is asked to contribute actively to processes of territorial socio-economic development. This debate is supported by compelling normative arguments about the benefits of such active contribution, as reflected in well-known concepts such as 'mode 2 knowledge production' (Gibbons et al. 1994), 'the triple helix' (Etzkowitz and Leydesdorff 1997; 2000), 'strategic research' (Rip 2004) or the 'third mission' of universities (Laredo 2007). Indeed, in their comparative review of a range of such knowledge production concepts, Hessels and van Lente (2008: 755) conclude:

> [T]he claim that the content of scientific research agenda is currently changing recurs in all diagnoses: all address a turn towards more relevant research, research that (sooner or later) may lead to applications in the form of innovations or policy. Furthermore, all approaches point to more interactive relationships between science, industry and government.

Despite widespread acknowledgement of these trends in academic knowledge production, there is little written around the practical aspects of achieving more 'relevant' research that is at the same time independent and academically rigorous. As a step in this direction, in a previous paper the authors proposed and explored a 'knowledge bridging' framework in a long-term case study of a group of researchers in the Basque Country region in Spain (Karlsen et al. 2012). They identified both micro-level changes among researchers and macro-level changes related to institutional entrepreneurship as critical elements in progressing from a simple bridging of knowledge between academics and practitioners towards the systemic co-generation of knowledge associated with 'mode 2 knowledge production' (Gibbons et al. 1994). This chapter deepens this work through a detailed analysis of the change process among researchers and regional development agents who have participated in three different long-term 'action research' processes in the Basque Country.

A central argument of the chapter is that action research can contribute to opening up the black box of interactive learning processes between academic research and regional actors. The cases presented are long-term projects developed with the clear goal of responding to research questions defined not by researchers alone, but together with policy makers. Indeed, the three projects are all oriented to change and share the goal of experimenting with how research can transform a local environment, impacting on socio-economic development processes. We analyse the evolution of these projects from being characterized initially by a fairly linear transfer of knowledge practices, to becoming a more integrated manifestation of the core action research principles of action, research and participation. They are hence case studies of change, with the main aim of the chapter being to shed light on how action research in the public policy sphere can be developed practically as a methodology for achieving research that impacts positively on socio-economic development.

2 THEORETICAL FRAMEWORK AND CASE METHODOLOGY

In Karlsen et al. (2012) the authors propose an analytical framework to understand how change takes place from Mode 1 to Mode 2 knowledge production (Gibbons et al. 1994). This framework sees 'bridging' as a first step in which researchers and policy agents meet. However it proposes that, for systemic and embedded processes of knowledge co-generation to emerge, this bridging must be supported by mutually re-enforcing changes in the approach and attitudes of individuals (action research), and in the configuration of institutions (institutional entrepreneurship). This framework is explored in the context of a long-term case study of a group of researchers in the Basque Country region in Spain. As a result of the applied analysis, the concept of 'bridging' in the framework is adjusted to re-occur throughout the transformation process towards systemic

Mode-1: Linear Transfer

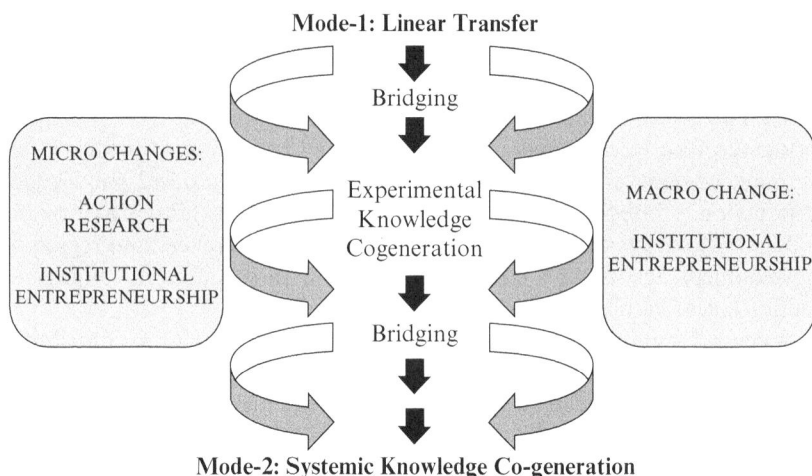

Source: Karlsen et al. (2012)

Figure 14.1   Knowledge bridging framework

knowledge co-generation, and the evolution of micro- and macro-changes is shown to be strongly interdependent (see Figure 14.1).

This framework has its theoretical roots in earlier work by Greenwood and Levin (2007) and Gustavsen (1992). Greenwood and Levin (2007) propose a co-generative action research model that consists of two ana-lytical phases. In the first phase the aim is to clarify an initial research question; i.e. to find out *what* the aim of the process is. Transition from the first to the second phase then occurs when the insiders (practitioners) and the outsiders (researchers) have reached consensus about the problem definition. The second phase takes place through dialogue between the participants to find a solution and test that solution through action(s); that is, to find out *how* the challenge will be addressed. This is not a linear process where the challenge is formulated and then the actions executed; rather, a dynamic process between the challenge and the actions is used to sharpen the research question, the challenge and the necessary actions in a mutual learning and reflection process. The model can be interpreted as a general model for planning and creating a common ground for action and change. Yet while it specifies communicative action, it does not specify how change can be identified or how it should take place.

Gustavsen's (1992) model on the other hand focuses on how to identify change. It connects changes in patterns of communication with changes in the issues that are defined as subject to development, and further with changes in work organization and in the selection and configuration of technological elements. The focus on the importance of language has also been referred to as a communicative turn in action research and working life research (Johnsen 2001). The main argument is that people are linked to each other through a process of shared meanings, and in this sense the research process is merged with a process of restructuring of language, which encompasses those who have to understand the research (Gustavsen 1992). According to Gustavsen (1992: 33) this can be done through dialogue where all participants share an interest in creating 'a good language', but he acknowledges that a change in language is not enough; it must be connected to practice through a process of understanding.

The case study employed in Karlsen et al. (2012) focuses on identifying and understanding the elements that made a change from linear knowledge transfer to systemic knowledge co-generation possible over a period of 11 years among a group of researchers. Three phases were identified, and were linked to micro-changes in attitudes and approaches alongside macro-changes in institutions. However, a deeper view of how change happened in the context of specific research processes, and of how researchers as well as practitioners changed during these processes, was absent. In this chapter we cover this gap by analysing in depth three specific research projects that have been at the heart of this experience of transformation towards systemic knowledge co-generation in the Basque Country. Each research project is treated as a case study in change, and four questions have been used to reflect on the critical elements that illustrate the change process. These questions are presented in Figure 14.2.

The case analysis is the result of an auto-reflexive process among the authors, different combinations of whom have worked together in developing the three research processes from their various inceptions. The reflection process has been based on two kinds of data. First, papers and articles published by the researchers during the course of the three

Questions
How is knowledge generated and transferred?
Who is defining the research questions and how are the questions defined by the actors?
How is the knowledge creation process organized?
Which kind of technology is used and how is it used?*

Note: *The word 'technology' is used following Gustavsen (1992), although in this specific case the word 'methodology' or 'technique' is more appropriate.

Figure 14.2   Questions to highlight key elements of change processes in knowledge creation

processes have made it possible to trace how the research team has evolved. Second, minutes of meetings, newsletters, emails and documents used during the research processes as means of communication between researchers and practitioners and in some cases among practitioners themselves have supported a reflection on how language and working practices have evolved. In the next section we briefly provide some contextual background, before turning to analysis of the three specific cases.

3   CONTEXT: CONNECTING RESEARCHERS AND DEVELOPMENT AGENTS IN THE BASQUE COUNTRY

The Basque Country is one of the 17 autonomous communities of Spain, with approximately 2 million inhabitants. It contributes around 6 per cent of Spanish GDP and has an important weight of manufacturing (around 22 per cent of GDP). A key characteristic of the Basque Country is its dense institutional framework, with three different administrative levels existing within the region, and influence also from the Spanish and European administrations. The Basque regional government has substantial autonomy to define industrial policy and is known for its proactive industrial policy during the last three decades. The provincial councils play a critical role in many policy areas and are responsible for collecting taxes. Finally, municipal authorities (especially in the bigger cities) and local development agencies promoted by them (in other areas) play an important role with respect to 'soft' policies such as support for networking, as they have the capacity to reach the final beneficiaries of such policies (specific firms). This institutional density can be considered an advantage if coordination between different levels is well developed. In particular the strong capillarity and autonomy at different policy levels facilitates closeness between policy makers, socio-economic agents and citizens, potentially enhancing participation and democratic processes in decision-making around development (Sugden and Wilson 2002). However, with weak co-ordination between the different levels, this characteristic can also be a source of inefficiency in policy design and implementation.

In this context, substantial efforts have been made to create infrastructures that give support to the regional innovation system (universities, technology centres, co-operative research centres). Yet an acknowledged weakness is the actual connectedness of different agents in the system, especially with regards the connections between firms and other knowledge agents and with regards the capacity for all agents to make external connections outside of the Basque Country (Orkestra 2011). Local development agencies and cluster associations are two key groups of intermediate agents that can play important roles in building such connections in the Basque context (Aranguren et al. 2010a, 2010b). Indeed, these two groups of agents have been the particular focus of a research agenda initiated around 12 years ago by researchers at the University of Deusto. Since 2006 this research agenda has been consolidated within Orkestra-Basque Institute of Competitiveness, an applied research centre with an explicit mission to orchestrate competitiveness processes with other agents, infusing these processes with academic knowledge.

Orkestra was founded in 2006 as an initiative of the Deusto Foundation, an institution devoted to making scientific knowledge available to society. It is supported by a group of stakeholders that include SPRI (the Society for the Promotion of Industry of the Basque regional government), the provincial council of Gipuzkoa, and several leading Basque firms. The University of Deusto also plays an important role: researchers forming Orkestra were drawn initially from the university and continue to teach there, and the Institute is physically located on the University campus. Supported by these stakeholders, Orkestra has the explicit aim of supporting activity from public administrations, socio-economic agents and all of the universities in the Basque Country in generating real improvements in the competitiveness of the region. A key challenge is maintaining an effective balance between working at the frontier of academic knowledge in regional competitiveness and working to improve the actual competitiveness of the Basque Country. It is a challenge of developing research in a way that will generate real change at the same time as enabling researchers to reflect and contribute to academic bodies of knowledge. Indeed, the need for specific approaches to meet these goals has been one of the driving motivations behind the analysis of knowledge co-generation processes in this chapter and is reflected also in several previous publications (Aranguren et al. 2012; Karlsen et al. 2012; Aranguren and Larrea 2011). In the next section we focus our analysis on three distinct processes that have integrally involved the cluster associations and/or the local development agencies: (1) mapping of clusters; (2) evaluation of cluster policy; (3) analysis of territorial competitiveness.[1]

4   THREE CASES OF CHANGE

The main aim of this section is to explore how change has happened in practice in three specific knowledge-generation processes by reflecting on the questions set out in Figure 14.2. We take each case in turn here and then discuss the synthesized findings in the concluding section.

4.1   Mapping of Clusters

The mapping of clusters in the Basque Country was initially identified as a concern by the stakeholders that established Orkestra, which led to the definition of two narrowly defined projects during the first year of Orkestra's operation. The first was to map 'traded clusters' using export data and a methodology developed by Porter (2003), which resulted in a report that identified and analysed the composition of the primary export clusters of the Basque Country (Aranguren et al. 2008a). The second was to map 'local clusters' using data on numbers of establishments in different sectors in each of the 250 municipalities of the Basque country, adapting the methodology of a study from Catalonia (Hernández Gascón et al. 2005). While both projects were conceived as one-off studies whose results would be diffused to the relevant agents through reports, the second project undertook a gradual transformation into a long-term process that would end up radically altering the mode of knowledge transfer and, as a consequence, the results of the study (Aranguren et al. 2011).

It became clear fairly early in the second project that there were significant difficulties in determining which sectors were related and which groupings of municipalities made most sense; in short there was a lack of detailed local and industry knowledge among the research team. Other studies have solved this problem by interviewing industry experts and then making judgements. However, the project coincided with awareness within the research group of: (1) a pool of local knowledge present within local development agencies and (2) the desire at the time of Basque Government policy makers to introduce a sub-regional element to their cluster policy. A decision was therefore made to re-orient the project from the production of a research report based on analysis of data, to a process involving policy agents from the local development agencies and the Basque Government. This decision led to the emergence over time of knowledge co-generation through a series of workshops and training sessions that combined theoretical knowledge with practical 'know-how'. In terms of how knowledge is generated, it has also been interesting to observe the combination of cognitive and emotional learning within this process, which had to cater for different expectations: while some agents approached it with a strong sense of engagement and enthusiasm for launching new projects; others were more reluctant and were looking for straightforward recipes for their already-defined problems.

There has been a corresponding evolution in 'how' and 'by who' research questions are defined. They were initially defined by researchers (with some arms-length interaction with Orkestra's stakeholders) on the basis of their theoretical and empirical understanding of the challenges facing the Basque Country. As the second project evolved into a collaborative process, however, the research questions became sharpened by the integration of knowledge and experience from the academic and practitioner perspectives. This led on the one hand to a strengthened focus on understanding in practice the relationships that lay behind observed statistical agglomerations of firms, and on the other hand to dropping the initial concern with producing a comprehensive mapping of Basque local clusters.[2] Related changes can also be observed in terms of organizing the knowledge creation process and the type of technology (or techniques) employed. Both projects were designed to be implemented by a team comprising a senior researcher alongside junior researchers and/or PhD students under their supervision; there was limited interaction envisaged with other agents during the research process. While the export-mapping project carried through this organization, the local mapping project evolved to incorporate mixed teams of senior and junior researchers, data and training support staff and technicians from local development agencies, each group with a differentiated role. The process was organized around a series of workshops in which researchers introduced concepts, techniques and visual data management/mapping tools, and practitioners discussed and applied these concepts and techniques to their own working contexts.

The workshop process thus provided an arena for combining knowledge and for sharpening the research questions towards more actionable outcomes. In this sense the need for specific knowledge transfer activities became unnecessary because the process itself was co-generating knowledge. This result can be seen in the fact that the envisaged comprehensive mapping report was never produced and diffused; rather, the research team wrote a report that reflected on the process of action research that had evolved over a four-year period (Aranguren et al. 2011). The results of the project were radically altered therefore, and became more 'relevant' in the sense of forming the basis for actions with socio-economic development impacts. Clear examples can be seen in the incorporation of new ideas from the workshops into projects being worked on by the local development agencies, including one case in which a cluster identified and analysed during the process has become part of the regional government's formal cluster policy to support its further development.

4.2 Evaluation of Cluster Policy

Interest among this group of researchers in the evaluation of the Basque cluster policy has its roots in a book analysing Basque Country competitiveness (Aranguren et al. 2003), which identified the high weight of small firms in the region and argued that they could become more competitive through co-operation. This led researchers to make initial contact with the policy makers responsible for the cluster policy of the Basque Government, a policy that aims to foster the competitiveness of groups of firms through co-operation by supporting the establishment and operation of 'cluster associations'. The motivation was to understand how this policy was developed (see Aranguren et al. 2006), and to analyse whether it was having an impact on SME competitiveness with the aim of contributing to improvement. In this sense the evaluation of the current cluster policy was identified as a critical, but complex, research agenda. This agenda was pursued initially by a group of researchers at Deusto University and later taken up as a core research line within Orkestra.

During the course of this still-ongoing research process several approaches have been used by researchers to evaluate the Basque cluster policy (Aranguren and Navarro 2003; Aranguren et al. 2008b; Aragón et al. 2010). Knowledge generation initially took place in a fairly traditional, linear way. The researchers designed projects using secondary data sources and/or collected primary data from the cluster associations. For example, a quasi-experimental evaluation approach was used to analyse two cluster associations: the Paper Cluster Association and the Electronics and Telecommunication Cluster association. In this approach the beneficiaries of the cluster policy and a control group of firms were identified using a statistical matching method, and their productivity growth and performance in areas like internationalization, innovation and quality were compared. The results showed that members of cluster associations performed in general better than non-members. This was complemented with a qualitative approach applied to the Paper Cluster Association with the aim of analysing some of the more intangible effects of the policy. Based on a questionnaire and in-depth interviews, the perceptions of cluster association members of the policy were analysed and the generation of social capital was identified as a key benefit of the policy but also a key challenge for the association.

After the creation of Orkestra, dialogue among researchers and the policy makers responsible for the Basque cluster policy led to the identification of a common interest around cluster policy evaluation as a key line of interaction between Orkestra and the Basque Government. Policy-makers in the Basque Government wanted to have evaluations of the cluster policy that would help them improve policy, and researchers were interested in deepening their existing research to overcome some of the acknowledged limitations. As a starting point for this work it was considered crucial by both parties (researchers and policy makers) that the cluster associations also saw the value of this research. A workshop was therefore held with the participation of 11 of the 12 cluster associations, where researchers presented the results of previous evaluation projects and instigated a dialogue around the value to all parties of ongoing evaluation. All of the associations considered evaluation to be relevant, particularly in an approach oriented to learning and improvement. Six of the 11 that participated in the workshop expressed interest in being part of a pilot case in 'participatory evaluation', which would bring together all policy stakeholders to consider the impacts of the policy as related to one specific cluster. The Aeronautics Cluster Association (Hegan) was selected, and this pilot case has developed into a knowledge co-generation process that is ongoing today (Aragón et al. 2011). Specifically, a series of workshops have been held with Hegan and its members, in which practical knowledge about the cluster's specific objectives and projects were combined with theoretical knowledge around issues such as social capital and other critical elements for cluster development. During this process a framework was defined and implemented to evaluate the cluster based on the level of development of social capital among members and its link to networking outcomes (Aragón et al. 2012).

Again we can observe a clear evolution from a research design for linear knowledge transfer to a process of knowledge co-generation that integrates the knowledge of researchers and practitioners. This is supported by a change in 'who' defines the research questions and 'how' they are defined. In the initial projects, before the creation of Orkestra, design was undertaken by researchers in isolation, based on their interest in analysing a policy relevant for their broader research on SMEs. This has evolved towards defining a participatory evaluation pilot process in open dialogue between researchers at Orkestra, cluster associations and Basque government policy makers, something that was possible due to the fostering of a long-term engagement between researchers and policy makers. In accordance with the process of participatory evaluation, the new knowledge generated was not only theoretical and cognitive, but there were several stages where emotional knowledge was crucial. For example, in one of the workshops there was confusion around the role of researchers and the consultants that were supporting the cluster association in their strategic planning, and in a later workshop it was initially difficult for firms to see the value of social capital indicators. In both cases there was a process of emotional learning among participants that was critical to moving forward with the research process.

In the transition from earlier evaluation approaches to current processes there has also been a change in how the knowledge creation process is organized and in the technology (or techniques) used. In the earlier projects, researchers defined and executed the research by themselves and then informed the cluster associations and policy makers of the results; there was a detachment of researchers from the agents being analysed. In the participatory evaluation project, knowledge was generated in interviews with cluster managers and policy makers and through workshops. Researchers were involved in a process *with* cluster associations and policy makers, and as such adapted their research to the timescales and working schedules of other agents. The involvement of other agents was not constant, however. The policy makers were heavily involved at the beginning, in the design phase, but following a change of government this involvement waned during the process. In the case of Hegan, involvement was high in discourse but low in action, although in this case it increased slightly during the process as the agents began to see the value more clearly. Regarding the technology (techniques) employed, in the first case researchers constructed research projects around the analysis of secondary data and interviews made to cluster members. In the participatory evaluation project a new social capital evaluation framework that is easily adaptable to other cluster policies was developed as a consequence of new knowledge generated through a co-generative process. Although the project generated some actionable knowledge for Hegan (for example it helped them identify pockets of the cluster where social capital was high or low), this new knowledge was scarce, in part due to the level of involvement of cluster agents in the process. Our interpretation is that the higher involvement of researchers and the lower involvement of practitioners resulted in co-generated knowledge with a greater theoretical component (specifically a social capital evaluation framework; see Aragón et al. 2012) than knowledge for action.

4.3   Analysis of Territorial Competitiveness

The third case refers to a process of analysing territorial competitiveness within the Basque Country, which started with participation by researchers at Deusto University in an EU Intereg project presented by Garapen (the association of Basque Local Development Agencies), jointly with partners from other parts of Europe. Within this framework Garapen asked the research team at Deusto to define and analyse a series of local competitiveness indicators in order to arrive at a framework and database to make diagnoses of competitiveness of the different counties in the Basque Country. Analysis was conducted for all Basque counties, which were grouped into typologies, and the results were published by Navarro and Larrea (2007).

Thus knowledge in this project was created by researchers using theoretical knowledge and secondary data analysis, with results transferred to society via the traditional publication route. However, the project coincided with one of the research team working also as a technician in Ezagutza Gunea, a network of firms, training centres, the local development agency, technological centres and the town council, located in one of the counties. Ezagutza Gunea was defining its strategic plan at that time, and to support this process the analysis was developed more deeply through a series of meetings between researchers and the network. In the part of the project developed with Ezagutza Gunea there was a different type of knowledge generation; the process led to knowledge co-generation in a way that meant that once the project finished there was no need to undertake a specific knowledge transfer activity.

Orkestra was founded at around the time when this process was finishing, and some of the researchers from the research team started working at Orkestra. This team saw an opportunity within Orkestra to develop a similar exercise to that developed in Ezagutza Gunea among the other counties in the Basque Country so as to generate capabilities and competencies to make strategic planning at county level. An agreement was signed with Garapen to develop a series of workshops with all of the local development agencies (LDAs) interested in improving in their capabilities to make strategic planning in their territories. Fifteen of the 32 LDAs participated in a series of five workshops where researchers presented the competitiveness framework, the database of indicators and so on, and the technicians from the LDAs used this input to develop an analysis of their own counties. This new approach facilitated a process of knowledge co-generation whereby new knowledge was generated in the arenas of dialogue that took place in the workshops. Researchers' theoretical knowledge and conceptualization capability was combined with technicians' practical knowledge, creating new capabilities. Emotional learning has also occurred and can be seen most clearly in the gradual adaptation of expectations among agents that initially entered the process with distinct perceptions of the usefulness of the workshops and varying levels of commitment. The results of the process were published in a chapter of the Second Competitiveness Report elaborated by Orkestra (Orkestra 2009).

As in the previous cases there has been a clear change in who determines research questions and how they are determined. In the initial Intereg project the framework and data analysis was posed by the researchers, in response to a general request from one of the agents (Garapen). The fact that one of the research team was also working for a network of agents in one of the counties being analysed led to a change in how the research questions were posed for that specific county, leading to a deepening of the analysis that contributed to the development of their strategic plan. Learning around the possibilities from co-generation of knowledge led to researchers proposing a widening of this process to all counties under an agreement between Garapen and Orkestra. At this stage the research questions were defined jointly among the researchers and Garapen, integrating the research interest in diagnosing territorial competitiveness with Garapen's interest in developing strategy-making capabilities at local level.

Related changes can also be observed in terms of the organization of the knowledge creation process and the techniques employed. The first project was designed to be implemented by a team of researchers; there was limited interaction envisaged with other agents during the research process, although in the evolution of the project there was interaction with the practitioners in Ezagutza Gunea. The second project was designed to incorporate mixed teams of senior and junior researchers, data and training support staff and technicians from local development agencies, each group with differentiated roles. The process was organized around a series of workshops in which researchers introduced concepts and techniques and practitioners discussed and applied these concepts and techniques to their own working contexts. The workshop process thus provided an arena for combining knowledge and for sharpening the research questions towards more actionable outcomes. In this sense the need for specific knowledge transfer activities became unnecessary because the process itself was co-generating knowledge. In this way the results of the project were more 'relevant' for actions with socio-economic development impacts. Clear examples of this are the different concrete projects and proposals that LDAs have presented to the provincial council and the Basque Government for funding (see Orkestra 2009).

5   CONCLUSIONS

The three cases have strong similarities, which is perhaps unsurprising given that they involved a group of researchers working in a commonly changing institutional context (the creation of Orkestra). All three cases started with a research question framed by researchers to be explored in a fairly traditional research project and then disseminated through publications. In each case, however, there was a key moment of realization among researchers that the usefulness of the research for agents (local development agencies, cluster associations and government policy makers) could be enhanced through a different kind of interaction. This led to fundamental changes in how the research processes proceeded, and ultimately in the types of results that were generated. There were several common features to these changes. Indeed, returning to the questions posed in Figure 14.2

Table 14.1   Summary of key elements of change processes in the three cases

Key questions	Key elements of change
How is knowledge generated and transferred?	From linear knowledge transfer to knowledge cogeneration From theoretical knowledge to knowing how From a cognitive approach to also emotional learning
Who is defining the research questions? How are the questions defined by the actors?	From research questions derived from literature to specific problem solving From specific projects to long term cooperation
How is the knowledge creation process organized?	From research teams to mixed teams From detachment to involvement Creating arenas: living laboratories and networks
Which kind of technology is used and how is it used?	Developing an approach to action research From knowledge transfer to competence building

(around which the case analyses were structured), the main lessons learned from the three cases are summarized in Table 14.1.

As can be seen from the case analysis these changes in the knowledge generation process led to different kinds of results and different kinds of socioeconomic impacts. In particular, where there were strong degrees of engagement between researchers and agents, a key result was seen in terms of building competences among agents and generating action-able knowledge that fed into concrete development projects that would not have happened without these processes (for example in the cluster mapping and territorial competitiveness cases). Where engagement was less strong or intermittent (for example in the cluster evaluation case) there was less actionable knowledge with capacity for concrete impacts in socioeconomic development processes and a higher theoretical component to the knowledge that was generated. The case analyses therefore raise an important issue of balance between theoretical and action components.

The approach to change in the three cases has been a long-term process where both practitioners and researchers have learned that it takes time to co-generate knowledge. Knowledge co-generation is a social and an emotional process, and this is especially so in change processes, where old cognitive patterns have to be replaced with new patterns in a collective, shared way. Change can only take place when everybody in the process realizes this and is prepared to change their behaviour. In this sense, the action research process applied in the three cases has been demanding because both researchers and practitioners have had to change their approach to research: the practitioners because they first wanted to get knowledge from the researchers in a linear way as a recipe of what to do; the researchers because they realized that their theoretical knowledge alone was not enough to have real-world impacts. Hence both parties had to change their cognitive patterns during the research process. This also implies that a long-term learning process is possible only if there is some continuity of people involved. In every process a 'knowing how' is developed that is very hard to share with people who have not participated, and thus there must be a team approach both among researchers and practitioners in co-generative processes.

These core issues of balance and the long-term nature of action research processes should be considered alongside a series of other specific implications from the analysis for the day-to-day work of academics that are responding to pressures to make their research more relevant. First, the institutional environment is important. In all cases the capacity to undertake workshops with practitioners was critical to developing actionable knowledge. Orkestra has given strong legitimacy in this sense, both in terms of attracting attendance and in terms of basic resources for such long-term processes (facilities, time). Second, the type of research outputs from knowledge co-generation processes is different, and this implies a different way of reporting the results. This can be seen in the types of reports produced, for example, which have changed quite substantially, and also in the types of academic articles that have been written (reflecting more on the process). Third, the development of more actionable knowledge requires a certain adaptation on the part of the researcher. In particular there is a need to adapt in terms of how the research project is 'sold' to agents – it is critical that they see the value early in the process – and to find a compromise between academic timescales and the timescales with which policy makers and intermediate agents are more accustomed to working. Finally, rather than replacing 'mode 1' research with 'mode 2' research, our analysis of the process of change in these three cases suggests that it is more a question of shifting balance between different types of knowledge production and transfer. More traditional modes of desk research and linear transfer do not cease to exist; rather they are complemented by new elements of co-generation that support more actionable knowledge and hence different kinds of socio-economic impacts. This can be seen in the fact that research results have been diffused through traditional academic publications in all three processes, alongside the emergence of new, related processes that facilitate the solution of problems identified with practitioners. In this sense our analysis supports Hessels and van Lente's (2008: 756) argument that 'we should not regard the changing modes of research as a one-dimensional development'.[3]

NOTES

1. We refer to research processes rather than projects, because in practice each has brought together several more discrete projects in a long-term evolution where it is difficult to distinguish between them.
2. The process developed only where there was engagement with local development agencies, and while it was based on an open call for participation by all agencies, take-up was not 100 per cent and the system of local development agencies also does not have 100 per cent coverage of the Basque territory.
3. See also Martin (2003) and Aranguren and Larrea (2011).

REFERENCES

Aragón, C., M-J. Aranguren and C. Iturrioz (eds) (2010), *Evaluación de políticas clúster: El caso del País Vasco*, Bilbao: Deusto Publicaciones.

Aragón, C., M-J. Aranguren, C. Iturrioz and J. R. Wilson (2011), 'Una metodología participativa para la evaluación, de la política clúster del País Vasco', in J-L. Curbelo, M. D. Parrilli and F. Alburquerque (eds), *Territorios innovadores y competitivos*, Madrid: Marcial Pons, pp. 319–42.

Aragón, C., M-J. Aranguren, C. Iturrioz and J. R. Wilson (2012), 'A social capital approach for network policy learning: the case of an established cluster initiative', *European Urban and Regional Studies*, doi: 10.1177/0969776411434847.

Aranguren, M-J. and M. Larrea (2011), 'Regional innovation policy processes: Linking learning to action', *Journal of Knowledge Economy*, **2**(4), 569–85.

Aranguren, M-J. and I. Navarro (2003), 'La política clusters en el país Vasco: una primera valoración', *Ekonomiaz*, **53**, 90–113.

Aranguren, M-J., M. Larrea and I. Navarro (2003), *Euskal Autonomi Erkidegoko Ekonomiari begira*, Donostia–San Sebastián: Deustuko Unibertsitatea.

Aranguren, M-J., M. Larrea and I. Navarro (2006), 'The policy process: Clusters versus spatial networks in the Basque Country', in C. Pitelits, R. Sugden and J. Wilson (eds) *Clusters and Globalisation: The Development of Urban and Regional Economies*. Edward Elgar Publishing, pp. 258–80.

Aranguren, M-J., C. Aragón, M. Larrea and C. Iturrioz (2008b), 'Does cluster policy really enhance networking and increase competitiveness', in Aranguren, M-J., C. Iturrioz and J. Wilson (eds) *Networks, Governance and Economic Development*, Edward Elgar Publishing, pp. 101–28.

Aranguren, M-J., M. Larrea and J. R. Wilson (2012), 'Academia and public policy: towards the co-generation of knowledge and learning processes', in B. T. Asheim and M. D Parrilli (eds), *Interactive Learning for Innovation: A Key Driver within Clusters and Innovation Systems*, Basingstoke: Palgrave Macmillan, pp. 275–89.

Aranguren, M-J., M. Larrea and J. R. Wilson (2010a), 'Trayectorias de Camino en la Gobernanza: Experiencias en Asociaciones Clúster y Redes en el País Vasco', *Ekonomiaz*, **74**(2), 160–77.

Aranguren, M-J., M. Larrea and J. R. Wilson (2010b), 'Learning from the local: governance of networks for innovation in the Basque Country', *European Planning Studies*, **18**(1), 47–66.

Aranguren, M-J., A. Azpiazu, M. Larrea, A. Murciego and J. R. Wilson (2011), *Identificación de clústeres: un proceso de investigación–acción*, Bilbao: Deusto Publicaciones.

Aranguren, M-J., M. Navarro, X. de la Maza and P. Canto (2008a), *Identificación de clústeres en la CAPV*, Bilbao: Deusto Publicaciones.

Etzkowitz, H. and L. Leydesdorff (eds) (1997), *Universities and the Global Knowledge Economy: A Triple Helix of University–Industry–Government Relations*, London: Cassell.

Etzkowitz, H. and L. Leydesdorff (2000), 'The dynamics of innovation: from national systems and "mode 2" to a triple helix of university–industry–government relations', *Research Policy*, **29**(2), 313–30.

Gibbons, M., C. Limoges, H. Nowotny, S. Schwartzmann, P. Scott and M. Trow (1994), *The New Production of Knowledge – The Dynamics of Science and Research in Contemporary Societies*, London: Sage.

Greenwood, D. J. and M. Levin (2007), *Introduction to Action Research*, 2nd edn, Thousand Oaks, CA: Sage Publications.

Gustavsen, B. (1992), *Dialogue and Development. Theory of Communication, Action Research and the Restructuring of Working Life*, Assen: Van Gorcum.

Hernández Gascón, J. M., J. Fontrodona Francoli and A. Pezzi (2005), *Mapa de los Sistemas Productivos Locales Industriales en Cataluña*, Barcelona: Generalitat de Catalunya.

Hessels, L. K. and H. van Lente (2008), 'Re-thinking new knowledge production: A literature review and a research agenda', *Research Policy*, **37**(4), 740–60.

Johnsen, H. C. G. (2001), *Involvement at Work: A Study of Communicative Processes and Individual Involvement in Organizational Development*. København: Handelshøjskolen i København.

Karlsen, J., M. Larrea, M-J. Aranguren and J. R. Wilson (2012), 'Bridging the gap between academic research and regional development in the Basque Country', *European Journal of Education*, **47**(1), 122–38.

Laredo, P. (2007), 'Revisiting the third mission of universities: toward a renewed categorization of university activities', *Higher Education Policy*, **20**, 441–56.

Martin, B. R. (2003), 'The changing social contract for science and the evolution of the university', in A. Guena, A. Salter and A. E. Steinmueller (eds), *Science and Innovation: Rethinking Rationales for Funding and Governance*, Cheltenham: Edward Elgar.

Navarro, M. and M. Larrea (2007), *Indicadores y análisis de competitividad local en el País Vasco*. Doc Ekonomiaz. Gobierno Vasco.

Orkestra (2011), *Basque Competitiveness Report 2011: Leading in the New Complexity*, Bilbao: Deusto Publications.

Orkestra (2009), *Second Report on the Competitiveness of the Basque Country: Towards an Innovation-based Competitiveness Stage*, Bilbao: Deusto Publications.

Porter, M. E. (2003), 'The economic performance of regions', *Regional Studies*, **37**, 549–78.

Rip, A. (2004), 'Strategic research, post-modern universities and research training', *Higher Education Policy*, **17**(2), 153–66.

Sugden, R. and J. R. Wilson (2002), 'Development in the shadow of the consensus: a strategic decision-making approach', *Contributions to Political Economy*, **21**, 111–34.

15. Where were you?

David G. Blanchflower

Inspiration is most likely to come through the stimulus provided by the patterns, puzzles and anomalies revealed by the systematic gathering of data, particularly when the prime need is to break our existing habits of thought.
Ronald Coase, Nobel Prize lecture (1991)[1]

All too few academic economists these days seem to be engaged in policy debates, and that seems especially true in the UK. Maybe that is because of perverse incentives, because promotion and reputation rest in large part on publication in prestigious journals that few people read. That may well be because the Research Assessment Exercise (RAE)/Research Evaluation Framework (REF) in the UK amounts to little more than top journal paper counting.[2] Sadly many of these papers are cited by few and are not written to solve a deep policy question and indeed, in some cases could even be summarized as an answer in search of a question and worthless. A 'major' contribution on a quite trivial technical point in the economics profession usually receives more approbation and attention, and even a salary increase than a small contribution to an important question. Trying to solve some narrow theoretical point may well be less than useless. The big emphasis on theory in many UK economics departments seems to have been a mistake, as it seems to have little impact and has done little or nothing to improve the human condition. Playing clever mind games, which is the equivalent of counting angels on pinheads, should be a hobby rather than an activity subsidized by the British taxpayer.[3]

Andrew Oswald (2006) examined citations in journals and found that the journal system often allocates high-quality papers into medium-quality journals, and vice versa. In the *American Economic Review*, which is perhaps the most famous journal in the discipline, he found that in its winter issue in 1981 more than one-third of the issue's articles had each been cited fewer than 20 times after a quarter of a century.[4] The very best papers in the other lower-quality journals had by then garnered far more mentions in others' bibliographies. Oswald concluded that 'it is dangerous to argue that publication in famous journal X means that a paper is more important than one published in medium-quality journal Y'.

Unless research is addressed to important policy questions the general public is entitled to feel they are not getting decent value for their investment. It is likely that the money would have been better spent delivering free childcare. I advise vice-chancellors and deans these days to ask every economist they interview the following question 'what problem is your research attempting to solve'? If they can't answer, or give an unsatisfactory response, don't hire them, period. It's perfectly okay to say that what is being examined is a hard question that may take a long time to solve, but it is not enough to say that what is being studied is how to add a squiggle to a squiggle. The university would be better off hiring someone who is working on how to cure cancer or ALS, which my father died from recently.

Sitting at the Bank of England as a member of the Monetary Policy Committee (MPC) from 2006 to 2009, trying to make interest rate decisions every month, was a lonely task; there was little or nothing academic economists had to contribute, I am afraid to say. I also learnt about the extent to which academic economists are not really engaged in the current policy questions. A major issue in 2008 was whether or not the labour market was tightening; none of my labour economist colleagues had been thinking about that. There were many more such issues that I needed help with, but was left high and dry, as the academic economics community is not engaged in the big economic questions of the day.

I am struck by how data releases drive the lives of economists out there practising in the real world and how little academic economists know about what they do. My life these days is very much based around data releases of the monthly unemployment and inflation numbers, the quarterly GDP numbers for the UK and the US and Europe, as well as reports by the Bank of England's agents; the EU monthly sentiment index; the Nationwide house price consumer confidence and house price indices; the Lloyds/HBOS house price index and the three purchasing manager's indexes for manufacturing, construction and services that come out on the first three days of the month, in that order. Plus there is material from the Bank of England on lending and the money supply each month. Then there are the quarterly Industrial Trends and Distributive Trades Surveys from the CBI and the quarterly survey from the British Chambers of Commerce. And that is only for the UK: there are indices for Europe on unemployment from Eurostat, as well as European PMIs and confidence indicators from Europe, including the German IFO index. Then there is what is happening in the bond markets to yields on ten-year bonds, as well as what is happening to bond auctions around the world. In addition there are speeches by various policymakers, especially central bankers around the world, plus the monthly interest rate decisions and statements and

Draghi, Bernanke and King's press conferences following these decisions. The average academic economist in a British university knows little or nothing about this, and hence is not a potential contributor to Bloomberg News or Radio 4's *The Today Programme*, *PM* or *The World at One*, Radio 5 Live, the BBC News Channel, or BBC 2's *Newsnight*. By the way, no need to be scared of Jeremy Paxman: I found him extremely pleasant and fair.[5] I have even become an expert on France.[6] Economists need to join the club, especially if they disagree, and engage in the public debate.[7] If you don't others will, and have, who know less.

A pretty good indicator of quality is the number of citations in the Web of Science as well as in Google Scholar where a paper cited a thousand times is a big deal.[8] According to RePec the ten most cited UK economists in order are as follows, with overall ranking among all 32 000 economists in the database in parentheses.[9] It is notable that with the exception of Chris Pissarides, who just received a Nobel prize, all are basically empirical – Besley does a mix of theory and empirics and was an external member of the MPC:

- (19) Richard Blundell (UCL)
- (39) Hashem Pesaran (Cambridge)
- (56) Steve Nickell (Oxford)
- (61) Steve Bond (Oxford)
- (64) Andrew Oswald (Warwick)
- (68) Tony Venables (LSE)
- (99) Tim Besley (LSE)
- (124) Mark P. Taylor (Warwick)
- (131) Chris Pissarides (LSE)
- (144) John Van Reenen (LSE)

Notably the UK has only seven of the 100 most highly cited economists in the world, according to this measure.

There is little engagement in the newspapers, where few academics write op-eds. Even fewer are prepared to go on TV and radio. I get to debate with the same old faces from the City of London: to this point the one major exception has been the fine transport economist David Newberry from Cambridge. In the US there is a long list of academics who write columns and appear on TV. The best known is Paul Krugman but also Bad DeLong, Barry Eichengreen and several of my Dartmouth colleagues including Doug Irwin and Matt Slaughter.

There are also many academics turned policymakers including Larry Summers, Robert Reich, Marty Feldstein and others. In part this is because there are a number of jobs for academic economists, including on the panel of economic advisors to the President, which has had a list of economic luminaries as chairman (Duesenberry, Ackley, Greenspan, Okun, Lazear, Romer, Bernanke, Mankiw, Hubbard, to name a few) as well as chief economist at the Labor Department (for example Holzer, Montgomery, Katz, Krueger, Lynch and Stevenson) and Abraham at the Bureau of Labor Statistics.[10] These are appointments that academics are given sabbatical leave to do from their home institutions for one year, as at the DOL, or two or three, as in the case of the Council. There is a tradition in both the US and the UK to take sabbatical leave to become members of the interest rate-setting committee at the Federal reserve, for example Mishkin (Columbia), Krosner (Chicago) and Blinder (Princeton) and at the Bank of England, e.g. Nickell (Oxford) and Besley (LSE). Ben Bernanke, Charlie Bean, Mervyn King and Stan Fisher resigned their academic jobs to take permanent appointments at central banks. A number of European academics have also become involved in the media, including Charles Wyplotz and Paul De Grauwe and some have taken up policy positions including Coen Teulings in the Netherlands, Wolfgang Franz and Christoph Schmidt in Germany and Bertil Holmlund and Lars Calmfors in Sweden.

There are important exceptions of course in the UK including Andrew Oswald and Marcus Miller at Warwick; David Bell from Stirling, Simon Wren-Lewis from Oxford, John Van Reenen from the London School of Economics (LSE) and Jonathan Portes from the National Institute of Economic and Social Research (NIESR), but the list gets pretty thin after that. These characters appear variously on TV and radio, write blogs and op-eds and some even tweet! Retired academics including Lords Skidelsky, Desai and Layard are especially active. It has to be said that the turnout for writing letters of complaint to various newspapers has been somewhat better. Analogously very few academic economists seem to have joined Twitter, which appears to have replaced blogging for the most part. Paul Krugman, for example, has over three-quarters of a million followers on Twitter.

So why the great fear of being engaged? Lack of self-confidence is one explanation. But economists spend their lives standing up in front of students explaining complicated arguments, so that doesn't wash. I suspect the big concern is that they will be forced to move outside their comfort zone and be asked questions about something else. That is a big mistake as first, they don't have to be drawn but second, and more importantly, even though they know little, they may well know more than anyone else. If the professionals are not prepared to contribute then the amateurs, including the politicians, get to take over.

This chapter is about the need for engagement and involvement of the economics profession in the problems of our day, principally on the macro economy, because that is where the most important problems are. We have been hit by a once-in-100-years' recession and the economics profession has largely been quiet. Why did so few people see this catastrophe coming and what should we do about it? In what follows I am going to discuss the policy mistakes and look for help. What should we do about rising unemployment? What is the best way to get youth unemployment down? How do we get the economy back to growth? Is there evidence that supports the contention that fiscal contractions are expansionary?

ECONOMISTS DIDN'T DELIVER

Where were economists in our hour of greatest need? Where were you? Asking a similar question, Paul Krugman says he is ashamed of economists and concluded as follows in his address at the University of Linz on 27 February 2012:

> I blame economists, who were incoherent in our hour of need. Far from contributing useful guidance, many members of my profession threw up dust, fostered confusion, and actually degraded the quality of the discussion. And this mattered. The political scientist Henry Farrell has carefully studied policy responses in the crisis, and has found that the near-consensus of economists that the banks must be rescued, and the semi-consensus in favor of stimulus in the initial months (mainly because the freshwater economists were caught by surprise, and took time to mobilize) was crucial in driving initial policy. The profession's descent into uninformed quarreling undid all that, and left us where we are today.
>
> And this is a terrible thing for those who want to think of economics as useful. This kind of situation is what we're here for. In normal times, when things are going pretty well, the world can function reasonably well without professional economic advice. It's in times of crisis, when practical experience suddenly proves useless and events are beyond anyone's normal experience, that we need professors with their models to light the path forward. And when the moment came, we failed.[11]

Wow!

The economics profession missed the big one – I suspect largely also because they had their eyes elsewhere and had become interested in theoretical niceties and had failed to follow Larry Summers' (1991) wonderful piece of advice about the need to confront theory with the data. He called it the 'scientific illusion' in empirical macroeconomics:

> [f]ormal empirical work which ... 'tries to take models seriously econometrically' has had almost no influence on serious thinking about substantive as opposed to methodological questions. Instead the *only* empirical research that

has influenced thinking about substantive questions has been based on methodological principles directly opposed to those that have become fashionable in recent years. Successful empirical research has been characterized by attempts to gauge the strengths of associations rather than to estimate structural parameters, verbal characterizations of how causal relations might operate rather than explicit mathematical models, and the skillful use of carefully chosen natural experiments rather than sophisticated statistical techniques to achieve identification. (p. 129)[12]

And later:

> Good empirical evidence tells its story regardless of the precise way in which it is analyzed. In large part it is its simplicity that makes it persuasive. Physicists do not compete to find more elaborate ways to observe falling apples. Instead they have made progress because theory has sought inspiration from a wide range of empirical phenomena. Macroeconomics could progress in the same way. But progress is unlikely as long as macroeconomists require the armor of a stochastic pseudo-world before doing battle with evidence from the real one. (p. 146)

The profession had become complacent, none more so than Bob Lucas, winner of the 1995 Nobel Prize in economics in his 2003 Presidential address to the American Economic Association who seems to have called it wrongly:

> Macroeconomics was born as a distinct field in the 1940s, as a part of the intellectual response to the Great Depression. The term then referred to the body of knowledge and expertise that we hoped would prevent the recurrence of that economic disaster. My thesis in this lecture is macroeconomics in this original sense has succeeded: its central problem of depression prevention has been solved, for all practical purposes, and has in fact been solved for many decades.[13]

In the summer of 2008, just before the crash of Lehmans, Olivier Blanchard, now chief economist at the IMF, published a National Bureau of Economic Research (NBER) working paper entitled 'The state of macro is good', which made no mention of bubbles or any real world data.[14] In it he argued that 'macroeconomics is going through a period of great progress and excitement', outlining what a typical article in macro looks like. No mention here of trying to test against data from the real world: calibration is just making things up because the model doesn't actually fit the real world:

> A macroeconomic article today often follows strict, haiku-like, rules: It starts from a general equilibrium structure, in which individuals maximize the

expected present value of utility, firms maximize their value, and markets clear. Then, it introduces a twist, be it an imperfection or the closing of a particular set of markets, and works out the general equilibrium implications. It then performs a numerical simulation, based on calibration, showing that the model performs well. It ends with a welfare assessment.

I have no idea what haiku-like rules are. I have been especially struck by the totally ludicrous claims made by Chari and Kehoe who seem to have entirely missed the plot.[15] If economics is not what Harberger in 1993 called an 'observational discipline', it is nothing.[16]

Over the last three decades, macroeconomic theory and the practice of macroeconomics by economists have changed — for the better. Macroeconomics is now firmly grounded in the principles of economic theory.

I would have hoped that macroeconomics would have been well grounded in the muddy waters of the data rather than being embroiled in arguments between the freshwater and saltwater kind of economics (Chicago and Minnesota vs Princeton and Harvard). Difficulties arise when a subject emphasizes theory over empirics. Theory is fine but we need to test it against data from the real world to see if it is actually true, rather than just elegant. Nobel Laureate Bob Solow as ever had it right in his summary of where macroeconomics has ended up:

> The other possible defence of modern macro is that, however special it may seem, it is justified empirically. This too strikes me as a delusion. In fact 'modern macro' has been notable for paying very little rigorous attention to data. I am left with the feeling that there is nothing in the empirical performance of these models that could come close to overcoming a modest scepticism. And more certainly, there is nothing to justify reliance on them for serious policy analysis.[17]

The consequences of this lack of understanding of how the real world operates has led to Western economies being unprepared for what was coming, especially because of their narrow focus on inflation. Of particular relevance are Paul De Grauwe's well-known comments in the *Financial Times* on 22 July 2008:

> There is a danger that the macro-economic models now in use in central banks operate like a Maginot line. They have been constructed in the past as part of the war against inflation. The central banks are prepared to fight the last war. But are they prepared to fight the new one against financial upheavals and recession? The macroeconomic models they have today certainly do not provide them with the right tools to be successful. They will have to use other intellectual constructs to succeed.[18]

The workhouse models for monetary policy analysis by central banks over the last decade are based largely on the New Keynesian Phillips Curve literature. This class of real business cycle models incorporates some nominal rigidities, but is actually more in the tradition of Friedman, stressing the importance of inflation expectations. However, there is little role for financial intermediation, money supply growth, asset prices and changes in the structure of wage setting, which inevitably limits their usefulness. These models have been poor tools for monetary policy makers.

Robert Skidelsky, in an article in the *Washington Post* in 2008, was spot-on in his criticisms of these various models:

> But what is in even shorter supply than credit is an economic theory to explain why this financial tsunami occurred, and what its consequences might be. Over the past 30 years, economists have devoted their intellectual energy to proving that such disasters cannot happen. The market system accurately prices all trades at each moment in time. Greed, ignorance, euphoria, panic, herd behaviour, predation, financial skullduggery and politics – the forces that drive boom–bust cycles – only exist off the balance sheet of their models. So mainstream theory has no explanation of why things have gone so horribly wrong.[19]

Lord Skidelsky goes on to suggest that to understand how markets can generate their own hurricanes we need to return to John Maynard Keynes. Is Skidelsky right? What is the actual evidence? Was the financial crisis predictable? It is perfectly possible that as economists we had insufficient understanding of the importance of herd behaviour in all of this, in housing and money markets, and that economics is too short of work on such phenomena.[20] Above all, was there something we economists could reasonably be expected to have said and then done well before the crash? Why didn't we pay more attention to tail risks? The events of the last 12 months represent a challenge to economists. Does mainstream theory have an adequate explanation of why things have gone so badly wrong? It is not clear that it does. It may well be time for a rethink.

COLLAPSE, RECOVERY, FLATLINING AND REVISIONS

I am particularly struck by how little engaged the economics profession has been on the causes and consequences of the Great Recession. Should we have spotted it coming? Given the profession in general failed to spot it, how much attempt has there been to address the failings in our economic models? Was it right to slash spending, as the 20 letter writers to the *Sunday*

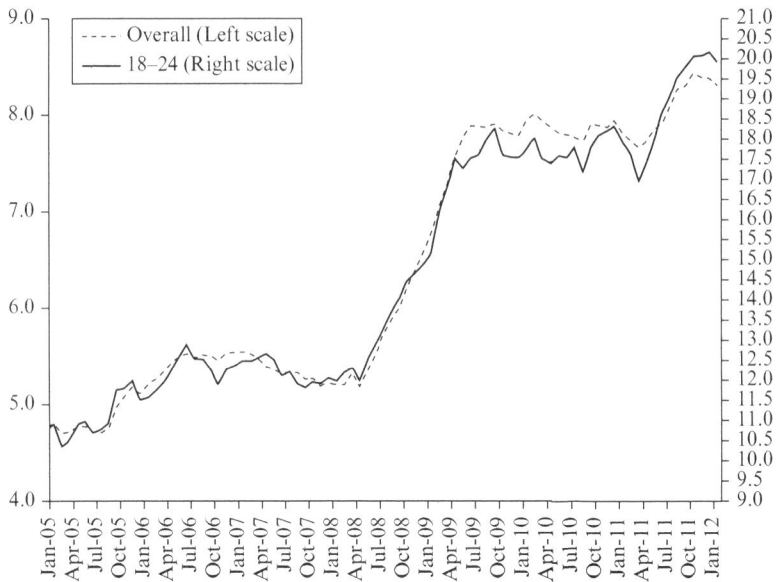

Figure 15.1　UK unemployment rates, 2005–12

Times in February 2010 wanted? Were the 60 economists who responded in a follow-up letter in the *FT* right? What has gone wrong? What policies should we be adopting right now? In the UK, should (Chancellor) Osborne change course – if so, how? Does (Shadow Chancellor) Ed Balls have the fix in his five-point plan? These are all questions that need addressing and, as far as I can tell, have not been.

It is certainly appropriate to take a look at the role of the Bank of England, including both the Governor and the MPC as well as why their forecasts have been so hopeless. Also the role of the Office of Budget Responsibility and its forecasts need to be examined. This is what I do in this section.

Figure 15.1 shows the increase in the overall UK unemployment rate and the youth unemployment rate since 2005. Unemployment jumped from 4 per cent in July 2005 to 8.2 per cent in July 2012, and from 1 423 000 to 2.67 million. One in five youngsters age 18–24 are unemployed. Youth unemployment dropped sharply after the Labour government introduced the Future of Jobs Fund and the Educational Maintenance Allowance targeted on reducing youth joblessness. Youth unemployment started rising again once the incoming coalition government abolished these programmes, which were working. In the US the unemployment rate increased to 10 per cent but is now falling with the latest estimate for

Table 15.1 Quarterly GDP and revisions as of May 2012 (%), quarter on quarter

	Preliminary	Latest	Revision
(a) Global Collapse			
2007Q4	0.6	0.2	−0.4
2008Q1	0.4	0.1	−0.3
2008Q2	0.2	−0.9	−1.1
2008Q3	−0.5	−1.8	−1.3
2008Q4	−1.5	−2.1	−0.6
2009Q1	−1.9	−1.5	+0.4
2009Q2	−0.8	−0.2	+0.6
(b) Darling Recovery			
2009Q3	−0.4	0.4	+0.8
2009Q4	0.1	0.4	+0.3
2010Q1	0.2	0.6	+0.2
2010Q2	1.1	0.7	−0.4
2010Q3	0.8	0.6	−0.2
(c) Osborne Collapse			
2010Q4	−0.5	−0.4	+0.1
2011Q1	0.5	0.5	−0.2
2011Q2	0.2	−0.1	−0.3
2011Q3	0.5	0.6	+0.1
2011Q4	−0.2	−0.4	−0.2
2012Q1	−0.2	−0.3	−0.1
2012Q2	−0.5		n/a
Average revision			
2006Q1–2012Q1			−0.1

September 2012 at 7.8 per cent. Youth unemployment is at 16 per cent but the duration of unemployment has risen.

Table 15.1 shows the loss in output in the UK since 2008, measured by changes in quarterly GDP measured as a quarter-on-quarter change. I split the table into three distinct parts:

(a) Global Collapse (2007Q4–2009Q2)
(b) Darling Recovery (2009Q3–2010Q3)
(c) Osborne Collapse (2010Q4–2012Q1)

GDP growth using the most recent estimates available in each of the three groups was −6.2 per cent; +2.7 per cent and −0.6 per cent respectively. The first period is the Global Collapse, which saw a collapse in output unprecedented since the 1930s. The second period, which I call the Darling Recovery, achieved growth of +2.7 per cent through a combination of fiscal and monetary stimulus. The final group is what I have termed the Osborne Collapse, which dates from the fourth quarter of 2010 and continues. It seems reasonable to use this as a starting point given that it takes time for policies to have an effect and the coalition was not formed until May 2010. Over the seven quarters since the end of 2010 growth has declined by 0.6 per cent and from the last quarter of 2011 the UK economy has been in a double-dip recession. There is some prospect that growth will be positive in 2012Q3, although a return to a triple-dip recession in 2012Q4 is not out of the question.[21]

The first column includes the preliminary estimate, which is reported, usually three weeks or so after the quarter is completed and covers only about 40 per cent of the economic activity which will be included in the more mature estimates published around 12 months later. For example the first estimate for 2012Q1 GDP of −0.2 per cent was reported on 25 April 2012. These numbers then enter into a revision cycle and are subject to revision for years ahead. Currently the Office for National Statistics (ONS) provides a revision triangle for these data as far back as 1992Q1, which last had a revision in September 2008.[22] The average size of revisions since 1993Q1 is +0.1 per cent and since 2006Q1 is −0.1 per cent. The reason for the upward revision is principally the change in the deflator from the Retail Prices Index (RPI) to the Consumer Prices Index (CPI). This did have an upward impact on GDP growth on average but it would be wrong, without knowing details of any proposed methodological changes and their impact, to assume that such revisions will be repeated.[23] I understand from the ONS that the large downward revision at Blue Book 2011 to 2008 growth rates was due to 'new data from various sources, including company profits from HM Revenue and Customs, being taken on in the balancing process'.

The definitive source on data revisions is a paper by Brown et al. They conclude:

> Although there is some evidence of historical upward bias in revisions, its extent and direction have not been stable or predictable. Further, any such bias appears to have been smaller since the mid-1990s, and insignificantly different from zero. Revisions are not sufficiently large, regular or predictable to be able to support any procedure of incorporating bias adjustments into early estimates.[24]

Despite this there has been some controversy over the quality of the data as some commentators claim to 'know' that these numbers will be revised upwards.[25] The best one can probably say currently is that any revision is likely to be small. But that is not to say that past revisions have been small, as is clear from columns 2 and 3 of Table 15.1. Column 2 of Table 15.1 reports the latest estimate while column 3 shows the extent and the direction of the revisions.

The revisions really do matter and this is something that academics really do need to pay attention to. The main findings in relation to the revisions are as follows:

1. Growth in 2007 was revised upwards strongly, by 0.4 per cent in each of the first three quarters. If I had known how strong growth was, in all likelihood I would have voted on the Monetary Policy Committee for further rate increases, particularly in the early months of 2007. The extent of the slowing at the end of 2007 that I observed now looks even sharper than it did, so it was probably right to start voting for rate cuts at the end of 2007.

2. Revisions moved the start of the recession earlier than it first appeared – from 2008Q3 to 2008Q2. The preliminary estimate for 2008Q2 that the MPC received in April 2008 was 0.2 per cent. In September 2011 that number was revised to −1.3 per cent suggesting that the recession had started but was not apparent from the official data. Tim Besley even voted for a rate increase from 5 per cent to 5.25 per cent in both July and August 2008, but surely would not have done so if he had known the economy had already entered recession. The preliminary estimate of −0.5 per cent really put the cat among the pigeons at the Bank of England at the end of September 2008, but more on that below. Interest rates were cut by 50 bp on October but panic would have really set in if we had known the latest number of −2.0 per cent. Given that 2008Q1 stands at 0.1 per cent at the time of writing (October 2012) it will only take a minor revision to move the start of the recession even earlier.

3. The biggest news is what happened in 2008, where the revisions make it clear that the recession was much deeper than first thought; Q1 was revised down from 0.4 per cent to 0 per cent; Q2 from 0.2 per cent to −1.3 per cent; Q3 from −0.5 per cent to −2 per cent; and Q4 from −1.5 per cent to −2.3 per cent. In short, aggregate initial estimates of −1.4 per cent were revised down to −5.6 per cent. Thank goodness we threw the kitchen sink at the problem, cutting rates from 5 per cent in October to 2 per cent in December.

4. The first two quarters of 2009 are still negative but revisions made the recession shorter. Growth achieved by Darling recovery in his five-quarter-long upswing was +3.1 per cent, revised up from +1.8 per cent. The stimulus worked.

5.   Then there is the Osborne collapse when over a six-quarter period the
     economy shrank by 0.2 per cent.

The scale of the drop in output is much greater than in the US. This
is shown in Table 15.2, which presents current estimates on the scale
of the shock across countries between 2008Q1 and 2009Q2.[26] The US
saw a GDP drop of 5.2 per cent compared with the drop in the UK
of 7.2 per cent. Germany, Italy, Portugal, Spain and France all had
smaller drops in output than the UK in part because of the size of the
UK financial sector (−5.6 per cent; −3.6 per cent; −3.8 per cent; −4.0
per cent and −6.7 per cent respectively). The UK drop was sixth largest
on the list, only smaller than in Estonia (−19.3 per cent), Ireland (−11.7
per cent); Finland (−10.6 per cent); Iceland (−9.2 per cent) and Denmark
(−8.2 per cent).

   The extent of the recovery, as documented in column 2 of the Table 15.2,
has been patchy across countries. In contrast a number of countries have
now restored the lost output – the list includes Austria, Belgium, Canada,
Germany, Mexico, Sweden and the US. Greece and Ireland are in especially bad shape being 9.4 per cent and 12.1 per cent respectively below
output at the start of the recession. The UK has not even restored half of
the drop in output after 48 months, which means that its recession will be
much longer-lasting than the Great Depression – which, as Figure 15.2
makes clear, was also over after 48 months.

THE CRISIS WAS FORESEEABLE

It really mattered that most macroeconomists had their eyes focused on
inflation and their DSGE ('Dynamic stochastic general equilibrium')
models and failed to notice what was happening around them. This was
especially true at the Bank of England, which has been run as a fiefdom
by Mervyn King.[27] In my view he made the Bank the bank for monetary
economics with little interest in regulation, market intelligence, talking
to bankers and hedge funds, or the data for that matter. That seems to
have been a major mistake, for which he must be held responsible. The
MPC failed to spot the greatest recession in all our lifetimes until they fell
over it. *Monetary policy failed.* Nobody, however, seems to want to take
responsibility.

   In an article in the *Financial Times* on 4 May 2012 Chris Giles argued
that as soon as King became governor in 2003, all that mattered was
monetary economics, and regulation was irrelevant. Financial stability
mattered primarily just for monetary policy:

Table 15.2   Cumulative quarterly GDP growth rates (%)

	2008Q1–2009Q2	2009Q3–2011Q4
Australia	2.2	6.2
Austria	–4.1	6.4
Belgium	–3.0	4.8
Canada	–3.7	7.2
Chile	–0.1	14.9
Czech Republic	–4.3	4.8
Denmark	–8.2	2.8
Estonia	–19.3	11.2
Finland	–10.6	8.1
France	–3.6	3.6
Germany	–5.6	7.3
Greece	–2.1	–7.4
Hungary	–6.5	3.3
Iceland	–9.2	1.5
Ireland	–11.7	–0.4
Israel	1.7	11.8
Italy	–6.7	2.0
Japan	–7.0	4.3
Korea	–0.6	12.7*
Luxembourg	–7.4	6.3
Mexico	–7.9	12.4
Netherlands	–4.5	3.1
New Zealand	–3.6	3.5
Norway	–3.4	3.5
Poland	3.4	10.3
Portugal	–3.8	–1.4
Slovak Republic	–5.9	9.4
Slovenia	–7.1	1.0
Spain	–4.0	0.2*
Sweden	–7.5	9.8
Switzerland	–1.6	5.4
Turkey	–7.4	19.8
United Kingdom	–7.2	2.9*
United States	–5.2	6.6*
Euro area (17 countries)	–5.1	3.6
European Union (27 countries)	–5.4	3.9
Argentina	2.3	20.7
Brazil	0.9	12.1
China	0.0	10.6
India	6.5	20.2
Indonesia	7.5	16.0
Russian Federation	–7.3	12.1
South Africa	–0.5	7.4

Note: *Until 2012Q1.

Source: OECD.

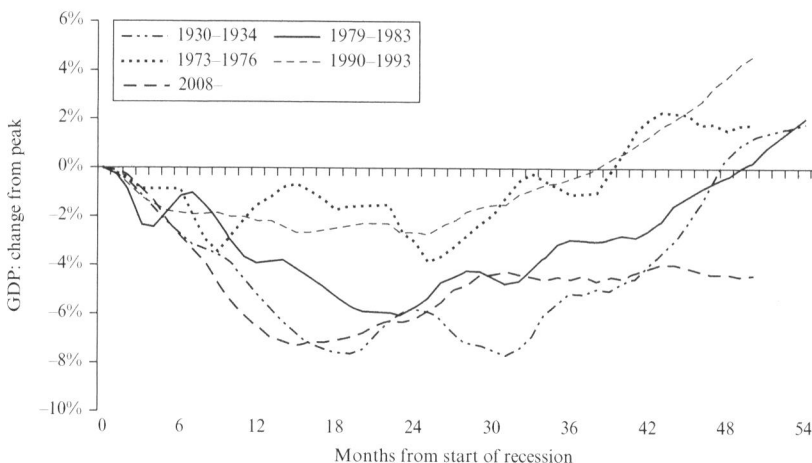

Source: NIESR.

Figure 15.2 GDP growth by quarter in various recessions

the staff became aware the new governor had big plans to remould the [Bank of England] in his own academic image. Already shorn of banking supervision and government debt management in the post-1997 changes, Sir Mervyn wanted to create a modern monetary authority concentrating on monthly decisions on interest rates. Although one of the BoE's two core purposes was 'to ensure financial stability', it seems he neither enjoyed nor fully understood the influence the BoE still had in calming financial excess by use of its powerful voice. Work in the financial stability division did not excite him and he told colleagues to 'operationalize' it, by which he meant simply writing and publishing two financial stability reports every year. Sir Mervyn demonstrated the low status he attached to such reports by not presenting them himself, unlike the inflation report, which he nurtured and presented as chief economist . . . Staff found presenting financial stability issues in front of the new governor frightening because of his apparent disdain for their work.

In a lecture on Radio 4's *The Today Programme*, King blamed Gordon Brown, the banks and the Financial Services Authority for all that happened.[28] No mea culpa here:

In August 2007 came the moment when financial markets began to realize that the emperor had no clothes. The announcement by the French bank BNP Paribas that it would suspend repayments from two of its investment funds triggered a loss of confidence and a freezing of some capital markets. A month later, the crisis claimed its first victim when Northern Rock failed. In the months that followed, there was a steady procession of banking failures culminating in the collapse of the American bank Lehman Brothers in September

2008. Financial waters, already extremely chilly, then froze solid. Banks found it almost impossible to finance themselves because no-one knew which banks were safe and which weren't.

And later:

> It's vital that we learn from the crisis. A good place to start is to ask, as the Queen famously did, 'Why did no-one see this coming?' The answer is extremely simple: no-one believed it could happen. Recessions were supposed to follow booms and high inflation, not periods of steady and sustainable growth with low inflation. There seemed to be no reason to expect the worst recession since the 1930s.

As a result, King claimed that the Bank of England really did spot the crisis but it was everyone else's fault. His mistake was not shouting loudly enough. No misjudgement there. No blame falls his way:

> That isn't to say we were blind to what was going on. For several years, central banks, including the Bank of England, had warned that financial markets were underestimating risks. So why, you might ask, did the Bank of England not do more to prevent the disaster? We should have. But the power to regulate banks had been taken away from us in 1997. Our power was limited to that of publishing reports and preaching sermons. And we did preach sermons about the risks. But we didn't imagine the scale of the disaster that would occur when the risks crystallized. With the benefit of hindsight, we should have shouted from the rooftops that a system had been built in which banks were too important to fail, that banks had grown too quickly and borrowed too much, and that so-called 'light-touch' regulation hadn't prevented any of this. And in the crisis, we tried, but should have tried harder, to persuade everyone of the need to recapitalize the banks sooner and by more. We should have preached that the lessons of history were being forgotten – because banking crises have happened before.

We pay the governor a large salary to have some foresight. No mea culpa here, which should surprise nobody. Sadly these claims don't seem to stand up to scrutiny.

Blaming Gordon Brown, the FSA and the banks simply doesn't wash. There is actually plenty of evidence suggesting that King personally missed what was going on. I do recall sitting at the same table in front of the Treasury Select Committee in March 2008 when these issues were raised. I went back to the transcripts and this is what I found.[29] Labour MP Andy Love asked him if we needed more regulation to which King replied, 'A brief answer would be do not have knee-jerk reactions but think very, very deeply about the causes of this crisis and whether levels of bank capital and the sort of financial system that generated this crisis does not require some action.' No 'we need more regulation there', from the rooftops or any place else. Obviously nothing was learned from the failure of Northern Rock.

I was also at the same hearing and was asked about the biggest risk to the UK economy:

> The difference between me and most of the members of the Committee in terms of the way the Inflation Report was written was my concern with risks to the downside, especially coming from the credit market. I guess from your earlier question, having seen what has happened in the US is that activity will drop dramatically and that would be something I do not want to see. My concern is that it is appropriate to take out some insurance and get ahead of the curve in the sense that the arguments made on the upside were that, but it seems to me those arguments apply on the downside too, so my concern would be one should make sure one is ahead of the curve so that later one is not in a position where something horrible happens, I do not want that to occur. My risks are to the downside and I have concerns that something horrible might come and I do not want that to happen. (Evidence to the Treasury Select Committee: David Blanchflower, 26 March 2008)

It isn't as if King and other members of the MPC weren't warned by a member of their own committee six days before the UK economy actually did enter recession on 1 April 2008.

At the Treasury Committee hearing on 26 March 2008, Love also asked King whether he was concerned that as the US was in recession it might spread to the UK. 'For us, far more important than the United States in terms of the impact on demand in the UK is the impact on the euro area because they have a weight three times larger than the United States in our trade-weighted index, so what happens in the euro area is much more important to us directly than the US economy.' I heard him claim that the UK had decoupled from the US many times. It had not, of course.

A month later I gave a speech for the David Hume Institute at the Royal Society of Edinburgh where I warned that I was 'particularly concerned that the UK exhibits broad similarities to the US experience'. I set out what I called four phases of the downturn in the United States based on data I had available up to 23 April 2008. The data are available also as an appendix to the paper.[30]

- *Phase 1 (January 2006–April 2007).* The housing market started to slow from its peak around January 2006. Negative monthly growth rates in house prices started to appear from the Autumn of 2006.
- *Phase 2 (May 2007–August 2007).* Substantial monthly falls in house prices and housing market activity including starts and permits to build were observed from late Spring/early Summer of 2007. Consumer confidence measures alongside qualitative labour market indicators, such as the proportion of people saying jobs are plentiful, started to drop precipitously from around September 2007.

- *Phase 3 (September 2007–December 2007).* Average hourly earnings growth started to slow from September 2007 as did real consumption. The growth in private non-farm payrolls started to slow. House price and activity declines sped up.
- *Phase 4 (January 2008–).* By approximately December 2007 the housing market problems had now spilled over into real activity. The US seemed to moved into recession around the start of 2008. There were big falls in house prices. In March 2008 housing starts were at a 17-year low. Foreclosure filings jumped 57 per cent in March compared with the same month of 2007. One out of every 139 Nevada households received a foreclosure filing in that month. California was second, with a rate of one in every 204 homes, with Florida third with a rate of one in every 282 homes being hit with a foreclosure filing. Mortgage application volume fell 14.2 per cent during the week ending 18 April, according to the Mortgage Bankers Association's weekly application survey. Refinance volumes fell 20.2 per cent on the week. Nominal retail sales and real personal disposable income had both fallen sharply since the start of the year. Real annual GDP growth in 2007Q4 was down to +0.1 per cent, from 1.2 per cent in 2007Q3. Spending on big-ticket items in the US tumbled. Labour market data released for the United States, for March 2008, showed the biggest drop in payrolls in five years, while applications for unemployment benefits increased. Declines in employment were concentrated in manufacturing, construction and financial activities.

In my speech I presented equivalent supporting data for the UK, suggesting there were a number of strong similarities with the US: the big difference is that in the UK the housing market was booming in 2006 and most of 2007:

- *Phase 1 (August 2007–October 2007).* House prices started to slow in 2007Q2 and 2007Q3. Housing activity measures also slowed from around October 2007.
- *Phase 2 (November 2007–January 2008).* Consumer confidence measures started slowing sharply from around October 2007. The qualitative labour market measures such as the REC Demand for Staff index also start slowing from around October 2007.
- *Phase 3 (February 2008–?).* In early 2008 the Halifax index and the RICS survey both suggested that house prices falls had started to accelerate. The Council of Mortgage Lenders (CML) announced that mortgage lending in March was down 17 per cent on the year. Loan approvals were down, and the RICS ratio of sales to stocks

was down from 0.38 in September 2007 to 0.25 in March 2008. Bradford & Bingley, Britain's biggest buy-to-let lender, had recently reported that some borrowers were finding it hard to repay their loans, so mortgage arrears were growing, reminiscent of what had been happening in the US. The latest figures showed that the number of people whose homes were repossessed in 2007 went up by 21 per cent. The CML said 27 100 homes, the highest figure since 1999, were taken over by lenders after people fell behind with repayments. According to data published by the British Bankers' Association the number of mortgages granted to homebuyers dropped last month by 47 per cent below the same month last year to its lowest level in more than a decade. Some 35 417 mortgages were approved for home purchase in March compared with 43 147 in February, a drop of 18 per cent.

Hourly earnings growth was sluggish – both the Average Earnings Index and Labour Force Survey measures were slowing. Total hours and average hours started to fall in early 2008. Claimant count numbers for February 2008 were revised up from a small decline to an increase. There was a growth in the number of part-timers who say they have had to take a part-time job because they couldn't find a full-time job – up 37 400 in March alone.

Even though the number of unemployed had fallen, the duration of unemployment appeared to be rising, which means that the outflow rate from unemployment had fallen. The numbers unemployed over six months in March 2008 was up 22 400 while the numbers unemployed for less than six months was down 47 400. As in the US, I noted that recent declines in employment in the UK are concentrated in manufacturing, construction and financial activities.

Phase 4 was 'coming'. More bad news was on the way, I argued. This is what I said:

> I think it is very plausible that falling house prices will lead to a sharp drop in consumer spending growth. Developments in the UK are starting to look eerily similar to those in the US six months or so ago. There has been no decoupling of the two economies: contagion is in the air. The US sneezed and the UK is rapidly catching its cold . . . Generally, forecasters have tended to under-predict the depth and duration of cyclical slowdowns.

Figure 15.3 provides some evidence that should have been hard to ignore. It plots the Halifax House price-to-earnings ratios, which took a big drop in May 2012 from 4.42 to 4.33 as house prices fell 2.4 per cent on the month.[31] The US housing market had started to collapse in 2006,[32] which

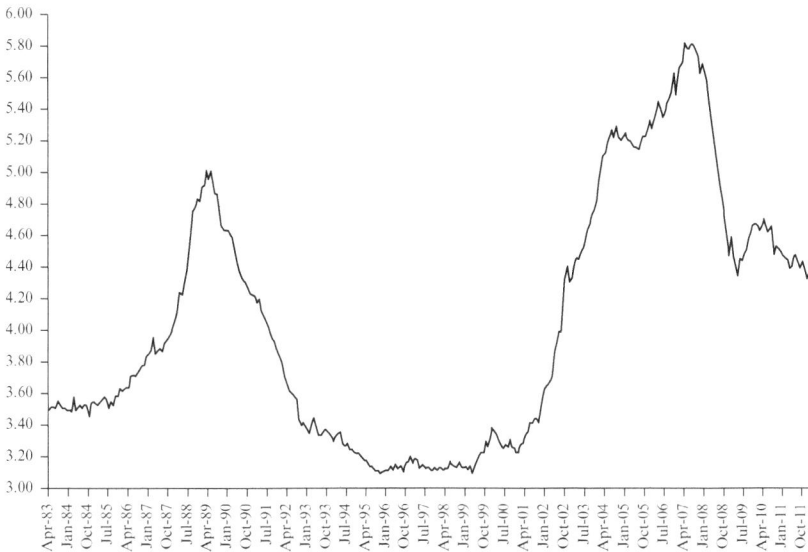

Figure 15.3   Halifax House price-to-earnings ratios

should have set alarm bells ringing given that the 1929 Great Crash started in the Florida housing market. UK average house price-to-earnings ratios had risen to unsustainably high levels. From 1983 to 2004 they averaged 3.4 but by July 2007 had reached 5.81. When King was interviewed in March 2008 the ratio had fallen to 5.44 and house prices were 5 per cent below their peak nine months earlier.

That should have been a wake-up call but not for King and the other members of the MPC who even by the beginning of September 2008, a week before the collapse of Lehman Brothers, had not spotted the big one and did not vote for rate cuts. Note that in the minutes of the September 2008 MPC meeting there is even a large section that argued for a rise in the bank rate:

> A case could be made for an increase in Bank Rate. There still remained a significant risk to inflation expectations from the expected short-term rise in CPI inflation. The recent fall in sterling, if sustained, might postpone the point at which inflation started to fall back sharply towards the target. High import price inflation and sterling's depreciation could be symptomatic of a weakening of confidence in the Committee's determination to return inflation to the target. An increase in Bank Rate now would emphasize the MPC's commitment to price stability and might result in an appreciation of sterling, relieving some of the upward pressure on import prices.

I ask you.

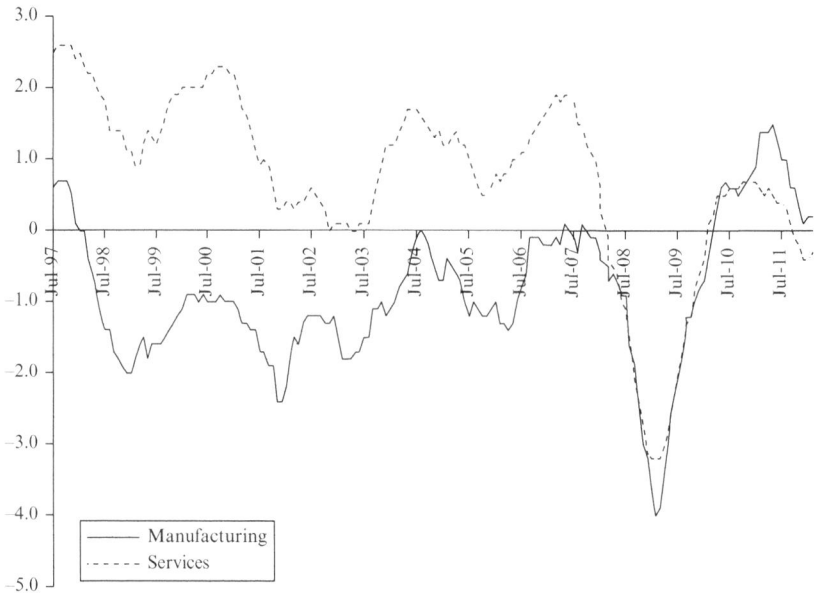

Figure 15.4   Bank of England's Agents' scores on employment intentions

House price-to-earnings ratios are only held up at these historically high levels by the very low interest rates, and if they were to rise this would have a downward and likely large impact on prices, which certainly look set to fall further. To get back to long-run averages would imply drops of at least 15 per cent and probably more given likely overshooting.

I also recall Governor King being questioned in September 2008 at another Treasury Select Committee session after the August 2008 Inflation Report that failed to spot the recession coming.[33] Mr Love again asked, 'On unemployment there have been some suggestions . . . that it may go up faster than the projections in the Inflation Report. Is that a worry to you? King's response was '*I do not think we really know what will happen to unemployment. At least, the Almighty has not vouchsafed to me the path of unemployment data over the next year*' (my italics). Unemployment had started rising in March of that year and would continue to do so for many months ahead and by that time and the Bank of England's agents scores on the labour market, had fallen off a cliff.[34] This is shown in Figure 15.4, which plots the Bank of England's Agents' scores for the state of the economy.

This is what I termed 'the economics of walking about' in a speech in 2007.[35] It follows on from a long tradition in Labour economics going

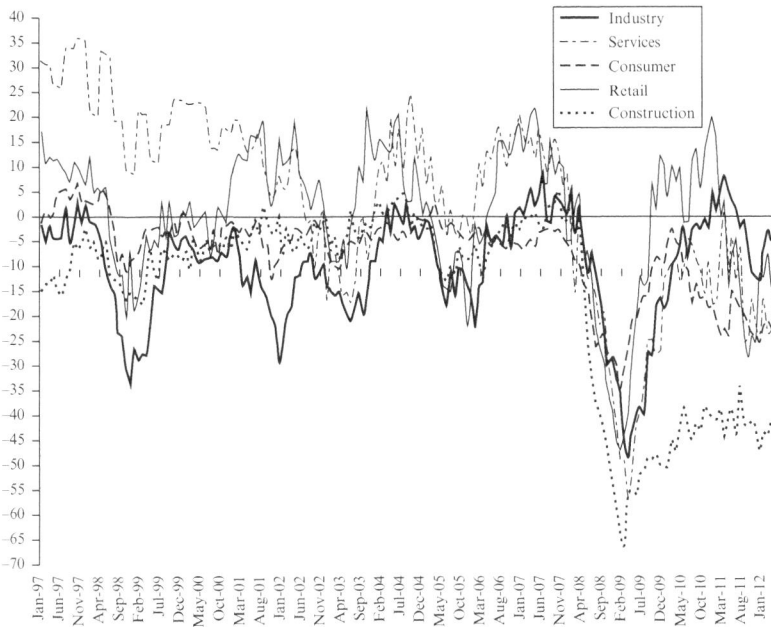

Figure 15.5   UK Economic Sentiment Index

back to the writings of the Webbs in the UK and the early American Labour economists Paul Douglas, John Dunlop, Clark Kerr, Richard Lester, Lloyd Reynolds, Sumner Slichter and Gregg Lewis. Clark Kerr encapsulated the spirit of these American labour economists when he said, 'Labour Economics will contribute more by helping to make a sense of reality than by building more castles in the air'.[36] At the time I very much felt I should give the MPC a dose of reality. The Bank's 12 Agents and their staff across the country report on their sentiment. The chart makes it clear that by the Autumn of 2008 employment intentions were spiralling downwards, both in manufacturing and services. These surveys were entirely consistent with other surveys of business and consumer confidence. Figure 15.5 reports surveys of four business groups – industry, services, retail and construction, plus an interview among consumers. All of these surveys had plummeted and were saying the same thing – the UK was headed to recession.

Finally, in contrast to the Governor of the Bank of England it appears that the men and women who ride on the Clapham omnibus did have some idea of what was going to happen to unemployment. They did walk about. Figure 15.6 reports the results from the EU survey of the responses to the question

Figure 15.6   The fear of unemployment

'what did the respondent think was going to happen to unemployment over the next six months?' It is reported as a balance that started to rise sharply from the end of 2007 and by July 2008 had reached its highest level since March 1993 when the unemployment rate was 10.6 per cent.

King and the other members of the MPC simply didn't get it, and they should have. But it was to get worse, because even after they missed the start of the recession they seemed unable to contemplate its scale or duration. We now turn to looking at the forecasts of growth by both the MPC and the OBR. For simplicity I ignore the inflation forecasts.

GROWTH FORECASTS

It is appropriate to look at the growth forecasts before and after the recession to see why the recession was missed and whether those errors have been fixed. There seems to be little evidence to support such a proposition.

Monetary Policy Committee

Figure 15.7 contains the famous MPC fan charts for growth. Figure 15.7(a) is the forecast from the August 2008 Inflation Report, which I initially

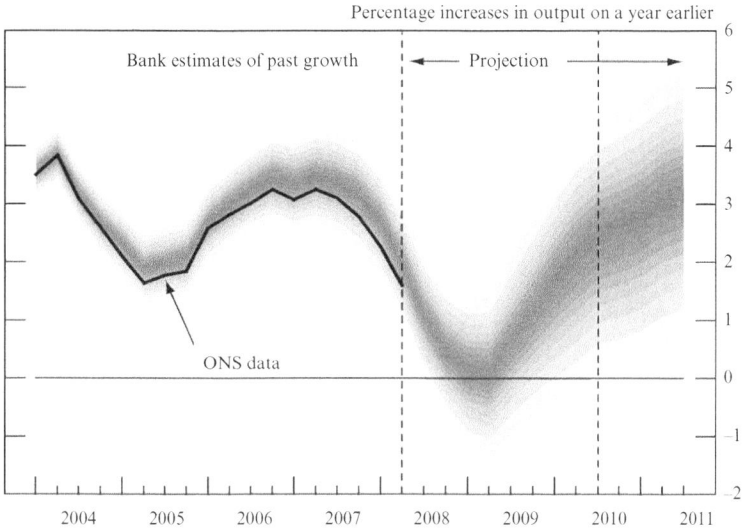

(a) August 2008. GDP growth at market interest rates

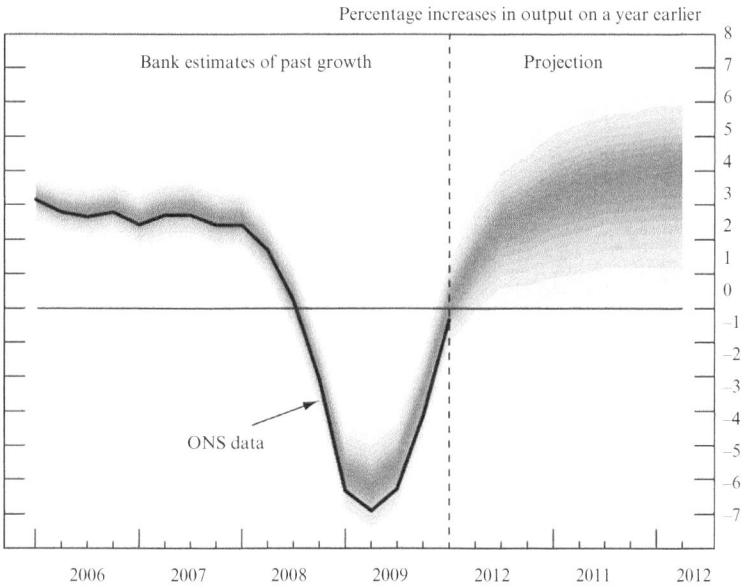

(b) May 2010. GDP growth at constant interest rate 0.5% and £200 billion asset purchases

Figure 15.7   MPC forecasts of GDP, 2008–12

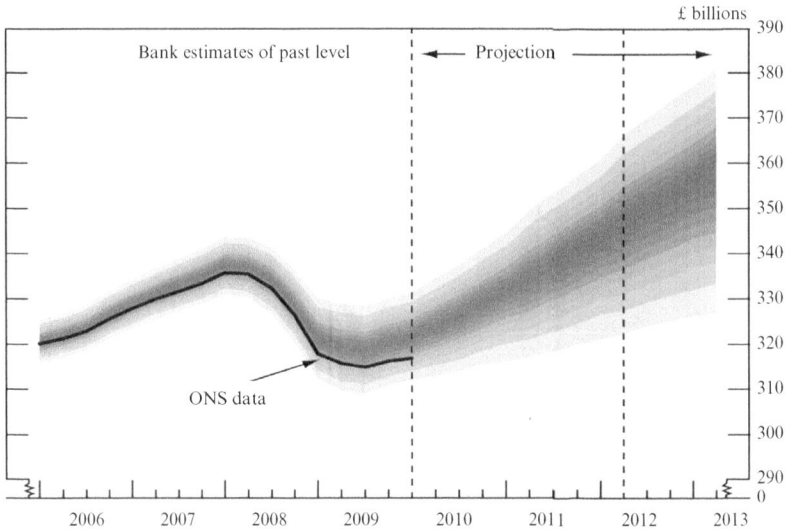

(c) May 2010. Projection of the level of GDP based on market interest rate expectations and £200 billion asset purchases

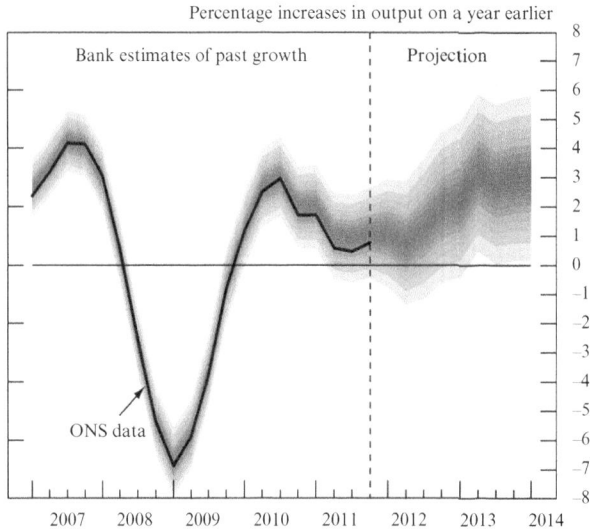

(d) February 2012. GDP growth at constant interest rate 0.5% and £325 billion asset purchases

Figure 15.7   (continued)

Percentage increases in output on a year earlier

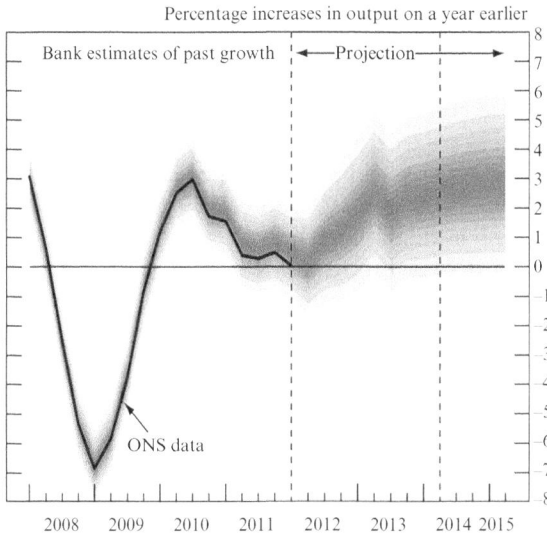

(e) May 2012. GDP growth at constant interest rate 0.5% and
£325 billion asset purchases

Figure 15.7 (continued)

signed up to, but then realized was far too optimistic. The Inflation Report itself doesn't contain the word recession. The central projection was that there would not even be a single quarter of negative growth, output would be restored quickly and trend growth would be restored by 2010. Data from the past – in what is called the *backcast* – will all be revised upwards, because the darker part of the fan is mostly above the dark line, which is the latest ONS estimate at the time of the forecast. A month later Lehmans had failed, and three months later interest rates had been cut to 2 per cent and eventually to 0.5 per cent. In March 2009 the MPC would embark on a programme of quantitative easing because the economy was in such bad shape. There were also loans to the Royal Bank of Scotland and Lloyds that the external members of the MPC were never told about.

Figure 15.7(b) is from May 2010, just before the coalition was formed, and it painted a pretty rosy picture. Recovery was nicely underway and trend growth was still headed the UK's way, but not before 2011. The MPC did not expect data for any of 2008 to be revised down but did expect data for 2009 to be revised up. Recovery, of course was going to be V-shaped, what else could it be? (the forecast was actually to look W-shaped or even more probably L-shaped if austerity were to hit).

Indeed the MPC projected that the level of GDP would be back to what it was at the start of the recession by the beginning of 2011. This can be seen in Panel C, which plots the level of GDP based on the market interest rate of 0.5 per cent and £200 billion of quantitative easing. The recovery date for the recession is obtained by drawing a line over from the start. If we refer back to Figure 15.2 this means that the MPC was projecting that the recession would be over in 36 months, essentially copying the growth path in the 1930s but with a much more rapid exit. It never looked like this would happen, and it didn't happen.

It didn't turn out so well for the MPC because, as we saw from Table 15.1, the GDP data for 2008 were revised heavily downwards. Chart D reports the February 2012 forecast. Growth in 2011 was not 3 per cent as predicted in both August 2008 and June 2010 but 0.8 per cent. But never fear, the economy is expected to spring back to life as the GDP data is expected to be revised upwards and growth data for 2012Q1 were expected by the MPC to be positive, but wasn't. Oh dear, here they go again – annualized growth of 5.5 per cent falls inside the fan while a negative number is ruled out. It looks very like the same mistake being repeated many times. I have said on many occasions that MPC growth forecasts are aspiring to be hopeless.

The most recent chart available at the time of writing, taken from the May 2012 Inflation report, is presented in Figure 15.7(e) and shows once again a highly bullish growth forecast. Astonishingly growth of 5.5 per cent is inside the 90 per cent confidence fan once again as early as 2013Q3 while zero or negative growth is outside it. Despite all the identified risks apparently from the euro area the committee decided that risks to inflation were balanced. On 22 May 2012 the IMF said that 'risks are large and tilted clearly to the downside'.[37] More astonishing still is the fact that even with that bullish growth forecast inflation is below the 2 per cent target at the two-year forecast horizon. This implies that the MPC should have loosened monetary policy further. This was a point made by the IMF a week later in its Article IV Consultation 2012 when it argued:

> Further monetary easing is required. Anemic nominal wage growth and broadly stable inflation expectations suggest underlying inflationary pressure is weak, providing space for greater monetary easing. That said, uncertainty about inflation dynamics and the strength of disinflationary pressure coming from the output gap imply risks that inflation could take longer-than-expected to return to target, with convergence being further delayed by additional monetary easing. Nonetheless, the cost of such a delay is likely to be low relative to the benefits of a more rapid closing of the output gap.

I have no explanation for why the MPC didn't act and start a new round of quantitative easing, other than sheer incompetence.

Why does the MPC continue to believe the recovery will be V-shaped, when it hasn't been up to this point? Is this a function of the models simply being mean reverting? That may have worked in the Great Moderation that occurred from 1997 to 2007, where a 25 bp tweak up or down did the job. I for one find it hard to see where growth comes from under current policies, so an L-shape looks to fit the data (Figure 15.2).

Office of Budget Responsibility

The MPC is not alone in being over-optimistic in its growth forecasts. Table 15.3 reports Office of Budget Responsibility forecasts at the time of the June 2010 Austerity Budget that killed off consumer and business confidence and destroyed growth. It didn't help that (Prime Minister) Cameron, (Deputy Prime Minister) Clegg and (Chancellor) Osborne claimed the country was bankrupt when it wasn't, or that it was like Greece, which is locked in monetary union. Greece by the way is ranked one-hundredth on the World Bank's *Doing Business* rankings, while the UK is ranked seventh.[38] There was never any empirical foundation for an expansionary fiscal contraction, which has turned out to be a *contractionary fiscal contraction*. The UK is now enjoying the weakest peacetime recovery in a century and is well behind the recoveries in other countries, including several euro area countries more directly impacted by the crisis, including Belgium, France and Germany.

The OBR forecast growth made respectively in 2010 of 2.3 per cent; 2.8 per cent and 2.9 per cent in 2011, 2012 and 2013, was revised down in February 2012 to 0.8 per cent; 0.8 per cent and 2.0 per cent. There has not been a resurgence in consumption or business investment as predicted, although the OBR continues to forecast that it will happen, even though it hasn't done so. The saving grace has been net trade but that seems set to worsen especially given the 5 per cent appreciation of the pound against the euro recently. Unemployment is higher and employment lower than predicted. It remains unclear why the OBR believes earnings are about to take off; they haven't and they won't, given the high levels of unemployment and the high fear of unemployment (see Figure 15.6).[39] Other forecasters are much less optimistic.[40] NIESR is forecasting zero growth in 2012 and 2 per cent in 2013 for example. According to the Treasury in April 2012 the consensus forecast for growth in 2012 is 0.6 per cent, and 1.7 per cent in 2013. Among City forecasters for 2012 Capital Economics and Standard Chartered are forecasting −0.5 per cent while Goldman Sachs are at the top end forecasting growth of 1.2 per cent driven principally by consumption, which seems highly unlikely. Among the non-City forecasts the lowest is NIESR at zero with Liverpool Macro the highest

Table 15.3   Office of Budget Responsibility's forecasts

(a) June 2010 Budget forecast

	Percentage change on a year earlier, unless otherwise stated						
	Forecasts						
	2009	2010	2011	2012	2013	2014	2015
Gross domestic product (GDP)	–4.9	1.2	2.3	2.8	2.9	2.7	2.7
Expenditure components of GDP							
Domestic demand	–5.3	1.6	1.4	1.9	2.2	2.2	2.3
Household consumption	–3.2	0.2	1.3	1.7	2.1	2.2	2.2
General government consumption	2.2	1.7	–1.1	–2.0	–2.3	–3.0	–2.1
Fixed investment	–14.9	–0.5	3.9	7.9	8.8	8.0	6.9
Business	–19.3	1.4	8.1	10.0	10.9	9.5	8.2
General government	15.7	–4.9	–19.0	–8.5	–6.6	0.6	2.0
Private dwellings	–19.7	–6.5	5.6	8.2	8.5	7.1	6.6
Change in inventories	–1.2	1.2	0.4	0.0	0.0	0.0	0.0
Exports of goods and services	–10.6	4.3	5.5	6.3	6.1	5.9	5.7
Imports of goods and services	–11.9	5.6	2.1	2.7	3.6	4.0	4.2
Inflation							
CPI (Q4)	2.1	2.7	2.4	1.9	2.0	2.0	2.0
Labour market							
Employment (millions)	29.0	28.8	28.9	29.2	29.5	29.8	30.1
Wages and salaries	–1.0	1.2	2.3	3.1	4.9	5.4	5.4
Average earnings	1.0	2.1	1.9	2.3	3.8	4.4	4.4
ILO unemployment (% rate)	7.6	8.1	8.0	7.6	7.0	6.5	6.1
Claimant count (Q4, millions)	1.6	1.5	1.5	1.4	1.3	1.2	1.1

(b) March 2012 Budget forecast

	Percentage change on a year earlier, unless otherwise stated						
	Outturn		Forecast				
	2010	2011	2012	2013	2014	2015	2016
Gross domestic product (GDP)	2.1	0.8	0.8	2.0	2.7	3.0	3.0

Table 15.3   (continued)

(b) March 2012 Budget forecast

	Percentage change on a year earlier, unless otherwise stated						
	Outturn		Forecast				
	2010	2011	2012	2013	2014	2015	2016
Expenditure components of GDP							
Household consumption	1.2	–0.8	0.5	1.3	2.3	3.0	3.0
Business investment	–2.1	0.2	0.7	6.4	8.9	10.2	10.1
General government consumption	1.5	0.3	0.5	–1.1	–2.1	–2.8	–2.7
General government investment	7.8	–13.0	–5.0	–3.6	0.1	0.4	–1.4
Net trade	–0.5	1.2	0.4	0.5	0.3	0.2	0.1
Inflation							
CPI	3.3	4.5	2.8	1.9	1.9	2.0	2.0
Labour market							
Employment (millions)	29.0	29.2	29.1	29.2	29.4	29.7	30.0
Average earnings	2.4	1.2	2.6	3.1	4.3	4.5	4.5
ILO unemployment (% rate)	7.9	8.1	8.7	8.6	8.0	7.2	6.3
Claimant count (millions)	1.50	1.53	1.65	1.64	1.52	1.35	1.19

Source: Office of Budget Responsibility (OBR).

at +1.4 per cent. Capital Economics expects growth of only 0.5 per cent in 2013.

One other issue that warrants attention is the extent of the cuts that the government has undertaken. New data from the International Labour Organization sheds light on the scale of the deficit reduction that has gone on in the UK. This is reported in Table 15.4 where the ILO has tried to create a comparable series across countries, which makes clear the extent to which the coalition has cut is deeper than other countries: more tightening has occurred in the UK than in the USA, Spain, Ireland and Greece or anywhere else for that matter, in 2011–12.

The main driver is public investment, which was down 2 per cent on the previous year. No wonder growth has tanked. So the claims that cuts haven't taken place look wide of the mark. Plus, at the time of writing, October 2012, the vast majority of the cuts haven't yet been

Table 15.4   Change in fiscal expenditures and revenues as a percentage of GDP by category between 2011 and 2012 (percentage points).

	Total expenditure	Total revenue
Australia	−0.5	1.3
Austria	−0.6	−0.1
Canada	−0.4	−0.1
Denmark	0.9	−0.6
Finland	0.7	1.7
France	−0.4	0.4
Germany	−0.3	0.6
Greece	0.2	1.6
Ireland	−1.8	−0.4.4
Japan	−0.8	−0.6
Korea,	−0.6	−0.4
Norway	0.2	−2.0
Portugal	−2.3	−0.9
Spain	0.9	−0.3
Sweden	−1.3	−2.3
Switzerland	−0.1	0.03
United Kingdom	−2.8	−0.3
United States	−1.7	2.2

Note: In the United States, value corresponds to change in spending on mandatory health. In France, the change is due to a reduction of special intervention social programmes, such as Aid for Social Housing (*aides au logement* (APL)), the Active Solidarity Revenue (*revenu de solidarité active* (RSA)) or the Disabled Adult Allowance (*allocation pour adulte handicapé* (AAH)). In Germany, figures correspond to the Federal Government budget plan and, in Sweden, to the Central Government budget plan.

Source: *ILO World of Work 2012*, Table 3.1.[41]

implemented. I am fearful what the effect on the economy will be if they are implemented as growth seems set to worsen, and the government still seems set on that course. The results of the local elections in April 2012 in which the coalition saw big losses, suggest that a rapidly developed plan B may be in the offing. More cuts, as some on the political right want, would likely be disastrous both in economic and political terms. There is little evidence to support the claims made by Liam Fox and others that slashing workers' rights would give a kick-start to growth. Firing people generally increases rather than deceases unemployment.[42]

CONCLUSION

The onset of the Great Recession in 2008 and the absence of any recovery in the UK represent a major challenge to economics. Why did it happen? Where did we go wrong? What policies are best to help the economy rebalance away from financial services, and in what direction should it be pointed? How can the models be made more realistic? How much of the macroeconomics we teach to our students has to be binned?

I am greatly concerned that the economics profession has had so little involvement in the major issues of the day. That has resulted, in my view in some of the worst economic policy errors in a generation. Economists need to focus on real policy questions rather than simply on publishing trivial technical extensions in academic journals. I suspect that will also mean a movement away from theoretical papers with no data to papers that involve empirical testing and the search for patterns in the data.

I have been very struck by the difference between what a City economists do on a daily basis and how little need they have to consult, or even read anything academic economists write. Academic economists for their part seem to me to have little knowledge of where the economy is and any interest in data revisions, qualitative surveys or even macro-forecasting. When I was at the Bank of England trying to work out whether the economy was collapsing I needed outside advice on what was going on in the economy but received little help. That needs to change and the profession needs to engage in the real world. We do need to know what went wrong with the macro-forecasts and why the macro models turned out to be so little help when they were needed most. The following advice from some of the most famous names in economics seems appropriate and may be helpful:[43]

> It is a good morning exercise for a research scientist to discard a pet hypothesis every day before breakfast. It keeps him young.[44] (Konrad Lorenz)

> In the case of the labour market, our preoccupation with price-mediated market clearing as the natural equilibrium condition may be a serious error.[45] (Robert Solow 1986)

> The vision I would like to carry away from this lecture sees economics as fundamentally an observational principle.[46] (Arnold Harberger 1993)

> Inspiration is most likely to come through the stimulus provided by the patterns, puzzles and anomalies revealed by the systematic gathering of data, particularly when the prime need is to break our existing habits of thought.[47] (Ronald Coase 1991)

> Good empirical evidence tells its story regardless of the precise way it is analysed. In large part, it is its simplicity that is persuasive.[48] (Larry Summers 1991)

> A full model and complete microeconomic foundation to wage adjustment with the power of the auction-model may never be forthcoming. If that is so we may have to look for regularities'.[49] (Charles Schultz 1984)

The move in behavioural economics to test people's behaviour rather than assuming they know what it is, is certainly to be welcomed. For the sake of the country academic economists need to become engaged in the policy debate. It really would help, of course, if Vice-Chancellors explicitly gave incentives, perhaps via pay increases or study grants, to encourage their faculty to become engaged in policy debates, on TV and radio and also in advising politicians and joining in national debates. It is not good enough to say you were working on something else.

The big worry going forward is what to do next? The MPC will clearly be concerned about the inflation risk and the slowing economy but the downside risk to activity looms large, which suggests they will have to push the trigger again. George Osborne's fiscal austerity has been a disaster, but what is the alternative? Doing too much in these circumstances is better than doing too little. We would have been in much better shape today if Mervyn King and the MPC had realized that in 2007 and 2008. Now is the time for economists to start speaking up. Become engaged. Think more about policy rather than focusing on minor twiddles. The British public is entitled to ask, 'where were you when we needed you?' Get busy.

NOTES

1. Coase, R.H. (1991), 'The institutional structure of production', *American Economic Review*, 82, pp. 713–19.
2. Andrew Oswald has argued that such exercises 'lead to short-term thinking; they make researchers focus on the names of journals rather than on ideas'. See http://andrewoswald.com/docs/oswaldraejan09.pdf (accessed 30 September 2012).
3. See Diane Coyle's Tanner lectures, 'The public responsibility of the economist' (2012), for interesting insights into the failings of both economics and economists in the Great Recession.
4. Andrew J. Oswald, 'An examination of the reliability of prestigious scholarly journals: evidence and implications for decision-makers', IZA Discussion Paper No. 2070, April 2006.
5. Allegedly, viewing figures are much higher when Paxman is the host.
6. http://www.bloomberg.com/video/92043651 (accessed 30 September 2012).
7. For example, Tory MP Grant Shapps tweeted me today to ask, 'so how long is it ok to go on borrowing £1 for every £4 spent?' My answer was, 'Depends what you spend

it on. Think about a large firm, presumably you think it ok for them to borrow to invest in a shipyard?' I wonder what other economists think? I don't know, as nobody engages.

8. For example, Alan Krueger, currently chair of the Council of Economic Advisers and Nobel Laureate Jim Heckman both have 12 papers with at least 1000 Google cites, and Heckman has one paper on sample selection bias with 14 700 cites (Heckman, James (1979), 'Sample selection bias as a specification error with an application to the estimation of labor supply functions', in James Smith (ed.) *Female Labor Supply*, Princeton: Princeton University Press).

9. http://ideas.repec.org/top/top.person.nbcites.html#pbl22 (accessed 30 September 2012).

10. http://www.whitehouse.gov/administration/eop/cea/about/Former-Members (accessed 30 September 2012).

11. http://krugman.blogs.nytimes.com/2012/03/05/economics-in-the-crisis/?pagewanted= all (accessed 30 September 2012).

12. Lawrence H. Summers, 'The scientific illusion in empirical macroeconomics', *Scandinavian Journal of Economics*, **93** (2), Proceedings of a Conference on New Approaches to Empirical Macroeconomics, June 1991, pp. 129–48.

13. R.E. Lucas, 'Macroeconomic priorities', *American Economic Review*, March 2003, pp. 1–14.

14. Olivier Blanchard, 'The state of macro', NBER WP14259, August 2008.

15. V.V. Chari and P. Kehoe (2006), 'Modern macroeconomics in practice: how theory is shaping policy', *Journal of Economic Perspectives*, Fall, pp. 3–28.

16. Arnold Harberger (1993), 'The search for relevance in economics,' *American Economic Review Papers and Proceedings*, 83, pp. 1–16.

17. Robert Solow (2008), *Journal of Economic Perspectives*, **22** (1), Winter, pp. 243–9.

18. De Grauwe, Paul (2008), 'Cherished Myths fall victim to economic reality', *Financial Times*, 22 July.

19. 'We forgot everything Keynes taught us', *Washington Post*, 19 October 2008.

20. For more on human imitation and herd behaviour see Andrew Oswald's CEP/LSE November 2011 lecture entitled 'Herd behaviour and keeping up with the Joneses', at http://andrewoswald.com/presentations.html (accessed 30 September 2012). A full set of references is available here: http://andrewoswald.com/docs/revHandoutOswald-HerdBehaviourLiterature.pdf. See also David G. Blanchflower, Andrew J. Oswald and Bert Van Landeghem, 'Imitative obesity and relative utility', *Journal of the European Economic Association*, 7, pp. 528–38, April 2009.

21. Over the period 2009Q4–2010Q4 Spain grew by 0 per cent, whereas from 2011Q4–2012Q1 Spain grew by +0.2 per cent – more than the UK despite having a 24 per cent unemployment rate.

22. http://www.ons.gov.uk/ons/publications/re-reference-tables.html?edition=tcm%3A77-258397 (accessed 30 September 2012).

23. 'Impact of changes in the National Accounts and Economic Commentary for 2011 quarter 2', Peter Patterson, Pete Lee and Malindi Myers, Office for National Statistics (ONS), 2011

24. 'Understanding the quality of early estimates of Gross Domestic Product', Gary Brown, Tullio Buccellato, Graeme Chamberlin, Sumit Dey-Chowdhury and Robin Youll, ONS, 2010.

25. http://www.newstatesman.com/politics/politics/2012/05/recession-deniers-it%E2%80% 99s-time-face-grim-reality-uk-plc (accessed 30 September 2012).

26. The US, the UK and the euro area all went into recession, in terms of a GDP drop in 2008Q2. The NBER dating group called the start of the recession at December 2007, based on the rise in unemployment.

27. http://www.newstatesman.com/economy/2009/09/mpc-bank-recession-king-rates and http://www.newstatesman.com/politics/2012/04/mervyn-king-tyrant-who-will-succeed-him-bank (both accessed 30 September 2012).

28. http://www.bankofengland.co.uk/publications/Documents/speeches/2012/speech567. pdf (accessed 30 September 2012).

29. http://www.publications.parliament.uk/pa/cm200708/cmselect/cmtreasy/453i/8032603. htm (accessed 30 September 2012).

30. http://www.bankofengland.co.uk/publications/Documents/speeches/2008/speech346. pdf (accessed 30 September 2012).

31. http://www.lloydsbankinggroup.com/media1/economic_insight/halifax_house_price_ index_page.asp (accessed 30 September 2012).

32. D. G. Blanchflower, 'Inflation, expectations and monetary policy', *Bank of England Quarterly Bulletin*, **48** (2), pp. 229–37, 2008Q2. Speech given in Edinburgh, 29 March 2008.

33. http://www.publications.parliament.uk/pa/cm200708/cmselect/cmtreasy/1033/8091107. htm (accessed 30 September 2012).

34. http://www.bankofengland.co.uk/publications/Pages/agentssummary/default.aspx (accessed 30 September 2012).

35. David G. Blanchflower, 'Recent developments in the UK economy: the economics of walking about', *Bank of England Quarterly Bulletin*, 2007Q2, **47** (2), pp. 317–29.

36. Clark Kerr (1988), 'The neo-classical revisionists in labour economics (1940–1960) – R.I.P.', in B.E. Kaufman (ed.), *How Labor Markets Work. Reflections on theory and practice by John Dunlop, Clark Kerr, Richard Lester and Lloyd Reynolds*, Lexington Books, p. 3.

37. http://www.hm-treasury.gov.uk/ukecon_imf_2012.htm (accessed 30 September 2012).

38. www.Doingbusiness.org (accessed 30 September 2012).

39. See David Blanchflower (1991), 'Fear, unemployment and pay flexibility', *Economic Journal*, May, **101** (406), pp. 483–96 and David Blanchflower and Chris Shadforth (2009), 'Fear, unemployment and migration', *Economic Journal*, **119** (535), February, pp. F136–F182.

40. http://www.hm-treasury.gov.uk/d/201204forcomp.pdf (accessed 30 September 2012).

41. Online at http://www.ilo.org/global/research/global-reports/world-of-work/lang--en/ index.htm (accessed 30 September 2012).

42. http://www.independent.co.uk/news/business/comment/david-blanchflower/david-blanchflower-slashing-employment-regulation-would-do-nothing-to-boost-growth-74 41395.html (accessed 30 September 2012).

43. These quotes were originally used as chapter headings in my joint 1994 MIT Press book with Andrew Oswald, *The Wage Curve*. They seem even more relevant in 2012.

44. Konrad Lorenz (1996), *On Aggression*, New York: Harcourt Brace Jovanovich.

45. Robert Solow (1986), 'Unemployment; getting the questions right', *Economica*, **53**, S23–S34.

46. Arnold Harberger (1993), 'The search for relevance in economics' (Richard T. Ely Lecture), *American Economic Review proceedings and papers*, **81**, pp. 1–16.

47. R.H. Coase (1992), 'The institutional structure of production' (Nobel prize lecture), *American Economic Review*, 82, pp. 713–19.

48. Larry Summers (1991), op cit.

49. L.C. Schultze (1985), 'Microeconomic efficiency and nominal wage stickiness' (presidential address to the American Economic Association, 1984), *American Economic Review*, **75**, pp. 1–15.

16. On leadership

Thomas Docherty

Let me begin with the words of a famous teacher. In a critique of the politics of Stanley Baldwin, who in his 1929 general election campaign adopted the motto 'Safety first', this teacher said, one Friday in March 1931, while walking with her pupils through the streets of Edinburgh, that 'Safety does not come first. Goodness, Truth and Beauty come first. Follow me' (p. 10). The charismatic teacher here is Miss Jean Brodie, the character made famous in Muriel Spark's novel, *The Prime of Miss Jean Brodie*.[1] Miss Brodie is, of course, a most dangerous precursor for any responsible educator to have.

Yet the problem does not lie in her concerns for the search for truth, goodness and beauty; rather, it lies in the ideas of 'following' and of leading that govern her practice as a teacher. The motto 'Follow me' figures quite highly among the worst things a teacher might ever say to her or his pupils. Her girls, the 'Brodie set', are to be charmed by the unconventional idiosyncrasies of the enigmatic leader that Miss Brodie sees herself to be; and she, in turn, is but a follower of some other, more dangerous political tendencies than those advocated by Stanley Baldwin, for she is an admiring follower of Mussolini ('one of the greatest men in the world', p. 44) and the fascisti.

On the walk that March day, she expounds her notion of education, which she sets against the practice of the head-teacher, Miss Mackay:

> Meanwhile, I follow my principles of education and give of my best in my prime. The word 'education' comes from the root *e* from *ex*, out, and *duco*, I lead. It means a leading out. To me education is a leading out of what is already there in the pupil's soul. To Miss Mackay it is a putting in of something that is not there, and that is not what I call education, I call it intrusion, from the Latin root prefix *in* meaning in and the stem *trudo*, I thrust. (p. 36)

The difficulty with this – Spark's irony – is that Miss Brodie is wrong in the matter of linguistic fact. The root she describes here is the root *educere* (to educe) and not *educare* (to educate). She is not talking about education, but rather about *educing*. Although close in some superficial respects, educing and educating nonetheless remain different; and the key difference has to do with leadership and following. To educe is to elicit or to infer, to bring a conclusion out of raw data; and in that sense, it is to 'draw out' or to lead out a reality from a mere raw or implicit potential. This needs 'leadership', in Miss Brodie's sense, in that it needs someone to spot the reality within the potential and to draw it out. Education, however, is not the mere realizing of potential; rather, it is the ongoing making of more and more potential, the never-ending desire to seek out *and to invent* the good, the true and the beautiful.

The key here lies in two notions of authority. To 'educe' is to assert one's own authority as the final word, with one's personal preference as final arbiter. Miss Brodie subscribes to such a view. She asks her set 'Who is the greatest Italian painter?' and they reply that it is Leonardo da Vinci. 'That is incorrect,' replies Miss Brodie. 'The answer is Giotto, he is my favourite' (p. 11). The 'authority' for this is nothing more or less than Miss Brodie's assertion: as 'the greatest' equates with 'my favourite', there can be no discussion, no proof or legitimation of the authority behind the statement – other, that is, than Miss Brodie's own charisma and force, or her institutional authority.

Against this would be a version of authority whose purpose is to give authorization to the views and thinking of others, or to bring them to the point where their voice is legitimate; and it is only this latter that can be called education.

The counterpart of leadership is now called, especially in the specialist jargon, 'followership'. Once more, we have an excellent literary example that might guide us, in a poem by Seamus Heaney. In a very early poem, 'Follower',[2] he writes of his relation with his precursor, his father. He describes how straight a line his father was able to plough, how skilled he was in leading his horse and his plough across the field and its furrows.

The last two lines of the poem show what happens in this situation, when generation speaks to generation, when they maintain a tradition and transfer a knowledge or an expertise:

> I was a nuisance, tripping, falling,
> Yapping always. But today
> It is my father who keeps stumbling
> Behind me, and will not go away. ('Follower')

In this moment, the poem becomes a poem about memory, about bearing the weight of the past; but also about how a follower, having learned something, becomes a leader and cares for the past. In leading, this leader bears the weight of the past on his back; aware that he is a leader *because* of the past, and able to look forward and make his own straight lines – in

Heaney's case, the lines of verse, turning back and forth like (but different from) the furrows of a ploughed field. He carries on the tradition of working the lines; but, as we also know from Heaney's most famous early poem, 'Digging', he exchanges the lines of the furrowed field for the lines of verse, of writing itself. It is thus – in this fundamental act of transformation – that this follower gains his authority, becomes an author.

These examples help us to understand that leadership and followership are charged with meanings well beyond the simple idea of being at the head or tail of a race, or of an army, or of a group or institutional body. In becoming a leader, one faces some fundamental issues. There are questions of responsibility to be addressed, of adequate answering for one's own past or for a more general tradition, of having appropriate experience, of being able to transform that experience in various ways (from ploughing to writing, say) such that something new is made possible. To lead does not mean to ignore all that has come before, but rather to have a peculiarly privileged relation to it. To lead requires a profound historical sense: a sense of one's responsibility to history. To lead is to be in a privileged position that brings with it a burden, but a burden called 'answerability'; and what is being answered is what has made one, among many other things. This is infinitely more than being 'accountable' for one's present decisions; and our contemporary notions of such 'accountabilities' are, sadly, a poor and entirely inadequate substitute for a real and substantive idea of what leadership entails. Perhaps above all, to lead means to assert a particular kind of break; and, in this, it is clear that the leader, insofar as she or he leads, cannot be simply the agent of another, more powerful force – even a force (like a government, say) to which she or he is to be held to account.

We can look at what this means for various qualities of leadership within the University. In some cases, the leader in question will be the Vice-Chancellor or President; but the leader may also be the Registrar. To leave it at this, though, will be to take a too narrow – too parochial – view of our question, for leaders crop up in many guises and in many situations. Thus, we need to look at the micro level and to consider the question in relation to teachers, students and colleagues; and also we should look at the macro level and ask about the wider authorities that shape the University institution, including funding councils, or education ministers and their associated political bodies. The fundamental question concerning leadership relates to the authority of the University as an institution within the much wider ambit of a society or a civilization, and thus to the legitimization of our search for the true, the good and the beautiful.

Let us begin elsewhere, and in another time.

1   ON TEACHING AND LEADING

On 18 October 1704, the philosopher Giambattista Vico, author of *The New Science*, gave one of his annual orations to the incoming student body of the University of Naples, where he held the position of Rector.[3] The annual oration was a kind of keynote address setting the academic credentials and priorities of the University; and in each of the addresses that he gave, Vico was at pains to iterate the foundational principles of his institution as well as to give leadership and to establish a kind of moral compass to guide the novices as they began their great courses and programmes of studies. He told the incoming novice students in Naples that year that the greatest benefit of learning is 'to be educated for the common good of the citizenry'. Their learning, and the teaching that goes with it, was not for private profit, but for the good of community.

What might Vico's lesson here mean for the profession of the teacher, indeed for the very conditions of education as a whole; and what might it imply for the question of leadership, not just in the Naples of the turn of the eighteenth century, but much more generally?

In earlier versions of the academy, the beginning teacher, seeking the authority to profess the discipline, was an apprentice. An apprentice learns a craft, but is also 'bound to serve, and entitled to receive instruction' from those already established in the craft. The two-way obligation here is vital: the apprentice is bound, but, once experienced enough, will be set free; the master is likewise bound, bound to give freely of her or his experience. In being thus bound together, like Heaney and his father, the generations together find what I will call the *intimacy of community*, and also the question of their responsibility for the community and its future. This – the necessity of establishing an intimacy of community – is already a fundamental precondition of citizenship. The apprentice is learning a craft, but also bearing it and its responsibilities, and thus becoming the guardian of its values; the master is attentive to her or his responsibilities towards the future in a community that extends beyond the academy, beyond the immediate environment in which he or she leads the apprentice, helping and shouldering where necessary.

However, as we know, we have by and large abandoned the idea of apprenticeship, and with it the idea of an intimacy of community between leader and follower that, were it present, we could call 'civilization'. Apprenticeship has been replaced with forms of bureaucratized teacher-accreditation, in the delivery of which inter-generational community is explicitly attacked in the name of endless supposed 'modernization'. Modernization, here, means that the practices that sufficed before the present day are irrelevant to the endemically changing situations in which we find ourselves: it is always 'Year Zero', and our forebears were less 'advanced' than we. With teaching accreditation all based on generic and abstract skills, the institutions drive a wedge between generations; and replace that inter-generational intimacy that we could call a living tradition with the ideal of a pledge, by the new teacher, of allegiance not to the subject or field, but rather to the institution and its abstract accreditation agencies.

Managerial 'modernization' assumes not only that the past is another country, but also that, as another country, it is under-developed; and, consequently, there is nothing to learn from visiting it. In short, 'modernization' is a cant term that is designed rhetorically to assert a force of authority – the authority of a Miss Brodie and her preferences, here, now – over the possibility of learning from the past, education, or even rational argument.

Instead, in fact, the purpose will now be to ensure that there is *no* allegiance between generations, and to require that the coming generation will form an allegiance with the much more abstract idea of 'modernization' itself, now raised to the level of being something like 'professional modernization'. The incoming teacher must break with her forebears and determinedly ignore any authority that their experience might offer, and must instead endlessly 'reform'; and she or he will do so according to the whims of those in control of the word 'modernization' – that is, the government and its agents, now acting like an authoritarian Miss Brodie, armed with the same charms and persuasive charisma.

These practices reduce the activity of teaching to a mere catalogue of mechanical operations; and the mechanic-in-chief is not the teacher, but rather an abstract and invisible agency that feels no need to argue for its methods. In this, the teacher becomes a pure (by which I mean mere) 'human resource', a simple and reduced element in the machinery, and one that has itself to be mechanized, routinized, and above all kept in check.

There is a consequent divorce between actual teaching and its alleged fundamental methods; and such a divorce has damaging effects for the question of leadership and authority. The model, based on the language of excellence, is replicated at other points in the structural organization of the University. Just as teachers must be taught to teach (though not by qualified teachers), so also our 'leaders' must have a form of leadership-accreditation (not based on anything called experience of engagement with their community). In the UK, there now exists a rather large armature that addresses the idea of leadership in higher education; and one very significant body involved in this is the 'Leadership Foundation for Higher Education', or LFHE.

The Foundation offers a number of 'tailored' programmes, all designed to address the very precise and specific circumstances of each individual who will follow their programmes. This tailoring, however, begins itself to look 'off-the-peg' as soon as one consults and considers their publicity materials. The organization runs a number of programmes; many of them designed in propaedeutic fashion to let a practitioner or participant move incrementally from one level of leadership to the next. Thus we have their flagship programme, the TMP or 'Top Management Programme', which has been followed by very significant numbers of existing Vice-Chancellors in the UK. However, before undertaking this course, it will really make sense if one follows the 'Senior Strategic Leadership' programme, which is partly designed for those who are already in such senior roles, with an eye to moving on to Vice-Chancellorship. Yet, it might make even more sense to start at 'Preparing for Senior Strategic Leadership'; and, lying 'under' this we will find, for example, the 'Head of Department' programme. Thus, there are multiple levels of leadership established, each with its corresponding programme, and each with its corresponding leader figure.

Two interesting things can be noted immediately. The first is that the publicity materials for all these look as if they have been prepared to a template: standardized recurring features include things like a '360-degree feedback loop'; 'practical tools, exercises and leadership techniques'; 'cross-institutional understanding'; 'a safe and supportive environment'; and 'action-learning sessions'. It may well be the case that these all apply at each and every level; but do they not also apply elsewhere, even in the classroom, say? In other words, these are *not* in fact specific to leaders at high strategic level; *nor* do they address the specifics of each level. The result here, however, is that this kind of activity is seen to be the preserve of higher-level leaders; and they also serve to homogenize all leadership as if it were all much the same thing. Generic abstraction, through which all differences are flattened into homogeneity, trumps the vagaries of the historically specific particularities that constitute the realities of any actual leadership situation.

Second, in the programmes designed by the LFHE, all the senior programmes make use of workshops. These are interesting because the workshops are all grounded in Shakespeare plays. If you are 'preparing' for senior strategic leadership, you work on *Macbeth*; if you have prepared and are now doing it, you work on *As You Like It*; and, if you've reached the TMP, you work on *Henry V*. In one way, obviously, the practising academic is delighted at this: the Vice-Chancellor is learning from the work of the English and Drama departments. Only, however, she is not. The plays are construed as allegories of leadership situations; and we are to learn an extremely limited number of things from them: the virtues of inspiration, rhetorical communication or persuasion, the ability to 'sell' an idea and secure buy-in, questions of ethical leadership; and so on.

The LFHE programmes all make extensive use specifically of workshops provided by Olivier Mythodrama, an organization dedicated to the use of drama – and especially Shakespeare – to help develop good leadership in business and the public sector. In one of the sample videos that are publicly available, Richard Olivier, a director and practitioner in the company, gives a lecture on 'The Pyramid of Power', in which he analyses Shakespeare's ancient Rome as an allegory of the shape of power. He indicates that Shakespeare mythologizes history, and quotes Joseph Campbell to the effect that 'myth is something that never was, but always is'. The lecture, as also with the lecture in 'inspirational leadership' deploying *Henry V*, proposes that there is such as a thing as an 'eternal myth of leadership'. This use of mythodrama is highly charged and highly significant.

We might set the question of mythodrama alongside other modes of learning, modes that might equally well involve an aspect of play or drama. Play, indeed, is central to learning; and it is important if we are to learn the details of leadership. Further, literature and the other arts can offer helpful structures that allow us to understand management at all levels. However, play, with its central guiding principles of fiction-making, need not drive us towards a subscription to myth or archetype.

Here, I take a lead from the scholarship of Frank Kermode. 'We have to distinguish', he writes, in *The Sense of an Ending*, 'between myths and fictions'.[4] It is important to hang on to the *provisional* nature of the fictions by which we will learn. 'Fictions can degenerate into myths whenever they are not consciously held to be fictive. In this sense anti-Semitism is a degenerate fiction, a myth; and *Lear* is a fiction' (p. 39). Leaving aside the troubling correspondence between myth learning and a certain anti-Semitism, we can see now the fundamental flaw in drawing up a 'myth' (especially an 'eternal myth') of leadership. Kermode again writes, 'Myth operates within the diagrams of ritual, which presupposes total and adequate explanations of things as they are and were; it is a sequence of radically unchangeable gestures. Fictions are for finding things out, and they change as the needs of sense-making change. Myths are the agents of stability, fictions the agents of change' (ibid.). Right through most of the management ideologies of leadership, there is an ongoing strain of 'change-management'; but the problem is that managerialist leadership such as that promoted through the LFHE erects the *myth* of the leader as opposed to the *fiction* of the leader; and myth presupposes keeping things as they are.

From this, we get the third and decisive point of interest. In all of this, the leader becomes a rather isolated, if potentially heroic, figure. This is so even when teamwork is being vaunted: the team consists of those who are the followers; the leader stands apart, above and beyond the fray. It is not that 'there is no "I" in team'; it is rather that ' "I" am not part of the team that I lead'. We see this very readily in the business world: hot-desking, for example, is extremely good for everyone – except the manager, who retains his own office space. This leader is heroic in that isolation, always presented as having to 'deal with' things that 'block' or 'stand in the way of' the vision or idea. The clear guiding principle underlying this is that the followers are nothing more than 'human resources' to be manipu-lated, even to be fooled by rhetorical legerdemain ('motivating' them), into the appropriate behaviour in order to fulfil the 'journey' presented by the leader-figure. The journey, however, is that of the leader alone; the 'troops' are but the resources required to get to the destination, that eternal myth called 'excellence'. Leaders decide things – in an abstracted form; and followers have to conform. This is not only a recipe for *hubris*; it is also a recipe for the unhelpful establishment of a fundamental division between the leader and her or his followers. Perhaps needless to say, it also offers a rather sad and desolate image of both the leader and his or her follower figures.

If we are indeed to modernize in any serious sense of the word, then we might start the process by trying to catch up with 1704, when Vico asserted – indeed, rather took for granted – that the University could establish a shared intimacy of community action, that it had a public function, and that such a function implied a relation to civic authority in a way that was designed to contest authoritarianism.

2   LEGALITY WITHOUT LEGITIMACY

In the film *Life of Brian*,[5] Brian is made into a reluctant leader of sorts: he is followed everywhere. In frustration, he decides to address his followers; and he tells them that they really do not need any heroes or leaders. They repeat his words, like schoolchildren reciting their lesson. 'You don't need a messiah', he shouts, 'you're all individuals'. 'Yes,' they shout back in perfect chorus, 'we're all individuals'. At which point, a little voice pipes up, '*I*'m not.' In the film, it is the very denial of individuality that produces individuality: it is the very denial of leadership that produces the singular individual capable of leading.

The underlying premise for my argument here is that we are facing something of a crisis of leadership in Higher Education in Britain, as also in the rest of the advanced economies. That crisis has been to a large extent provoked by what we might call 'the rise of the managerialist class'; and the result of that onward march and triumph of the archetypal members of that class is that instead of leaders, we have managers; instead of followers, we have resources.

We need to be clear on this, to prevent possible misunderstandings. Managerialism is the very opposite of managing: managerialism is that mind-set that would put in place a system that generates decisions, and all that is then required is the bureaucratic operation of the decision-machinery. By contrast, managing depends upon individuals working in cooperation with each other. In managerialism, there is no possibility of collegiality, and thus also no possibility of leadership: the bureaucratic arrangement means that no one is ever responsible for anything, since is it a mechanism that is being operated only. In managing, by contrast, leadership becomes possible; but it becomes possible precisely because the establishment of relations among colleagues is required. Those relations, built on the primacy of actual material and personal contact and engagement, depend upon mutual trust. Managerialist 'leadership' eliminates trust or the need for trust from the activity; and it thus degenerates into forms of authoritarianism or, as it might better be called, leadership without legitimacy.

As virtually anyone within the sector now knows, we operate within a highly bureaucratized system. This, while it may appear to offer some organizational benefits, actually operates in ways that militate against proper leadership. The key to an understanding of this lies in what we can call the demise of argument or debate. One way of leading any large organization, such as a University, is to find rational principles for moving towards the future development and ongoing work of the organization. Habermas would describe this in terms of our being able to have systematic argument, from widely differing points of view.[6] The aim is to provide legitimacy for the operation of the organization, as well as to ensure that all participants share in equally committed fashion to the work carried out.

The way this works, in a rational fashion, is for arguments to be laid out in public. The argumentative positions must be articulated without prejudice or bias, and simply as what each participant sees as the better case, based on established facts and desired end-points. Participants then try to persuade each other, and to do so without any coercion, threat, or force other than the force of the argument itself. If the parties can establish a consensus on these grounds, then, according to Habermas, the result is the expression of a rational will; and it will offer us the benefit of commitment from all parties and a clear sense of an agreed direction for the organization. As a further corollary, the debates must be kept under review, in case of changing circumstances or the emergence of new and different argumentations.

This is not how things happen. Given the distance between leaders and followers in our institutions, and given that they effectively operate in incommensurable realms of discourse, such dialogue and debate is never among equals. A Brodie-style authority is asserted, but very indirectly. It is rather difficult in many cases to bring about consensual agreement. In terms of the politics of management, the decision then is to abandon the very pursuit of rationally agreed plans. Instead, what we have is an agreement regarding much lower-level and seemingly peripheral matters: agreement regarding *procedures* or *processes.* Sometimes the agreement in question here is even agreement about procedures for reaching agreement about plans – the plans themselves hovering ghost-like in the background, but never being openly discussed. The logic then is that the leadership can substitute an agreement about a procedure for an agreement regarding a plan. While it may look *as if* we are debating matters of academic substance, we are in fact *limited* to a mere discussion of the 'best practice' in terms of how we reach decisions in general. To agree to move things in accordance with a specific set of procedures becomes *the equivalent* of agreeing to substantive change or stability itself; for, if the procedures by which the plan is agreed are shown to conform to the (agreed) processes for making decisions, no one need ever discuss anything of substance any more. This is bureaucracy.

Habermas worried that many societies might operate entirely legally, but without legitimacy: that is, they establish laws, but the laws have not been arrived at through a rational process of examining substantive argument involving participants. Bureaucracy moves a step further. Instead, then, of providing an argued case for something that can have the force of consensually agreed *law*, we have abandoned the principle of having law – and certainly for establishing legitimacy – in this way. Weaker than a law is a 'guideline', or a 'code of practice'; and these are essentially matters or procedural protocol. Given that these are not *laws*, they do not need to be argued for: they are 'merely' guidelines or codes. However, once we do have such guidelines or codes, they start to assume the *force* of law, and to operate precisely *as if* they were laws that have been arrived at in rational fashion. The result is that our bureaucratized and mythic leadership may have *power* but that it now has grounding neither in *legality* nor, certainly, in anything approaching what Habermas would regard as *legitimacy.*

Leadership is thus established essentially on the basis of something no more substantial than gossip, or 'news management' as it is sometimes called. Slavoj Žižek has written about how this operates, in his book, *The Puppet and the Dwarf.*[7] There, he discusses the more extreme political forms that this kind of leadership has taken in world history; and, alarmingly, he finds the model in the manner of governance operated by Stalin. He points out that Stalinism operated as a 'strictly centralized system of command'; but the problem for many of the cadres was that, frequently, no clear order would be given. Instead, Stalin provided vague hints and general guidelines or, in Žižek's terms, nothing more substantial than a mere 'sign' (p. 105). The enthusiastic cadres, eager to curry favour, would typically over-respond, as if the sign were in fact an order. Thus, for example, there might be the placing of an anonymous derogatory comment regarding someone or some event in *Pravda*, or some ostensibly very minor matter of culture would be referred to in praiseworthy terms; and it was up to the cadres to 'interpret', to find the meaning behind the signal. Stalin, thereby, is of course absolved of specific responsibility: he did not give the order as an order at all. There is, in fact, no need now to issue orders: the cadres intuit the general trajectory, and maintain their own authority and legitimacy by fulfilling orders that have not been given.

This then becomes a system of leadership. Citing Sheila Fitzpatrick's *Everyday Stalinism*, Žižek goes on to indicate that 'important policy changes were often "signalled" rather than communicated in the form of a clear and detailed directive' (p. 106). In this, the leader can get things done, can remain 'above' the fray ('excellent'), and can also appear even to be critical of the actions carried out by the cadres. This leader shows, in the words of Žižek, a basic 'mercy' against the power of the law itself. He then goes on:

> Is it not a fact that showing mercy is the only way for a Master to demonstrate his supralegal authority? If a Master were merely to guarantee the full application of the law, of legal regulations, he would be deprived of his authority, and turn into a mere figure of knowledge, the agent of the discourse of the university. (pp. 110–11)

Now, it would clearly be a mad exaggeration to suggest that Vice-Chancellors are Stalinist. However, it is not at all a wild suggestion to indicate that the methods of leadership have certain structural similarities: in Fitzpatrick's extremely troubling terms, that a certain Stalinist practice has become 'everyday'. Specifically, they both engender and indeed are grounded in authoritarianism rather than authority. First, there is the 'excellence' in which the leader-figure hubristically exceeds the bounds of the institution, establishing a division between the worlds inhabited by leaders and followers. Second, there is the assumption of a power, but without the corresponding responsibility (for responsibility belongs to the realm of the enthusiastic cadres, or 'middle-managers'). Third, there is the ostensible 'enabling' of the cadres, whose 'job' is to so internalize the signs that they can, in turn, replicate the system of authority at work. Finally, while they may be legal, they lack legitimacy.

More commonly, we have that system whereby leadership now implies an identification of the local leader (in our case, a Vice-Chancellor, say) with a more 'central' leader (say, a government official). The resulting leadership looks rather peculiar. A useful example to highlight what is at stake here comes in an address to the Association of University Administrators from the President of Universities UK in April 2009 when the then-Labour administration was requiring that all academics demonstrate fully the 'impact', beyond the walls of the academy, of the research that they undertake. The President's speech had him assuming the position of a government minister, and asking whether the arts and humanities community had done enough to demonstrate that they should be funded according to these new impact-driven criteria: 'if you were sitting in the Treasury, you would ask: do we need 159 institutions doing humanities and social science research?'. The question is not one that is meant to elicit dialogue and debate. More recently, in an attempt to defend the supposed 'independence' of the 2010 Browne Review Committee, one of the two Vice-Chancellors on the group explained that, while there had been no direct interference by government, nonetheless the Review would have been doomed had the Committee not taken into account and internalized in their deliberations the fact that they expected government to be making massive cuts in the teaching budget for the University sector. The cadres were doing what they were told, without the necessity of anyone telling them to do it.[8] The structure here is akin to that described by Žižek in the political sphere; and, crucially, those who should be 'leading' their organizations now 'lead' by internalizing a logic that has been neither debated, nor discussed, nor even established.

In the end, we have what is properly called a system of the delegation of guilt and blame. This is the proper description of bureaucracy. It is clearly anathema to rational leadership; and, equally clearly, it deserves no followership.

3   ON LEADING TOWARDS FREEDOM

It should be obvious from the foregoing that there is a major problem concerning leadership in the academy. In the increasingly dominant view, we have Vice-Chancellors who style themselves as CEOs and call the University a 'business'. In doing this, they try to give credence to an entire ideology of competitive aggression. In some cases, the competitive aggression is not just directed at other institutions that they wish to trounce in league-tables; rather, it becomes the *modus operandi* within the institution itself, with departments and individuals competing against each other in the interests of . . . That sentence is actually difficult to complete in any meaningful way: it is not at all clear whose interests are served by aggressive competition in this sphere. It might be worth recalling our leadership to a service of fundamental intellectual principles.

There is a long history of anti-intellectualism in Britain; and that now manifests itself most evidently in a mistrust of the University that has been established as an ideological norm in our conservative cultures. The real question for the sector is how we might rehabilitate the University as an institution worthy of respect, treated as an institution of at least equal importance alongside the vague 'business' that our governments demand that it serve. The idea that the University is there as a service-provider for this vague world of business is extremely short-sighted; and, worse, it limits the possibilities that the University might have to offer to the wider social sphere. It reduces the idea of 'service' to an extraordinarily narrow range; and that reduction not only damages the University, but also damages the whole of the social and public sphere of which it is an integral part.

We might seek something different, based not on aggressive competition but rather on the intimacies of cooperation and trust. At this historical moment, the University finds itself endlessly trying to justify its existence, rather than assuming a role as occasional leader and constant servant-leader of the society in which it finds itself. The logic of the position that I am advancing here, however, is that the leader is indebted to the follower for any power that she or he has; in brief, the power lies neither with leader nor follower but with their relatedness, their shaping of an intimacy of community in the pursuit of justice and enhanced freedom. This kind of leader establishes the kind of authority validated by Arendt,[9] an authority that gains obedience without any loss of freedom; but I go further, to argue that leadership is leadership if and only if it enhances freedom and extends it. It is not enough simply to protect existing freedom; the point of leading is to offer freedom more widely.

What might this mean in the University? It means, above all, finding out what the constituency wants to do. It means encouraging dissent rather than conformity; and this dissent becomes the language that shapes possible futures, and keeps them open. It means challenging authorities, especially those that are illegitimate or that assume the position of Jean Brodie. At the present time, we urgently need the University to assume this kind of servant-leadership if it is to establish its legitimacy – the legitimacy of the life of the mind and even of thinking itself – as an important element in the public sphere. That is, we need the authority of the institution as a bulwark against the forms of authoritarianism that threaten not just the University but the whole of our public life, the whole of our social, cultural and political communities.

NOTES

1. Penguin Books, 1965 (initially published in *The New Yorker* in 1961).
2. In Heaney, *Opened Ground* (Faber and Faber, 1998).
3. *On Humanistic Education (Six Inaugural Orations, 1699–1707)*, edited and translated by Giorgio A. Pinton and Arthur W. Shippee (Cornell University Press, Ithaca, 1993).
4. Frank Kermode, *The Sense of an Ending* (Oxford University Press, 1966).
5. Monty Python film, directed by Terry Jones (1979).
6. Jürgen Habermas, *Legitimation Crisis*, translated by Thomas MacCarthy; Heinemann (1976).
7. Slavoj Žižek, *The Puppet and the Dwarf* (MIT Press, Cambridge, MA, 2003).
8. Reported in *The Times Higher Education*, 21 October 2010.
9. Hannah Arendt, *Between Past and Future* (Penguin, 1993).

Index